The University as Urban Developer

Cities and Contemporary Society

Series Editors: Richard D. Bingham and Larry C. Ledebur,
Cleveland State University

Sponsored by the
Maxine Goodman Levin College of Urban Affairs
Cleveland State University

This new series focuses on key topics and emerging trends in urban
policy. Each volume is specially prepared for academic use, as well as
for specialists in the field.

The University as Urban Developer

Case Studies and Analysis

David C. Perry and Wim Wiewel

editors

LINCOLN INSTITUTE
OF LAND POLICY
Cambridge, Massachusetts

M.E.Sharpe
Armonk, New York
London, England

Published in cooperation with the Lincoln Institute of Land Policy.

Library of Congress Cataloging-in-Publication Data

The university as urban developer : case studies and analysis / edited by David C. Perry and
Wim Wiewel.
    p. cm. — (Cities and contemporary society)
  Includes bibliographical references and index.
  ISBN 0-7656-1541-X (cloth : alk. paper) — ISBN 0-7656-1641-6 (pbk.: alk. paper)
  1. Community and college—United States—Case studies. 2. Urban universities and
colleges—Environmental aspects—United States—Case studies. 3. Community develop-
ment, Urban—United States—Case studies. 4. Real estate development—United States—
Case studies. I. Perry, David C. II. Wiewel, Wim. III. Series.

LC238.U546 2005
378.1′03—dc22   2004026589

Printed in the United States of America

The paper used in this publication meets the minimum requirements of
American National Standard for Information Sciences
Permanence of Paper for Printed Library Materials,
ANSI Z 39.48-1984.

BM (c)	10	9	8	7	6	5	4	3	2	1
BM (p)	10	9	8	7	6	5	4	3	2	1

Contents

Part I
Introduction

Part II
The Campus and the City:
Neighborhood, Downtown, and
Citywide Development

Section 1. The Campus and Its Neighborhood

v

Part IV
Lessons Learned

List of Tables, Figures, and Maps

Tables

Figures

Maps

Foreword

Factories have left the cities. Regional department stores have been replaced by national chains. Local banks have been bought by regional banks that have, in turn, been bought by national banks. The suburbs are growing faster than the cities and are increasing their political clout. Urban universities, however, rarely abandon their cities. Thus it is no wonder that those of us interested in the development and redevelopment of our nation's cities are very interested in the real estate activities of colleges and universities.

Universities, whether they are public or private, internationally acclaimed research institutions or the primary training grounds for the metropolitan area, face a complicated set of constraints and expectations. Universities serve the public (e.g., by training teachers or brain surgeons, or informing the views of future citizens, or creating and passing on our culture) and yet they can also put a strain on city services and the goodwill of their immediate neighbors. Can they do whatever they want? Must they always constrain their actions to meet the wants of those on their doorstep? Can we legitimate their presence in the city only if we can put a dollar value on every contribution? These questions are meant to illustrate some of the competing demands that the nation puts on its universities.

The cases presented in this volume are a part of a larger set of activities in The City, Land and The University Program at the Lincoln Institute. As a whole these activities are viewing land development from 360 degrees. We are interested in the university's expansion beyond its borders, and we want to understand that action within the context of the university's mission and culture. In addition we are interested in the immediate neighbors, their dreams for their neighborhood, and how they might coexist with a more powerful institutional neighbor. And we are interested in the ways that city government can articulate a development path that requires contributions from and delivers benefits to all the city's residents.

The intellectual leadership for this project came from two friends and colleagues, David Perry and Wim Wiewel. They are among the reasons that I am glad that knowledge production is a social endeavor.

Rosalind Greenstein
Cochairman, Department of Planning and Development
Lincoln Institute of Land Policy
Cambridge, Massachusetts

Preface

The University as Urban Developer: Case Studies and Analysis is the product of a multiyear collaborative project of training, professional development, and research designed to contribute to our understanding of the role of the university in urban real estate development. Early on in the collaboration between the editors and the Lincoln Institute of Land Policy, we learned that there is neither a rich professional pedagogy, nor a core body of urban research, nor a well-developed professional practice focused on the real estate development practices of universities and the impacts such practices have on the long-term development of cities.

One of the elements of our approach has been the development of a Universities as Developers Workshop, organized as a joint project of the Great Cities Institute at the University of Illinois at Chicago and the Lincoln Institute, based in Cambridge, Massachusetts. The results of three such workshops with top-level university land and development officers have confirmed the mixed state of professional and academic understanding of urban university development practices and the substantial need for published work in these areas.

Obviously another element of our collaboration is this book. University-based land development is clearly a significant element of urban formation—colleges and universities are becoming increasingly active in acquiring and developing property, adding not only land and buildings but also commercial ventures to their asset base. There are multiple strategies, goals, and forms of practice, as well as varied implications of such university activity for the institutions themselves and for their communities and cities. We certainly hope we have addressed some of these conditions of university/city development in this book, adding to the available levels of professional communication, development, and scholarly research. We also hope the studies included here will help scholars and administrators alike to register and better understand the significance of the university presence in urban development and enhance the state of development practice.

Continued active attendance at our national workshops has shown that there is keen interest in the topic and a real need for organized, extended study. Participants have argued that there is no central source of knowledge on the subject. This book is our attempt to meet these needs. As such this collection serves to initiate an intellectual and professional literature. Such an undertaking is not an easy one, and we have benefited greatly from the work and support of our colleagues at the Great Cities Institute and from our long-standing and deep collaboration with our colleagues at the Lincoln Institute. To everyone at both institutes we are profoundly grateful.

Most important, we want to acknowledge our collaboration with Rosalind Greenstein of the Lincoln Institute. She has been our intellectual partner and program officer. With her we have produced an emerging workshop curriculum as well as this book. The book has benefited as well from the research support of Lynn Stevens and Barbara Sherry at the Great Cities Institute, and research assistants John O'Neil, Lynn Peemuller, Claire Gron, and Kristen Kepnick. We learned much from the advice and feedback of Scott Levitan, Alice Boyer, Henry Webber, Elizabeth Sisam, Thomas Lussenhop, Alicia Berg, and David Dixon. The assistance of Allegra Calder, Rajesh Pradhan, and Lisa Cloutier at the Lincoln Institute was very important to the project, and the editorial assistance of Ann LeRoyer, also at the Lincoln Institute, has made the book far better. We are extremely grateful for the guidance and support of Richard Bingham and especially of our editor at M.E. Sharpe, Harry Briggs.

David also wants to thank Judith Kossy, who has been supportive of the efforts of time, distance, and distraction that combine to make family life while working on such an enterprise far less interesting than it should be. Wim thanks the Georgetown University Library, which graciously provided space while he was writing the final chapter; and most of all Alice Boyer whose involvement in this project has been life-changing.

David C. Perry   Wim Wiewel
Great Cities Institute   University of Baltimore
University of Illinois at Chicago

Part I

Introduction

1

From Campus to City

The University as Developer

David C. Perry and Wim Wiewel

> *"Higher education, including the research complex . . . has become the most critical single feature of modern society."*
>
> —Talcott Parsons, as quoted in Stefan Muthesius,
> *The Postwar University: Utopianist Campus and College,* 2000

The University, Its Mission, and the City

Few would quarrel with the value of the university to society, and many would even join Talcott Parsons in his claim of the singular social importance of institutions of higher education. The university has long been one of Western civilization's key institutions. Along with local government, the firm, and the church, among others, universities contribute in multiple ways to modern urban society (Van der Wusten 1998). The university is a significant source of received knowledge or wisdom, the primary site for the debate over change in the intellectual order, and an incubator of revolutions in science and technology. Just as important, the university is considered a center of culture, aesthetic direction, and the moral forces shaping the "civilized" society. Universities also contribute in important ways to the economic health and physical landscape of cities, serving as all but permanent fixtures of the urban economy and built environment.

Such contributions to social formation, however, have not left the university in an unambiguous position relative to its urban environment. Almost from the beginning, the relationship between the university and its surroundings has been as conflictive as it has been important—captured most commonly in the timeworn phrase of "town-gown" relations. In part this is understandable, since the university as a site of knowledge has often seen itself as something of an enclave, removed enough from the immediacy and demands of modern life to produce the knowledge and information with which to better understand society and the science and technical inventions that ultimately transform it. For some this meant that the purpose of the modern research university was to create a community of scholars removed from the "turmoil" of the city and free "from the distractions of modern civilization" (Graham 1898, as quoted in Bender 1998, 18). For others this meant an unresponsive, disconnected, and alienated institution with a decidedly antiurban bias. Especially in the United States, there has been an impulse to build campus environments (even in cities) with "an affinity with the purified, safe and calm life of the suburbs" (Bender 1998, 18).

This impulse has been tempered in return by a new, more modern, and equally historically grounded tradition that views the university in quite different terms: as a product of its relationship with the city and its urban surroundings, with a strong belief "in a university *of,* not simply *in,* the city. But that does not imply that it ought to be or can be the same thing as a city" (Bender 1998, 18). This call for a clarified understanding of the "university of the city" takes on a host of meanings. In a very real way the fundamental intellectual mission of the university cannot be understood outside its context. To subscribe to the view that the university is purely an "ivory tower" or "wholly self-contained" is both wrong and unrealistic because the lion's share of the truth a university seeks to transmit, the knowledge it concerns itself with, is not of its making. It comes from outside the campus—from other institutions and other scholars. Even the knowledge produced by a university's scholars is "not for their contemplation exclusively. . . . What is essential in a university—knowledge—must be drawn from and offered to students, teachers and investigators in other parts of the world. Intellectually, no university can be wholly self-contained" (Shils 1988, 210).

At the same time, while the prevailing model of university development has historically been the pastoral campus, university land development cannot be conducted in a "wholly self-contained" way anymore than the educational mission can. The urban university is an urban institution—not only in terms of the transmission of knowledge, but in many other ways as well. The "university of the city" (Bender 1998; Cisneros 1995) with a "land grant mission" (McDowell 2001; Crooks 1982) serving as an "engaged" institution (Kellogg Commission 1999; Harkavy and Puckett 1994; Maurrasse 2001) with "urban goals" (Klotsche 1966; Nash 1973; U.S. Congress House Committee on Banking, Finance and Urban Affairs 1992; U.S. Congress House Committee on Education and Labor 1977; Grobman 1988) is a recurring theme of academic leadership and literature, especially in the late twentieth century.

This search for knowledge (and engagement), the production of knowledge, and the training of society occurs in large, complex, physically expanding, and economically important environments. The research group Initiative for a Competitive Inner City (ICIC) reports that in 1996 there were well over 1,900 universities and colleges in the core of U.S. cities (2002, 7), and their combined budgets comprised more than 68 percent of the more than $200 billion spent annually by universities nationwide (NCES 2002, ch. 3, 3). The total in 1999–2000 constant dollars was $216.3 billion. Put another way, as of 1996 urban universities were spending about $136 billion on salaries, goods, and services, which is more than nine times what the federal government spends in cities on job and economic development (ICIC 2002, 7). Universities consistently rank among the top employers in metropolitan areas and, in some cases, they are a city's top employer. Universities also are among the largest and most permanent sources of land and building ownership in the city—indeed it is estimated that, using original purchase price as a referent, urban colleges and universities at present own over $100 billion in fixed assets (current market value would be several times higher) (ICIC 2002, 8).

While the overall impact of universities on regional development is becoming better understood, their impact on central cities "remains relatively unexplored" (ICIC 2002, 6) and the role of the university in real estate development is equally underexplored (Pinck 1993; ICIC 2002; VerMeulen 1980; Wolfe 1986). Nowhere is the complex, often conflicted nature of the university as an urban institution more evident than in its real estate development practices. The claims of campus development and expansion are often practiced as, or at least perceived to be, decisions made in relative institutional isolation, mirroring the pastoral traditions of campus and ivory tower (Bender 1988; Muthesius 2000; Dober 1991, 2000). University developers acquire land and build structures that contribute to a *campus,* responsive to the core mission or the demands of the "ways of knowledge," the disciplines, the sciences, and the new modes of discovery they require and the technologies they fuel (McDowell 2001). Universities find their main constituencies in their faculty, their students, and increasingly their alumni and donors. Their first development responses are those that meet the requirements such constituents have for the campus—what attracts good students and faculty and retains them and what donors will support (Dober 2000; Webber, chapter 4 in this volume).

Against such *internal* logic of development is an equally evident *external* logic. Because universities are among the largest landowners and employers in cities, as well as major consumers of private goods and public services, they have a host of external constituents. Both indirectly, in light of the institution's educational mission, but quite directly and dramatically, in terms of the university's physical location, economic relations, and political demands, these constituencies often assert every bit the same level of claims on the university as they do on the firm, the church, or public agencies in the city. Therefore the role of the urban university is an important and complex one—mixing the institutional demands of both academy and city.

The political, economic, intellectual, and ethical elements that make up the challenges and opportunities of real estate development comprise one of the university's most important areas of institutional practice. This book serves as an initial exploration of such practice, offering a rich array of cases that provide an opportunity to understand significant elements of university administration, finance, community relations, and development, and also contribute to our understanding of urban institutions more generally, placing an emphasis on the undeniable importance of the roles universities play in the growth and development of the city. To write the cases, we have assembled scholars, academic leaders, university development experts, practitioners, real estate development specialists, and community leaders who use their varied experience and scholarship to describe a host of university practices, community responses, and policy initiatives that comprise much of contemporary university real estate development. Taken together their approach here is both contextual and evaluative, serving as one of the first efforts to treat university real estate development as "a new area of academic as well as applied inquiry" (Wiewel and Perry, chapter 17 in this volume).

The book sets out to contribute to this new area of academic and professional study in four ways. First, we seek to add to the general academic conversation on the place of the university in the city, from the perspective of what motivates the university to enter the urban real estate development process. More precisely, does the particular educational mission of the university and its obligations to students, faculty, and researchers, and the scholarship they seek, combine to require different or higher standards of institutional procedures and ethics in real estate deals?

Second, a major part of the book concentrates on how the university, through its land and building policies, embeds itself in (some critics might say "ignores") the larger urban development process. Put another way, university real estate development has come to be perceived as an important part of the community development process. Thus a substantial part of this book is committed to a discussion of the ways university real estate practices engage such processes at key levels of urban spatial development, including the neighborhoods that surround the university, the development of the urban core or downtown business district, and larger citywide development strategies of which university-city real estate collaboration is meant to be a part.

A third purpose of this collection is to drill more deeply into the practices of university real estate development, using as a starting point the particular issues of real estate acquisition and development that universities face as they undertake different types of land and building deals. The chapters written to address these topics are meant to provide fine-grained assessments of decision making, financing, and community relations practices. While each of these sets of practices is important, if there is a "first practice" among them it is finance, and therefore special attention is paid to the different mechanisms universities use to fund their real estate transactions.

A fourth goal is to establish a critical or evaluative tradition within which to build a long-standing and reflective understanding of the university as developer. Therefore the book closes with chapters that set guidelines for institutional and practice-based evaluation of university real estate development. We use the rich combination of analysis and experience demonstrated by the contributors to this collection to provide a synthesis of best practices and lessons learned. The final chapters are meant to be more than capstones to this collection. We hope they will serve as an early assessment of a previously understudied area and a bridge to future academic analysis and professional understanding of universities as developers.

The Campus and the City: Neighborhood, Downtown, and Citywide Development

If there is some semblance of academic and professional tradition to be found in past university development practices, it is most likely in the scholarship and practice of campus design and planning. And if there is a single term that seems to capture the logic of university development practice, it was and remains the term "campus," the Latin word for field. "Campus became common as an expression for an ensemble of buildings for higher education. Thus campus indicates primarily location. The term underlines the self-containedness of the institution and thus its separateness" (Muthesius 2000, 24). The source of this self-containedness was derived from the perceived nature of the intellectual mission of the institution and the "separateness" of the campus working to ensure the academic "community" or enclave in the service of that mission.

Historian Thomas Bender takes these notions of university as campus further. He suggests that in the all but universal adherence to the developmental principle of the campus, American universities, even the urban ones, came to embody the tradition of "Anglo American pastoralism"—where the academic mission is carried out in and around the "green" or the quad: a setting that links faculty and students to their respective disciplinary buildings and dorms, but keeps them unlinked and away from the city (Bender 1988). Thus the campus and its planning, argues Paul Turner (1984), is the thoroughly American tradition of university architecture and design, albeit a decidedly anti-urban one (as referenced by Bender 1988).

During the era of educational reform following World War II, the tradition of campus planning as the ideal form of university urban development became something of a "science." Ironically what started as essentially a figment of American antiurbanism became the paradigm for postwar urban university development. Richard Dober, in his seminal 1963 book *Campus Planning,* describes how university campuses are built through "logical building increments," or academic, housing, or administrative units, laid out in large relatively flat settings and of a scale to facilitate pedestrian-auto linkage. Above all this new campus, argues Dober, must be "green—providing relief from the communal life of the institution and removal from the stress of the general conditions of modern society" (Dober 1963, as quoted in Muthesius 2000, 26).

Writing more recently Dober (2000, xvi) continues to describe the ideal landscape of university development as a "green carpet upon which buildings are placed, or . . . articulated as a device to extend a building design concept into open space, with a garnish for an architectural feast." As such the campus green remains, for university planners like Dober, a central feature of university land development. It serves as a signature element in the strategies to make colleges and universities better able to "attract and retain faculty and students, advance educational program and research programs, energize fund-raising appeals . . . demonstrate environmental concepts and ethics . . . and strengthen the campus as a community design asset" (Dober 2000, xviii).

It follows, therefore, that university development, informed by such ideals, could easily exacerbate historic town-gown conflicts, often running at odds with the broader urban and community development agendas of the city. This is certainly borne out in the first several chapters of this collection, which show how the development requirements of the modern urban campus are no longer served by a developmental celebration of traditional American pastoralism. The notion of campus is changing and the ways it is planned and built reflect new needs of the communities—both academic and urban—that study, work, or live in and otherwise use university-owned buildings and land.

There are many reasons for these changes. First, the campus tradition, built as it has been on a model of the university separate from its surroundings, created the potential for long-term, serious conflict between the university and its neighbors. It is not uncommon to hear communities angrily critique universities for their imperious, unresponsive development policies and intrusive real estate impacts. Second, university capital requirements increasingly dictate that real estate development projects be mixed-use in nature—blurring the edge of the old campus and the purposes of new buildings, creating projects that are part academic and part commercial, and making the traditional notion of the campus more a thing of the past. Third, university development projects today are often projects of community and city redevelopment as well as educational projects. As a result it is not uncommon for citywide planning, design, and development goals to become key elements of university development plans.

In short, university real estate practices may be driven by internal goals of campus design, academic program needs, and endowment, but there are very few projects, on campus or off, that do not register an impact on the city. Therefore, the chapters in Part II explore the ways successful university real estate practices have come to depend on the quality of relationships the institution must maintain: with its neighborhood (see chapters 2–4); in the central business district or inner city (see chapters 5–7); and through targeted models of university-city-state collaboration meant to have a downtown, citywide, or even regional impact (see chapters 8–10). The cases in these chapters cover a full range of urban universities in North America, detailing the experiences of public and private institutions, research universities of long-standing elite status, and new public-private university collaborations with a community mission. The chapters also describe the ways new university real estate development projects are embedded in regional development strategies, cultural and sports strategies, and new blends of research and community service.

The Campus and Its Neighborhood

The first three chapters in Part II are case studies of the fundamental tension between the university as *campus* and its neighboring surroundings as *community*. Each case offers a clear history of the ways universities have come to find that successful real estate development requires responsive collaboration with their residential and commercial neighbors. Each chapter also explores the historical connections between university real estate development and urban renewal and public land clearance. Each case serves as evidence of how broader, national trends in the organization and application of community development principles are finding their way into the university-community real estate development relationship.

The realization that successful real estate development requires collaborative community development did not come easily to major urban research universities. In chapter 2 Sabina Deitrick and Tracy Soska describe a four-decade struggle between the University of Pittsburgh and its immediate Oakland neighborhood as a period that forever altered the university's dependence on traditional campus planning and corollary practices, including unilateral decision making regarding land development and campus expansion. The case describes how the university's mobilization of resources, powers of eminent domain, and insularity of traditional campus planning goals were challenged, first by protesting grassroots organizations and then by the formal creation of new community development organizations in the neighborhood. Deitrick and Soska describe the transformation of both university *and* community as each moved from "reactive modes during the period of conflict and confrontation" to a new era of university-community collaboration, often mediated with the help of city hall leadership or state planners. Put another way, the authors suggest that this case of community-based university real estate expansion is the story of "how an 800-pound gorilla learned to sit with—and not on—its neighbors."

The importance of university-community partnerships in the development process is also at the heart of Peter Marcuse's and Cuz Potter's study of Columbia University in chapter 3. Columbia, like the University of Pittsburgh, is truly an 800-pound gorilla when it comes to comparing its landholdings to that of its neighbors. Columbia is the third largest landowner in all of New York City and, in many respects, as a landowner and investor, report Marcuse and Potter, it "has acted no differently than any other landowner; it has invested in real estate for its financial return." But it is also different from other urban landowners in that it is one of the largest, most prestigious institutions of learning, in the city and in the nation, and at the same time it is located near the vibrant African American community in Harlem and the Dominican community in Washington Heights. Through a study of the university's Audubon Biomedical Science and Technology Center, Marcuse and Potter provide a clear picture of how another 800-pound gorilla was made to sit with and not on its neighbors.

The requirements of biotechnology and science made the development of the Audubon Center a necessity for the research university, and yet Columbia at first could not and later would not build the Audubon facility without responding to the demands of major political and community opposition requiring that the renovated facility meet the needs of science *and* community. In telling this story of modern university land development, Marcuse and Potter draw out three threads that affect not only Columbia but also other universities as they seek to blend campus with community:

1. its concern with meeting its own institutional needs by first housing its students and faculty and then providing space for university-related economic activities;

2. the involvement of those students (and some faculty) in issues dealing with the university's role in the community; and
3. the reactions of the surrounding poorer communities to the universities' activities.

In chapter 4 Henry Webber offers a review of fifty years of university-
community development history in his case study of the University of Chicago. Over time, Webber explains, the university has become "deeply involved
in efforts to improve communities surrounding its campus." The reason for
such efforts, early on, could be chalked up to enlightened self-interest as the
neighborhoods surrounding the university declined, in some cases precipi-
tously, and the very attractiveness of the university to faculty and students
was threatened. These efforts, he suggests, "have generally been successful,
but not without controversy or great cost." University forays into the community development process in the 1950s and 1960s were, like those of many
university development efforts, appended to the demolition and land clearing tenets of urban renewal. Like other urban renewal efforts these actions
were met with stiff, vocal community resistance. By the 1990s the urban
economy had changed and a somewhat chastened university employed a very
different, more engaged strategy in the context of "Chicago's growing attractiveness, the increasing role of city government in neighborhood planning, and improved commercial and residential real estate markets [that]
allowed the university to work with partner neighborhoods to improve communities without costly and institutionally difficult real estate interventions."
Therefore, Webber reports, university development today is

> highly influenced by the community development movement and features
> a comprehensive set of initiatives designed to make neighborhoods attrac-
> tive to potential residents by ensuring good schools, safe streets, good trans-
> portation and attractive housing choices . . . While real estate initiatives are
> part of a comprehensive strategy of supporting high-quality communities,
> they do not dominate.

The University and the Central City

Just as university real estate development practices emerged as ingredients
in the changing patterns of urban renewal and community development planning, they also became key features of inner city and central business district
(CBD) development. The decline of central cities during the last half of the
twentieth century was especially pronounced in CBDs and the declining residential areas and derelict industrial zones closely linked to them. In chapter 5

Brian Coffey and Yonn Dierwechter describe the development of an entirely new campus for the University of Washington at Tacoma, located on a 4.6-acre "economically depressed, high-crime district that included a large homeless population and several vacant or underutilized buildings." The new campus is surrounded by warehouses, low-income housing, and port facilities.

In telling the story of the building of a new campus entirely in this setting, Coffey and Dierwechter give us a new model of campus design where the major principles are not those of a traditional campus of greens and quadrangle, "hermetically sealed off from its surroundings," but a cluster of educational facilities that "mix in seamlessly with commercial, retail, and service functions. For example, university buildings house restaurants, taverns, bookstores, and related outlets. Expansion plans call for continued allocation of space to be leased to business establishments." The case of the University of Washington at Tacoma is one where a decidedly different approach to the campus meets the functional needs of a new university and becomes a "major reason for the reurbanization of the inner city." Urban real estate development approached from this substantially more contextual vantage point becomes a practice that includes consideration of the following factors:

> the university's impact on historic preservation; the role of the university in promoting economic renewal; land use issues and concerns related to the development of the site; and the perceived role the university plays in community development, particularly as related to social welfare and equity.

If there is a case that clearly builds upon and amplifies the findings of Coffey and Dierwechter, it is the Auraria Higher Education Center in Denver. In chapter 6 Robert Kronewitter, one of the master planners of this unique higher education site, describes a development collaboration that locates four very different institutions of higher education, from community college to graduate research institutions, in a new multifunction campus located in a deteriorated historic site, all rationalized through urban renewal. The result is a multi-institutional campus that blends historic preservation with large-scale capital infrastructure investment to meet the educational needs of 33,000 students and serve as "a functional and visual contribution to the revitalization of the Denver CBD." Kronewitter reports that this type of university real estate development requires public-private partnerships among commercial, tourism and education leadership, with the buildings of the campus again serving a mixture of academic and community uses.

If the campus planning process in Tacoma emphasized a real estate development that stretched the concept of what a university campus would look like, the Auraria campus completely changes the notion of whose campus the university developers were building. The campus plan becomes, in Kronewitter's assessment, a part of Denver's urban master plan. With buildings and land shared by four institutions, the Auraria Higher Education Center becomes both a physical manifestation of what is new in inner-city development and a physical manifestation of new linkages in higher education as well.

In each of the preceding chapters, indeed in all the chapters so far, there is a clear message: university real estate development is a political process. Without a good understanding of local politics and what it requires, development will be far more difficult if not impossible to carry forward. Elizabeth Strom approaches this topic of the politics of university real estate development comparatively in chapter 7. She studies "the experiences of the University of Pennsylvania and Temple University, two large institutions situated just outside Philadelphia's central business district, which have become increasingly committed to urban development and community revitalization activities."

The chapter starts with the assumption that "the institutional health of an urban university is inextricably bound to the health of its surrounding community" and compares the differences, successes, and challenges to be found in and between the community-university politics of Temple, the public university, and Penn, the private university. Strom finds that Penn's variety of community-based initiatives, ranging from buying from local vendors to highly visible student learning contracts with community groups and schools, makes it "easier for the institution to achieve its own goals, including campus expansion," citing specifically the university's relations with the city council when buying large tracts of inner-city land. Temple ignored, at its peril, the interests of elected officials and concerns of the state delegation, making the obvious link to both local and state politics even more a part of the university's development process. Through this comparative assessment, Strom illuminates clear leadership channels in politics that must be adhered to; such communication structures are never more apparent than in the politics of real estate. In light of the need to mobilize political support for a real estate project, Strom also reports that while universities often have goals similar to private developers, their nonprofit status requires a more nuanced list of strategies to accomplish the development objective.

The University as a Collaborator in Urban Development

A common theme running through chapters 2–7 is that university real estate development requires collaboration with and between a full array of public and private actors. The next three chapters build on Strom's political study, offering an assessment of the politics and practices of negotiation, the characteristics of leadership, and the institutional conditions of political and financial management of risk that comprise successful university real estate development.

More than most functions of university development, successful large-scale real estate initiatives require strong institutional commitment and benefit from the full attention of senior institutional leadership. This certainly is born out in a study of Georgia State University in chapter 8. Lawrence Kelley and Carl Patton explore the university's development strategy for building and renovating a substantial number of university buildings as part of a several-billion-dollar renewal effort in downtown Atlanta. The authors describe how a city without a downtown master plan benefited from a university that took over the downtown planning process and became, through its own real estate redevelopment efforts, the lead institution in the overall central city redevelopment process. The case centers on the work of a new "planner president" at Georgia State who used the claim that the "university should be a part of the community and not apart from it" as the guiding principle for the university's first strategic master plan. Kelley and Patton suggest that the plan identified a full agenda of university and urban renewal issues that required, for its execution, a rich constellation of university, private, and state governmental partners who "built support, utilized two private foundations to float bond issues, leveraged private funds, and developed the expertise to rebuild (the university) and downtown Atlanta." Kelley and Patton describe such development as a product of many factors: politically active university leadership, focused strategic planning, and the mobilization of fiscal resources through innovative public and private investment mechanisms. Of the three, they argue, university leadership comes first.

Leadership also plays an important role in the comparative tale of three cities (Indianapolis, Louisville, and St. Louis) and their universities found in chapter 9, by Scott Cummings and his colleagues. They highlight the central role university real estate development can play in building and expanding campus infrastructure, and in rebuilding cities themselves. They compare the experiences of three universities (Indiana University-Purdue University at Indianapolis, the University of Louisville, and Saint Louis University) and find them to be important examples of how universities use large-scale urban land clearance programs and citywide goals of redevelopment to advance their own real estate development agendas.

In telling the stories of these institutions of higher education and their cities, the authors chart a comparative pattern "of public-private partnerships in which the universities were critical intermediaries." The chapter describes how university leaders are able to imbed their institutional development agendas into large citywide redevelopment agendas based on the arts, enter-tainment, sports facilities, and tourism. In each of these cities, educational administrators emerge as "major political players in the urban regimes and coalitions promoting redevelopment." Cummings et al. describe processes that require innovative university development arrangements and public-private partnerships with a citywide range of actors including private inves-tors, federal agencies, and municipal and state governments. As a result the authors find university real estate development to be a complex process where "both political and financial risks . . . must be strategically managed when universities become players in larger development agendas."

However, university real estate development strategies that are closely linked to larger urban development agendas require more than leadership, planning, and the management of risk. They also require skillful negotiation between public and private partners to carry out the mix of academic-commercial projects that are making up larger and larger parts of university development. In his case study of Ryerson University's attempt to build a mixed commercial-university building on university land in Toronto's Dundas Square, David Amborski, in chapter 10, examines negotiations between the university, the private developer, and the City of Toronto. In the process uni-versity real estate practitioners encounter complex, often conflicting require-ments of private commercial development and of the university that must be reconciled if a deal, both financial and programmatic, is to be struck. Such negotiations go to the heart of how to plan, build, and ultimately manage mixed-use university buildings. Amborski's case study is a good example of how the resolution of university goals and mission with the proprietary goals in the building of new campus-city structures has become an important in-gredient in good real estate practice.

University Development Practices: Acquisition, Finance, Development, and the Deal

To understand the role of the university as developer, it is important to inves-tigate the issues that affect a university's acquisition and development prac-tices and how these issues manifest themselves in day-to-day activities, according to Ziona Austrian and Jill Norton. This important assertion estab-lishes one of the key elements of the larger research agenda for urban real estate development and sets the topic for Part III. In these chapters the con-tributors attempt to examine the microlevel practices of university real estate development: What are the issues that drive university acquisition and devel-opment practices? How are these practices manifest in day-to-day activities, both inside the university and externally, as the institution engages the city?

Three general areas of practice in universities are of concern in this set of five chapters. Austrian and Norton first provide an overview of the complexity of acquisition and development practices and the multiplicity of institutional levels and community contexts within which they occur. The next two chapters focus on what some consider to be the real meat of the acquisition and development process: financing the deal. The last two chapters address the question, "Who's in on the deal?" They explore the ways universities must create new partnerships with the private sector, city, and community to make a development work, as well as the need to create whole new public-private entities or development agencies.

Using such criteria as public-private status, enrollment size, geographic location, and the characteristics of surrounding neighborhoods, Austrian and Norton, in chapter 11, studied five universities using a national survey that provided a more fine-grained assessment of both the independent factors that influence university real estate development and the impact that such factors have on particular higher education real estate practices. The key independent factors they find are university leadership, the land development motivations of the institution, and the physical and policy environments in which the university finds itself. The authors argue that these factors help shape key real estate practices of decision making, financing, and community relations, along with assessing the types of real estate projects university developers undertake.

Understanding the different mechanisms universities use to finance their real estate transactions is especially important, and the next two chapters offer clear cases of how different institutions (public and private) have approached major downtown mixed-use development projects. Larry Kurtz's account, in chapter 12, of the leasing practices of the University of Toronto's affiliate Victoria University is an instructive description of the benefits of employing lease finance strategies as mechanisms for building both university facilities and university endowment, as well as contributing to the economic development of surrounding urban residential and commercial communities. Most of the case studies in previous chapters have dealt with the large-scale real estate deals conducted by rather large institutions of higher education. Through his analysis of three different real estate initiatives, Kurtz seeks to answer a host of finance questions and show how small universities can participate in urban real estate development.

Kurtz raises the following questions: How does a small arts/theological university come to be a major landowner and commercial landlord in the middle of Canada's biggest city, Toronto? What does it take to turn university property into endowment real estate? And what impact does the university as developer have on its surrounding community? The answers are found in Kurtz's detailed description of the lease finance practices that allowed his small urban university to employ a land development strategy that was one part "acquisitive, expansionist instinct" and one part "control of development" that turned into a "quasi-sacred trust" of institutional endowment. Kurtz gives ample evidence of the benefits that can accrue to an institution when it begins its real estate efforts with the assumption that leasing rather than selling its property holdings is a preferred long-time development strategy.

In chapter 13 Kenneth McHugh extends our concern for the study of the midsize urban university as well as large research institutions, with his case study of development policy at DePaul University in Chicago. The chapter is a study of financial practices meant to address complex preservation and mixed-use rehabilitation projects. McHugh describes the acquisition and rehabilitation process conducted by DePaul, in partnership with the City of Chicago, which produced a model mixed-use development effort between the university, the city, and the commercial sector. The complex array of university-city fiscal strategies described in the case are at once unique and, yet, in their innovative mix of financial obligations and public incentives, instructive of the new ways acquisition and development practices can benefit from addressing the concerns of new markets of education and commerce. The result is the redevelopment of one of the largest historic buildings in the heart of downtown Chicago. Now known as the DePaul Center, the project has helped transform an important building and section of Chicago's downtown Loop area and also helped elevate DePaul, according to McHugh, "from the 'little school under the El tracks' to its position as the largest Catholic and ninth largest private university in the nation."

Addressing the successful implementation of financial mechanisms in successful university-community deal making, Allegra Calder, Gabriel Grant, and Holly Muson, in chapter 14, concentrate on "who's in on the deal (and why)." Their study of Boston's Northeastern University and a mixed-use housing project at the Davenport Commons for students and neighbors identifies the stakeholders who *need* to be in the real estate collaboration, if it is to succeed. The case suggests that recognizing and trying to satisfy different, even apparently competing, interests may not sink a project; rather it may be the only way to accomplish it. In the Northeastern-Davenport case all interests were able to claim success: "The university added nearly 600 beds to its strained inventory; the city successfully disposed of long-underused parcels of land in a manner that helped the city's affordable housing problem; and the local residents won a number of concessions, including home ownership rather than rental units, a lower overall density, and greater transparency with respect to the university's master plan." Calder, Grant, and Muson conclude with the observation that "the fact that all involved were able to claim some level of victory allowed the project to be built and will make it easier for Northeastern to pursue future development in the area."

David Dixon and Peter Roche, in chapter 15, also discuss creating the climate to "do the deal." Their case study of The Ohio State University's Campus Partners organization explores this special development agency created to facilitate the university's participation in community real estate development. Campus Partners is organized to carry out significant land acquisition and financial, political, and administrative practices for the university in order to redevelop the neighborhood next to the campus. Quite often universities have neither the authority nor the staff expertise to attend to the full range of matters relating to real estate development and expansion off the campus. This was certainly the case at OSU, which determined that it would be advantageous to engage in large-scale projects of mixed-use development and neighborhood housing revitalization. This initiative can certainly be viewed as a prime example of how a nationally recognized university can become actively involved in "stemming the tide" of urban decline through community revitalization. Dixon and Roche report, however, that the real estate development projects at OSU were really more examples of "enlightened self-interest," where the university's recognized needs for a "crime-free," "vital" community that would "enhance the quality of student life" and help "attract top students and faculty" represented the real drivers of development. For the university to effectively enter the community development process, it needed to establish its own community development corporation, Campus Partners. Today this quasi-university agency is designed to carry out the tasks of day-to-day development, construction management, marketing, and operational activities of complex university real estate initiatives.

Lessons Learned

In their review of the fourteen case studies in this collection, Wim Wiewel and David Perry conclude, in chapter 17, that university real estate development constitutes a new academic topic and a new area of applied research. Therefore it is very important to provide both conceptual and case analyses, as well as a summary or overview that sets some parameters for evaluation. This last part of the book begins the academic conversation about guidelines for institutional and practice-based evaluation of university real estate development.

The conflictive place of the university in the city, especially as it relates to land development practices, requires an assessment of the ethics or institutional responsibilities of the university. The preceding case studies focused almost exclusively on the practices of those who conduct the university's real estate business. The issue of how closely does or can this business hew to the larger mission of the university, to serve the requirements of teaching and research, and the broader public interest, is worthy of consideration. In part this goes to the heart of the debate over just how engaged a university should or can be with its surrounding city and still maintain, both physically and programmatically, the independence required for the production of knowledge. Is the tension between academic mission and the proprietary impulses of real estate development resolved when a university takes the path of enlightened self-interest?

Even a casual reading of the cases in this volume gives rise to a host of other questions: How much real estate should a university own and develop? Is there an upper limit? Does the role of the university as developer change when the project is considered part of the educational infrastructure? Does the university take on a different set of obligations when the project is strictly an income-generating part of its endowment portfolio? Finally, are there conditions when real estate development ceases to be a worthy institutional function?

As Rachel Weber, Nik Theodore, and Charles Hoch suggest in chapter 16, university officials "must address the ethical ambiguities and challenges encountered when their universities act as developers." They evaluate the case studies with an essay meant to describe why and how "ethics matter in university real estate deals." Such ethics are not abstractions—they are toughly honed institutional parameters that come to guide (or sometimes not play a role in) university real estate development. For example, in chapter 15 Dixon and Roche describe an institutional ethic of enlightened self-interest. Weber, Theodore, and Hoch suggest that the "practical ethics" of university real estate development are "situational, negotiated by deliberation among shifting stakeholders inside and outside the university." The norms that must obtain in each situation can be summarized in the following ways: Does the deal fit the basic purposes of the university and those it serves? Does the deal offer good market value for the university as a competitor in the real estate market? Does the deal treat the relevant parties fairly? Further, the authors suggest that any transaction in such a situational setting must be guided by conditions of reciprocity, that is, a balance of costs and benefits in the transaction between the parties, and transparency, where the communication channels between the parties are open, clear, and well-serviced.

Wiewel and Perry review the rich analysis and experience coming from the many vantage points of the previous chapters and provide the reader with a synthetic essay of best practices and lessons learned. They find that universities are highly proactive, internally motivated institutions that have, over time, joined with a broad range of partners and intermediaries and used a full and sophisticated array of financial planning and development practices to accomplish their developmental ends. The real estate development projects that universities seek to develop today appear almost limitless, although the main reasons university developers look to acquire land and build on it remain the expanding demands integral to their core mission. But, as the cases here show, a substantial share of urban university projects now are mixed-use development efforts that physically blur the edge and structure of the campus. Wiewel and Perry offer a summative bridge to more work in both the academic analysis and professional understanding of universities as developers. As such, the chapter is an early assessment of the state of knowledge and practice in this important, albeit nascent, academic field.

References

Bender, Thomas, ed. 1988. *The university and the city: From medieval origins to the present.* New York: Oxford University Press.

Bender, Thomas, 1998. Scholarship, local life, and the necessity of worldliness. In *The urban university and its identity: Roots, locations, roles,* ed. Herman Van der Wusten, pp. 17–28. Dordrecht, Netherlands and Boston: Kluwer Academic Publishers.

Cisneros, Henry. 1995. *The university and the urban challenge.* Washington, DC: U.S. Department of Housing and Urban Development, and Rockville, MD: HUD USER.

Crooks, James. 1982. The AUU and the mission of the urban university. *Urbanism Past and Present* 7(2): 34–39.

Dober, Richard P. 1963. *Campus planning.* New York: Society of College and University Planners.

———. 1991. *Campus design.* New York: John Wiley.

———. 2000. *Campus landscape: Functions, forms, features.* New York: John Wiley.

Grobman, Arnold Brams. 1988. *Urban state universities: An unfinished national agenda.* New York: Praeger.

Harkavy, Ira, and John L. Puckett. 1994. Lessons from Hull House for the contemporary urban university. *Social Service Review* 68(3): 299–321.

Initiative for a Competitive Inner City (ICIC). 2002. *Leveraging colleges and universities for urban economic development: An action agenda.* Boston: CEOs for Cities.

Kellogg Commission on the Future of State and Land-Grant Universities. 1999. *Returning to our roots: The engaged institution.* New York: National Association of State Universities and Land-Grant Colleges.

Klotsche, J. Martin. 1966. *The urban university and the future of our cities.* New York: Harper & Row.

Maurrasse, David J. 2001. *Beyond the campus: How colleges and universities form partnerships with their communities.* New York: Routledge.

McDowell, George R. 2001. *Land-grant universities and extension into the 21st century: Renegotiating or abandoning a social contract.* Ames: Iowa State University Press.

Muthesius, Stefan. 2000. *The postwar university: Utopianist campus and college.* New Haven: Yale University Press.

Nash, George. 1973. *The university and the city: Eight cases of involvement.* New York: McGraw-Hill.

National Center for Education Statistics (NCES). 2002. *Digest of educational statistics.* Washington, DC: U.S. Department of Education (http://nces.ed.gov).

Pinck, Dan. 1993. (Re)emerging roles for developers: Universities as partners. Real *Estate Finance* 10(2): 62–64.

Shils, Edward. 1988. The university, the city, and the world: Chicago and the University of Chicago. In *The university and the city: From medieval origins to the present,* ed. Thomas Bender, pp. 210–30. New York: Oxford University Press.

Turner, Paul Venable. 1984. *Campus: An American planning tradition.* New York: Architectural History Foundation.

U.S. Congress. House Committee on Banking, Finance and Urban Affairs. Subcommittee on Policy Research and Insurance. 1992. The Role of Urban Universities in Economic and Community Development: Hearing Before the Subcommittee on Policy Research and Insurance of the Committee on Banking, Finance and Urban Affairs, House of Representatives, One Hundred Second Congress, First Session, October 28, 1991. Washington, DC: U.S. Government Printing Office.

U.S. Congress. House Committee on Education and Labor. Subcommittee on Postsecondary Education. 1979. The Urban Grant University Act of 1977: Hearings Before the Subcommittee on Postsecondary Education of the Committee on Education and Labor, House of Representatives, Ninety-Fifth Congress, Second Session, on H.R. 7328. Washington, DC: U.S. Government Printing Office.

Van der Wusten, Herman, ed. 1998. *The urban university and its identity: Roots, locations, roles.* Dodrecht, Netherlands, and Boston: Kluwer Academic Publishers.

VerMeulen, Michael. 1980. The university as landlord. *Institutional Investor* 14(5): 119–122.

Wolfe, Robert J. 1986. When a university becomes a developer. *Real Estate Finance Journal* 2(1): 56–61.

Part II

The Campus and the City:
Neighborhood, Downtown, and
Citywide Development

2

The University of Pittsburgh and the Oakland Neighborhood

From Conflict to Cooperation, or How the 800-Pound Gorilla Learned to Sit with— and not on—Its Neighbors

Sabina Deitrick and Tracy Soska

In the summer of 2002, two separate but interrelated events occurred in the Oakland neighborhood that surrounds the University of Pittsburgh. The first was a retrospective exhibition, "Designing Oakland," which showed a century of plans and planning in the neighborhood known as Pittsburgh's traditional cultural center (Carnegie Museum of Art 2002). The visitor's attention was drawn to several models, largely centered on and conceived by planners for the University of Pittsburgh. Chancellor Edward Litchfield's plan of 1958 portrayed an expanded university with new buildings extending well into Oakland's residential neighborhoods. Championed as "a new era for Oakland," the plan reflected the university's desire to become "a great university" (Breachler 1958, 2). The second, bolder proposal for Oakland, known as the Panther Hollow project, included an entire skyscraper laid on end and a technology park of hanging gardens, the "first city of the 21st century" (Faust 1963, 7). These visions for university expansion slated several areas bordering the campus for clearance and redevelopment (Breachler 1958; Pittsburgh Regional Planning Association 1961).

The third campus plan was less imaginative in scope but no less expansive. Designed by the Pittsburgh architectural firm Deeter Ritchey Sippel, the University Master Plan of 1968 extended Pitt's campus in two directions, sprawling up the hill from the upper campus and extending deep into the heart of Oakland on the southwest side next to Forbes Field, then home of the Pittsburgh Pirates baseball team.

Though architecturally different, the Litchfield plan of 1958 and Deeter Ritchey Sippel master plan of 1968 envisioned similar changes for the university and the neighborhood:

- a University of Pittsburgh both spatially and academically larger than the original institution, with new buildings grouped by academic discipline and activities;
- more student residences to house the growing student population;
- demolition and redevelopment of several Oakland residential areas, including the Forbes Field area, which would become available for redevelopment when the Pirates moved to their new home near downtown; and
- views of the nearby Oakland neighborhoods as spaces for university expansion, treating the community "like barren ground" (Phillips 2002). This was the university as the 800-pound gorilla.

The second event occurred just a few blocks away from the Oakland exhibit. The university opened a new building on the southern part of campus called Sennott Square, housing "multipurposes" including academic and nonacademic functions for both university and commercial uses. This opening culminated a cycle of planning, community resistance, and organizing that coincided with the plans on display at the museum. The building's location, called the "two-block area," had been "a battleground for university-community sparring that spanned the tenures of four chancellors" (Hart 2000, 11). Reflecting on that history and the evolution of university-community relations over the period, Chancellor Mark Nordenberg proclaimed at Sennott Square's dedication that the project represents a "tangible reflection of our new era of partnership and progress within our community" (Sammons 2002, 2). This was the university that learned to sit with its neighbors.

This case study analyzes the planning and real estate development processes of the University of Pittsburgh from the 1960s onward and its relationship with its Oakland neighborhood. Relations between the institution and the community evolved over this period, as both underwent a series of changes reflecting different eras and institutional shifts. Two key themes influenced these changes. First, in 1966 the university became a quasi-public institution. This "public-ization" began a gradual process that changed its role and identity from private to public actor in the city and region. Second, the external context of community planning was changing in the 1960s, as cities and communities battled bulldozers and urban renewal. The Oakland community was undergoing its own mobilization toward organizational and political changes like many places in America at that time. The university's early plans, showcased in "Designing Oakland," led to conflict and then confrontation. Over time the community and university moved through an uneasy and uneven process toward cooperation and collaboration. The Sennott Square dedication represented the culmination of the changes in the university in an era of cooperation, a shift from what Thomas Bender calls "the university in the city" to a "university of the city" (Bender 2002, 150).

Context: The Oakland Neighborhood

Oakland and the University of Pittsburgh (Pitt) were no strangers to grand plans. In the nineteenth century, former resident Mary Schenley donated 300 acres to establish a park, and the city added more land centered on a plaza in the Schenley name (Coyne et al. 1974). Andrew Carnegie selected Oakland for his library, museum, and lecture hall in the late 1890s and for his technical school a few years later. At the turn of the twentieth century, local businessman Frank Nicola conceived of Oakland as Pittsburgh's City Beautiful Civic Center and attracted the University of Pittsburgh in 1908 with its plans for an "Acropolis on the Hill" (Breachler 1958; Lowry 2002). By 1920 Oakland laid claim to the region's cultural and civic center (Lubove 1995). A few years later the university began construction on the forty-two-story gothic Cathedral of Learning, dubbed the world's tallest education building.

The Oakland neighborhood expanded with these developments as many residents worked in the nearby educational and cultural institutions or sports stadiums. By 1950 some 22,000 people lived in Oakland, with 8,452 in the core area next to the university. Gradually this concentration of activities began to weaken as the city planned to build a new sports stadium near the downtown and move the Pirates baseball team from their Oakland home at Forbes Field. The city also embarked on plans for a new cultural district in the heart of the CBD (Hart 2000). Oakland's economic base was changing, as was its former residential base of primarily family home owners and long-term renters. While over 80 percent of Oakland's population lived in their residence for more than five years in 1950, the figure dropped to just over 50 percent by 1960 (Dolan 1993). The trend toward more short-term residents and rental properties was under way, and by 2000 central Oakland's population fell to 5,281 as many residents moved to the suburbs. The university's plans would accelerate this trend.

Pitt's plans in the 1960s began the first period of conflict between the institution and the neighborhood. The fanciful hanging gardens and technology park were never realized, and only a few buildings in the 1958 comprehensive plan were built: Lawrence Hall, Litchfield Towers dormitory, and Hillman Library (see Map 2.1). The university was facing financial distress,

Map 2.1 **Oakland Neighborhood and Major University of Pittsburgh Real Estate Projects**

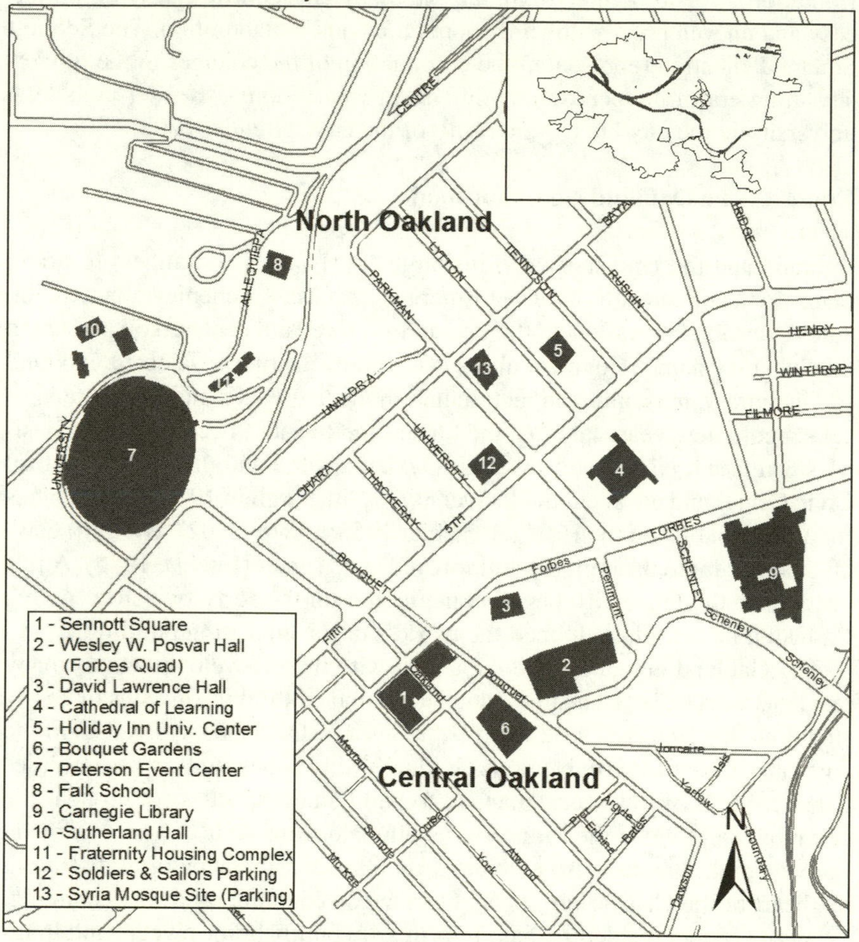
North Oakland
Central Oakland
CENTRE
ALLEQUIPPA
PARKMAN
LYTTON
TENNYSON
RUSKIN
HENRY
WINTHROP
FILMORE
UNIV DR A
UNIVERSITY
OHARA
THACKERAY
5TH
BOUQUET
FORBES
Forbes
Fifth
Oakland
Bouquet
Schenley
Meyran
Semple
Atwood
York
Joncaire
Yarrow
Argyle
Bates
Dawson
Boundary
N
1 - Sennott Square
2 - Wesley W. Posvar Hall (Forbes Quad)
3 - David Lawrence Hall
4 - Cathedral of Learning
5 - Holiday Inn Univ. Center
6 - Bouquet Gardens
7 - Peterson Event Center
8 - Falk School
9 - Carnegie Library
10 -Sutherland Hall
11 - Fraternity Housing Complex
12 - Soldiers & Sailors Parking
13 - Syria Mosque Site (Parking)

Source: Map was prepared by Andrew Aurand, graduate student, Graduate School of Public and International Affairs, University of Pittsburgh.

and the chancellor was forced to resign. The Commonwealth of Pennsylvania had to step in to absorb Pitt as a "state-related" institution, about the same time it took over Temple University in Philadelphia (see chapter 7 in this volume).

Conflict and Confrontation

The change in university status from private to quasi public changed the institution after 1966. Under Chancellor Litchfield the university had planned to expand the physical campus and increase enrollments to 22,000 (PRPA 1961); public-ization accelerated both processes. Enrollments doubled in six years and the number of full-time students exceeded previous projections.

Public-ization meant a new role for the state in the institution, with executive and legislative bodies involved through finances, governance, reporting, and appropriations. Some of these changes were felt immediately, while the impact of others became evident later in the development process. Tuition dropped by over two-thirds, and the public contribution rose to 50 percent of the university's operating budget by 1971 (Kobosky 1974). Through the General State Authority (GSA), the state planned over $100 million in campus construction projects and could act on behalf of the university to use eminent domain to acquire the land. In 1967 the GSA purchased land near Forbes Field, a two-block area bounded by Forbes Avenue, Bouquet Street, and Oakland Avenue (Hart 2000; Roling 2002).[1]

The new chancellor unveiled the University Master Plan of 1968; it was less expensive and less expansive than Chancellor Litchfield's 1958 plan, but targeted the same parts of Oakland for campus expansion (Roling 2002; Shaw 1973). The key areas for expansion plans were the two-block area, as the eminent domain area near Forbes Field came to be known, and an area near the campus in a north Oakland neighborhood.

The university proceeded using the traditional approach to planning of that time: finalizing a plan internally, focusing on formal organizations, and ignoring grassroots and noninstitutional interests (Shaw 1973; Kobosky 1974). The university unveiled its master plan to the Oakland Chamber of Commerce, the city's planning department, and Model Cities, none of which expressed serious reservations with the plan. The university then requested funding from the state but was blindsided by what occurred next—Oakland residents were extremely upset by both the master plan and their exclusion from the process.

Parts of the University Master Plan of 1968 proceeded without incident, including new buildings on Pitt's existing campus, but plans for other areas created conflicts in the community. For example the campus expansion plans called for new student housing for the larger enrollment, roughly 1,500 students, to be housed in a new Hillside dormitory located in the upper campus (Spatter 1992). The project was to take part of the private Falk School's playground (ironically, a private school operated by the university's School of Education), located in a congested area that included nearby residents and the Veteran's Hospital, which had already encroached on the neighborhood with its own expansion. The university informed the Falk School's director of its plans in 1970, and the school principal, school supporters, and residents quickly began to organize and complain to the university (Shaw 1973; Roling 2002).

The second area of conflict was around Forbes Field, the two-block area extending into the community. The master plan called for a four-phase development, part of it a contracted version of the Litchfield plan with a new law school and a quadrangle of professional schools. The imposition of eminent domain, the acquisition of property, the lack of relocation of residents, and the destruction of Forbes Field provided the sparks for neighborhood residents and activists. Community opposition at the grassroots level emerged and organized as the confrontation with the university intensified. In many areas across the country, community efforts to battle eminent domain and redevelopment resulted in new community development corporations (CDCs) in affected neighborhoods, and Oakland followed this path (Gittell and Wilder 1999).

Opponents to the Hillside dormitory project came together in a series of meetings in September 1970, forming People's Oakland. As students, professors, architects, lawyers, and others joined the Hillside residents in fighting the university's expansion plans, the focus of the group expanded to include the future of Forbes Field and the feared disappearance of Oakland (Coyne et al. 1974; Hart 2000; Phillips 2002). The leaders of People's Oakland summarized their approach as finding "small technicalities" that create delays and can kill a project (Phillips 2002).

The community was helped by political changes in Pittsburgh. Peter Flaherty defeated the Democratic machine candidate for mayor in the primary and won the general election in 1969 (Lorant 1978). His campaign platform emphasized a redirection for Pittsburgh toward its neighborhoods and away from the nonresidential projects of the famed Pittsburgh Renaissance (Lubove 1995). Dubbed "a new folk hero" by the *New York Times* (Lorant 1978, 62), Mayor Flaherty changed the planning department to reflect his focus on neighborhood involvement and issues (Lurcott and Downing 1987). Planners from the city aided community activists in Oakland (Kobosky 2002; Phillips 2002). Flaherty also battled the expansion of other nonprofit organizations, as the city feared losing more taxable properties.

Using political channels and creating delays advanced the community's agenda. In January 1971 People's Oakland filed an objection with the planning commission to the university's conditional use application on the Hillside dormitory project. The planning commission delayed approval of Pitt's plans until the city, community, and university discussed and agreed on the plans. The community also proposed alternative reuse plans for Forbes Field, which Pitt rejected. People's Oakland lobbied state officials in Harrisburg to stop the university's demolition of Forbes Field (Hart 2000; Phillips 2002). Support from then governor Milton Shapp, another independent Democrat, and a lack of state development monies caused the state to suspend funding for Pitt's construction projects until the university could work with the community on a new plan.

The community's tactics worked. The university abandoned its master plan, including plans for the contested two-block area and the Hillside dormitory, and agreed to relocate buildings to other sites. It entered into a joint planning process with the community and the city, mediated by a GSA official and described as "a new era of cooperation" (Dunlop 1973). The state was interested in approval of a joint plan, having invested significant funds in the master plan and facing rising construction costs. The community agreed to end its battle to save Forbes Field but persisted in defining the border of Pitt's new construction to be Bouquet Street—the eastern edge of the two-block area held by the GSA. Furthermore the university agreed to "the development of new commercial space and 'people-oriented' space in the Forbes Field area" (Shaw 1973, 24).

Early outcomes were achieved: the Law School and professional schools buildings were located to new sites; Pitt agreed to pay the city an amount for city services (instead of payments in lieu of taxes); and People's Oakland created a new community planning organization, Oakland Directions, Inc. (ODI), as a permanent joint planning process in Oakland, with community, university, and city planning representatives in leadership and activist roles (Kobosky 1974; Phillips 2002). ODI secured public and private funding for the process, which centered on a number of issues including the two-block area still owned by the state but now freed from university expansion pressure by the reduced Forbes Field–area expansion. In 1972 the university and community settled on a new plan for the area, which was to include 17,000 square feet of space for the community and 35,000 square feet for the university (Coyne et al. 1974, 8). The university was to maintain the buildings, which would also include the local office of the GSA.

Over the period of conflict and confrontation, the university underestimated the political strength of the community and the changed politics of both city and state officials. A 1973 analysis of the process concluded that "[t]he University . . . proceeded without effective organization and planning, thus compiling a record of what now is seen as comic opera episodes which made the University appear intransigent and uncooperative and may have assisted the organizational efforts of the adversaries to campus expansion" (Shaw 1973, 10).

The university also misunderstood its own role as a newly public institution. One informant characterized the university coming out of its private status as "grand style with a lot of vision and little practical ability to make things work." Through the period of conflict, university community and public affairs were handled by the Office of Physical Plant, which lacked expertise in these areas. While individuals in the institution recognized the changed environment in which the university was working, an early proposal to establish a community policy (1970) was not enacted (Shaw 1973). Since the university was forced into joint meetings with the community by the city and state, Pitt planners had to change their understanding of what was meant by participating formally with the community. After abandoning the 1968 master plan and Forbes Field project, the university established an Office of Public Affairs responsible for the joint planning process and communications with the community, city and state (Kobosky 1974).

The university did expand greatly over the 1960–80 period, increasing from 64 to 110 acres, mostly on the former Forbes Field site (Hart 2000). The number of buildings increased from 23 to 40 over the same period, although most were within the university boundaries and not a threat to Oakland: the Nursing School, Chevron Hall, Crawford Hall, Hillman Library, Learning Research and Development Center, Benedum Hall, Graduate School of Public Health, and Trees Hall.

An important question about this process is: since most of the university's construction plans were realized, did the community influence real estate development at the university? The evidence from sources and interviews points to a qualified yes. The activism stopped the physical expansion of the 1968 master plan. At the same time the field of planning itself was changing. Community involvement was increasingly required for major development plans from the local level to federal government programs. Politics in older industrial cities and at the state level was also changing as independent Democrats took power. The community understood political changes better than the university did and made connections with city and state governments. The conflict also changed the community, which began to develop its own planning process for Oakland.

The university viewed itself as detached, in part due to its history as a private institution, and was not as capable a political player in a public arena. The university required a much longer time to adapt to its public-ization process than the short time of its legal incorporation into the Commonwealth system. One former university official felt that if the university had become state-related years earlier, "[p]erhaps then the University would have been acclimated to functioning as a public agent and the circumstances of 1971 would have been avoided" (Kobosky 1974, 66). That inexperience proved costly for the University Master Plan of 1968. Ultimately, though, the delays pushed the university into a joint planning process with ODI that produced new development plans acceptable to community and its public partners and a new process for future planning.

On the Road to Collaboration, or Crisis

In 1980 ODI published *The Oakland Plan* (ODI 1980), a neighborhood-generated plan that offered both a process of community organization and a set of goals for the community. It set boundaries for institutional development and portal areas and focused on revitalization, transportation, and continued joint planning. It created a CDC, the Oakland Planning and Development Corporation (OPDC), to carry out neighborhood development. During the 1980s the Oakland plan guided development, with the CDC working on residential development and the university working on expansion within the boundaries established by the plan. University-community relations finally had calmed down.

Oakland and other Pittsburgh neighborhoods continued to receive strong support from Pittsburgh's next mayor, Richard Caligiuri. He promoted a second downtown renaissance—Renaissance I largely rebuilt the downtown in the 1950s and early 1960s—and a more grassroots renaissance in the neighborhoods (Lubove 1996). This focus brought dollars to the neighborhoods for infrastructure and physical improvements and seeded the capacity of community organizations to become development specialists (Jezierski 1990; Ferman 1996).

OPDC succeeded in this environment and built more than 200 units of affordable housing in the 1980s (Phillips 2002). It secured funds from national foundations and other private and public sources, and found a development partner in an Oakland-based private developer. National Development Corp. was identified with Pittsburgh's political leadership and had completed large developments in the region. It became a major development force in Oakland through partnering with OPDC to complete various neighborhood priorities, building housing, improving the neighborhood's western portal, and working with the university (Barnes 1991).

During the 1980s a crisis erupted in the region's steel industry as the city's industrial base collapsed. More than 100,000 jobs were lost between 1980 and 1986, many in the hard-hit steel towns in the industrial Mon Valley (Deitrick 1999). The university turned its attention to this crisis and focused on regional job loss and economic restructuring (University of Pittsburgh 1983). Pittsburgh's economic base was shifting to services, particularly technology, health, and education (Mitchell-Weaver 1992). Its traditional public-private growth partnership, famed for the two Renaissance projects, represented a corporate planning model focused largely on real estate development (Ferman 1996; Sbragia 1990). As a major regional employer and research institution, Pitt became part of an urban regeneration agenda stressing economic restructuring (Sbragia 1990). Both Pitt, with biotechnology

and health research, and Carnegie Mellon University, with software and ro-
botics, were central to a new, state-financed economic development project,
the Pittsburgh Technology Center (PTC) (Allegheny Conference 1984; City
of Pittsburgh 1985). Part of the university's attention to real estate matters in
the 1980s centered on the PTC, located on the site of a former steel plant.

In Oakland the university's role was more limited during this period. It assisted OPDC in setting up a development loan fund to help complete housing
and other projects and acquired key boundary properties to bank for future use
(Yeager 2002). The university worked with National Development on several
projects, including the Soldiers and Sailors Memorial Hall underground parking lot, Sutherland Hall dormitory, and the PTC (Barnes 1991). When the university was concerned with the lack of hotel space in Oakland, National
Development built the Holiday Inn/University Center and later the Oakland/
Forbes Avenue Hampton Hotel, another component of the western portal improvement (Barnes 1991; Yeager 2002). Though sharing a development partner, the university and the CDC never secured a partnership to develop housing
in Oakland, something that some speculate might have helped to slow Central
Oakland's continued slide to absentee property ownership (Phillips 2002).

Despite the joint planning process, Oakland was not always involved in
university real estate plans. As the 1980s came to a close, Oakland's tense
community-institution relationship flared once again as the university, the
medical complex, and National Development eyed the historic buildings of
Oakland's City Beautiful period for new expansion.[2]

Cooperation and Collaboration, After a Rocky Start

By 1990 the accord between the university and the community to engage in
joint planning had weakened. Established leaders in both groups who first
battled then brokered relationships with each other over two decades had
moved on or stepped down. ODI had become less active with organizational
and community changes, and a new chancellor lacked experience with what
had preceded him. The university had no formal mechanisms or senior officials in place for working with the community, and relations with both city
and neighborhood were handled on an ad hoc basis. As the joint planning
process stalled, so did the process of public-ization of the institution at the
community level. As one university official noted, "in 1991 it wasn't that
those ties [university-community] had been severed, but those ties had atro-
phied" (McManus 2002). Central Oakland had also changed. The trend toward more rental properties that began in the 1950s accelerated in the 1970s
and 1980s. Student renters and absentee landlords dominated the housing
market, and housing conditions were deteriorating rapidly. By 1990 only 16
percent of Central Oakland residences were owner-occupied (Dolan 1993).

The decade began with a firestorm: the purchase and razing of the Syria Mosque, a community treasure located in Oakland's civic center area. The university was effectively in competition for the building with itself, as the medical complex (later called UPMC) and the university sought separately to acquire the property. The medical side prevailed and its development partner, National Development, purchased the building. Despite an eleventh-hour attempt to save the building through historic landmark status, the politically connected developer obtained a valid demolition permit two hours before the historic status nomination. Though UPMC purchased and razed the building, the community targeted its ire at the university and its secrecy.

Two developments in 1992 put joint planning back on both the community and institutional agendas, and the attempt to produce the first university plan since the University Master Plan of 1968 was aborted in 1971. First, the Syria Mosque episode forced the university to realize that it needed to restart its community outreach activities and develop a clear and structured approach to communications (McManus 2002). The Oakland Agreement Committee became the first in a series of formal and informal groups to discuss Oakland and university relations and planning (see Table 2.1). Second, the City of Pittsburgh, weary of reviewing institutions' plans on a project-by-project basis, required city institutions to submit for approval a master space plan before any new construction would be permitted. Because of the requirement for community participation in planning, the two changes became interwoven (see Table 2.2).

The new chancellor, Dennis O'Connor, assigned the Plant Utilization and Planning Committee (PUP) of the university senate to the master planning task. PUP produced an initial master plan in 1994, but the city's Planning Commission rejected it because it lacked a comprehensive housing strategy and transportation management plan. Even without such agreement on strategic planning, the university was on the move, having increased student housing on campus with the opening of a new dormitory, Sutherland Hall, in 1992 and new buildings in which to relocate fraternities from North Oakland to the campus.[3] This development still was not enough: estimates of demand for student housing found a 2,200-bed gap between supply and demand (Dolan 1993). Oakland residents continued to press their concerns about student housing and transportation issues. A year later the planning commission revisited the 1994 plan and gave conditional approval, pending the development of the housing and transportation strategies (Sajna 1995; Wilds 2002). The community was pushing for a commitment to construct more new student housing over the next four years, and PUP set up a subcommittee, the Community Input into the Master Plan (CIMP), to gain community input into the master planning process. Through its meetings in the community, CIMP realized that the community wanted to discuss more than just the master plan.

Table 2.1

Planning Groups in the 1990s

Planning group	Composition	Tasks/outcomes
Oakland Directions, Inc. (ODI)	Community groups, city, university, institutions	The Oakland Plan (inactive by early 1990s)
Plant Utilization and Planning (PUP)	University senate subcommittee—faculty, staff, and administration	1994 Master Space Plan 1995 Master Space Plan 1995 Oakland Housing Plan 1995 Transportation Study
Community Input in the Master Plan (CIMP)	Oakland's community organizations working with PUP and university	1995 Master Plan community input to plan
Oakland Agreement Committee (OAC)	Community organizations and university; City-facilitated (grew from CIMP)	Non-university development 1995 Oakland Housing Proposal
Oakland Community Council (OCC)	Coalition of Oakland's community organizations (grew out of/replaced CIMP)	1997 Master Space Plan community input to plan
Facilities Planning Committee	Internal university administrative committee	1997 Master Plan
Oakland Improvement	City-led group, community organizations, university, institutions	Non-university development strategy (OIC) 1998 Oakland Improvement Strategy—housing, zoning, and public corridors
The "Eli" Group	Forum between university and Oakland organizations focused on university development impacting Oakland	"Two-block area" student housing and Sennott Square; ongoing university developments
Oakland Task Force (OTF)	Long-standing but little-used forum from Caligiuri era; community organizations, city, university, Oakland institutions, Allegheny Conference on Community Development (corporate leaders planning group)	Became proactive late 1990s; Schenley Plaza and other institutional and noninstitutional developments in Oakland

Table 2.2

University of Pittsburgh and Oakland Community Plans in the 1990s

Plans/proposals	Date	Participants	Comments
Oakland Historic Core	1992	City of Pittsburgh–City Council	Reaction to demolition of Syria Mosque
Interim Planning Overlay District Proposal	1992	City of Pittsburgh Planning Department and Oakland resident groups	
Initial University Master Plan	1994	University of Pittsburgh administration	Rejected by city Planning Commission
Oakland Housing Strategy	1995	Oakland Agreement Committee— university and Oakland groups	
University Master Housing Plan (revised)	1995	University Plant Utilization and Planning Committee, university administration	Received conditional Planning Commission approval
Bigelow Boulevard Closing Proposal	1996	University of Pittsburgh, City of Pittsburgh, Oakland groups	Reopened after six-month trial period
University of Pittsburgh Plan: 1998–2007	1997	University of Pittsburgh Facilities Planning Committee	Plans for two-block area include multipurpose facility and new student housing
Pitt Master Space Plans	1998	University Implementation Committee	Revisions of 1995 plan; integrated space and academic plans
University Comprehensive Housing Strategy	1998	University with input from Oakland community	Updates master plan to include new student housing on two-block area
Oakland Improvement Strategy	1998	Oakland community partners, institutional partners, funders, and City of Pittsburgh	Action plan for Oakland, focusing on design and zoning, created Oakland Business Improvement District (OBID)
Final Master Space Plan	1999	University, City of Pittsburgh, Oakland groups	Revised 1999–2000 to meet Planning Commission stipulations

The PUP/CIMP process created change in both the university and the community. The university began to realize that the community was more than one or two vocal organizations, and it needed a process to "institutionalize community input" (Jones 2003). Likewise the community began to see a decentralized university and had to act differently than when dealing with one or two individuals. To bridge these gaps, university and community representatives formed the Oakland Agreement Committee (OAC). Reminiscent of the old ODI, city planning officials facilitated the discussions, centered on housing and transportation issues absent from the 1994 master plan. As OAC set out its housing priorities, the group melded into the Oakland Community Council (OCC), a more formal organization with more community members. The university and OCC continued discussions about university planning, particularly the student housing issue (OAC 1995). Dissatisfied with the pace of the university's plans, some community members felt the process was failing and they left.

In 1995 the university was instructed by its Board of Trustees to begin a ten-year facilities plan, a comprehensive review of all capital priorities of the university on its campuses with short-, medium-, and long-term priorities and their costs spelled out. The provost sought to insure that the facilities plan was guided by the university's academic plans to ensure a strong rationale for funding and long-term success. The plan, completed by senior administration, laid out $362 million in capital projects (Steele 1996; University of Pittsburgh 1997). In 1996, one year before the final report, the committee reviewed the plan with internal and external sources. For external review the city and OCC provided input into the plan, especially regarding student housing issues and other issues focused on Oakland.

In the university's Facilities Plan approved in 1997, the long-disputed two-block area would be developed, with a multipurpose academic building (MPAC), a convocation center (later sited elsewhere), and new student housing, which became the university's chief building priorities in the latter half of the 1990s (University of Pittsburgh 1997). Resources remained the sticking point until the state committed $135 million over five years for Pitt's facility projects (Barnes 1998). Combined with a capital campaign and other funding reserves, the university now had the resources to realize its plans. Community opposition continued, however, as the time frame for development remained unconfirmed. The university, on the other hand, was single-minded in its commitment to press forward and implement its plans. The need to reinvigorate the university-community relationship became an important part of the implementation process, including maintaining continuity of relations and engaging senior administration in this dialogue (Golomb 2002; McManus 2002).

During this period the university underwent another change in leadership, as Dennis O'Connor resigned and Mark Nordenberg was appointed chancellor in 1995.[4] Nordenberg received a mandate from the Board of Trustees to expand the university's involvement in regional economic and community development, especially with neighborhoods on the university's borders (University of Pittsburgh 1996; Wilds 2002). Promoting community quality of life in Oakland became an important part of the university's transformation into a public institution.

Oakland also remained on the city's agenda as the city sought another planning process with community and institutional participation. Rather than updating the 1980 ODI-produced plan, the OCC decided to focus on three areas raised by OAC: housing, zoning, and public corridors. With financial support from the institutions and the city, the group produced *The Oakland Improvement Strategy* (Focus Communications 1998). The university took a major role in implementing dimensions of the strategy by helping to fund a new Oakland Business Improvement District (OBID), contributing to OPDC's development fund, and sharing the costs with the city of a building inspector assigned to Oakland (Focus Communications 1998).

Just after assuming office the new chancellor oversaw yet another community imbroglio. The university proposed closing Bigelow Boulevard, a main thoroughfare through the central campus. The city agreed to the closure, but the community saw the closing as another university land grab. The university was allowed to close the boulevard for a sixty-day trial period, but it was subsequently reopened by the city. In private, many residents supported the closing as pedestrian friendly; but publicly they felt that "the University should not be allowed to move forward with what it wanted until the community got what it wanted," which was student housing on campus and improved transportation management (McManus 2002).

In accordance with the 1997 facilities plan's priorities, the university revised its housing strategy and finally satisfied the community's demands for immediate housing construction (University of Pittsburgh 1998a; 1998b). The construction of the first phase of new housing received highest priority, at a cost of $5.3 million for the initial phase scheduled to open in 1999. Bouquet Gardens, as the project became known, would house 500 students in garden-style apartments. The university finally realized that key to completing any projects in the future would be the passage and construction of new student housing.

After the missteps noted above, the university again revamped its procedures to work with the community. Chancellor Nordenberg appointed Eli Shorak, under the vice chancellor for business affairs, to serve as the point person with the community on construction projects. A relative "new kid on the block," Shorak had no "baggage" with the community, but lacked experience in community and city planning (Garvey 2002; Shorak 2002). His mandate was "to get those buildings built" (Shorak 2002). Though inexperienced, he learned from university personnel, community representatives, and city officials. He spoke directly with and for senior administration in his relations with the community and the city, and unlike previous community liaisons Shorak was able to make commitments for the university. The community had never had this level of coordination with the university (Shorak 2002; McManus 2002).

Community input on the former two-block projects included design changes and parking. The facades of Bouquet Gardens were redesigned to fit the neighborhood context, and student residents were banned from the residential parking program. Community needs for short-term parking were built into the new multipurpose building. The Oakland Improvement Strategy stressed the need for improvements in the Forbes Avenue commercial corridor, and MPAC addressed these concerns with designs for 18,000 square feet of retail space.[5] The university also had to deal with the contentious process of relocating community organizations from the two-block area to other parts of the neighborhood. OPDC, OCC, and OBID moved into a university-owned building that OPDC now owns. The university also helped People's Oakland purchase a building for its use by donating $100,000 toward the purchase.

By the end of the decade, the university had learned to sit with its neighbors. Shorak and OCC met biweekly to discuss the university's real estate concerns so that the community would have a regular dialog and input on issues. The group, dubbed the "Eli meeting," represents what informal channels can achieve through regular communications. The group had input into design changes of Bouquet Gardens and MPAC, now called Sennott Square. The meetings continue to address important issues such as problematic landlords, code enforcement, and zoning.

In 2001 the university moved its football games to the new Heinz Field, home of the Pittsburgh Steelers. It razed Pitt Stadium for the construction of a new convocation center that was formerly planned for the two-block area. This upper campus development opened up space for a new dormitory for 1,000 students, and the plan was supported by the community. While many alumni and business owners opposed the move, the university was doing what the Pittsburgh Regional Planning Association plan for Oakland had called for in 1961—but then they were looking to move Pitt football to the then newly proposed Three Rivers Stadium.

Not all disputes have been settled or settled amicably. Despite new dormitory space, the persistence of student overcrowding and absentee landlords means housing conditions continue to deteriorate in Central Oakland.[6] Some residents remain suspicious of any moves by the university, given their long history, and one Oakland leader felt the university is "not going to tell you anything" about any real estate project (Potts 2002). Nonetheless, over the decade the joint planning process between the university and the community emerged stronger than it had been in the early 1990s. The university now participates in yet another Oakland planning process, the Oakland Task Force, a formal organization that is implementing the *Oakland Improvement Strategy*. The task force aims to restore Oakland as a "showplace," with its City Beautiful roots. The university will be a major investor in the public projects of this effort. In addition the university was a recipient of a U.S. Department of Housing and Urban Development Community Outreach Partnership Center (COPC) grant in 2000 to work with community partners on revitalization efforts throughout Oakland. The public-ization of the University of Pittsburgh has matured.

University-Community Partnership: Sitting with Neighbors in the New Millennium

We find two main themes affecting university and community planning and its changes: the university's adaptation to its role as a newly public institution—its public-ization—and the evolution of the planning process in both the Oakland community and university, which began in reactive modes during the period of conflict and confrontation. The university found itself in an unfamiliar public role and opposed by growing community activism as it tried to expand in the Oakland community. Conflict and confrontation led to a city- and state-brokered joint planning process that grew into a more collaborative initiative in the years that followed. The community was learning to plan for its future development while the university was learning to be a public partner in planning with its neighbors.

Leadership changes in both the community and the university resulted in new contentions and the need to revisit the joint planning process in the 1990s. After some rocky years the university established more effective structures for communicating and working with the community. A new process of city planning required greater public input into the university's plans and resulted in some community needs being met. The university now targets investments with benefits for both university and community, and participates in the community planning process with greater commitment, including financial support. Looking back on the original plans for Oakland, many of the earlier visions for the University of Pittsburgh have come to fruition, but it was not just real estate development that changed (Dolan 1993). The changing planning process proved to be significant in transforming the university into a public institution.

The University of Pittsburgh, like many urban universities, has matured and recognized that the university and the community are inextricably linked. As the university came to understand the practical nature of community politics, recognizing and respecting the process of community problem solving and the political power of the community, it was able to assume a broader community development role. The 800-pound gorilla has learned to support and engage in collaborative planning through university-community partnerships forged over four decades, and the University of Pittsburgh now sits with, not on, its Oakland neighbors.

Notes

1. Pitt was quoted as saying the university was not involved in property acquisitions or negotiations with property owners (Spatter 1969). However several informants disputed that statement, claiming that the university had front people working for them. The process sped up speculation in the neighborhood, either waiting to be acquired by the university through the GSA or holding properties for depreciation cycles and swapping with other landlords (Phillips 2002).

2. Located between O'Hara Street and Fifth Avenue, these institutions were noted much earlier by the Pittsburgh Regional Planning Association (1961, 18), which recommended that should these institutions wish to leave their building, "reuse should be by the University of Pittsburgh."

3. The university's request for approval for the Sutherland Hall dormitory gained approval from the city's Planning Commission, but after that all city institutions were required to have an official master plan in place before additional construction projects would be approved.

4. Nordenberg was first appointed interim chancellor in 1995; his appointment was made permanent in 1996.

5. This was the space devoted to community uses in the two-block area. Now the community wanted retail to improve the commercial corridor and place the community groups in new locations.

6. Absentee landlords and property speculation continue to increase in Oakland. A University of Pittsburgh neighborhood development class documented nearly two decades of property swaps by a core group of absentee landlords (Feathers 2001).

References

Allegheny Conference on Community Development. 1984. *A strategy for growth: An economic development program for the Pittsburgh region.* Pittsburgh: Allegheny Conference on Community Development.

Barnes, Tom. 1998. Oakland residents oppose Pitt expansion. *Pittsburgh Post-Gazette,* January 22: A9.

———. 1991. Spotlight plays on Oakland developer: Mosque dispute raises firm's low profile. *Pittsburgh Post-Gazette,* April 25: 6.

Bender, Thomas. 2002 *The unfinished city: New York and the metropolitan idea.* New York: The New Press.

Breachler, Edwin. 1958. Here's how Oakland's face is changing. *Pittsburgh Press,* December 14: 2.

Carnegie Museum of Art. 2002. *Designing Oakland.* Heinz Architectural Center, Pittsburgh, June 22–September 22.

City of Pittsburgh and Allegheny County. 1985. *Economic development strategy to begin 21st century: A proposal for the Commonwealth of Pennsylvania.*

Coyne, Mike et al. 1974. Oakland residents under stress, organized for survival. *New Sun,* Pittsburgh, March 13–26: 1.

Deitrick Sabina. 1999. The post-industrial revitalization of Pittsburgh: Myths and evidence. *Community Development Journal* 34(1) (January): 4–12.

Dolan, Anthony. 1993. Central Oakland: Winning the battles but losing the war. Unpublished manuscript, Graduate School of Public and International Affairs, University of Pittsburgh, April.

Dunlop, Beth. 1973. Pitt, residents begin new era of cooperation. *Pittsburgh Press,* October 1: 4

Faust, William. 1963. Panther Hollow project. *Pittsburgh Press,* November 24: 7–8.

Feathers, Ruth. 2001. *Meyran Avenue.* Pittsburgh: University of Pittsburgh, Graduate School of Public and International Affairs, February.

Ferman, Barbara. 1996. *Challenging the growth machine.* Lawrence: University of Kansas Press.

Focus Communications. 1998. *The Oakland Improvement Strategy,* vol. 2, appendices. Pittsburgh, PA, December.

Garvey, Martha. 2002. Personal interview. President, Oakland Planning and Development Corporation, September 18.

Gittell, Ross, and Margaret Wilder. 1999. Community development corporations: Critical factors that influence success. *Journal of Urban Affairs* 21(3): 341–361.

Golomb, Susan. 2002. Personal interview. Director, Department of City Planning, City of Pittsburgh, September 16.

Hart, Peter. 2000. The two-block area. *University Times.* University of Pittsburgh, March 16: 9–12.

Jezierski, Louise. 1990. Neighborhoods and public-private partnerships in Pittsburgh. *Urban Affairs Quarterly* 26(2): 217–249.

Jones, Robin. 2003. Personal correspondence. Former Director, Urban Studies Program, University of Pittsburgh; now at University of South Florida, Tampa, April 25.

Kobosky, Bernard J. 1974. Institutional/community relations in an urban setting: The University of Pittsburgh experience. Ph.D. dissertation, University of Pittsburgh.

———. 2002. Personal interview. Executive Vice President, Public Relations, University of Pittsburgh Medical Center, July.

Lorant, Stefan. 1978. *Pete: The life of Peter F. Flaherty.* Lenox, MA: Authors' Edition, Inc.

Lowry, Patricia. 2002. Places: In Oakland, a lust for land and a penchant for plans. *Pittsburgh Post-Gazette,* June 29: C6.

Lubove, Roy. 1995. *Twentieth-century Pittsburgh: Government, business, and environmental change,* vol. 1. Pittsburgh: University of Pittsburgh Press.

———. 1996. *Twentieth-century Pittsburgh: The post-steel era,* vol. II. Pittsburgh: University of Pittsburgh Press.

Lurcott, Robert H., and Jane A. Downing. 1987. A public-private support system for community-based organizations in Pittsburgh. *Journal of the American Planning Association* 53: 459–468.

McManus, Dennis. 2002. Personal interview. Executive Director, Institute of Politics, University of Pittsburgh, July 24.

Mitchell-Weaver, C. 1992. Regional development in southwestern Pennsylvania. *Canadian Journal of Regional Science* 15(2): 131–146.

Oakland Agreement Committee (OAC). 1995. *A proposal for a housing strategy for Oakland.* Pittsburgh, September 26.

Oakland Directions, Inc. (ODI). 1980. *The Oakland plan: A citizens' planning process.* Pittsburgh: Oakland Directions, Inc. and Urban Design Associates.

Phillips, Sandra L. 2002. Personal interview. Vice President, Manchester Bidwell Corporation, Pittsburgh, July.

Pittsburgh Regional Planning Association (PRPA). 1961. *A plan for Pittsburgh's cultural district, Oakland.* Pittsburgh: Pittsburgh Regional Planning Association.

Potts, Jonathan. 2002. Revitalizing Oakland: A tough test of universities, community. *Pittsburgh Tribune-Review,* July 5: A1.

Roling, Jay. 2002. Personal interview. Community and Governmental Relations, University of Pittsburgh, July.

Sajna, Mike. 1995. City Planning Commission approves university master plan, but adds several stipulations. *University Times* 27(17): April 27: 7.

Sammons, Amanda. 2002. Chancellor, mayor, others dedicate Sennott Square. *Pitt News,* University of Pittsburgh, September 6: 2–4.

Sbragia, A.M. 1990. Pittsburgh's "third way": The nonprofit sector as a key to urban regeneration. In *Leadership and urban regeneration: Cities in North America and Europe,* ed. Dennis Judd and Michael Parkinson, vol. 37, pp. 51–68. *Urban Affairs Annual Review.* Newbury Park, CA: Sage.

Shaw, Paul C. 1973. *Truth, love and campus expansion: The University of Pittsburgh experience.* Pittsburgh: University-Urban Interface Program, June.

Shorak, Eli. 2002. Personal interview. Associate Vice Chancellor, University of Pittsburgh, August.

Spatter, Sam. 1969. New expansion by Pitt year off, Posvar says. *Pittsburgh Press,* January 11: 2.

———. 1992. City planners seek greater control over future developments. *Pittsburgh Press,* February 16: H16.

Steele, Bruce. 1996. New building, renovation plan proposed for campus. *University Times* 29(1): August 29: 1.

University of Pittsburgh. 1983. *Recommendations for southwestern Pennsylvania's regional development strategy for the 1980s and 1990s: University of Pittsburgh chancellor's conference proceedings,* Pittsburgh.

———. 1996. Partnering in community development. Resolution of the Board of Trustees, University of Pittsburgh, February 22.

———. 1997. *University of Pittsburgh facilities plan: 1998–2007.* Pittsburgh: University of Pittsburgh, April.

———. 1998a. *University of Pittsburgh: Comprehensive housing strategy.* Pittsburgh: University of Pittsburgh, June.

———. 1998b. *University of Pittsburgh: Comprehensive housing strategy.* Pittsburgh: University of Pittsburgh, August.

Wilds, John. 2002. Personal interview. Community and Governmental Relations, University of Pittsburgh, June.

Yeager, John. 2002. Personal interview. Associate Professor and Director, Institute for Higher Education Administration, School of Education, University of Pittsburgh, August.

3

Columbia University's Heights

An Ivory Tower and Its Communities

Peter Marcuse and Cuz Potter

Columbia University is one of the three largest landowners in New York City, after the Catholic Church and the city government itself (see Map 3.1). In its role as owner and investor in real estate, the university has acted no differently than any other landowner: it has invested in real estate for its financial return. In its role as a major institution, Columbia has interests no different from any other institution: to meet the spatial requirements that its own activities determine. Here it is similar to a profit-motivated business entity in having to meet its own needs for space and location, but differs from them, as does a museum or a hospital or a church, in that its bottom line is measured in terms other than dollars.

In a number of ways, however, Columbia, as a university, differs from all of these other private and nonprofit entities in relation to its real estate interests. First, because its core activities involve the long-term presence of young people, often away from home for the first time in their lives, it is an accepted obligation of the university to take care of their accommodations, and, if not *in loco parentis,* to provide for their security in a fashion at least adequate to maintain the desirability of the institution as a place for others to request admission. Its role in providing housing for its faculty, while perhaps seeming to be intuitively similar, is in fact no different from the role of any large employer seeking to attract and hold employees in its service.[1]

Second, because its core activities involve young people at a high educational level, generally with wide-ranging curiosity and sympathies, and because its faculty is likely to have within its ranks many interested in issues of social policy and equity and attentive to issues in their surroundings, what a university does that affects those surroundings is likely to engage the attention of its members and influence its policy. Third, because of its scale Columbia has a greater impact on its residential surroundings than almost any other nonprofit or single profit-making landowner in the city.

Map 3.1   Columbia University and Selected Affiliates' Properties in Northern Manhattan

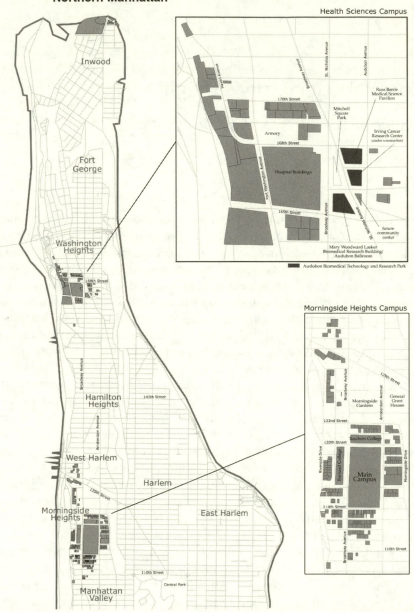

Source: Data from the New York City Department of Planning PLUTO database.

A fourth way that Columbia is different from most other institutions, whether public, nonprofit, or private, is in the location of its two northern Manhattan campuses next to lower-income communities. The main campus in Morningside Heights is adjacent to Harlem, an overwhelmingly African American community that has long been an icon of African American life, while the Health Sciences Campus in Washington Heights is in the center of a vibrant, predominantly Dominican community. These two communities differ, however, in their sense of permanence. The historical significance of Harlem to the African American community has created a sense of rootedness and place, while Washington Heights is perceived by some members of the Dominican community as a temporary base of action from which to amass the capital necessary to return to a comfortable life in the Dominican Republic or across the river in New Jersey.

Three important threads affecting Columbia University's development activities are of particular interest to us here: (1) its concern with meeting its own institutional needs by first housing its students and faculty and then providing space for university-related economic activities; (2) the involvement of those students (and some faculty) in issues dealing with the university's role in the community; and (3) the reactions of the surrounding poorer communities to the university's real estate activities. Those concerns run throughout the evolution of Columbia's policies toward development and arise in roughly chronological order. This chapter does not deal with Columbia as a real estate developer or investor per se, where the motivation for the university's actions is profit as a property owner/landlord,[2] although the profit-making motivation enters strongly into its desire to expand its biomedical facilities, nor with other aspects of the university-community relationship, also interesting.[3]

The Evolution of Community Relations

When Columbia University moved from the current site of Rockefeller Center in 1897 to the property that it had purchased from the Bloomingdale Insane Asylum on Morningside Heights, that neighborhood was relatively undeveloped. Other institutions soon followed: Teachers College, Barnard College, the Union Theological Seminary, the Institute of Musical Art (now the Julliard School), and the Jewish Theological Seminary. When the subway finally reached them in 1904, the neighborhood was rapidly transformed into a middle-class apartment-house neighborhood. Morningside Heights remained middle-class until the end of World War II, when low-interest mortgages were introduced through federal legislation and middle-class families began their exodus to the suburbs. The vacuum left behind was filled by

African Americans, who were moving into northern cities at the time, and Puerto Ricans, who were beginning to migrate in large numbers. The low rents, building deterioration, and presence of SROs (single room occupancy buildings) also attracted elements considered undesirable, such as drug addicts and prostitutes.

To counteract the negative impact these developments were expected to have on their primarily white and middle-class constituents, the institutions in the neighborhood banded together in 1947 to form Morningside Heights, Inc., now called the Morningside Alliance. Their chief objective was to halt the "encroachment of Harlem" (by which they meant the spread of the slums from predominantly African American and Puerto Rican Harlem and Manhattanville, now West Harlem) by upgrading housing conditions in the neighborhood (Dolkart 1998, 329). Contemporary real estate pressures, followed by urban planning wisdom and supported by federal funding provisions, advocated urban renewal—the technique of the wholesale demolition of buildings in designated slum areas, most often without any provisions for the relocation of their previous low-income tenants—and the construction of grand new developments that were to revitalize the areas (Schwartz 1992).

Morningside Heights, Inc. subscribed to the planning logic of its day. Among its projects, in 1951 the institutional alliance undertook the sponsorship of Morningside Gardens, a slum-clearance project that replaced two blocks of older residential buildings north of 123rd Street between Broadway and Amsterdam with a subsidized middle-class housing cooperative. In conjunction with this construction, the New York City Housing Authority initiated a low-income, urban renewal–based public housing project of ten high-rise buildings across Amsterdam to the east. The combined effect of the buildings completed in 1957 was to wall off, visually if not literally, Morningside Heights from Harlem to the north.

Columbia University appeared to follow a similar approach to stanch the deterioration of housing and increasing racial change occurring to the south, east, and west of its main campus. After a dozen scattered purchases in the late 1950s and very early 1960s, in 1962 the university began aggressively purchasing buildings between 112th and 119th streets to expand its facilities through clearance and reconstruction as an East Campus and a South Campus. At an early stage in the process the university implemented a policy of purchasing the thirty-three SROs that existed to its west in 1961 for conversion or demolition to "rid the area of the objectionable features of these properties" (Columbia University 1979, Appendix A, 2). The university and local institutions perceived these buildings as havens for alcoholics, prostitutes, and drug addicts, thereby contributing to blight (Dolkart 1998, 333). In the 1960s the university purchased nine buildings, converted five of them for other uses, and tore down four. By 1979 it had purchased a total of twenty-three buildings and torn down at least nine.[4]

New York City tenancy laws, while protecting the rights of residential units and forcing Columbia to adopt a strategy of slowly turning over vacated apartments to university affiliates, made it relatively easy to evict SRO tenants whose tenancy the laws did not protect. The displacement of an estimated total of 6,800 residents between 110th and 115th streets, most of whom were African American and Puerto Rican, was a major ingredient in the ensuing political battle against the university's perceived heedlessness about its impact on the local community (Kahn 1970, 88). The battle was fueled by four factors:

1. The university cleared the properties between 116th and 118th streets and Amsterdam and Morningside and constructed its East Campus there.
2. Political activism was surging in the city and across the nation.
3. Morningside Heights, Inc. took a limited proposal from 1966 and expanded it into a plan for the wholesale redevelopment of all mid-blocks from 111th to 116th streets and from Riverside Drive to Morningside Drive.
4. The precipitating event was Columbia's efforts to build a gymnasium in Morningside Park, a public park at the edge of Harlem, that would allow only limited access by Harlem and non-Columbia Morningside Heights residents.

These efforts galvanized the local community and the student body, culminating in massive protests and the occupation of university buildings in the spring of 1968 by students opposed to the university's policies. The situation was eventually brought under control only by calling in the New York City Police Department. These events jolted the university into an awareness that the communities surrounding its campuses must be taken seriously, leading to an abandonment of the gymnasium and the South Campus proposals, a virtual moratorium on property acquisitions, and a policy of keeping a much lower profile in the community.[5]

The university began to look for alternatives and commissioned I. M. Pei's architecture firm to prepare a new master plan to address the university's housing and spatial demands with development contained on the main campus. In 1970 Pei proposed several innovative underground developments and two enormous dormitory towers on the existing campus, which were never built. Housing became increasingly scarce as the decade wore on. In the wake of the New York City Department of City Planning's 1971 Upper West

Side Development Plan, and perhaps the university's own real estate activities, Morningside Heights underwent gentrification and became more desirable to middle-class residents not affiliated with the university. The housing crisis was exacerbated by the university's conversion of some residential units to nonresidential uses, the increasing size of the student body, the growing desirability of university housing to students, and an informal commitment made effective in 1975 to guarantee university housing to all incoming freshmen. All these factors combined to produce an ongoing housing crisis in which commitments to provide housing for undergraduates were broken in the late 1970s.

This event and growing faculty frustration over housing triggered a spate of introspective studies and a new master plan. This new plan (prepared by Abeles, Schwartz, Hackel and Silverblatt in 1981–82) redefined the university's concept of the "maximum return" on its investment in housing and the commercial spaces that were often located on the first floors of its buildings. Although the Office of Institutional Real Estate reported in 1979 that "Maximum return on investment is *not* the primary objective in either the acquisition or maintenance of these buildings" (emphasis in original), the Rosenthal Report prepared in 1980 states that these buildings were "considered part of the University's investment portfolio and [were] expected to generate income" (Columbia University 1980, 10).[6]

Supporting the Rosenthal Report's findings, other documents report that the real estate office obtained net return on equity ranging from 3.2 to 6.9 percent from 1973 to 1978 (Columbia University 1979, 8). The financial team that assumed office in 1978 viewed these returns as too low, however, and aggressively increased the rents on university-owned housing units (Columbia University 1983, Appendix 1, 3), averaging over 11 percent annually from 1979 to 1981 (Columbia University 1983, 7). Commercial spaces were also expected to provide a positive revenue stream and were leased with an effort to maximize rents (Abeles 2003; Columbia University 1979). Consequently establishments were not geared primarily to provide optimally for the needs of students and faculty. Ironically the new plan, which was developed in complete secrecy through a series of meetings with a handful of select university representatives to avoid the "intramural sports" of community participation that had hamstrung earlier plans, was to prove more conducive to community development than any other plan to date.

The 1982 plan had four features pertinent to this study. First, it recommended a "deck of cards planning system" in which the university picked the randomly dealt cards up off the table (i.e., buying properties cheaply and quietly as they become available) and then considering how those cards fit into its hand (the university's broad plan). The second feature was the argument that the university could measure the return on its properties only in terms of its true bottom line—education and research. Consequently it suggested that the university accept lower rates of cash returns on its commercial properties and rent them to tenants whose businesses would provide for the needs of university affiliates and create the environment necessary to attract top-notch faculty and students. Third, the plan recommended streetscape improvements, especially to the median strips on Broadway. The final feature was the creation of a technical assistance operation to assist local property owners in expanding or renovating their properties. This idea would serve the dual purposes of anticipating political opposition and further improving the local housing stock. These four core recommendations reflected a growing trend in institutional planning, which had abandoned the grand reconstruction plans of urban renewal and replaced them with smaller interventions that provided amenities to improve the quality of life for both university-affiliated individuals and the community at large (Educational Facilities Laboratories 1980).

The university steadily implemented these recommendations in the 1980s and early 1990s, a period of little new construction and much renovation. The area's appearance was improved by upgrading the median strips on Broadway with new plantings and benches, by harmonizing the facades of its commercial spaces on Broadway, and by bringing in a significant number of new commercial tenants, including restaurants and cafes, bookstores, a video rental and record store, a sporting goods store, and others that accord with the results of surveys of university affiliates. The university also has remained committed to instituting avenues of communication to balance the needs of the university with the desires of the community, including the preparation of a Framework for Planning developed in conjunction with several community members to guide university development.

Since the mid-1990s, spatial pressures for housing and offices have triggered a steady flow of new construction and property acquisitions.[7] None of the new building proposals was well received by the community, however, in part because of the building designs. Using the development rights permitted to it under New York City zoning law, the university has built or is building at least three 17- to 19-story residential buildings above 116th Street in the middle of blocks, far taller than and out of character with surrounding buildings. Most of the new buildings meet housing demands, though a new business school building and law school extension have been built on Amsterdam Avenue at 115th and 116th streets, and a building for the School of Social Work is under construction at 122nd Street and Amsterdam. The university has begun to extend its reach south of 112th Street with the development of a 12-story building that will house faculty and a private K–8 school that the university hopes will help attract key faculty. The university has discussed proposals extensively with the community groups and residents and has striven to balance the needs of the community with its own internal demands. For instance the university has stated that the new K–8 school will serve children from the wider community in addition to the children of Columbia affiliates, and the university is, at no charge, renovating two adjacent historic buildings that will be used for housing for nonaffiliates of Columbia (Marshall 2001).

The 1982 development study also made similar recommendations for revitalizing the Washington Heights neighborhood surrounding the Health Sciences Campus, which was experiencing a different type of spatial pressure. The plan recommended pushing the campus eastward across Broadway to incorporate four blocks on the west side that the university already owned, and went even further to boldly encourage the university to actively purchase all properties west of Broadway to create a "river to river community" (Abeles 2003). The university chose not to adopt this aggressive expansion, however, perhaps out of sensitivity to the surrounding community. The other major proposals contained in the Washington Heights study paralleled its recommendations for the Morningside Heights campus: upgrade the streetscape and improve the retail mix around the campus to provide then-lacking services and amenities for the affiliated and nonaffiliated community and generate street life that would revitalize the area (Wiener 2002).

The Audubon Biomedical Science and Technology Center

At the Health Sciences Campus, the early 1980s saw two major developments that added significantly to the university's desire for space and its ability to attract researchers and funding. First, the Bayh-Dole Act passed in 1980 allowed academic and research institutions to license and commercialize the discoveries of their researchers. Both universities and the researchers they employed and hoped to attract perceived this potential commercialization of technologies to be a significant source of revenue. The second major development was the sudden rise of biotechnology. Since major discoveries in molecular biology during the 1970s, the biotechnology field has grown at an incredible rate and the number of biotechnology patents has increased at an exponential rate. The annual number of new biotechnology patents increased from 1,265 in 1977 to 8,374 in 1997. Predictions based on current growth rates indicate there will be a "daily doubling of knowledge" in the biotechnology field (i.e., number of new patents) by the year 2016 (Oliver 2000, 56–59).

For Columbia University the development of a commercial biotechnology incubator in proximity to the Health Sciences Campus became a major

priority. Without an incubator the university feared it would lose its researchers and consequently its funding. The funding for scientific research in the
biotechnology field is supplied directly to researchers associated with various research institutions by the National Institutes of Health (NIH), one of
eight health agencies of the Health Sciences Services in the U.S. Department
of Health and Human Services. Most universities, including Columbia, supply little funding to their researchers directly; the researchers must finance
the bulk of their research through these NIH grants. The university depends
on these funds to support its laboratory investments and expand its capabilities and must therefore attract researchers who can obtain this funding. Since
the Bayh-Dole Act and subsequent success stories—including Columbia
University's Richard Axel, founder of Sentigen—top researchers now demand the availability of incubator lab space to commercialize their discoveries. Already in cramped quarters, Columbia needed to expand its Washington
Heights facilities (Gipson 2002).

Washington Heights, centered on 168th Street, is situated at one of the
highest and narrowest points on the island of Manhattan. Always an immi-
grant neighborhood, Washington Heights has been the home of German Jews
in the 1930s; Puerto Ricans, Cubans, Haitians, Koreans, and Russians in the
1940s, 1950s, and 1960s; and Dominicans since the 1980s.

Perhaps the most prominent landmark on Washington Heights is the
Audubon Ballroom, located at the center of the neighborhood between 165th
and 166th streets and Broadway and St. Nicholas Avenue. To its west lies the
bulk of the twenty acres that comprise Columbia University's Health Sciences Campus, and to the east lies a dense, low-rise residential neighborhood. The Audubon, consisting of a theater and a ballroom designed by
Thomas Lamb for the Fox theater group, opened in 1912 and has served as a
venue for celebrities such as Lucille Ball and Mae West. Its delicate and
intricate terra-cotta ornamentation, including fox heads and Neptune, has
recognized architectural significance. The ballroom served the Puerto Rican
community during the 1950s, but its primary historical significance arises
from the fact that in 1965 Malcolm X was assassinated as he gave a speech in
the ballroom.

Despite its importance the Audubon was neglected and deteriorated along
with much of the neighborhood over the decades following the assassination. The block itself had become a gathering place for the homeless, drug
users, and others who further diminished the value of the site for prospective
developers (see Figure 3.1). Apparently unprofitable, the site was acquired
by New York City in the mid-1970s for back taxes owed. In the early 1980s
the unused second-floor ballroom was deteriorating while the ground floor
was home to the New York Housing Preservation and Development

Figure 3.1 **The Audubon Ballroom, c. 1985**

Source: Photo by Jonathan Smith.

Department, and the remainder was rented out by the city. Other tenants included the San Juan Theater, which showed Spanish-language movies and later was converted into a mental health center by the city, a synagogue in the basement, and an ESL (English as a Second Language) school (Gipson 2002).

The city-owned site was the crucial element in the university's 1982 plan to expand across St. Nicholas Avenue and incorporate four blocks from 165th to 168th streets on the west side, for three reasons. First, the long sliver of Mitchell Square Park and the Audubon block separated the main campus from these parcels. Because of the pedestrian-daunting width of the two avenues that meet at the northern tip of Mitchell Square Park, 165th Street south of the Audubon Ballroom would be the main pedestrian conduit from the hospital complex across Broadway to both the proposed development and the residential and commercial area to the east. Second, the decrepit appearance of the Audubon Ballroom, the drug dealing surrounding it and the park, which at the time was a virtual camp for homeless men affiliated with the nearby 1,000-bed Armory shelter, acted as an imposing psychological barrier isolating the campus from the community. Finally, as the area from 165th to 168th streets along Broadway serves as the Health Sciences Campus's front door, these unattractive qualities also discouraged the investment that would contribute to local economic development and the university's

Figure 3.2 **Audubon Ballroom and Mary Woodward Lasker Medical Research Building, April 2002**

Source: Photo by Cuz Potter.

expansion (Wiener 2002; Gipson 2003). In fact Columbia had a matching sunset grant from the Sherman Fairchild Foundation for the phase-two development of the Russ Berrie Medical Science Pavilion on the northernmost block between 167th and 168th streets and Audubon and St. Nicholas avenues that was contingent on the rehabilitation of the Audubon site.

The Audubon Biomedical Science and Technology Park was conceived as a five-phase project that would produce five buildings with more than 600,000 square feet of research laboratory space at a cost that would exceed $300 million. Three of the buildings were to be academic research buildings and two would provide commercial incubator spaces. For the reasons listed above, phase one would be the Mary Woodward Lasker Biomedical Research Building that would house the biotechnology incubator known as the Audubon Business and Technology Center, generally referred to as the Audubon Center (see Figure 3.2.).

New York City and New York State also recognized the growing importance of biotechnology and were seeking to capitalize on the city's high concentration of medical research facilities by supporting a biotechnology incubator. Both agreed with Columbia that the site of the Audubon Ballroom would be appropriate for such a development. The university received an early financial commitment in the mid-1980s from Governor Mario Cuomo and approached the city with it (Gipson 2003). Though the retention of biotech start-ups was the city's main objective, the potential for economic development in Washington Heights contributed to the ensuing commitment to grant Columbia a ninety-nine-year ground lease for the Audubon, to grant $1.2 million outright, and to invest $10 million through the New York City Public Development Corporation. The New York State Urban Development Corporation was prepared to invest $8.1 million toward the $25 million redevelopment of the Audubon Ballroom site. Though this total of $18.1 million was technically an "investment" that would generate returns for the city and state through operating profits, in practice it amounted to a subsidy because the incubator's below-market rents were not expected to produce any returns for the Audubon Center. The university claimed that it lacked funding and felt it necessary to find a private investor to move forward with the project. As none were forthcoming and the Sherman Fairchild Foundation grant's sunset was approaching, the university discovered and committed $4.5 million of its own funds and obtained $2.5 million in debt financing to start the project.

In keeping with the university's recently adopted low-profile approach to community relations, the project plan was developed through close and quiet cooperation with the local Community Board 12 and city and state agencies. The university ultimately proposed a six-story research building offering 100,000 square feet of laboratory and office space for both biotechnology start-ups and established pharmacies and 10,000 square feet of ground-floor retail. The original building was to be demolished because of the high cost of preservation efforts, estimated to be $10 million. However Columbia recognized the Audubon Ballroom's significance as the site of Malcolm X's assassination and consulted with appropriate state and city agencies and with Malcolm X's widow, Dr. Betty Shabazz, who supported the project. The university proposed the creation of a permanent memorial and proactively established a $250,000 medical scholarship fund for African American students in Malcolm X's name; it later committed to doubling the fund (Kantrowitz 1990). Mayor David Dinkins was not satisfied with simply a memorial, however, and worked out a compromise that would have saved a portion of the ballroom. The Audubon ballroom holds significance for the African American community as a whole and for some African American residents of Washington Heights, but it does not resonate strongly in the Dominican community and therefore was not a significant barrier to its approval of the proposal.

The project plan was certified by the New York City Department of City

Planning in 1990, initiating the six-month Uniform Land Use Review Process (ULURP), which allows the local community board and the borough president to give their nonbinding approval or disapproval of a proposal before it goes to the New York City Planning Commission for an initial vote. In practice the process provides an opportunity for various political powers to modify the proposal to more accurately reflect their interests by extracting concessions from the developer. The municipal body ultimately required to act on proposals in 1990 was the Board of Estimate. That board was to be disbanded that year, however, since it had violated the one-person, one-vote rule in the selection of members; it would be replaced by an expanded New York City Council. The Board of Estimate was scheduled to vote on the Columbia proposal for the Audubon Center at its very last meeting on August 16, 1990. This deadline put pressure on the university to ensure that the proposal made its way safely through the ULURP process and the Board of Estimate vote, so the time-consuming and expensive process would not have to be reinitiated with an untested and unfamiliar political body.

Columbia's relations with the Washington Heights community have historically been far less confrontational than those with the Harlem community. Community residents were hostile toward the hospital several decades earlier, because many of them were not able to obtain proper care there, but Columbia had recognized the importance of working with the community because of its experience at the Morningside campus. To ensure that all went smoothly in the Audubon case, a model of the full future development was presented to the executive committee of the community board, which objected to several aspects, including the creation of a superblock by merging two blocks together and the lack of attention to the park. The university strove to incorporate these concerns by eliminating the superblock and initiating discussions with the city about park improvements. Dr. Betty Shabazz spoke to the community board of her support for the proposal.

The university also made a series of small deals with local political leaders that facilitated the acceptance of the university's proposal, including an agreement to allow the construction of a community facility on a triangular parcel between St. Nicholas Avenue and 165th and 166th streets, although it did not pledge to develop the facility. The university's relations with local figures have been described as "family" since the relationship persists and each member must find a way to work with the others (Gipson 2003). The only anticipated difficulty in moving forward was the relocation of existing tenants, which Columbia actually achieved without much difficulty (Wiener 2002). In addition to the university's efforts to accommodate the community, one possible explanation for their amicable relations is the relatively short-term tenure of many local Dominicans. Because they come to the neighborhood with little intention of remaining for a long time, they may be less invested in the neighborhood. They may view the area's largest employer as an important source of the money they need to move away. Another factor may be the student base of the Health Sciences Campus, which is less inclined to protest than the younger, undergraduate students in Morningside Heights.

Other obstacles, however, did emerge. The flourishing of hip-hop culture in the late 1980s promoted a much broader awareness and appreciation of Malcolm X's contributions to American society. The full force of this consciousness came to bear on the unfortunately timed introduction of the project to the community at large—around the twenty-fifth anniversary of his assassination. The first public hearing before the community board on April 4, 1990, erupted into shouting matches at times. Soon afterward the December 12th Movement, an African American activist group from Brooklyn named for the date of a 1987 protest against police brutality in Newburgh, New York, held a series of Friday-night protests at the site (Kantrowitz 1990). It also has been suggested that Sonny Carson, a noted African American activist and leader of the December 12th Movement, had a falling out with Mayor Dinkins and therefore saw the destruction of the Audubon Ballroom not only as the erasure of a major landmark of American history but also as a political opportunity to build his political base (Gipson 2003). Apparently many Columbia students from the main campus in Morningside Heights also made the trek uptown to join their protests (Kantrowitz 1990).

Protests also were held by organizations concerned with historical preservation, including the Municipal Arts Society and the Sugar Hill Historical Society. They strongly opposed the demolition of the original structure, arguing that its terra-cotta ornamentation should not be lost (Kantrowitz 1990). Other local residents were concerned with the perceived risks of genetic research to the health of the surrounding community, perhaps not realizing that such research was already being actively pursued in Columbia-Presbyterian Hospital's nearby laboratories (Gipson 2002). Concern about biohazards subsided after the university gave a tour of similar facilities already in operation in the hospital complex (Berlin 2003). After a number of additional hearings, Community Board 12 unanimously approved the proposal amid a great deal of disruption by protestors, and the ULURP process moved forward.

The most dramatic moments arose as the fateful Board of Estimate vote approached on April 16. Though she had publicly supported the original proposal from the beginning, Manhattan Borough President Ruth Messinger, perhaps with an eye to the mayoralty for which she subsequently ran, became involved in support of the preservation position proffered by the Municipal Arts Society, including the preservation of Puerto Rican cultural history associated with the ballroom and the selection of an appropriate monument to Malcolm X. She employed an obscure law to veto the disbursement of the $8.1 million in funds that had been committed by Governor Cuomo years previously and were being channeled through the Port Authority of New York and New Jersey, unless her conditions were met (Bass 2003; Purdum 1990). This about-face and brinkmanship induced the *Daily News* (1990) to write an infamous editorial likening her to Lady Macbeth, washing her hands of the guilt of having supported the project up to this point.[8] On August 16 the proposal submitted to the Board of Estimate met her conditions. The city would donate the funds necessary to preserve the facade, and Columbia would incorporate a community health center, a Malcolm X museum, and a community arts center into the building. Consequently one of the Board of Estimate's last actions was to approve the construction of the Audubon Biomedical Science and Technology Center. The ninety-nine-year ground lease between the city and the university was signed in 1992.

The Audubon Center has by all accounts been successful. Malcolm X's memory has been preserved at a historically significant location. Rare terracotta ornamentation has been preserved. The incubator, which has had no vacancies since it first opened in 1995, has been home to several highly successful biotechnology companies. Homeless people are seldom seen in the park and never in large numbers. And perhaps most important, the Audubon Center has revitalized the streetscape and community through both physical and social improvements.

In negotiating the lease with the city, Columbia continued to strive for a deal that incorporated the additional public infrastructure improvements requested by the community. Mitch Gipson, then representing the New York City Economic Development Corporation, argued that such improvements would naturally take place since the city had invested so much in the project. Around 1997–98, the Parks Department and the Manhattan Borough President's Office spent over $1 million to improve Mitchell Square Park, located just north of the Audubon Center. In 1999 and 2000, several traffic islands were planted with trees and shrubs, and the Broadway medians were given minor facelifts to arrest structural decay (Gipson 2002).

Pedestrian activity has increased as this area has become a local shopping destination. Gipson, now executive director of the Audubon Center, played a major role in this revitalization. He was instrumental in ensuring that the retail space in the center was rented to a healthy mix of businesses that serve the surrounding community, thereby integrating the university's development into the community. One principal achievement was convincing Chase Manhattan Bank, which was closing its local branch, to relocate to the Audubon building. Another was to bring several successful restaurants from the neighborhood to larger spaces in the building, thus facilitating their expansion and offering a critical amenity for university employees. A third achievement was the establishment of the first coffee shop in the neighborhood. Finally, the Barnes & Noble bookstore was moved to the center from its insulated location within the Health Sciences Campus, and it began stocking a selection of Spanish-language books that would be of interest to local residents. These retail developments succeeded in bringing desperately needed pedestrian traffic to the area from the campus, the hospital, and the neighborhood as a whole.

These improvements, in tandem with the general reduction of crime in the region, has led to an influx of middle-income residents and a rise in median family income.[9] This transformation has included displacing some lower-income residents and improving conditions for others, in part due to the economic growth of the 1990s. The Armory Track and Field Center, now one of the premier U.S. indoor track facilities, formerly warehoused about 1,000 homeless males in the hall where the revived indoor track is now located. With economic recovery after the 1990–91 recession, this questionable method of sheltering the homeless was abandoned gradually by the Dinkins administration, and the building now shelters only about 100 males.[10] On the other hand, Mitch Gipson reports, "the building on the southeast corner at 165th Street and Broadway was transformed into an SRO by a previous owner who probably had trouble renting the spaces to long-term renters. It was poorly run, as many are, and housed drug addicts, among others." It was taken over by the Volunteers of America, which has a reputation for transforming such facilities into safe, clean apartment buildings with efficiency apartments, services, and short-term leases for low-income residents (Gipson 2002).

The university's community-oriented approach did not achieve complete success, however. The second and third buildings of the Audubon Park were planned to incorporate community-accessible, ground-floor retail like that in the Audubon Center, but ultimately the buildings have directed their focus inward. The completed Russ Berrie Medical Science Pavilion includes a small coffee cart (run by a tenant in the Audubon Center), an outpatient clinic, and the office of the Genome Center. The third building, the Irving Cancer Research Center, is slated to provide only a small commissary that will serve only building tenants (Gipson 2003).

Construction has yet to begin on the community center, though supposedly funds from outside the university have been committed and designs developed. Several important community organizations have found space in the Audubon Ballroom and Daniel Galvez has painted a mural there, but progress on the Malcolm X museum has stalled. Zead Ramadan (2003), the current chair of the area's community board, suggests that, in light of persistent attempts that have failed to move the project forward due to the intransigence of the Mayor's Office and Columbia University, some groups have abandoned their efforts to locate the museum in the ballroom. Meetings between representatives of the Mayor's Office, the university, the Empire Development Corporation, and the community board may begin to break this impasse. Columbia University, which has established a Malcolm X research center, is reported to be holding high-level, internal discussions about how to develop the museum. As of this writing, however, the museum still has no location for its physical construction, although it has limited programs under way.[11]

Conclusion

Since World War II, Columbia University's approach to institutional expansion and community development has gone through major changes, in its strengths and weaknesses, often paralleling broader trends in urban planning. Reacting to a perceived decline in neighborhood quality and safety around the main campus in Morningside Heights as the white middle class fled to the suburbs and African Americans and Puerto Ricans moved into the apartments left behind, Columbia and the other large institutions in Morningside Heights embraced the federal urban renewal program's slum-clearance approach. The university's outright disregard of the surrounding community's interests and needs put a spark to the tinderbox of political activism in neighboring Harlem and in its own dormitories and classrooms. This perceived outrage culminated in the tumultuous events of spring 1968, forcing the university to completely rethink its relationships with the community. After a relatively quiet decade of withdrawal during which Columbia dramatically reduced its real estate purchases, the university faced a housing crisis and began to expand once again. To avoid the failures of previous policies, the university adopted a commissioned plan that called for community development through small interventions that improved neighborhood quality as the university's real estate register lengthened.

Similar recommendations were made in the subsequent economically driven expansion phase at the Health Sciences Campus in Washington Heights, which was isolated in an area of low incomes and high drug abuse. The proposal entailed a university effort to extend its influence across Broadway from its own campus and build a mutually beneficial relationship with the surrounding community by providing retail services that would both enhance safety by increasing pedestrian traffic and provide needed retail activity. To accomplish its own aims, the university saw the necessity of building support for the project among community residents, representatives, and politicians. Despite their efforts the significance of the Audubon Ballroom, where

Malcolm X had been assassinated in 1965, ignited protest from black activists and preservationists, most of whom were from outside Washington Heights, pulling city and state politicians into the fracas. The intervention of an active community-oriented political figure led to a hard-negotiated deal that preserved the terra-cotta facade and was expected to renovate the decaying ballroom as a Malcolm X museum.

The Audubon Center has been an unabashed success for the university and in 2003 remains the city's first and only operating biotechnology incubator. The construction of the center and the concurrent economic boom have contributed to an influx of middle-income residents and the outflow of homeless and low-income residents. The immediate vicinity is now a much more attractive and lively retail destination for Columbia staff and students as well as those now living in the neighborhood. Whether the full scope of the promises held out to the community will be realized, however, has yet to be seen.

Notes

1. There is an interesting legal question involved here. Nonprofit institutions are exempt from real estate taxes to the extent that the usage of the real estate is in pursuance of its nonprofit, here educational, purpose. When New York University invested in Mueller Spaghetti, for instance, its income and the property owned for the production of spaghetti was not tax exempt, but was treated as a normal business use—even though its net result was the enhancement of the ability of the university to provide education. The same argument might be applied to the provision of conventional housing for faculty members or any other employees. Certainly it benefits the university; but so would tax exemptions for the returns on its investment in Mueller Spaghetti. And if housing for faculty members is per se an educational purpose, why should not housing owned by a faculty member be as tax exempt as housing owned by a university and provided to that member? But the law seems quite settled on the point.

2. Robert McCaughey, professor of history at Barnard College, has done much recent work on the topic. His conclusion is: "Columbia operated as a real estate venture for a significant part of its history . . . [Its portfolio included] property that has now become . . . the former World Trade Center. Columbia did play the real estate market with skill . . . including the purchase of land . . . [including] what is now the ITT building for $63,000 . . . [and the purchase and later sale of] Rockefeller Center."(From notes by Nancy Kwak on McCaughey's talk, University Seminar on the City, January 30, 2002).

3. The Columbia experience is rich on many other issues related to real estate development and university-community relations. They include the role of the university in primary and secondary education for its own affiliates and for other residents of its surrounding community; the provision by the university of community facilities, from athletic fields to gyms to meeting spaces to emergency shelter to parking, which could or could not be shared between the university and its surrounding community, and the inverse use by university affiliates of those facilities provided for public use; the availability of university services, from classes to social services to

health services to security to urban planning, to unaffiliated residents of the surrounding community, and again the inverse use by university affiliates of those services publicly provided.

4. The university purchased a total of ninety-two buildings between 1962 and the turbulent events of 1968.

5. Only fifteen buildings were purchased during the entire decade of the 1970s, most of them SROs.

6. The Rosenthal Committee, consisting of senior faculty, was appointed to review the university's policies of housing for its affiliates (Columbia University 1980).

7. At least seven properties were acquired in Morningside Heights and West Harlem between 1998 and 2001, the latest date for which figures were provided by the university.

8. *Macbeth* was playing on Broadway at the time (Purdum 1990).

9. The area has experienced a significant decline in crime: drug activity has moved to other locations, robberies declined 57.6 percent from 1994 to 2002, and burglaries went down 78.7 percent for the same period. For up-to-date figures see www.nyc.gov/html/nypd/html/pct/ cspdf.

10. See Armory Track and Field Center Web site (www.armorytrack.com/history.htm).

11. For current information, see the Malcolm X Museum Web site (www.the malcolmx museum.org).

References

Abeles, Peter. 2003. Telephone conversation. Urban planning consultant long active in New York City. March 25.

Allah, Dasun. 2003. Sonny Carson dies. *Village Voice,* January 1–7. Available at www.villagevoice.com/issues/0301/allah.php/.

Anakwe, Simon. 1990. Dr. Shabazz not consulted by those trying to save Audubon. *New York Amsterdam News,* March 17.

Audubon Update. 1995–2003. Available at www.cumc.columbia.edu/news/audubon/.

Bass, Richard. 2003. Personal conversation. Former staff member for former Manhattan Borough President Ruth Messinger. February 18.

Berlin, James. 2003. Telephone interview. Chair of Transportation Committee, Community Board 12, New York City. April 10.

Biotechnology Industry Organization. 2002. Available at www.bio.or/er/statistics.asp/, February 27.

Center for Biotechnology. 2002. *The empire state development-industry cluster reports: Biotechnology and pharmaceuticals.* Available at http://life.bio.sunysb.edu/biotech/nybi/index.html, March 12.

Center for an Urban Future. 1999. *Biotechnology: The industry that got away.* New York City: Center for an Urban Future. September.

Columbia University. 1949–1971. Reports of the Registrar.

———. 1979. *Background paper on the scope and administration of institutional real estate,* May 24.

———. 1980. Task Force on University Housing, Albert J. Rosenthal, Chair, May.

———. 1980–1981. Committee on Community Relations, Minutes, April 4, 1980 to March 20, 1981.

————. 1983. University Senate Panel on Housing and Rental Policy, Final Report, March 21.

————. 1990. *The Audubon research building,* March 15.

————. 2001. *By-Laws, statutes, and rules of the university senate.* Available at www.columbia.edu/cu/senate/, June 2.

Daily News. 1990. Raze the Audubon? Yes, but . . ." March 19.

Dolkart, Andrew S. 1998. *Morningside Heights: A history of its architecture and development.* New York: Columbia University Press.

Educational Facilities Laboratories (EFL). 1980.*Campus and community.* New York: EFL.

Ernst & Young Economics Consulting and Quantitative Analysis. 2000. *The economic contributions of the biotechnology industry to the U.S. economy.* Prepared for the Biotechnology Industry Organization, May.

Gipson, Mitch. 2002. Personal interview. Executive Director of Audubon Business and Technology Center. March 8.

————. 2003. Personal interview. March 28.

Gleason Center for State Policy. *Will NYS miss the biotech train?* Available at www.cgr.org.

Kahn, Roger. 1970. *The battle for Morningside Heights.* New York: Morrow.

Kantrowitz, Jeffrey. 1990. Audubon meeting erupts into shouts. *Columbia Spectator,* April 5.

Landmarks Preservation Commission. 1981. *Low Library, Columbia University designation report* (LP-1118). New York: City of New York.

Marshall, Lauren. 2001. *Columbia News,* October 5.

Mayor's Task Force on Biomedical Research and Biotechnology. 2000. *Initial report,* January.

McCaughey, Robert. 2002. Talk, Columbia University Seminar on the City, January 30.

Nelson, Margaret. 2002. Personal interview. Real Estate Coordinator, Brooklyn Economic Development Corporation. March 11.

New York Amsterdam News. 1990. Move the Audubon project, February 10.

New York City Investment Fund. 2001. *Market demand study for commercial biotechnology, biomedical and bioinformatics facilities in New York City.* February.

Oliver, Richard. 2000. *The coming biotech age: The business of bio-materials.* New York: McGraw Hill.

Purdum, Todd S. 1990. To borough chief, ballroom issue is no waltz. *New York Times,* August 16: B1.

Ramadan, Zead. 2003. Telephone interview. Chair, Community Board 11, Manhattan. April 18.

Renner, James. Audubon Ballroom. Available at www.washington-heights.us/ links/ frame.php?url=http://www.hhoc.org/hist/.

Rockefeller Center. Available at www.rockefellercenter.com.

Rousselot and Walker. 1979. Background paper on the scope and administration of institutional real estate.

Saunders, Chery1.1981. Columbia's influence on the Morningside Heights community. Term paper, Columbia University.

Schwartz, Joel. 1992. *The New York approach: Robert Moses, urban liberals, and the development of the inner city.* Columbus: Ohio State University Press.

Wiener, Geoffrey. 2002. Personal interview. Assistant Vice President, Planning and Project Development, Columbia University. March 5.

4

The University of Chicago and Its Neighbors

A Case Study in Community Development

Henry S. Webber

Since 1950 the University of Chicago has been deeply involved in efforts to improve the communities surrounding its campus by significantly influencing public safety, commercial development, education, parks and recreation, and residential real estate. These efforts have generally been successful, but not without controversy or great cost.

This case study charts the evolution of the university's community strategy over the past fifty years. It begins with a background section describing the university, the surrounding neighborhoods, and the university's goals for community redevelopment, focusing on two strategies of university-community relations. First is an urban renewal strategy characterized by direct institutional action to transform large land areas through demolition and rebuilding. Implemented in the late 1950s and early 1960s, this strategy led to the demolition and rebuilding of central Hyde Park and to the university obtaining twenty-six acres on the northern edge of Woodlawn. Second is a model characterized as supporting the development of high-quality communities. This strategy is highly influenced by the community development movement and features a comprehensive set of initiatives designed to make neighborhoods attractive to potential residents by ensuring good schools, safe streets, good transportation, and attractive housing choices. If any of these elements are missing, the strategy fails. While real estate initiatives are part of a comprehensive strategy of supporting high-quality communities, they do not dominate. Elements of this strategy began in Hyde Park as early as the 1950s, and by the late 1990s had been expanded to include the surrounding neighborhoods.

The chapter concludes with a discussion of the evolution of the university's community strategy over time. The strategy predominantly reflected the circumstances facing the university and the mid–South Side Chicago neighborhoods during the relevant periods. Urban renewal was a specific response to a crisis facing the area and the university in the 1950s, and it involved extensive real estate intervention by both the city and the university. By the 1990s the City of Chicago's growing attractiveness, the increasing role of city government in neighborhood planning, and improved commercial and residential real estate markets allowed the university to work with partner neighborhoods to improve the communities without costly and institutionally difficult real estate interventions.

Background

The University of Chicago was founded at the very end of the nineteenth century. Endowed by John D. Rockefeller and leading Chicago industrialists and merchants, the university quickly became among the wealthiest and most prestigious institutions of higher learning in the United States. Within a few years the tradition of awarding Nobel Prizes to university faculty and graduates was well established.

In addition to its role as an intellectual and cultural center, the university quickly became an economic force on the South Side of Chicago. The university offered an undergraduate program and many graduate and professional programs, and it operated a large teaching hospital on its campus. Estimates indicate that by 1950 between 15,000 and 20,000 university faculty, students, and staff worked or attended school at the Hyde Park campus.

All large universities with adjacent major hospitals are important economic forces in their cities. A distinctive feature of the University of Chicago is the strength of its relationship with the Hyde Park neighborhood. The vast majority of its faculty, most of its students, and many staff live close to campus in a neighborhood only 1.5 miles long and 1 mile wide (see Map 4.1).

Before beginning a discussion of the relationship between the university and the community, it is helpful to describe the basic geography of the area. The University of Chicago was originally located primarily in southwest Hyde Park between 55th and 59th streets and east of Cottage Grove Avenue. A second area, between 60th and 61st streets, grew rapidly after 1960 and now runs from Cottage Grove Avenue to Stoney Island Avenue. Bisecting these two parts of the university is the Midway Plaisance, a one-block-wide, mile-long public park designed by Frederick Law Olmsted. The Woodlawn neighborhood begins on the south side of the Midway and runs south to 67th Street.

Hyde Park has four major residential areas. The area from 55th to 59th streets, west of the Illinois Central (IC) railroad tracks and Cottage Grove, is called the Golden Rectangle. The area contains fine single-family houses, condominiums, and apartments. North of 55th Street between the IC and

Map 4.1   **The University of Chicago and Its Neighbors**

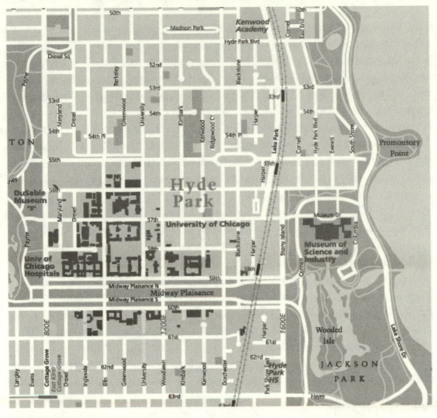

Source: Chicago CartoGraphics.

Cottage Grove is Central Hyde Park, traditionally the least wealthy area containing a mix of cottages, apartment buildings, and single-family homes. Between 47th and 51st streets, Cottage Grove, and the IC tracks is South Kenwood. Settled around the turn of the century, South Kenwood was once one of the most prestigious areas of the Chicago region, and many of the original mansions remain. Between the IC tracks and Lake Michigan is East Hyde Park, an area of high-rises and six-flats which was once the center of the Chicago Jewish community.

The commercial areas of the neighborhood have been focused along 53rd and 55th streets with a small commercial strip near the university on 57th Street. West of Hyde Park is Washington Park, a very large public park. The population of the Hyde Park-South Kenwood area in 1950 was 71,689; in 2000 it was 42,723.

University-Community Relations Before Urban Renewal

The University of Chicago and the Hyde Park neighborhood grew up together in the period just after the turn of the twentieth century. The neighborhood originally contained high-end housing stock, but by 1930 there were already signs of decline. In 1945 the university recognized that the deterioration of the neighborhood was a pressing concern. Between 1940 and 1950 Hyde Park lost many of its distinct advantages relative to other city neighborhoods (Rossi and Dentler 1961). Chancellor Hutchins, in his State of the University message in 1945, reported, "For the last fifteen years, the university neighborhood has steadily deteriorated, until today, I am ashamed to say, the university has the unfortunate distinction of having the worst-housed faculty in the United States" (Levi 1961a).

Hyde Park was not the only neighborhood surrounding the university that was in decline by 1950; Woodlawn also was struggling. Despite its physical proximity, Woodlawn had never been as intimately tied to the university as Hyde Park was. The housing stock was less robust than in Hyde Park or Kenwood, and very few university facilities were located south of 61st Street. Nevertheless a number of university faculty lived in Woodlawn, and 63rd Street was a thriving commercial strip. Settled as a stable middle-class community, Woodlawn began to decline during the Depression, when many of its apartments were cut up into smaller units that could attract lower rents. During World War II the decline accelerated as industrial workers drawn to Chicago poured into Woodlawn, creating overcrowded conditions (Silberman 1964).

Even the broader city, while not in decline, was a challenge to the university during this period. Chicago was a gritty industrial city, not the gleaming service center it would become. As Chancellor Kimpton said in a State of the University message addressing the problem of bringing distinguished faculty to the university, "Here I believe the difficulty is the city of Chicago itself. Broad shoulders, freight-handlers, and hog butchers are not everyone's dish of tea, if you will allow me to mix a neat metaphor" (Levi 1961a).

Urban Renewal in Hyde Park

By 1951 the university saw itself facing problems much more pressing than the gradual erosion of neighborhood quality. In Hyde Park these problems were rapid demographic change and rising crime rates. From 1940 to 1960 the lure of war-production jobs, changes in southern agriculture, and the postwar industrial boom brought large numbers of African Americans to Chicago. In this twenty-year period Chicago's African American population

jumped from 278,000 to 813,000. Prior to the late 1940s restrictive covenants confined African Americans to a handful of increasingly overcrowded
"black belt" neighborhoods on the South Side of the city.[1] With the end of
restrictive covenants, however, African Americans could move to nearby white
neighborhoods, although they were often denied mortgages and their limited
incomes forced families into subdivided apartments, for which they would
be forced to pay exorbitantly high rents. One of these neighborhoods was
Hyde Park-Kenwood (Perloff 1955). Between 1950 and 1956 the black population of Hyde Park-Kenwood grew from 4,300 to 30,000 and the white population dropped from 67,000 to 47,000 (Levi 1961b). Citizens of all races
were concerned with this rapid racial change. Local religious leaders and
leading citizens formed the Hyde Park-Kenwood Community Conference
(HPKCC) in response to changes and to support integration in Hyde Park.

From the perspective of today, the racial change in Hyde Park in the 1950s
was a step toward the racially integrated community that Hyde Park would
become. In the 1950s, however, rapid racial change was alarming to both the
university and the Hyde Park community. Community after community on
the South Side of Chicago was moving from all white to all African American with stunning speed, along with declines in per capita income. The concern was that Hyde Park was on its way to becoming a ghetto neighborhood
(Cohen and Taylor 2000). It would be impossible, it was thought, to recruit
students and faculty to a university in a ghetto, and the evidence supported at
least some of these concerns. In the early 1950s the poor condition of the
university neighborhood was one of the major factors causing a sharp decline in enrollment in the undergraduate program and the loss of prominent
faculty (*Hyde Park Herald* 1954; Boyer 1999).

Crime was also a major concern. From 1952 to 1959 the Hyde Park Police
District had among the four highest crime rates among the thirty-nine police
districts in the city (International Association of Chiefs of Police 1967). Later
analysis questioned the reliability of all crime reporting from this period,
and crime actually declined in the years prior to the beginning of urban renewal, but perception is crucial. Residents saw themselves as surrounded by
crime, much of it associated with the aging and decrepit commercial strips
along Lake Park Avenue and 55th Street, immediately north of the campus.

From the perspective of university leadership and many community leaders, university action to improve the neighborhood was necessary (Sagan
2002). In 1952 the university established the South East Chicago Commission (SECC) in response to the kidnapping and attempted rape of the wife of
a faculty member. Concerns about crime were rampant, and in the wake of
this crime 2,000 Hyde Parkers jammed Mandel Hall on the university campus demanding action. The university initially directed the SECC to take a

number of specific steps: improve street lighting; organize a police observer corps; inspect local taverns for legal compliance; undertake a physical survey of the neighborhood; embark on a conservation and rehabilitation program for specific blocks and buildings; organize block groups; design a program to curb the activities of youth gangs; and set up a program of cooperation with other agencies including the Chicago Crime Commission and the South Side Planning Board. Within a few years real estate activity came to dominate the agenda of the SECC.

The first director of SECC was Julian Levi, a member of a prominent Hyde Park family and the brother of Edward Levi, who became provost and later president of the university and then served as attorney general of the United States. Julian Levi both designed and implemented the university's program of urban renewal. Among his many skills was the use of public policy to benefit the university community. It was Levi, for example, who secured for the university the power to use eminent domain to purchase private homes in southwestern Hyde Park for university expansion.

In 1958 the City of Chicago approved SECC's urban renewal plan. The plan area included 885 acres, of which 101.2 acres were to be cleared. The goal was to meet the needs of the university for expansion and to create a neighborhood that would allow the university to continue to recruit from among the strongest students and faculty in the world. The tools were both land clearance and conservation. The lack of land for expansion had been a major university problem for years, and urban renewal offered the opportunity for a solution. Besides university expansion, the objectives of urban renewal were to reduce densities in the Hyde Park-Kenwood area generally and to raise residential and service standards (especially in the area near the university) so as to attract upper-middle-income families (Perloff 1955). With the strong support of Mayor Richard J. Daley, the city not only passed the plan but also funneled more than $30 million in federal and local urban renewal funds into Hyde Park-South Kenwood, a large percentage of the total urban renewal funds available to Chicago (Levi 1961b).

Many aspects of urban renewal in Hyde Park-Kenwood were implemented quickly. The seedy commercial strips and dilapidated apartment buildings along Lake Park Avenue and 55th Street were razed, along with a number of scattered blocks and buildings. Many side streets were converted for one-way traffic or blocked by cul-de-sacs and dead ends designed to curtail travel through the area by outsiders. The university purchased more than 700 units of housing for student use and built a new dormitory. Two new suburban-style shopping centers were built, and a nonuniversity local hospital added a large outpatient center.

The greatest changes were along 55th Street, including a modern high-rise apartment complex and a series of modern townhouses designed for university faculty. Further to the west landscaping was installed, a new fire station and churches were constructed, and a social service agency built a residential facility. Not surprisingly some plans were never fulfilled. The urban renewal plan, for example, called for a major expansion of George Williams College, but instead the college left the neighborhood in the early 1980s. The university itself never built some planned graduate student housing. By 1961, however, more than $47 million in public funds had been spent along with $35 million in private support. In the process a total of 2,500 neighborhood families had been displaced (Levi 1961a).

Across the city reactions to urban renewal were mixed. The City of Chicago saw the Hyde Park effort as a model for what urban renewal could do in other parts of the city. The NAACP, the liberal wing of the Catholic Archdiocese, and various community activists were opposed to it. Monsignor Jack Egan, the legendary Chicago community activist, spoke for the Archdiocese in arguing that too many resources were flowing into Hyde Park to the exclusion of the rest of the city (Hirsch 1998).

Within the neighborhood there was also great debate, although it was more about specific elements of the plan than about the need for dramatic changes. The HPKCC had been very active even before the formation of the SECC, and there was intense public concern about the future of the neighborhood. Surprisingly, the decision to reduce density and rebuild 55th Street aroused only moderate debate.[2] The focus of sharp debate was on motives and public housing. The HPKCC and the SECC disagreed sharply over the number of public housing units to be rebuilt in the neighborhood, with the SECC arguing for as few as possible and generally prevailing (Hirsch 1998).

Overall the university and most of the active political community agreed that Hyde Park was threatened, that dramatic action was necessary, and that achieving a racially integrated community of high standards was a worthy goal for spending great resources and justifying the considerable displacement of lower-income African American residents. As the local newspaper wrote in an editorial, "This expenditure of money and human discomfort should be made only for a justifiable cause. The *Herald* believes we have this cause. We believe that a demonstration that neighbors of all races can live in a community of peace and self-respect is worth whatever price must be paid" (*Hyde Park Herald* 1958). What is most striking about the debate over urban renewal in Hyde Park is how little of the debate seemed to focus on what is now seen as the central flaw in urban renewal—the displacement of many African Americans from the neighborhood.

Evaluating the success of the Hyde Park urban renewal plan of the 1950s and 1960s is difficult. The plan, as important as it was, was only one strategy

for neighborhood revitalization in the neighborhood, and many other strategies were employed over the next few decades. Some conclusions can be
drawn, however. In terms of its goals of obtaining the land necessary for
institutional expansion and preserving a community where a world-class
university could thrive, urban renewal was successful. Urban renewal re-
versed very negative demographic trends in Hyde Park during a period where
every other mid–South Side neighborhood in Chicago was sharply declining. The community's goal of a sustained integrated community of high standards was achieved, a very rare accomplishment across the country.

On the other hand, mistakes are worth noting and many residents did not
fare well. Through the work of Jane Jacobs (1961), the Hyde Park urban
renewal model with its reduction in vibrant street activity became a national
symbol of what not to do in urban planning. The elimination of the only
large commercial strip very close to campus helped make campus life dull,
particularly for undergraduates. Perhaps most important, the displacement
of many African Americans from the neighborhood and the perception that
the university was acting dramatically only in response to a rise in the African American population led to deep tensions between the university and the
African American communities of Chicago that persisted for decades.

Urban Renewal in Woodlawn

In Woodlawn, too, demographic changes were accelerating long-term trends
of decline. Between 1950 and 1960 the white population of Woodlawn fell
from 48,000 to 8,000 while the African American population increased from
6,000 to 51,000 (Levi 1961a). African Americans were moving into Chicago in record numbers from the South via the Illinois Central, whose tracks
ran through Louisiana, Mississippi, Tennessee, and Kentucky straight into
Chicago. The last stop on the line before the Loop was Woodlawn's 63rd
Street Station, which became the postwar port of entry for thousands of
newer African American immigrants to the city. By 1960 East Woodlawn
was overwhelmingly African American, and, while vibrant, was also economically depressed.[3]

In July 1959, a year after the approval of the Hyde Park Urban Renewal
Plan, the SECC announced the South Campus Plan. This plan was designed
to raze a number of the apartments and commercial buildings between 60th
and 61st streets and replace them with a line of new structures that could be
used as teaching and research facilities and parking lots for faculty and staff.
The most prominent of these was to be the Law School quadrangle, attached
to an existing undergraduate dorm on one side and bounded by a new headquarters of the American Bar Association on the other. Several side streets

that once crossed north onto 60th Street would be cut short at 61st Street, creating a series of barriers between the Midway and university campus to the north and the Woodlawn neighborhood. Once completed, the South Campus Plan would effectively extend the university campus across the Midway, which would then become a part of the university's landscape. Approximately 1,000 families would have to be relocated.

The plan was greeted by a firestorm of opposition. A new and powerful community organization, the Temporary Woodlawn Organization (TWO, later called The Woodlawn Organization), led the fight to stop the university plans for expansion. Monsignor Jack Egan and the Catholic Church were fully engaged, as was Saul Alinsky, the legendary community organizer and former student at the University of Chicago. Several of the most important African American community leaders grew to prominence out of this struggle, including Bishop Arthur Brazier and Reverend Leon Finney. TWO pioneered many of what would become the most effective community organizing techniques of the 1960s: rent strikes, picketing of overcharging retail merchants and overcrowded public schools, and sit-ins at prominent corporate offices. As with many political controversies, the reasons for the firestorm were complex. For Jack Egan the forced relocation of African Americans in order to meet the institutional needs of the university was a reprise of the battle over urban renewal in Hyde Park. For others the battle was an early skirmish of the civil rights movement in Chicago and the right of African American communities to have input into decisions that affected their communities. In Woodlawn, unlike Hyde Park, the university did not have a base of community support. It was seen as an invading force and a symbol of institutional dominance.

Eventually TWO and the university compromised over the South Campus Plan. In 1964 TWO dropped its opposition to the plan in exchange for the university's promise to avoid owning or operating any real estate in Woodlawn south of 61st Street and its support of efforts to develop a large subsidized housing project on both sides of Cottage Grove Avenue from 60th to 63rd streets (Bowley 1978). This development is now known as Grove Park. The original plans called for 762 units, of which 504 were built.

The resolution of the debate over the South Campus Plan led to other university involvements in Woodlawn as well. In the early 1970s the university provided a no-cost, long-term lease on an almost nine-acre university site to TWO for a mixed-income housing project. A Woodlawn experimental public school district was later developed jointly by Woodlawn community leadership and the university. The university initiated numerous human and social service programs but maintained a role of junior partner and did not take on any real estate role. The south campus of the university developed, but it remained on the campus edge.

Supporting High-Quality Communities

By the early 1970s the university stepped back from its overriding concern for community issues. During urban renewal the chancellors and other senior officers of the university spent an extraordinary amount of time and university resources on community issues. With the end of that era, the university reduced its emphasis on community development.

Despite this shift in focus, the university continued to maintain an active community role in Hyde Park-South Kenwood, although it changed over time. The university was no longer developing plans for dramatic changes in land use for large areas. Instead the focus turned to building demand for housing among members of the university community and middle- to upper-class citizens of all races. Successful neighborhood revitalization strategies depend on inducing people with choices to live in selected communities. For Hyde Park-Kenwood to prosper, it needed to be made attractive. The university embarked on a comprehensive effort to improve Hyde Park and increasingly the surrounding neighborhoods through a number of initiatives.

The single most important area of university intervention was public safety. Even after urban renewal there was a widespread sense that the neighborhood was very unsafe. In December 1968, for example, there was a crime wave in Hyde Park that culminated in the shooting of a local alderman and five sexual assaults against University of Chicago students in a one-month period. The university negotiated an agreement with the City of Chicago whereby the campus security force became a fully licensed police department within the borders of Hyde Park-South Kenwood. The university staffed its police department sufficiently to achieve a two- to three-minute response time to any call. The cost was several million dollars a year, but, it was argued, if crime could not be controlled it would be impossible to maintain Hyde Park as a family neighborhood and to attract faculty and students to the university.

Commercial and retail development was another area of attention. In the early 1980s the university became increasingly concerned about the decline in the Hyde Park Shopping Center, built during urban renewal. The university purchased, renovated, and later twice expanded the shopping center. In making this purchase the university's motives were primarily noneconomic. Faculty, staff, students, and other residents would not want to live in a community without a good grocery store and basic commercial services. Similar reasoning led the university to purchase selected other commercial parcels, including much of the small shopping area along 57th Street close to the campus, and to actively market Hyde Park to selected retailers and restaurants.

Investments in education were a third major strategy. Hyde Park has long had a network of very strong private schools, notably the University of Chicago Laboratory Schools. No neighborhood can be successful without strong public schools, however, and over time the university became an advocate and developed a rich network of programs to support public schools.

The university also sought to attract other institutions to Hyde Park, with mixed results. Hyde Park became one of the major centers of theological education in the country, for example, with seven seminaries in addition to the University of Chicago Divinity School. On the other hand, the American Bar Association, which during urban renewal built its headquarters on the university campus, moved downtown in the 1980s.

Residential real estate continued to have a role in the university community strategy. The focus, however, was generally limited to problem buildings. The SECC continued a vigorous program of code enforcement and the university made selected purchases of particularly bad or threatened properties. After purchase the university in most cases renovated the buildings for student or staff housing. By the late 1990s the university owned almost 2,000 units of graduate student, faculty, and staff housing, and almost 1,000 undergraduates lived in dorms located away from the main campus. The most important and successful neighborhood real estate efforts after the urban renewal period was the effort to support a talented local developer in revitalizing Regents Park, a 1,100-unit apartment building on the Lakefront at 50th Street that was riddled with management and physical problems. Given the size of the property and its prominent location, it was believed that a failure to save Regents Park could be a fatal blow to East Hyde Park. This effort was notably successful and Regents Park is now the premier large apartment building in the neighborhood.

These efforts to support developing a high-quality community were effective. Median family income in Hyde Park grew by 48.3 percent from 1960 to 1990, far more than the 9 percent growth in Chicago as a whole. The neighborhood remained stable and integrated with the percentage of African Americans in Hyde Park-South Kenwood remaining at 47 percent for the period from 1960 to 1990.

Despite the progress, however, the University of Chicago continued to lag behind many other leading universities in community attractiveness. In good part the problem was the macroenvironment. Between 1950 and 1990 the population of Chicago declined by more than 837,000 residents. No other U.S. city has ever lost so many individuals in a forty-year period, although the percentage of population decline has been greater elsewhere. The south and west sides of the city saw great declines in population and median income. East Woodlawn and North Kenwood-Oakland, along with many other city neighborhoods, were depopulated. It was surprising that Hyde Park did as well as it did, but not surprising that most of the university's energy was focused there rather than the surrounding areas. In a declining economy, investing outside of Hyde Park-Kenwood would not likely have been successful.

The major factor influencing the community strategy of the University of Chicago over the past few decades occurred in the mid-1990s, when Chicago experienced rapid growth in its economy. After decades of declining population, the city of Chicago began to grow, adding 127,000 residents in the decade of the 1990s. Employment in the central business district also increased and neighborhoods in the core of the city began to rebound. Many cities improved in the 1990s, but Chicago improved more than most.

Within the university positive factors also were at work. New university leaders were keenly interested in urban revitalization, and the stock market boom of the 1990s created a new resource base. Crime declined across the country and receded as an issue, making cities less scary places. The city government increasingly focused on neighborhood development, and for the first time in half a century housing markets were moving in the university's favor. Throughout the south and west sides of the city, where neighborhoods had declined for decades, new housing began to sprout up. A total of 582 units of new market-rate housing were built in Hyde Park in the 1990s; all were independent of university sponsorship.

In terms of relationships with community groups and the process for engaging in its community work, the university also evolved over time. The SECC developed a strong executive committee and became a quasi-independent voice on development issues in the neighborhood. New community organizations arose in North Kenwood-Oakland and Woodlawn, and senior university staff sat on the boards of some of these organizations. Reflecting the national trends toward a more pluralistic community development process, the university worked assiduously with outside partners and elected officials.

With the sharp improvement in the economy of the city and the revitalization of housing markets, the university set a goal of Hyde Park-Kenwood becoming a competitive asset to the university. Vibrant communities north and south of Hyde Park, particularly in North Kenwood-Oakland and Woodlawn, were a necessary part of that strategy. By itself Hyde Park-South Kenwood's population base was simply too small to support the university community's demand for entertainment and retail. In addition the rapid escalation of housing prices in Hyde Park in the 1990s priced many university staff and some faculty out of the market. A revitalized Woodlawn was increasingly recognized as important to the development of the university's south campus.

The City of Chicago joined with community groups and a strong local alderman to develop a detailed plan for revitalizing North Kenwood. In support of these efforts, the university started a public charter school in North Kenwood. This school, and a public school with which it shares a large historic building, have both been very successful and are drawing new residents to the neighborhood as well as providing excellent education to the children of long-term residents. With the support of the community, the university police service area was extended to include much of Woodlawn and North Kenwood-Oakland. The university also provided loan guarantees and technical support to community groups for residential and commercial housing development in surrounding neighborhoods and greatly extended its employee housing programs, encouraging university employees to purchase homes in North Kenwood-Oakland, Woodlawn, and Washington Park. An academic community development program was established at the university in 2001, generating research and preparing graduates who were committed to the field.

How different is the university's current community strategy from the strategies of the urban renewal period? Quite different, one could argue. Consider two examples. In late October 2002 the university opened a combination bowling alley, pool hall, restaurant, and tavern on the first floor of its parking garage on 55th Street. The bowling alley is directly across the street from the commercial strip torn down during urban renewal (that site is now a landscaped park). The bowling alley is open to the public, brightly lit, and sells a lot of beer. The goal of the project is to enliven the campus area and increase the level of activity. This is the exact opposite of the strategy for the same area during urban renewal. Similarly the plan for the Midway crafted jointly by the city and the university included extensive public involvement and has an explicit goal to draw people to the Midway and make it a great public park for the university, the Hyde Park and Woodlawn communities, and the entire South Side of the city. The first major project, a year-round skating rink, draws from all of these communities.

An Evolving Community Strategy

How can one explain the changes in the University of Chicago's community strategy over the past fifty years? The interests of the university have been consistent: creating and sustaining a neighborhood that would attract and retain very high-quality students, faculty, and staff. Universities, at all times, tend to be risk-averse, reluctant to take controversial stands, and sensitive to criticism.

Within this context three factors explain the evolution of the University of Chicago's community strategy since 1950. First are changes in the external environment. The 1950s were desperate times for the South Side of Chicago and the university. The university was worried, and with reason, about its ability to survive as a world-class educational institution. Enrollment was declining and neighborhoods around the university were becoming devastated. This created the impetus for bold, decisive, and in some ways severe action. By the 1990s much had changed. The South Side was becoming more attractive, city government was more capable, and the university's community partners had developed real capacity. In this more positive environment the university concentrated on building neighborhood amenities rather than fighting neighborhood trends. In a sharply contracting economy, for example, new retail is unlikely to be successful no matter how well designed. In an expanding economy new neighborhood amenities draw new residents, and partnership becomes an important theme.

The second factor influencing the university's community strategy has been the growth of knowledge in the community development field that is now established with a body of learning and literature. Some of the planning mistakes of urban renewal would not be made today. The importance of neighborhood revitalization as opposed to land clearance is now apparent, and community involvement is now a standard.

Third and last are the effects of history. The decisions made by the university during urban renewal, combined with larger social and political forces in Chicago, led to a set of tensions between the university and the African American communities of Chicago that have plagued the university for decades. African American students and faculty have been reluctant to come to the university, due in part to the lingering perception of hostility in the surrounding neighborhoods. At a time when the university is committed to becoming more diverse, its community strategy must evolve to reflect a new sensitivity to its predominantly African American neighbors.

Notes

The author gratefully acknowledges the research assistance of David S. Finch and the comments of Bruce Sagan, Allison Davis, Richard Saller, and Geoffrey Stone.

1. In the 1930s the university supported the use of restrictive covenants (Cohen and Taylor 2000).

2. Harvey Perloff, in a critique of urban renewal distributed to the entire community by the *Hyde Park Herald* in August 1955, raised perhaps the most profound objections to the urban planning ideas contained in the 55th Street plan, arguing instead for greater commercial activity and the creation of a "town center." There is no evidence that his objections, which appear to be quite reasonable by modern planning standards, were influential, however.

3. West Woodlawn, in the area west of Cottage Grove, was much less affected by economic decline than East Woodlawn and remained an intact neighborhood of brick bungalows.

References

Bowley, Devereux. 1978. *The poorhouse: Subsidized housing in Chicago, 1895–1996.* Carbondale and Edwardsville: Southern Illinois University Press.

Boyer, John. 1999. *Three views of continuity and change at the University of Chicago.* Chicago: University of Chicago.

Cohen, Adam, and Elizabeth Taylor. 2000. *American pharaoh.* Boston: Little, Brown and Company.

Hirsch, Arnold. 1998. *Making the second ghetto: Race and housing in Chicago, 1940–1960.* Chicago: University of Chicago Press.

Hyde Park Herald. 1954. University of Chicago fights decline on B.A., area fronts. August 25: 1.

———. 1958. Editorial: Brave New World, May 14, p. 2.

International Association of Chiefs of Police. 1967. *A survey of security services.* Chicago: University of Chicago, May 14: 2.

Jacobs, Jane. 1961. *The death and life of great American cities.* New York: Random House.

Levi, Julian. 1961a. The neighborhood program of the University of Chicago. Monograph, August.

———. 1961b. Statement to the Board of Trustees, October.

Perloff, Harvey. 1955. Urban renewal in a Chicago neighborhood: An appraisal of the Hyde Park-Kenwood renewal program. *Hyde Park Herald,* August.

Rossi, Peter H., and Robert Dentler. 1961. *The politics of urban renewal: The Chicago findings.* New York: Free Press.

Sagan, Bruce. 2002. Personal interview, November 25.

Silberman, Charles. 1964. *Crisis in black and white.* New York: Random House.

5

The Urban University as a Vehicle for Inner-City Renewal

The University of Washington, Tacoma

Brian Coffey and Yonn Dierwechter

The precipitous decline of the American inner city in the short space of the last half of the twentieth century undoubtedly constitutes one of the nation's most profound contemporary challenges. This is particularly true for neighborhoods that abut central business districts (CBDs), such as derelict industrial zones and blighted residential areas, where the value of underutilized public infrastructure and private building stock measures in the trillions. In the "postfederal" era, creative and sustainable reutilization of these inner-city resources is increasingly necessary.

City-based universities have multiple opportunities to address this challenge. As universities are embedded in broader urban development processes, though, they necessarily engage with the tensions inherent in these processes. Inner-city investment practices often dramatically change previous land uses. In some cases this can lead to "contested ground" (Davis 1991), pitting inner-city neighborhoods concerned with social equity against downtown "growth coalitions" concerned with wealth generation (Logan and Molotch 1987; Dreier and Ehrlich 1991; Krumholz 1999). Even within relatively harmonious and putatively successful settings, tensions typically arise. How the inner-city university relates to these wider development dynamics provides a fertile but heretofore largely unexplored research terrain.

Within this context, this chapter considers the impacts of the University of Washington, Tacoma (UWT) as a land developer on inner-city Tacoma from physical, economic, and social perspectives. Topics included in the discussion are the changing urban landscape and the university's impact on historic preservation; the role of the university in promoting economic renewal; land use issues and concerns related to the development of the site; and the perceived role the university plays in community development, particularly as related to social welfare and equity.

The analysis is based on university records, public documents, news reports, questionnaires, and detailed interviews with community leaders. The interviews included conversations with approximately thirty political leaders, government officials, architects and developers, stakeholders in the area, community activists, directors of nonprofit agencies, and others in positions to influence decisions or affect the development of downtown Tacoma. For example interviewees included the mayor of Tacoma, planning and economic development officials from both city and county offices, the director of an affordable housing agency with dozens of units in the vicinity of the university, the director of a major social service agency located near the university, members of neighborhood councils, the commercial realtor who acquired land for the university, and a major developer of properties in downtown Tacoma. The interview process began with the administration of a scaled questionnaire to which individuals were asked to agree or disagree along a five-point scale with a series of statements about UWT's impact on economic development, downtown revitalization, the allocation of public monies, and UWT's role within the community. In an open-ended discussion interviewees then were asked to elaborate on their responses. Typically interviews lasted from one to one and one-half hours.

Based on the data generated, our overall assessment of UWT's investment activities to date is positive. However we also highlight emerging tensions, especially between neighborhood-based and downtown-oriented actors. Given these tensions we conclude that, notwithstanding the remarkable successes to date, "UWT as developer" may have to consider more closely its broader urban responsibilities as it simultaneously pursues an expanding development agenda in the coming years.

The University of Washington, Tacoma

In the late 1980s a decision was made to locate a new campus of the University of Washington in Tacoma, a city of approximately 180,000 people located thirty miles south of Seattle. A forty-six-acre site at the southern edge of Tacoma's CBD was designated as the home of the new campus, an area that largely consisted of older warehouses and vacant land. Surrounding land uses included a warehouse district to the south, a low-income neighborhood to the west, and an industrial port district to the east. The site and its surrounding neighborhood were viewed as an economically depressed, high-crime district that included a large homeless population and several vacant or underutilized buildings.

Interestingly the site chosen for the campus was not initially among the final sites identified as the best possible locations by the Siting Advisory Committee composed of seven business and education leaders. Approximately twenty locations were considered and four sites were eventually identified as finalists. One was located on vacant farmland in a small community abutting Tacoma. This site's relatively remote location was cause for concern, however, and there was considerable economic and political pressure to locate the campus in Tacoma, especially in the downtown area (Maynard and Voelpel 1989; Gillie 1989). Thus in the end this suburban location was not judged a viable option.

The other three sites were in Tacoma proper. One was on the west side of the city adjacent to a community college, a location ultimately rejected because of limited room for expansion and neighborhood opposition (Gillie 1989; Godchaux 1990). The other two were in the downtown area. One was in a low-income residential neighborhood about one-quarter mile from where the university now stands and, in the end, was rejected because of land use constraints (Maynard 1990). The remaining site overlapped the university's present location but it avoided an area of old warehouses (many of which were vacant) on the main artery running south from downtown. Late in the decision-making process, however, city officials convinced the siting committee to consider using the warehouses (Sullivan 2003). The lobbying effort paid off and the final recommendation incorporated them. This selection was deemed the site that would provide the best access for commuting students (University of Washington, Tacoma 1990), and urban renewal was also a consideration. News reports and comments from officials and developers indicated that the inner-city location had the greatest potential to stimulate efforts to revitalize the city center (Hadley 1990a, 1990b, 1990c). The final decision was "hailed . . . as an important step for downtown's economic renaissance" (Godchaux 1990) and as one that offered the "potential to develop a historic city campus . . ." (Maynard 1990).

Land acquisition for UWT began in 1990. By 2002, 65 percent of the site had been acquired at a cost of approximately $20,000,000 (See Figure 5.1). Groundbreaking for the university took place in 1995 and it officially opened in 1997. Between 1995 and 2002 nearly $100,000,000 was spent for warehouse renovation and new construction, creating a core campus of twelve buildings. In 2002 another $40,000,000 was allocated for rehabilitation and renovation of five nearby buildings as part of the university's continued expansion.

The Campus Landscape: Aesthetic and Functional Dimensions

The most obvious impact of any major development relates to its physical place in the urban fabric, especially in areas marked by widespread dereliction.

Figure 5.1 **Tacoma, Washington, and the University of Washington, Tacoma Campus**

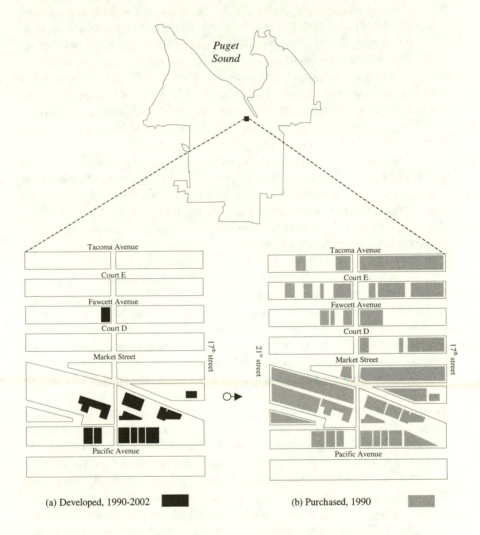

(a) Developed, 1990-2002   (b) Purchased, 1990

Two important dimensions relate to UWT's physical impact on Tacoma's long-derelict inner-city neighborhood: the aesthetic and architectural quali-ties of the campus as a major project in historic preservation; and the func-tional design of the campus environment, particularly as it relates to reurbanization and integration in the immediate area (cf. Wansborough and Mageean 2000).

Historic Preservation and Urban Aesthetics

From the vantage point of 2002, UWT's brief history already provides an excellent example of how preservation and aesthetic objectives can be realized. As an educational institution, UWT's primary mission has been to address insufficient and inequitable access to upper-division baccalaureate education in the South Puget Sound region (Chance 1988). But the impact of UWT goes well beyond this social objective. In addition to supporting the economic revitalization of downtown Tacoma, of which more in a moment, UWT also represents a highly successful experiment in large-scale historic preservation and urban aesthetics.

Tacoma had saved two downtown theatres in the early 1980s, but the key preservation event before UWT was the restoration of Union Station, along Pacific Avenue (See Figure 5.2). This newly refurbished facility (a federal courthouse today) sat across from arguably the most striking "street wall" in the city: a collection of long-abandoned warehouses that nonetheless possessed enormous potential for adaptive reuse (Miles et al. 1988). The unified character of the warehouses, built mainly between 1890 and 1903 on land owned originally by the Northern Pacific Railroad, exhibited a strong sense of place and visual harmony (despite the dereliction).

UWT's architects and urban designers built on these aesthetic strengths, even as they overcame practical problems, including an active rail line, serious public safety issues, irregularly shaped buildings, curved roads, and service corridor requirements. In the end the exteriors of the warehouses were largely preserved, and the building interiors now house classrooms and offices. Lines of vision toward the nearby Thea Foss waterway on Commencement Bay and the CBD, respectively, were also well articulated. Indeed this overall effort was recognized in 1999 with two major design awards: the American Institute of Architects (AIA) Honor Award for Urban Design and the National Preservation Honor Award from the National Trust for Historic Preservation. Not surprisingly Tacoma stakeholders appear nearly unanimous in their admiration for the preservation and aesthetic achievements of the campus, especially given the scale and speed of the transformation. Arguably this success (despite initial political opposition) has made future preservation initiatives in Tacoma and the wider Puget Sound region much easier. At the very least it has demonstrated the contribution to inner-city revitalization that large-scale historical preservation is capable of making.

Campus Design

The overall design of the campus environment also addressed many functional objectives in the immediate area. In particular the AIA award noted

Figure 5.2 **University of Washington, Tacoma and Adjacent Developments, 1990–2002**

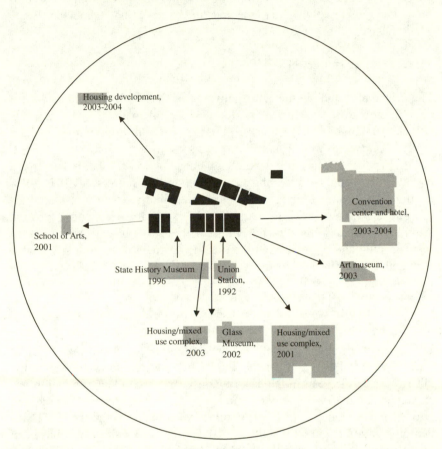

the original aim to create both a university campus and a mixed-use commercial district. This aim is being realized steadily, as the warehouse stock, particularly along Pacific Avenue, facilitates multiple uses, and educational facilities mix in seamlessly with commercial, retail, and service functions. For example university buildings house restaurants, taverns, bookstores, and related retail outlets. Expansion plans call for continued allocation of space to be leased to business establishments.

In this sense UWT has been a major reason for the reurbanization of the inner city. Thus while the campus master plan superimposes axes that support an orthogonal street grid appropriate to a university setting, UWT is "not a typical campus of greens and quadrangles," hermetically sealed off from its surroundings (Ellsberg and Fysh 1992). The industrial character of the campus is pronounced, integrating UWT into the surrounding urban fabric, helping to attract visitors to the area and contributing appreciably to the economic impact of the campus.

The Economic Impact of UWT

The principal economic impact of universities like UWT is their long-term contribution to the formation of human capital in local labor markets (Blackwell, Cobb, and Weinberg 2002), but there are more immediate and concrete impacts as well. This section discusses two economic impacts. First, UWT is a powerful magnet at the center of consumption thresholds that stretch over a large region. By attracting cash from nonlocal sources, UWT is influencing the economic character of adjacent neighborhoods; it is also contributing to the urban, regional, national, and even global economy through multiplier effects (Weisbord and Pollakowski 1984). Second, by pulling in this spending and by improving the local investment climate, UWT is also stimulating adjacent developments, including "big-ticket" projects such as museums and large-scale housing projects.

Spending in the UWT Area

UWT serves a rapidly growing urbanized region, the South Puget Sound area. UWT enrolled approximately 2,000 full- and part-time students in the 2001–2 academic year. In the past several years the student population has expanded about 15 percent per annum, a trend that is expected to continue into the next decade. If funding commitments remain strong, the UWT student population could hit 6,500 by 2010. Faculty and staff growth has been commensurate. From a small group of founding figures, today UWT employs 94 full-time faculty and 124 full-time staff.

What does this past and expected expansion imply for the economy of inner-city Tacoma? One way to answer this broad question is to focus on retail behavior in the immediate UWT area. Table 5.1 shows the results of a survey of students, faculty, and staff conducted in August and September 2002. On average, students reported that during the regular term they visit the UWT campus 3.5 times per week and spend about $13 over this same period of time (a figure that will probably grow as more types of businesses locate in the immediate area). Faculty and staff visit the campus on average 4.4 times per week and spend $17.85 over this same period of time. Spending is disproportionately food-related across all groups, a finding we would expect from this particular population. Unfortunately for the local retail sector, though, adjacent shops still benefit less from student, faculty, and staff purchases than many would like.

Making inferences to the general UWT population, we estimate that, again with reference to the regular term, students make about 7,000 visits per week to the UWT campus while faculty and staff make about 950 visits. This generates an average of approximately $26,600 in direct student spending each week and $3,855 for faculty and staff—well over $900,000 during the thirty weeks that constitute the three main academic quarters at UWT (October through June). Multiplier effects amplify this impact because they capture the size of the total effects of spending in a given area, calculated as direct effects + indirect effects + induced effects (See Table 5.1). The total effect of spending in the UWT area, then, is estimated at $56,700 per week, or about $1.7 million over the three academic quarters. If the student population actually expands to about 6,500 by 2010 (with commensurate growth in faculty and staff) this figure could mushroom to somewhere between $6 and $7 million (using 2002 dollars).

Just how much of this estimated $1.7 (or future $6–7) million in total spending might actually benefit the urban and regional economy is difficult to determine without more detailed analysis of sourcing patterns. Students, faculty, and staff were asked to list the outlets they typically frequent over the regular term. Chain outlets such as Starbucks, Taco Del Mar, and Subway constituted more than half of these responses (54 percent) for the numerically more important student population. This is not surprising, but chain stores do far less for local economies than most people imagine—a point first established by Gunn and Dayton-Gunn (1991) in their analysis of the local (and in their view largely negative) economic impact of a typical McDonalds (cf. Shuman 1998). All the same, continued expansion of the UWT campus will certainly stimulate locally owned businesses in the urban economy along the (rough) quantitative lines suggested above, adding to the ongoing revitalization of the inner city. The shape of this sector will also reflect to some extent what students, faculty, and staff now consider to be desirable, but at present unavailable, retail and service facilities. More (and more varied) types of restaurants topped this list, but respondents also wondered why there were not more convenience or grocery stores and retail clothing outlets, among other types of businesses.

Associated Development

All this positive economic activity has improved investor confidence. Most community leaders agree that UWT has been a catalyst for continued development in the southern portion of downtown Tacoma, although the university

Table 5.1

Spending around the University of Washington, Tacoma Campus, 2002

Home	Students		Faculty and staff[1]	
	Average days on campus per week	Dollars/week[2]	Average days on campus per week	Dollars/week[2]
Tacoma	3.7	13.30	4.6	18.00
Pierce County	3.2	13.10	n/a	n/a
Another county	3.5	13.50	4.1	16.40
Average	3.5	13.30	4.4	17.85
Total (Year 2000–1)	7,000	26,600	950	3,855
Multiplier = 1.9[3]	—	49,400	—	7,325
Total impact	1,482,000 (30 weeks)	220,000 (30 weeks)		

Source: Survey conducted by the authors, August–September 2002.

[1]Part-time employees and adjunct faculty are excluded from the analysis.

[2]The mid-point of numerical bands (e.g., 12.50 for 10–15) were used to calculate the averages presented above.

[3]Multiplier typically used in the literature on tourist impacts.

was not the first element of the district's renaissance. Prior to the university's opening, two major projects were completed in the area: the 1992 renovation of Tacoma's historic Union Station for reuse as a federal courthouse, and the construction of the State History Museum, which opened to the public in 1996 (Figure 5.2).

These two projects represent an investment of approximately $90,000,000 and likely affected the decision to locate UWT on its current site. However, once the university opened in 1997, a number of nearby projects quickly followed. Within five years Tacoma's Museum of Glass opened to national acclaim (Graves 2002); construction began on a new art museum; a convention center was sited adjacent to the university; at least two major housing projects providing dozens of apartments, townhouses, and condominiums came under construction; and a new arts high school was located near the university (Figure 5.2).

In addition to these developments, a major architectural firm located in the area because of the university's presence; a nearby warehouse was renovated to provide more than 120,000 square feet of office space; loft apartments were created in another warehouse space; and an esplanade was built along the waterway just east of the university (Bruce Dees and Assoc. 2001). Future development plans include a hotel adjacent to the new convention center and a new marina-condominium project near the glass museum (Card 2002; Gillie 2002).

While it is difficult to say precisely what development can be directly attributed to the university's presence, it is clear that the establishment of the campus changed attitudes about the area and had a significant effect on investment decisions by both the public and private sectors. Besides the investment in the university itself, hundreds of millions of dollars in public and private investment in projects immediately surrounding the campus came on the heels of campus construction. It is easy to argue that there is a causal relationship; at the very least, one can make the case that if UWT was not the catalyst for this investment that it accelerated the process, bringing about change in a few years that might otherwise have taken decades (see Szymanski 2002).

Community leaders support this view. Responding to a scaled questionnaire related to downtown development, they share the sense that the university is significantly (though not singularly) responsible for the changing face of the CBD (See Figure 5.3). There is strong agreement that without the presence of the campus the southern portion of downtown would be experiencing limited economic activity, less development, and weaker investor confidence. As originally intended the campus is viewed as more than an educational resource. It is also considered to be an economic development engine, although there are some attendant frictions associated with this engine.

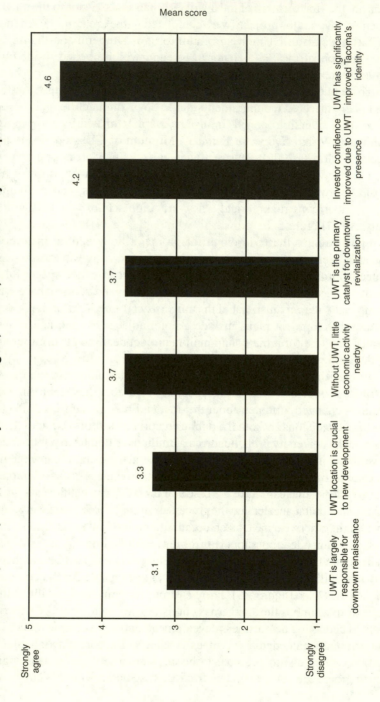

Figure 5.3 **Leadership Perceptions, University of Washington, Tacoma, and Central City Development**

Friction Amid Adulation

While the community overwhelmingly supports the university and views it as a major catalyst in the rebirth of Tacoma, interviews with community leaders have brought to light a number of underlying concerns related to community relations, the role of the university vis-à-vis community needs, and university impediments to the planning and development process. These concerns are not unusual, as the literature on the political economy of progressive urban development suggests (Clavel 1985; Keating 1986; Krumholz 1999).

Transparency and Community Relations

One such issue relates to individuals who hold or have held property within the bounds of the campus (i.e., landowners whose property has been purchased by the state or who are waiting what is assumed to be that inevitable result). A number of property owners accuse the university of being heavy-handed in the acquisition of land. They argue that threats of litigation prompted some owners to sell at submarket prices. Further, property owners note that at the outset the university defined the entire site to be developed without giving a timeline for the acquisition of land. Planners for the university have noted that the entire site may take as long as a century to fully develop. Embittered landholders in the area charge that in taking this approach the university has effectively stopped development and depressed the market because potential buyers and developers realize that the university might condemn a parcel at any time and require it to be sold.

Property owners feel that this strategy has prevented land values throughout the forty-six-acre site from increasing despite the fact that some of the parcels will likely not be developed for decades. Further, some landholders feel that this vagueness on the part of the university is a calculated technique designed to hold values down and, hence, allow the university to acquire land as cheaply as possible. For example, one landowner indicated that he asked the university about its plans for his building and was advised that the university would not be interested in his property until sometime between 2005 and 2025. Thus he does not know if his property will be acquired in a few years or a few decades. He argues that this time span is such that he is unable to plan for future improvements and uses of his building. However others suggest that this argument may not be entirely accurate, because any improvements made would increase the value of the parcel and that increase would be reflected in the amount the state would be required to pay for the site at a later time.

Related concerns include charges that UWT has not shared information with stakeholders affected by university actions and that they have made decisions without consulting those impacted. Poor communication on the part of the university appears to have soured relations between the institution and a small group that resents what is often perceived as arrogance or bullying on the part of the university.

Planning and Land Use

Another area of concern comes from city and county planners and developers who feel that the lack of a timeline for acquisition, the banking of land and the resultant limited private development of the site is poor planning practice. Architects, planners, and developers bemoan the fact that the university has no interim plan for the undeveloped portion of the site, particularly the portion that will not be developed until the university nears completion in 50 or 100 years.

It is argued that leaving buildings unoccupied and vacant parcels undeveloped on such a large tract of land creates a "hole" in the area that in turn impedes the development process. Several interviewees suggested that interim development by the private sector involving buildings or other land uses with life spans of twenty to thirty years should be considered for portions of the site. However the university has shown little interest in pursuing such an approach.

Social Equity

Executives of local nonprofit agencies, members of neighborhood councils, and neighborhood activists also have voiced questions about university actions or inactions. As has happened in other cities, however, these groups raised a different set of concerns than those that troubled planners, developers, and stakeholders (Clavel 1986). A common theme raised by these individuals is that the university has tended to ignore social issues and problems in the city to the extent that in some cases a sense of distrust has developed. For example it was argued that in the late 1980s and early 1990s the city, in collusion with university officials, allowed the neighborhood around the proposed site to deteriorate so that land values would decrease, thereby allowing the university to acquire land at bargain prices. Others have suggested that the university avoids social issues because it is too closely aligned with business leaders in the city and wants to avoid dealing with matters that may be controversial or contrary to their interests.

While no evidence could be found to support either of the above notions, there is little doubt that community leaders from the social service and neighborhood renewal arenas feel that the university has failed to live up to expectations that it would work to improve the lot of Tacoma's disadvantaged and disenfranchised residents. This sentiment was expressed by the majority of interviewees who focused on issues of social welfare and social justice. Members of these groups noted that the African American community did not relate to UWT. They questioned why the university was not more visible in Tacoma's poorer neighborhoods, and they argued that the university tends to cater to a view that higher education is an upper-end jobs provider.

Some of these interviewee comments are especially instructive. One individual referred to the university's economic development and business relationship as "Faustian" in nature. Another argued that the university needs more public criticism. A third concluded that UWT is a "CBD place" with little interest in the city's neighborhoods. Indeed many neighborhood-oriented actors, even those who were broadly sympathetic to UWT, expressed this last view with some frequency: UWT is "doing its thing," as one observer put it, but with a "limited sense" of neighborhood issues and dynamics.

Further, the view that economic development generated by the university resulted in service-wage jobs for the city's poor was a common concern; so too was the view that unless economic development plans included policies designed to raise the standard of living and quality of life of the disadvantaged, then those plans were destined for failure (cf. Keating and Krumholz 1991). This same group feels that much of the economic development funding that goes into downtown Tacoma (particularly the university district) comes at the expense of poor neighborhoods that reap few of the benefits generated by downtown renewal (see also Atash 1988).

These perceptions indicate that there is a decidedly sociospatial dimension to views held about the university, its role in the community and its economic development impact. The differences of opinion are distinct between neighborhood-oriented leaders (e.g., neighborhood council members, social service providers, and advocates for disadvantaged populations) and downtown-oriented leaders (e.g., architects, developers, economic development officials, and politicians).

Neighborhood-focused actors are much more likely to argue that downtown development diverts money from needy neighborhoods, that downtown development dollars would be better spent elsewhere in the city, and that the downtown renaissance is spatially limited in that its effects have little impact on the city's neighborhoods (See Figure 5.4). Further, neighborhood-oriented players feel strongly that the university has a special responsibility to deal with social issues affecting the city but that it has not met that responsibility.

Figure 5.4 **Downtown versus the Neighborhoods, Tacoma**

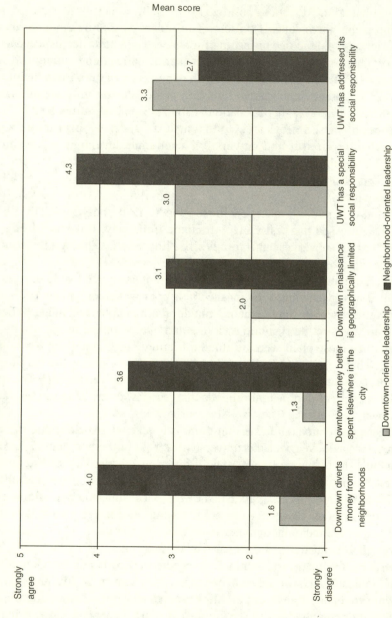

Mean score

Downtown-oriented leaders are less likely to agree that this is the role of the university, but they sense that the university has played an important part in dealing with the city's social ills.

The extent to which these criticisms are valid is unclear. The university is still a relatively small institution and further research is needed into the politics of Tacoma's recent renaissance. However, perceptions do matter. The university needs to take steps to increase its visibility in the broader community and to make the public more aware of what it is doing in the social arena, or it will face mounting cynicism and criticism as it expands its activities in the coming years (Mullins and Gilderbloom 2002). In our estimation, without such efforts the potential for friction between the university and this segment of the community will continue to grow.

Conclusions

There is little question that the University of Washington, Tacoma has been a major economic force in the recent redevelopment of downtown Tacoma (Anderson 2000). The university has been a significant contributor to historical preservation; it has spawned retail activity in a previously economically depressed section of the inner city; it has spurred investment in major public and private developments surrounding the campus; and it has brought a mix of uses and users to the area who have come to live, work, study, or recreate. In short it is a classic example of bringing together the criteria that Jane Jacobs (1961) argues are necessary for healthy, viable urban districts.

UWT's impact as an economic development engine is difficult to overestimate. In a few short years it has brought about a degree of renewal, rehabilitation, and regeneration that is rare in most of America's central cities. Given the rate of change and the investment to date, it is easy to imagine that within a decade Tacoma's downtown will earn a national reputation as an attractive and livable center offering an appealing quality of life. The change has been dramatic. Tacoma finds itself in the enviable position whereby investment and development now generate more investment and development, creating a cycle of growth that most U.S. central cities seek but never achieve. In short, as an economic enhancement strategy, the decision to locate the campus in the inner city of Tacoma was brilliant.

Further, UWT enjoys remarkable community support. The city's leadership in particular views the university as a key reason for the reversal of Tacoma's overall fortunes—a significant contribution for an institution whose primary mission is social, not economic. In fact this broad support likely shields the university from criticism that some express on an individual basis, but that rarely appears in the media or in public forums. Nevertheless major concerns exist about UWT as a developer and there is a sense in some quarters that expectations are not being met, particularly in regard to disadvantaged neighborhoods (cf. Rubin 1998). To enjoy continued goodwill the university would do well to reach out to all segments of the community in a visible and meaningful way.

References

Anderson, P. 2000. "City of destiny": Tacoma is finally destined for a turnaround. *Los Angeles Times,* November 12: B4.

Atash, F. 1988. Providence. *Cities* 5(1): 24–32.

Blackwell, M., S. Cobb, and D. Weinberg. 2002. The economic impact of educational institutions: Issues and methodology. *Economic Development Quarterly* 16(1): 88–95.

Bruce Dees and Associates. 2001. *Thea Foss Esplanade.* Available at www.bdassociates.com.

Card, S. 2002. Tacoma: downtown turns around. *Tacoma News Tribune,* June 24: A1.

Chance, W. 1988. Higher education needs in the greater Tacoma area. Unpublished consultant's report to the South Puget Sound Higher Education Council. September.

Clavel, P. 1985. The local state: Hartford, Cleveland, and Berkeley under populist rule in the 1970s. *Community Development Journal* 20(2): 120–128.

———. 1986. *The Progressive City.* Thousand Oaks CA: Sage.

Davis, J.E. 1991. *Contested ground: Collective action and the urban neighborhood.* Ithaca, NY: Cornell University Press.

Dreier, P., and B. Ehrlich. 1991. Downtown development and urban reform: the politics of Boston's linkage policy. *Urban Affairs Quarterly* 26(3): 354–375.

Ellsberg, H., and G. Fysh. 1992. Campus goal is to transform, not destroy, downtown. *Tacoma News Tribune,* July 19: B1.

Gillie, J. 1989. Fight for UW campus: Lesson in higher economics. *Tacoma News Tribune,* June 26: B2.

———. 2002. Downtown projects: The whens and wheres. *Tacoma News Tribune,* July 2: A8.

Godchaux, E. 1990. UW's downtown site wins state's final ok. *Tacoma News Tribune,* November 15: B1.

Graves, J. 2002. Museum of glass draws world's eye. *Tacoma News Tribune,* July 2: A1.

Gunn, C., and H. Dayton-Gunn. 1991. *Reclaiming capital: Democratic initiative and community development.* Ithaca, NY: Cornell University Press.

Hadley, J. 1990a. UW looks at 3 more branch campus sites. *Seattle Post-Intelligencer,* February 22: B2.

———. 1990b. UW settles on half-dozen prospective branch sites. *Seattle Post-Intelligencer,* March 17: B1.

———. 1990c. Downtown Tacoma picked for UW campus. *Seattle Post-Intelligencer,* November 15: A11.

Jacobs, J. 1961. *The death and life of great American cities.* New York: Random House.

Keating, W. D. 1986. Linking downtown development to broader community goals: An analysis of linkage policy in three cities. *Journal of the American Planning Association* 52(2): 133–141.

Keating, W.D. and N. Krumholz. 1991. Downtowns plans for the 1980s: The case for more equity in the 1990s. *Journal of the American Planning Association.* Spring: 136–152.

Krumholz, N. 1999. Equitable approaches to local economic development. *Policy Studies Journal* 27(1): 83–95.

Logan, J., and H. Molotch. 1987. *Urban fortunes: The political economy of place.* Berkeley: University of California Press.

Maynard, S. 1990. UW decides downtown or TCC will get campus. *Tacoma News Tribune,* March 17: A1.

Maynard, S. and D. Voelpel. 1989. Fife makes finals for UW Branch. *Tacoma News Tribune,* September 16: A1.

Miles, M., P. Tillet, G. Grulich, and J. Webber. 1988. *Trackside: preserving railroad station warehouse districts: A comparative study of seven cities.* Tacoma: Department of Community Development, City of Tacoma.

Mullins, R., and J. Gilderbloom. 2002 . Urban revitalization partnerships: Perceptions of the university's role in Louisville, Kentucky. *Local Economy* 7(2): 163–176.

Rubin, V. 1998. The roles of universities in community-building initiatives. *Journal of the American Planning Association* 17(4): 302–311.

Shuman, M. 1998. *Going local: Creating self-reliant communities in a global age.* New York: The Free Press.

Sullivan, M. 2003. Personal interview. February 21.

Szymanski, J. 2002. Help for boyhood neighborhood. *Tacoma News Tribune,* March 15: D1.

University of Washington, Tacoma. 1990. UW Branch campus study: Tacoma area: Site evaluation report. Unpublished report.

Wansborough, M., and A. Mageean. 2000. The role of urban design in cultural regeneration. *Journal of Urban Design.* 5(2): 181–197.

Weisbord, C., and H. Pollakowski. 1984. Effects of downtown improvement projects on retail activity. *Journal of the American Planning Association* 50(2): 148–161.

6

Auraria Higher Education Center and Denver Inner-City Development

Robert Kronewitter

Auraria is an inner-city campus in Denver shared by three teaching institutions: University of Colorado at Denver (UCD), primarily a graduate school; Metro State College Denver (MSCD), primarily a four-year undergraduate college; and Community College of Denver (CCD), which offers two-year associates degree programs. A fourth institution, the Auraria Higher Education Center (AHEC), was formed in 1971 to represent the other three institutions as a single voice for planning, developing, and managing their new campus for more than 33,000 students.

Auraria is rich in influence and assets, such as historical legacy, proximity to downtown, and access to major highways and mass transit routes. From the outset the construction of the new Auraria campus was seen as a way to help revitalize the Denver central business district (CBD). However there were major obstacles. The revitalization of Denver's inner city was problematic and subject to dramatic boom-bust cycles; economic conditions, interest groups, alliances, and decision makers changed frequently; and public scrutiny was intense. The governance of the new campus was not clear, funds were limited, and schedules were tight. Out of necessity AHEC decisions were made quickly and they had to be exact, appropriate, acceptable, and representative.

This chapter describes the process and significant aspects of how four unique institutions with diverse roles and missions worked together to plan and design the Auraria campus. The time frame of this case study begins in approximately 1971, when AHEC was formally established (the first building opened in 1976) and ends in 2000, when major campus development was completed.[1] The chapter describes the final product and offers examples of how surrounding development, third-party collaboration, community interests, and inner-city values contributed to the development of both the campus and the broader Denver CBD. The chapter concludes with a description of Auraria's successes and a summary of how such accomplishments can serve as lessons that can be applied to the development of other inner-city universities.

Background

The Auraria campus was named after and constructed on the site of the first settlement in the region named Auraria: a gold mining boomtown founded in 1858. The discovery of gold attracted 100,000 people to Colorado (then part of the Kansas Territory) over the next two years. In 1859 gold prospectors moved to the opposite side of the creek and started a rival mining town, which they called Denver City. In 1860 the towns merged under the adopted name of Denver. Although incorporated in the Denver CBD, Auraria retained its own character and identity for the next 100 years. Severe flooding decimated Auraria in the late 1860s and 1870s and flooding continued through 1965, when improved flood-control measures were incorporated. However the damage had been done and the Auraria neighborhood was experiencing severe blight, making it a prime candidate for urban renewal.

In 1965 the state General Assembly created the Colorado Commission on Higher Education (CCHE) with a mission to "avoid needless duplication of facilities and programs and to achieve the best utilization of educational resources" (Abbott 1999). Nevertheless in 1966 MSCD opened its doors in rental space; CCD was located in numerous buildings scattered on the city's south side; and UCD was housed in adaptive reuse space on the north side of the Denver CBD. Academic programs were fragmented and the institutions were paying more than $2 million per year in rent (Cameron and McFadyen 1977, 124).

In 1968 the new executive director of CCHE, Frank Abbott, and others proposed a single campus for all three teaching institutions, where they would share use of space and resources. A fourth institution, AHEC, would be created to "plan, construct, own, lease, operate, maintain, and manage all of the physical plant, facilities, building, and grounds" (Abbott 1999, 119).[2] This type of governance was unprecedented and the scope of the undertaking was immense. AHEC, acting as developer, would take responsibility for managing the campus so the three teaching institutions could focus on their teaching missions.

In 1969 CCHE hired Lawrence Hamilton to direct the project and determined that, initially, funding would come from three sources: a federal and city urban renewal program, private donations, and state appropriations. It was demonstrated that annual expenditures exceeded tax dollars generated from the blighted community. Consequently in 1969 Denver citizens voted and approved a bond issue to cover the city's share of urban renewal expenditures. The U.S. Department of Housing and Urban Development (HUD) had never financed a project with a multi-institutional management structure. Considerable convincing was necessary, but HUD funding was approved by 1971 (Cameron and McFadyen 1977, 125). Historic Denver Incorporated, a private nonprofit organization incorporated in 1971, encouraged preservation and raised funds for historic renovation. An initial state appropriation of $2 million for planning and land acquisition was approved in 1970, and in 1971 the governor signed a bill legally establishing AHEC.

By 1972, with questions of governance, early finance, and the process of integrating programs from three institutions resolved, Hamilton hired Chicago architect Jacques Brownson to direct the planning and design. The planners found that the amount of space needed for the individual institutions could be reduced by 33 percent if facilities were shared on a single campus. The initial construction budget of $40 million was the largest capital construction appropriation in Colorado at that time. The project was put on a fast track to make use of available funding and to avoid renegotiating existing institutional lease agreements. The goal was to acquire land and to plan, design, and construct almost 1 million square feet of academic space between 1972 and 1976.

Planning meetings with community groups, students, and institutional representatives were held, programs were finished, and a consortium of five architectural firms was hired. It was necessary to complete designs even before land was acquired and to start construction before all land was vacated. The few residents still living in the Auraria community were relocated to their choice of new neighborhoods and were paid generous allowances made possible by the Relocation Assistance and Real Property Acquisitions Policy Act of 1970 (Cameron and McFadyen 1977, 125–126).[3]

The three academic institutions were still skeptical of the management structure. In 1974 the University of Colorado Regents called a meeting of the respective governing boards for clarification, and the governor and Joint Budget Committee of the state legislature reaffirmed the original decision: the Auraria Board would own, control all space allocations, and manage all of the facilities for the three institutions, which would maintain their own identities and academic and administrative functions. By 1976 relocation was completed and the buildings opened on schedule. It would take another twenty years to vacate all roads, relocate traffic, establish mass transit, complete historic renovation, complete second-phase construction, and provide landscaping, exterior lighting, and signage.

Process

Representation

The Auraria Board included appointees by the governor and a delegate from the governing boards of each teaching institution. The Auraria Foundation, with a separate board, was established to facilitate property and real estate transactions. Another group, the Auraria Institutional Executives Committee (AIEC, later AEC), included the chancellor of UCD, the presidents of MSCD and CCD, and the executive director of AHEC. The AIEC met every two weeks to discuss academic needs, campus issues, major campus plans, and economic concerns. The committee presented its concerns and decisions at monthly meetings with the Auraria Board. A subcommittee of board members reviewed plans and designs and then presented recommendations to the full board for approval. The AHEC executive director was on all of these boards and committees.

Faculty members from each teaching institution participated with AHEC in planning and programming the spaces required for academic and special needs. Furthermore, AHEC personnel who were on the faculties or lectured at the university or colleges and faculty from the teaching institutions were on AHEC committees. Depending on the situation, faculty committees included representatives from one or more of the institutions, such as to help select consultants or produce plans for campus designs and community connections. Master plans were presented at Auraria Board meetings (open to faculty) and to special faculty committees to ensure their involvement. The University of Colorado (system) Design Review Board (DRB), made up of faculty and leading design professionals, also was invited to contribute to the planning and design of Auraria.[4]

AHEC represented all 33,000-plus students on the campus regardless of where they were enrolled. As early as 1973 students were represented on the Auraria Academic Coordinating Committee. Special Auraria Board meetings addressed student issues and later student representatives sat on the Auraria Board and AHEC committees. The Student Advisory Committee to the Auraria Board (SACAB) formed subcommittees for the student union, food services, child care, events, and the bookstore. SACAB represented all three institutions and became a unified and persuasive voice on campus issues. Individuals or groups of students worked directly with decision makers and had direct access to nonacademic divisions including planning, design, and the AHEC executive director's office (see Figure 6.1). Students provided innovative solutions for student lounges, participated in the planning of campus-community bicycle routes, helped prepare internal and community pro-

Figure 6.1 **North Classroom Work Session**

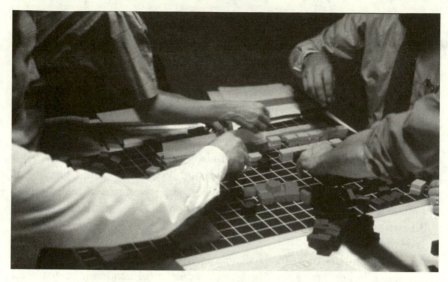

Source: AR7 Architects, Denver, Colorado.

grams for student centers, and helped establish a child care center in the adjacent community.

There was collaboration between AHEC, the teaching institutions, and community decision makers, who ranged from small neighborhood groups to high-level city and state government officials. AHEC succeeded in its goal of obtaining key leadership positions on major planning committees for the City Master Plan and for the development of such projects as the Cherry Creek Corridor, Platte River Valley, Denver Light Rail, and the Denver Center for Performing Arts (DCPA). Members of interest groups working together one day could be opposing each other the next. For example, at one point AHEC teamed with the Denver Rapid Transit District to develop a monorail and at the same time was opposing its plans to store buses on the campus. Negotiating skills and development strategies for maintaining long-term relationships were essential to assure future alliances. AHEC's voice in all aspects of campus and city issues gave it the ability to influence decisions and protect its interests. Through their strong community ties and development strategy, AHEC decision makers knew when to stand firm, when to compromise, and when to give in.

Information flow to and from Auraria was critical to understanding the needs and concerns of the of the community and to make fast, responsible

decisions. AHEC staff joined high-profile community organizations and committees such as Downtown Denver Incorporated, Denver Housing Authority, Denver Urban Forest, Light-Rail Stakeholders Committee, American Institute of Architects (AIA) Board of Directors, and AIA Urban Design Committee. Auraria also established internal committees to deal with community issues such as historic preservation. The Auraria Foundation and the public relations departments of AHEC and the three institutions were heavily involved in community affairs. The Auraria Board and the Foundation invited community leaders as board members, and neighborhood stakeholders participated on various AHEC committees so that plans, presentations, and development strategies could be modified to reflect public interests before they were announced or publicized. Conflicts of interest still arose but there were few surprises and proposals met with less resistance because of this continuous sharing of information with the community.

Leadership

The Auraria Board had high expectations, confidence in a succession of AHEC executive directors, and a no-nonsense attitude about getting the job done. The directive from the top was simple and the message was clear: "Get the campus built and we will support you." Meeting institutional needs and fostering long-term relations with the surrounding community were implied and obvious. Executive directors were given substantial latitude in how to get the job done—that is, considering they were in a fish bowl being watched by three partner institutions; state, local, and federal government agencies; and every major interest group in downtown Denver.

Auraria's success was grounded in strong leadership and the effective delegation of authority. Classical leadership attributes included an established vision and distinct roles for staff decision makers. The Auraria Board provided clear direction and key board members worked closely with strong executive directors. Together they identified government, education, and community decision makers needed for coalition building on such objectives as relocating highways, developing a monorail, and preserving historic green space. Well-defined principles, guidelines, and objectives were produced to deal with conflicting ideas.

Decision Making

The Auraria Board was committed to the idea that institutions funded with tax dollars and incentives have a responsibility to make planning decisions in the public interest and to make wise, financially sound investments. Like

any public agency or private developer, AHEC had the right to present itself
and the teaching institutions in the best possible light, providing accurate
information and honest answers to questions. Confidentiality and the timing
of the release of information were critical tools for decision makers. Auraria's
plans evolved from public input, public scrutiny, and an understanding of
community needs. In fact there were debates over who best represented the
citizens of Denver—AHEC or Denver's city government.

At many universities the system or process (means) for completing tasks
determines what goals (ends) can be achieved. Frequently at Auraria the ends
defined the means. Typical questions included: "what are the most idealistic
goals; what constraints must be overcome; how are goals achieved; and, if
necessary, how do we tactfully change the system to reach those goals?"
This is not to say the ends justified the means. Legal, procedural, and ethical
conflicts were inevitable. Powers of eminent domain were cited diplomati-
cally during negotiations, and decisions frequently went beyond merely ethical
debate to straddle the line between legal versus illegal. Throughout, however, the process was designed to be morally right and to serve not only the
teaching institutions but also the community at large. Planning and design
were oriented toward determining the ideal solution and consequences, and
then ensuring that the process was representative and met the highest standards of development.

Master Planning

The original Auraria master plans were visionary, assuming idealistic but
somewhat unrealistic goals such as moving railroad tracks, realigning highway viaducts, widening Cherry Creek, or constructing an access road around
the perimeter of the campus. Although the teaching institutions participated
informally in the planning process, there was minimal transparency as plans,
information, politics, and coalitions seemed to change daily. There was a
concern that misinterpretation of fast-changing information would interfere
with coalition building or effective decision making; to add to the confusion,
it seemed that there was little chance of Auraria's plans becoming real.

Later, master planning became more traditional and more transparent as
planning constraints were alleviated and real alternative solutions developed.
For example, twenty-one options for relocating traffic to the north side of the
campus were proposed and evaluated publicly. Institutional and community-
based committees presented clear alternatives with related benefits and consequences, such as multiple options for the siting of buildings that were
prepared and evaluated by the institutions and other campus stakeholders.

As major issues were resolved, planning again moved away from the traditional and became even more transparent. A typical campus plan reflects the role and mission of a single university with a certain level of synergy between the university, the planners, and the plan. At Auraria intense scrutiny came from multiple stakeholders, including three different institutions with different, usually uncompromising, ideals as well as students and other groups representing campus-wide interests. There were situations where the president of one institution wanted to achieve a particular goal but the president of SACAB, representing 33,000-plus students from all three institutions, wanted to achieve a conflicting goal. As planning became more adversarial, planning decisions had to become more detailed and defensible. The solution was to increase the number of presentations to stakeholders and to planning and design professionals.

More than eighty professionals with expertise in campus design were consulted and they contributed their experiences from hundreds of campuses with thousands of students and faculty. AHEC staff also visited, compared, and analyzed plans and designs from hundreds of other campuses. Various plans were presented to the community at Metro on the Mall, Downtown Denver Inc., and the Denver Botanic Gardens and Art Museum. Presentations were even given in China to leading Chinese planners and architects. Over a ten-year period, the national AIA Committee on Design had extensive input into Auraria planning, and plans were frequently presented to academic groups; the University of Colorado DRB; and local, regional, and national events sponsored by the AIA and Society for College and University Planners. Portions of the plan were published in the book *Campus Design* by Richard Dober (1992), and in national and international magazines. With each review the master plan was refined. Many comments were heard over and over again, but with each presentation new ideas evolved and old ideas were reconfirmed.

Product

Auraria was always envisioned as a positive functional and visual contribution to the revitalization of Denver's CBD. Buildings such as the St. Francis Center, St. Cajetan's, and the King Center for Performing Arts were designed to accommodate community functions. The largest campus population densities were located on the edges of the campus, positioning potential customers close to restaurants and retail in the Lower Downtown Historic District. Auraria provided more than 30,000 potential new customers per day, counting students, faculty, and staff, so pedestrian connections were improved to ease their access to downtown destinations. Landscaping provided a park-like ambiance, and buildings were kept low to allow sun into outdoor spaces and preserve views of the mountains and campus towers. Roofs of campus buildings were to be the same color, to provide continuity and enhance views from downtown buildings. View planes were established from neighborhood streets looking toward special campus features such as historic buildings or landscaped entrances (see Map 6.1).

The overall goal was to construct as much as possible, as fast as possible, for the lowest possible cost (Brownson 1976). To reduce costs and speed construction, the designers established a system to maximize the use of repetitive materials and dimensions. An economical 30-foot x 30-foot structural grid was planned over the entire campus. Columns were located on the grid intersections and beams were standardized at 30 feet. Standardized building materials such as bricks, lights, and tiles would fit on 5-foot and 1-foot modules within the 30-foot grid (Brownson 1973). Large building footprints minimized the cost of expensive exterior walls and maximized interior flexibility. Building plans also utilized existing infrastructure such as sewers, water lines, and streets. The concept resulted in high densities and well-defined open spaces without reliance on high-rise buildings, expensive elevators, and extensive life safety systems. Auraria was able to achieve some of the lowest construction costs in the country, at approximately half of what was being spent on other campuses.

There was considerable debate at the beginning of the planning process about whether Auraria should be conceived as an urban campus, leaving the street system in place with buildings aligning sidewalks, or as an urban park, which would locate buildings sensitively within a large open green space. Early planning studies extending several miles in each direction of the campus showed a lack of park space in the center of Denver. Thus the new campus designed as a park would help fill this void and provide neighboring residents and city workers with access to Auraria's landscaped open spaces and recreation facilities.

Some of the greatest successes at Auraria came from a partnership with the Colorado Department of Highways. The Auraria Board developed a different vision from many universities that fail to take a serious interest in highway design and end up surrounded by nondescript or obtrusively designed roads. Auraria looked at highway construction as an opportunity to provide a new entrance to the city, enhance the image of the campus, and eliminate vehicles from the campus core (see Figure 6.2). For example, a bridge replacement program using federal funds reconstructed four major bridges across the Platte River Valley that carried more than 50,000 cars per day through or next to the Auraria campus and in and out of the Denver CBD.

A coalition including Auraria, the Army Corps of Engineers, community

Map 6.1   **Auraria Higher Education Center Campus Plan, 1995**

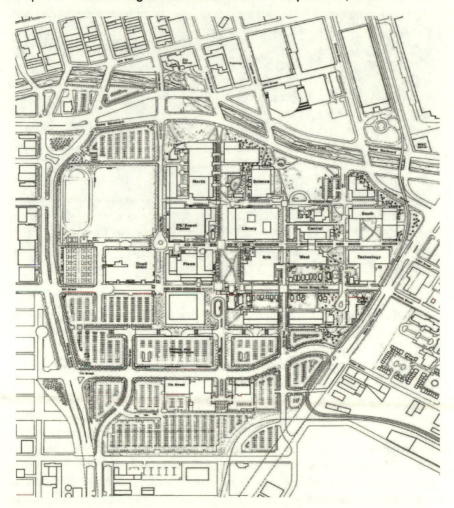

Source: Used by permission of the Auraria Higher Education Center.

interest groups, and federal, city, and state governments worked to divert traffic to the new Auraria Parkway, vacate seven major streets traversing the campus, and use the vacated space for programs or parks. Other features included visually upgrading bridge designs and planting more than 2,000 trees to enhance traffic corridors. Impacted streets in the Denver CBD also received new trees, special brick paving, historic lights, and historic street furniture. Railroad tracks were relocated, lengths of viaducts reduced, and a campus ring road designed and constructed. Auraria agreed to accommodate

Figure 6.2 **Auraria Parkway, Denver**

bus parking and storing on campus. In return the Regional Transportation District (RTD) agreed to help pay for a new transit-way with appropriate landscaping and signage. Difficult issues of phasing construction were confronted and resolved. Trees, lawns, pedestrian walkways, preserved open spaces, and landscaped median strips were incorporated to help unify and enliven the campus. Subsequently functions such as the Coors Classic Bike Race and Denver Grand Prix were held on the Auraria Parkway and other campus streets.

Substantial research yielded valuable records that documented the remnants of historic landscaping and other development in the area. After the discovery of gold in the late 1880s, Denver experienced ten years of boomtown growth, but during this tremendous period of expansion not a single park was constructed. In the early 1900s Denver embraced the City Beautiful Movement, creating a picturesque parks and parkway system based on the designs of internationally famous landscape architects Burnham, Olmsted, Kessler, and DeBoer (Denver AIA 1986, 1–9). As the campus plan evolved during the 1970s and 1980s, AHEC became a leader in the grassroots movement to revitalize the Denver Parks and Parkway System and especially Speer Boulevard, which in the early 1900s was one of the country's most picturesque parkways.

Speer Boulevard, with the richly landscaped Cherry Creek forming the center median, bordered Auraria's longest edge, so the preservation and res-

Map 6.2   **Speer Boulevard Bisects the Auraria Campus**

Source: Used by permission of the Auraria Higher Education Center.

toration of historic plantings and landscape principles became a cornerstone for campus landscape design. Presentations to city officials, interest groups, and residential and retail neighbors recommended use of historic streetlights and historic planting patterns to recreate Speer's original grandeur. As a result of these efforts, Speer Boulevard has received both national historic and local landmark designation, and a beautiful edge to the campus has been restored (see Map 6.2).

Historic buildings at Auraria also became significant assets. Three beautiful churches were designated as historic landmarks, and two of them were carefully renovated for both campus and community uses. Also preserved were some of Denver's oldest houses, beautifully detailed with handcrafted

Figure 6.3   **Ninth Street Park Sketch, Denver**

Source: Used by permission of the Auraria Higher Education Center.

masonry, exquisite doors and windows, and intricate cast-iron fences. A twelfth-hour effort by Historic Denver Incorporated (HDI) and AHEC saved several houses from demolition. CCHE agreed to enter an agreement with HDI to restore, protect, maintain, and ultimately donate the houses to the state. The Denver Urban Renewal Authority (DURA) deeded the property to AHEC, which in turn subleased the land to HDI, which then raised money for construction and developed the project (Cameron and McFadyen 1977, 127).

There were two significant aspects to this project. First, a private historic agency was acting as the developer, and second, HDI obtained a grant from the Land and Water Conservation Fund of the U.S. Interior Department, which required that the site was preserved in perpetuity. UCD faculty provided historic research and designed special site and architectural features for the houses, which were renovated into offices, conference facilities, a faculty club, and a student café, providing Auraria with 35,000 square feet of space at no cost to the taxpayers. The historically landscaped neighborhood now features original cast iron fences and repaired sandstone walks and granite curbs, as well as new but historically accurate benches, picnic tables, gaslights, and fountains. The historic Ninth Street Park has become a quiet contemplative retreat in the center of a bustling city (see Figure 6.3). It is one of the most popular places on campus and the most frequently visited historic site in Colorado. Many universities strive to rescue beautiful campus lawns and open spaces from the infringement of building expansions, but Auraria has been fortunate that its historic houses and surrounding landscapes were legally preserved and are on the National Register of Historic Places.

A private developer was hired to renovate another prized Auraria asset: the Tivoli Brewery, originally called Sigi's. This was the oldest brewery in the state, constructed in 1866. Along with the Turnhalle Opera House, constructed in 1882, the brewery was part of a thirteen-building complex that was a favorite nightspot for Denverites. Severely damaged by flooding and neglected because of a strike, the Tivoli had closed in 1969. A cost-value analysis concluded that the magnitude of the damage eliminated it from being a candidate for state, university, or student funding. AHEC was not deterred, however, and saw the Tivoli as an opportunity to provide income, recreation, and entertainment. One obstacle was a city ordinance forbidding the serving of liquor within 500 feet of an educational facility, but AHEC argued that the Tivoli (requiring multiple liquor licenses) was actually on the campus, thus negating the 500-foot requirement. In another challenge DURA saw the brewery project as a commercial venture on tax-free property and would not approve the necessary contracts (Abbott 1999, 129). AHEC filed a suit through the attorney general's office, resulting in a legal interpretation that AHEC as an educational agency, not DURA, had the right to determine what was "necessary, accessory, and supportive to higher education." AHEC thus got the green light to develop the property.

AHEC turned to the private sector for funding and renovation services, signing an agreement with Trizec Corporation Ltd. to develop Tivoli as a regional entertainment center. The renovated Tivoli complex, with some of Denver's most prestigious restaurants and most popular theaters, would serve the surrounding community for sixty-two years and then revert to being a campus-run facility. Over this time period tenants would pay fees to AHEC. Private money was used for commercial benefit, but in the long term Auraria would gain 350,000 square feet of needed building space. Some areas of the complex were constructed of high-quality materials and details that have stood the test of time. Other areas were not renovated or were of poor construction quality, leading to skyrocketing operational and maintenance costs.

The Tivoli development eventually experienced significant financial losses due to renovation costs, the economic recession caused by soaring gas prices in the mid-1980s, lack of student-oriented retail, and lack of supporting community functions, such as housing, retail, and cultural facilities. The teaching institutions at Auraria saw this situation as an opportunity to use student funds to buy back the Tivoli and then use state funds to renovate the existing student center into classroom and office space—an option that was already part of the campus master plan. In 1991 students voted to approve the use of student fees for this renovation, and multiple staff, faculty, and student committees began to work with the architects. The Tivoli reopened in 1994 as one of the country's largest student centers that also retains retail, recreational, and cultural functions serving the surrounding community (Fetter 1996).

Parking was a major issue for Auraria's 33,000-plus commuting students and the surrounding community, which by 1988 included Mile High Stadium (Denver Broncos football) and McNichols Arena (Avalanche hockey and Nuggets basketball). AHEC, these neighbors, the city, numerous city interest groups, and local residents collaborated to solve various parking issues, in part by proposing to share campus parking with Mile High Stadium. More than 1,500 student cars were parked at the stadium during the week with trolleys shuttling students to and from the campus. On Sundays buses carried spectators from Auraria parking lots to Broncos games in the stadium. However the trolleys were expensive to operate and cost-value studies showed that constructing a parking structure on campus would be less expensive in the long run.

AHEC led the way in proposing the private development of a lightweight monorail connecting the municipal stadiums, Auraria, the Denver Center for Performing Arts (DCPA), and the 16th Street Mall, a pedestrian transit mall running the length of the Denver CBD. At the time the Tivoli had been developed into a successful regional entertainment center accommodating some of Denver's finest restaurants. With the monorail a person could park at Auraria, dine at the Tivoli, and ride the monorail to a sports event or a performance at the DCPA. Analyses of alternative systems and economic feasibility studies concluded that the monorail project was viable if passengers paid a small fee. However the monorail was designed to cross and then parallel Speer Boulevard for a short distance, which meant that impacts on the historic landscape would have to be resolved. Sensitive negotiations were already under way to obtain federal funds to pay for new Speer viaducts, and some feared that publicizing additional historic issues might compromise viaduct negotiations. Consequently the monorail project was abandoned.

The implemented alternative to the monorail project was the combination of a new parking structure, new shared parking lots, and new light-rail stations connecting the Auraria campus to the metropolitan light-rail system. A slight increase in parking fees in all Auraria lots and low-cost construction enabled AHEC to purchase the bonds to pay for a new parking structure for almost 2,000 cars. New parking lots for 1,500 cars on the edge of the campus are shared with the adjacent Pepsi Center, which is the new stadium for the Colorado Avalanche (hockey) and the Denver Nuggets (basketball). The shared parking agreement generates income for AHEC and helps meet parking needs for both the campus and the Pepsi Center, which hosts more than 200 events per year.

AHEC took every opportunity to use third parties to develop land or programs, provide income, or increase the value of its land. For example AHEC partnered with the Catholic Church in a plan to channel grant money to the church in return for its donation of the St. Francis Conference Center plus operating capital to Auraria. The Franciscan Friars would transfer the center to AHEC and pay $200,000 per year, from the May Bonfils Stanton Trust. Additional income would come from leasing St. Francis office space to the campus ministries and renting conference space for campus events. AHEC would use these sources of revenue to pay off a promissory note to the Friars and to pay for building management and maintenance. A portion of this funding was later used to relocate the historic Golda Meir house to the campus.

In another case Auraria owned a building adjacent to DCPA, but did not have the funds for renovation; DCPA needed expansion space for rehearsals and back-of-house functions, but did not want to lease space. The two institutions decided to turn the building into a condominium. DCPA would buy the lower floors for its needs and the proceeds would be used by AHEC to renovate the top floor for classroom and office uses. Auraria also generated income by leasing its downtown buildings to the other institutions and state agencies and by developing event space on campus for community conferences, meetings, movies, art shows, weddings, and recreational activities. Students also initiated programs, including child care and child development centers available to the community, and received a million-dollar interest subsidy grant from DURA (Cameron and McFadyen 1977, 127).

Conclusions and Lessons Learned

Auraria has had a major positive impact on Denver's inner city, including development of community functions, historic landmarks, access to the Denver CBD, and beautiful parks and parkways. The Auraria campus also has been a catalyst for the development of neighboring housing, retail, and cultural facilities. The unusual organizational structure and the strong leadership provided by AHEC and the teaching institutions have been very effective in defining their vision and interrelationships and in making the right decisions quickly. The lessons learned in this experience can be summarized in four categories.

1. *Emphasize community collaboration.* Collaboration and information sharing enabled Auraria decision makers to be aware of community responses to their plans even before the plans were presented publicly. Decision makers learned when to place emphasis on institutional interests, when to emphasize community interests, and when to compromise.

2. *Create a vision.* The Auraria leadership and planners had clear directions, well-scrutinized plans, and written design guidelines. Decision makers knew when their decisions were directly aligned with policy and when they had to obtain an interpretation from the AHEC executive director or the Auraria Board. Extraordinary efforts were made to accomplish goals; there were always a hundred reasons not to do a project, but there were also people who listened to those reasons and then provided the perseverance and creative solutions to get the job done anyway.

3. *Leverage assets and search for opportunities.* Auraria's leaders made every effort to maximize benefits from the site's assets and to discover opportunities for campus and community enhancement. They leveraged the assets to form numerous third-party coalitions to generate income, create value, and bring programs to the campus. They found opportunities for community plans to promote Auraria's interests and for campus plans to reflect community interests, such as providing public parks and designing both sides of public streets on campus edges to beautify both the community and the campus.

4. *Involve diverse stakeholders.* Faculty, students, neighbors, and most of all professional consultants were valuable contributors to Auraria's planning process, especially when they were given time and provided with pertinent information and resources to make decisions. There was a feeling that if a campus plan or design could not withstand professional criticism then it would not withstand the test of time. Excellence and professional scrutiny were stressed more than internal politics and opinions.

Auraria has been a major success, with space-sharing and operational efficiencies resulting in cost savings to students and taxpayers. One out of every five college and university students in Colorado is studying on the Auraria campus. Over the past ten years Auraria has received more than forty-five awards for its plans, designs, and community collaboration, and it continues to contribute to the Denver CBD. Auraria demonstrates that inner-city universities have an enormous and varied capacity for community-related campus development. Its success has been based on the search for opportunities and the implementation of creative solutions.

Notes

1. Robert Kronewitter, author of this chapter, was the campus architect from 1983 to 1996.

2. Alternative ideas suggested a campus for MSCD only or the creation of a single nationally prominent research university. There was considerable debate and analysis to determine what space was to be shared.

3. Experiencing severe blight, the number of dwelling units declined from 823 units in 1940 to 386 in 1960 and 134 in 1968. Approximately 155 families and 250 businesses were relocated, with 96 percent electing to remain in Denver. Surveys showed that almost all relocated residents and businesses were satisfied with the relocation process.

4. The Design Review Board included private consultants Hideo Sasaki and Bill Muchow and faculty consultants John Prossor and Dwayne Nuzum. Sasaki became a paid adviser to AHEC.

References

Abbott, Frank. 1999. *The Auraria Higher Education Center, how it came to be.* Denver: Auraria Higher Education Center.

Brownson, Jacques. 1973. *Auraria Higher Education Center, 1973–1976.* Denver: Auraria Board of Directors.

———. 1976. *Site development master plan.* Denver: Auraria Board of Directors.

Cameron, Robert J., and Galen G. McFadyen. 1977. New college facilities, new in-town vitality. *Journal of Housing and Community Development,* March: 124–27.

Denver AIA Urban Design Committee. 1986. *Denver's Speer Boulevard: A revitalization.*

Dober, Richard. 1992. *Campus design.* New York: John Wiley & Sons.

Fetter, Rosemary. 1996. *Brief history of Auraria, celebrating 20 years of innovation.* Denver: Auraria Higher Education Center, Office of the Executive Director.

7

The Political Strategies Behind University-Based Development

Two Philadelphia Cases

Elizabeth Strom

The institutional health of an urban university is inextricably bound to the health of its surrounding community. Universities are therefore motivated to work toward the improvement of their neighborhoods. Engaging in such work requires cultivating a range of political relationships. This chapter examines the experiences of the University of Pennsylvania (hereafter called Penn) and Temple University, two large institutions situated just outside Philadelphia's central business district, which have become increasingly committed to urban development and community revitalization activities.[1]

Penn and Temple grew out of different traditions and serve different constituencies. Penn, a member of the Ivy League, traces its roots back to the eighteenth century and its residential campus draws high-achieving students from all over the country. Temple was founded in 1884 as an evening school for poor students studying for the ministry. Over time it lost its religious affiliation but remained a school that catered to working people. In 1965 the school became affiliated with the state university system. Both universities are involved in neighborhood development on many levels: they are themselves developers of a variety of projects on or near their campuses; they have worked closely with other developers investing in their areas; they have had a "seat at the table" when public officials carry out neighborhood improvement plans; and they have created hundreds of community partnerships that are aimed at bettering their neighborhoods (see Maps 7.1 and 7.2).

When universities become engaged in community development activities, they are thrust into new relationships with community stakeholders and elected officials. Crafting and sustaining these relationships, then, becomes a focus of institutional activity. This chapter examines the political strategies

Map 7.1   **Temple University Main Campus**

Source: www.temple.edu/maps. Used by permission.

these universities have used, first to carry out urban renewal schemes in the 1960s, and more recently to implement a variety of neighborhood improvement programs throughout the 1990s. These case studies make it clear that political strategies have changed over time. They also show that the ability of

Map 7.2   **University of Pennsylvania Campus**

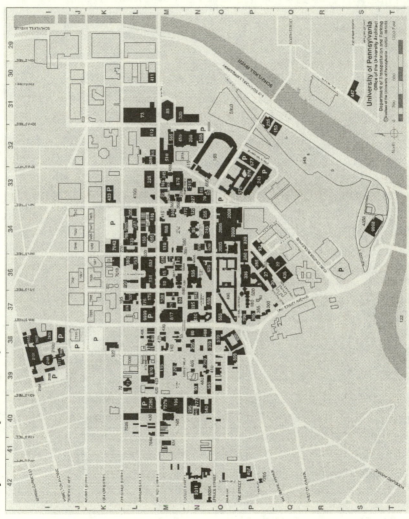

Source: Facilities and Real Estate Services, University of Pennsylvania. Copyright © Trustees of the University of Pennsylvania. Used by permission.

a university to create a positive political climate depends on internal conditions (most notably the quality of institutional leadership and availability of financial resources), as well as external conditions (including the quality of local political leadership and the socioeconomic conditions of the community). Finally they suggest that public and private universities may face different constraints and take advantage of different opportunities when operating in the political arena.

Development in a Post–Urban Renewal Era

Both Penn and Temple made extensive use of the federal urban renewal program, administered in Philadelphia by the Redevelopment Authority (long chaired by Penn trustee Gustave Amsterdam), in the 1950s and 1960s. Section 112 of the revised legislation authorizing the program made special provision for projects centered on university expansion: the federal government allowed cities to "count" university investment as part of the local match required to leverage federal funds. This gave city officials great incentive to seek out university partners, just when universities, concerned about deteriorating conditions in their neighborhoods and anticipating increased enrollments, had become actively engaged in campus planning. Partnering with city officials who could use local eminent-domain powers and federal funds to acquire and clear sites, both universities benefited enormously. Over 45 percent of Penn's total square footage today was added during the 1960s and 1970s, much of it as a result of publicly sponsored redevelopment powers, and many of Temple's buildings were erected under the auspices of urban renewal.

But the methods used by renewal officials—large-scale clearance and displacement with limited community consultation—generated opposition to institutional expansion in North and West Philadelphia. This opposition grew by the late 1960s into outright resistance marked by protests by community residents as well as students. Since the demise of urban renewal, urban universities have had to figure out ways to achieve the goals of campus expansion and neighborhood renewal using different tools. Lacking a pool of redevelopment funds, scrutinized by wary elected officials and viewed suspiciously by neighborhood interests, development-oriented universities have had to reassess their expansion needs, forge new relationships with public officials, and reconsider their posture toward their communities.

In the 1980s both schools were at critical junctures in their institutional lives, making them all the more sensitive to the conditions in their communities. After rapidly expanding in the 1960s, Temple's enrollments were declining as the most talented students in the region were seeking other public campuses. Peter Liacouras took office as president in 1982, determined to transform the school from a shrinking commuter college in a deteriorating neighborhood to a robust state university campus. He was often quoted as saying, "We could become a glorified community college. That might not be a bad thing, but we wouldn't need 60 percent of the people here" (Weyrich 1998, 17). Key to effecting this transformation, he believed, was upgrading the North Philadelphia campus, both by expanding university facilities and by stemming the decline of the surrounding neighborhood. Liacouras spelled out his priorities in a 1984 public memo following a meeting with Mayor Wilson Goode. He sought the city's support in creating a high-tech industrial park; expanding the school's athletic facilities; and generally improving the Broad Street corridor, the city's main north-south axis that was the entry point to the Temple campus (Temple University 1986). Less publicly, Temple officials also sought to expand dormitory space,[2] and to improve the sorts of amenities (i.e., dining halls and recreation centers) that attract students to campus.

Penn, always a prestigious institution, had seen its academic fortunes improve in the 1980s. Penn researchers were increasingly productive, with total research and development support more than doubling from $94 million to $189 million between 1980 and 1990. Penn's humanities, medicine, business, and engineering strengths, among others, propelled the institution's national and international reputations. By the end of the 1980s, Penn was a truly global institution, one of the few in Philadelphia. The school's leadership recognized that sustaining this position required new facilities and a livelier, more appealing neighborhood. In the mid-1980s, Penn President Sheldon Hackney began working to strengthen the university's connections to its neighbors, throwing the full weight of the institution behind a robust series of community partnerships (eventually brought together under the Center for Community Partnerships). His successor, Judith Rodin, appointed in 1994, went even farther. As she sought to promote university and university-related development at the edges of the campus, she also embarked on a series of initiatives to improve housing, education, and security in West Philadelphia.

While both schools came into the 1990s with similar campus expansion agendas, Penn encountered far less resistance to its development plans. The school still controls a great deal of property it acquired during the urban renewal era, and new sites became available near the medical complex when a municipal hospital and the city's civic center both closed. University officials have expressed reluctance to expand the campus westward, where they are likely to encroach on established residential neighborhoods, but the school owns or can reasonably expect to own sufficient land to the east to secure its expansionary interests. Building on land it already controls, the university has been able to add classrooms, laboratory and recreation facilities, and a retail complex without needing more than routine public support.

Temple's geopolitical situation is considerably different. The school has several campuses inside and outside of the city, but its main North Philadelphia campus is far smaller than Penn's. It controls little surplus property and is surrounded by housing projects on the north and south and the regional railroad tracks to the east. In theory the school could expand westward, and a visitor to the area noting the many empty lots and abandoned buildings west of Broad Street might think this would be a natural area for expansion. But property ownership in this area is highly dispersed, with dozens of owners controlling small parcels on each block, creating barriers to site assembly. In contrast, property ownership to the east of the Penn campus is less dispersed, dominated by public, institutional, and commercial owners. Assembling large parcels west of Broad Street would require the city to use its condemnation powers against hundreds of owners on Temple's behalf, in a neighborhood already disposed to think the worst of the university. It is hard to imagine that either district or citywide elected leadership would be prepared to spend the political capital needed to undertake such an effort. Moreover, in the agreements the school signed to end protests against urban renewal in 1970, Temple officials agreed to limit the school's expansion; all efforts to loosen these restraints have met with resistance. As one long-time community activist told a reporter, "If they just stay where they are, it would be good. If they tried to move north, south, east or west, it would be bad, and the community would confront them immediately" (Dean 1998).

Strategies: How Temple and Penn Mobilize Support for Development

Penn and Temple, like other urban universities, seek to shape land uses and land use policies in their cities. In this regard they are like other place-based corporations, using whatever resources they can bring to bear to influence those who regulate land use. But their interests and strategies are distinctive. Private investors have two very blunt and effective weapons at their disposal when they seek to extract favorable action from public officials. They can threaten to move (Kantor and Savitch 1993), and they can reward and punish elected officials by targeting campaign contributions. Universities, however, are not mobile. As Judith Rodin has written, "Ultimately, urban universities cannot change their address. Most have too much invested in physical facilities and too much history in their communities to want to do so, anyway" (Rodin 2001).[3] Moreover, as public or nonprofit institutions, they cannot give financial support to electoral candidates.

Finally, for-profit developers can comfortably pursue strategies designed purely to maximize financial returns without encountering conflict with their shareholders, their employees, or their consciences. Even elected officials generally understand that private developers are in the business of making a profit, and don't expect them to engage in participatory decision-making processes or solve social problems. Universities, whether public or nonprofit, are in a very different situation. Elected officials and community residents expect them to behave in public-oriented ways; their own constituents (students, faculty, alumni, and trustees) demand corporate behavior that is consistent with the high-mindedness thought to be characteristic of liberal arts values. Held to a higher standard than for-profit developers, development-oriented universities must achieve similar goals using different methods. If they are to win friends for their campus and neighborhood improvement schemes, they must find more nuanced ways to forge alliances.

Service and Outreach

Temple and more notably Penn have both sought to win support by becoming engaged in a variety of community-service programs. Penn has been on the cutting edge of university-sponsored community development activities with its West Philadelphia Initiatives, an interlocking series of programs designed to address the area's security, educational, housing, and economic development needs (Lussenhop 2001; Rodin 2001). Penn made direct investments in commercial and campus infrastructure and pursued numerous operating polices designed to improve local quality of life. Both universities have developed extensive relationships with the troubled public school system. Penn actually built and now manages one school, in hopes of improving the level of elementary education in the immediate community while also making the school's West Philadelphia neighborhood a more attractive place for families to live. Penn also has supervisory contracts with the school board to oversee several other schools. Temple's contract with the school board gives it responsibility for five local schools, where university personnel are involved in curriculum development, after-school activities, and other programs.

Both universities offer a number of academic programs featuring different styles of service learning. Penn's Center for Community Partnerships, run by Dr. Ira Harkavy, represents a national model for incorporating community-based activities into the curriculum, and giving such activities academic legitimacy. Penn offers some seventy-five such courses, and counts 200 different campus-community partnerships in its portfolio. Temple has recently broken ground on a community education building that will house a variety of community-based programs; the school's Web site also lists over 100 courses and programs through which Temple students can engage in community outreach. Penn and Temple students and faculty can be found staffing community centers, tutoring in public schools, and providing outpatient care in medical school clinics, just to give a few examples.

Both Temple and Penn are actively engaged in promoting local business development as well. Temple has contributed both technical assistance and capital in an effort to upgrade the commercial strips surrounding the campus. Penn has similar small-business development programs, and it has also boosted the local economy through its Buy West Philadelphia program. Created in 1986 this initiative makes purchasing from local vendors a high priority throughout the institution. Buy West Philadelphia doesn't merely compile lists of local vendors; it works actively with small businesses so they increase their volume of sales to the university, and requires some large, national suppliers to form partnerships with local companies to administer their Penn-related contracts (ICIC 2002, 17–19).

Such partnerships have multiple motivations. To some, service learning and community outreach should be an emblematic feature of a liberal arts education, and the leadership at both schools sincerely embraces this view. In addition such programs are valued as practical training for students in a variety of fields where such practice is essential. Such initiatives also have a real public relations value to universities. At the most superficial level, the schools can point to their many community-directed programs to show that they are giving back something to neighborhood residents. Many residents consider universities to be less than ideal neighbors; apart from the more dramatic tensions over urban renewal, West and North Philadelphia residents have often complained about traffic, parking, and disruptive behavior of students. Programs that offer concrete benefits to communities can improve a university's image among those who live nearby.

On a less tangible level, community outreach programs can help the university win political support that may, in the long run, make it easier for the institution to achieve its own goals, including campus expansion. Penn's economic development director told researchers that the school's outreach efforts helped its relations with the city council, specifically citing the school's negotiations with the city over the purchase of the civic center (ICIC 2002, 17). Those who benefit directly from university programs are less likely to join the opposition when the university seeks to close off a street or erect a new building. Elected officials whose constituents feel well served by university-sponsored services have less incentive to win political points by demonizing the school as it seeks to expand. There are limits to the political value of such programs, however. One knowledgeable observer suggested that North Philadelphia community organizations are happy to take advantage of whatever in-kind services Temple is willing to offer, but still remain suspicious of any new development plans. But each partnership represents another relationship that anchors the school in the community, and this complex web of relationships provides a good basis for building political support for projects essential to the university's growth.

Direct Institutional Engagement in the Political Process

The presidents and government relations officials of both universities work hard to cultivate positive political relationships, although this is not as straightforward as it sounds. Philadelphia is a politically fractious city. Not only do institutions need to reach out to their council representatives, but they (especially state-funded Temple) must also attend to the concerns of at least one state representative and one state senator. Pennsylvania's large lower chamber means that a university's development may cross districts, in which case additional state representatives must be considered. In some instances an area's representatives have been rivals, so that a close relationship with one alienates another.

Simply doing good work in the community is not enough. Universities must make an active effort to build relationships based on small but crucial understandings. Elected officials must be kept informed. The worst thing that can happen to an elected official, says one university representative with extensive political experience, is to hear about something for the first time from an unhappy constituent. Elected officials are credited for positive developments in the area, thanked at groundbreakings, photographed at award ceremonies, and given the best seats at university sporting events. One university respondent noted that an elected official once told him, "You'll be able to get a lot done here in the community as long as you don't care about taking credit for it."

Even the manner of communication with the "electeds" is part of the relationship. At both schools it is understood that contact with the local council representative must go through one of two or three top officials. If an elected official begins receiving calls from dozens of people up and down the school hierarchy, the relationship will be damaged. Because this endeavor is so complex, both schools have government and community relations staffs with experience at the local, state, and national levels; high-level administrators are frequently drawn from the ranks of the public sector as well.

Building Relationships through Intermediaries

University leaders have been able to build political relationships from service on boards and committees. All the top administrators at Penn and Temple serve on a variety of nonprofit boards and government commissions, from the boards of local community development corporations, to the United Way, to the board overseeing the city's Empowerment Zone. Just about every city commission has a Penn or Temple official on it. Judith Rodin was asked to serve on Mayor John Street's transition team, and Street's first economic development initiative was to create an agency, chaired by Rodin, charged with luring high-tech companies that would build on the city's university- and hospital-based research.

This sort of service on the part of top officials brings multiple mutual political benefits. University representatives can often bring expertise and respectability to an organization. Their participation helps smaller neighbor- hood groups get taken seriously by funders and political leaders, and can give weight to higher-level efforts as well. The news report announcing Street's economic development initiative, for instance, notes the importance of Rodin's appointment as giving the agency "heft" (Gorenstein and Burton 2001). Temple officials serve on the Empowerment Zone board and are included in virtually all North Philadelphia development efforts. By agreeing to serve in these roles, university officials win the goodwill of political and community leaders. They also get the opportunity to meet and develop relationships with a wide variety of city stakeholders, and these relationships can be immedi- ately beneficial or bring advantages down the road.

Universities also reach beyond their paid administrators when seeking to win political friends. Faculty, alumni, and trustees can all be political assets. Many local and state politicians have had some kind of connection to these two schools. For example, former mayor Ed Rendell received his BA from Penn, and Mayor Street received his law degree from Temple. These kinds of personal connections don't translate into automatic political support, how- ever. Some observers believe that Rendell went to great lengths to avoid showing favoritism toward Penn, and as a city council representative John Street carried on a running war with Temple.[4]

University trustees often are chosen precisely because they are economi- cally and politically prominent and can help the university realize its civic goals. Penn trustee Gustave Amsterdam was the chair of the city's Redevel- opment Authority throughout the 1960s, which no doubt helped the school navigate the complex urban renewal process. Temple trustees also have been able to bring important resources to bear in the resolution of political con- flicts surrounding campus expansion efforts. A Temple trustee who was also the president of First Pennsylvania Bank was able to organize a bridge-loan fund that enabled a nonprofit community development corporation to build a housing project that helped end a political impasse over urban renewal in 1970. Another trustee used his close connections to Ed Rendell to bring the mayor in to mediate between the university and then-councilman John Street, hammering out the compromise that allowed the construction of Temple's long-delayed recreation complex, now known as the L. When crime became a pressing concern in North Philadelphia and Temple officials were unable to get increased police patrols at nearby bus and substations, Temple board chair F. Eugene Dixon, a prominent Philadelphia-area businessman with high-level political and social connections, met personally with the police commissioner to bring attention to the school's problems.

Finally both universities have created institutional partnerships through which to carry out important development and community improvement tasks. Penn spearheaded the creation of the University City District, which provides much of the sanitation and security services for the area; this organization includes representation of the other large West Philadelphia institutions, as well as smaller businesses and community organizations. Housing, community development, and education programs also work cooperatively with local groups. Temple has fewer institutional neighbors with which to work, but has also learned to take advantage of existing resources. A well-respected local nonprofit developer, Beech Corporation, is currently renovating several multifamily houses to serve as student apartments just west of the campus's Broad Street border. Whereas the school's efforts to build dormitories have always encountered community resistance, and plans to build facilities to the west of Broad Street have been greeted by near universal opposition, this project has not come under fire. Apparently community activists are willing to see student housing constructed west of Broad, providing it is built and owned by a local entity.

We can see the importance of nurturing good relationships when we look at situations in which they have not prevailed. Penn encountered its share of community displeasure over development during the 1990s, for example, when Penn bought the old civic center from the cash-strapped city and made plans to demolish it (the new Pennsylvania Convention Center had made it obsolete). More recently a group called Neighbors Against McPenntrification has protested a number of matters, including efforts to create an historic district in West Philadelphia and plans to upgrade retail along 40th Street.[5] But these flare-ups have not, since the last days of urban renewal, forced the school to derail or even seriously revise its plans. Because Penn enjoys an excellent relationship with its city council representative, complaints from these fringe community groups have not erupted into political battles.

In contrast, strains between Temple and its neighbors have proven more politically costly. John Street, who represented Temple's neighborhood in city council for eighteen years, was frequently at war with the university, most notably with its former president, Peter Liacouras. Typically when

Temple would propose a project that took it outside of its zoned Institutional Development District, Street would put up roadblocks to the project until he had exacted concessions from the school, usually in the form of community projects.[6] Beginning in 1985, when Street held up the construction of a research and development center to be funded by Bell Telephone, through the 1990s, when a major recreation complex and two dormitories were built only after extensive negotiation, Temple found itself in the unpleasant situation of carrying out its neighborhood development plans in opposition to its closest elected official. Street is known, even among his allies, as a stubborn man who insists on having things done his way (Bissinger 1997). But community battles with Temple predated Street's tenure; in insisting that school officials and their associates have greater consideration for the concerns of the neighborhood, he was no doubt reflecting his constituents' views.

Temple president Liacouras, who is considered as pugnacious as Street, made many tactical errors as he sought to move his development agenda forward. Even sympathetic community residents complained that he would present a plan as a *fait accompli,* leaving Temple's neighbors no sense that they could have any input. He spent some eight years battling John Street to get approvals to build a large recreation center on West Broad Street. Hoping to manage an end run around Street's opposition, he convinced the state legislature, which was funding much of the project, to declare it a state project, thus eliminating the city's zoning authority. But the city still retained other kinds of authority over the site so Liacouras's strategy managed to infuriate Street without actually removing him from the approval process (Goodman 1995). It seems that only a change in personnel (Street was elected mayor in 1999 and Liacouras stepped down as Temple president in 2000) and extraordinary fence-mending efforts on the part of current Temple president David Adamany have made possible a less-fractious relationship.

Conclusions: Political Strategies of Public and Private Universities

Urban universities must cultivate a number of relationships on many different fronts to maintain the friendships that will allow them to carry out their development plans. Perhaps surprisingly these circumstances have been similar for Penn and Temple. One might think that Temple, the school founded to provide evening education for the city's humble strivers and a state school that must be adept at working with political leaders to ensure its support, would be less enmeshed in town-gown hostilities than Ivy League Penn, but this has not been the case. If anything, suspicion of Temple is greater among North Philadelphia residents and leaders than is suspicion of Penn among its

West Philadelphia counterparts. Explanations for these differences have as much to do with the schools' histories in their communities as with their public or private status.

First, although Penn's main campus is larger than Temple's, Temple expanded very rapidly in the 1960s. It had earlier been a small player in a densely populated residential neighborhood, and overnight it became an expanding university in a shrinking neighborhood struggling to stabilize. Moreover, North Philadelphia is a poorer, more deteriorated part of the city than is West Philadelphia. Whereas about 20 percent of West Philadelphia residents live below the poverty line (Rodin 2001), in the North Philadelphia communities closest to Temple the figure is over 50 percent (Young 2000). Thus Penn is a long-time anchor in a relatively organized community, whereas Temple has a shorter history in a more volatile neighborhood, producing very different kinds of relationships in the two cases.

West Philadelphia, moreover, is home to several nonprofit institutions (most notably Drexel University), and Penn has worked effectively with them, earlier through the West Philadelphia Corporation and more recently through the University City District. This cooperation allows Penn to extend its impact, and it also serves to deflect potential community opposition from the university to the larger West Philadelphia institutional network. By contrast Temple is essentially the only major institution in its area. It has fewer natural allies as it pursues its development agenda, and community leaders are more likely to focus their energies on scrutinizing its actions. Fairly or not, many neighborhood residents look to local institutions to provide the benefits that, much to their frustration, their city government has failed to provide; in North Philadelphia the service deficits are very great, and Temple becomes the target of local dissatisfaction.

Third, Penn students and faculty may have a greater sense of connection to West Philadelphia than Temple students and faculty have to North Philadelphia. Although Penn students and faculty are drawn from around the nation and the world, most students live on campus or nearby and many faculty live in nearby communities. Indeed when Penn negotiates with community groups, it is often negotiating with Penn faculty and staff who are also neighborhood residents. Temple students, on the other hand, are far more likely to hail from Philadelphia or its nearby suburbs. Most commute to school and feel little attachment to the neighborhood, although there is a growing student presence on campus. Temple faculty, likewise, seldom seek housing in the public projects and dilapidated row houses surrounding the campus.

Finally, Penn's resources and its institutional independence enable it to become active in community programs to a degree beyond the reach of Temple officials. As a well-endowed, financially stable, private institution, Penn's leadership has the flexibility to invest its resources as it sees fit. Penn officials are quick to point out that there are many demands on their resources, and in interviews all have rejected the idea that they have simply bought their way to improved community relations. And to be sure, recent Penn presidents have exercised effective leadership in West Philadelphia, formulating and carrying out well-integrated programs that have deservedly won widespread support. Penn has a greater ability than Temple to fund community development initiatives and underwrite the costs of other projects that help promote good relations, from student internships to paid community relations staff, to sanitation and security services. Moreover, Penn has the stability to commit itself to long-term projects.

At least some of Temple's political difficulties of the 1980s and 1990s were self-inflicted, and Liacouras's hard-knuckle tactics at times might have hurt the university's interests. As a state school, Temple battles each year with the legislature for its funding; it has less flexibility in deciding how this money is spent and is less able to commit its resources to long-term projects. North Philadelphia residents, and many elected officials, however, expect Temple to duplicate Penn's level of community investment, and they are disappointed when Temple fails to meet this standard.

For both Penn and Temple, expanding their campuses and upgrading their surroundings have been closely tied to their core institutional missions for several decades. Both have sought to accommodate new facilities and introduce amenities that make campus life more attractive, and both have relied on multifaceted political support to achieve these goals. In seeking support for their development activities, these universities pursue strategies similar to those of other developers seeking to cultivate good relations with elected officials who are important to realizing their goals. But universities have to rely on a more nuanced list of strategies to achieve these goals, strategies that are relatively similar for public and for private universities.

Notes

1. Interviews with university and civic leaders familiar with the University of Pennsylvania and Temple University have provided some of the information in this chapter.

2. Community members were especially suspicious of Temple's efforts to provide housing for more of its students or staff, fearing that their presence would transform the neighborhood in ways that would not benefit current residents.

3. During his battles over Temple's recreation center, Peter Liacouras did once threaten to relocate many of Temple's programs to its suburban campus (Weyrich 1998). This threat was not taken very seriously, but it indicates how poor relations between Temple and city officials had become.

4. Indeed Street's ill will toward Temple University, and particularly its recent

past president Peter Liacouras, was inflamed by his close connections to the school. In the mid-1980s Street was serving on the city council and teaching part-time at the Temple Law School, when the press reported that he still owed the school several thousand dollars in unpaid student loans. Street, according to one interviewee, always believed that Liacouras had provided this information to the press to embarrass him, and the incident fed a mutual antipathy.

5. The group complains that Penn promotes gentrification in surrounding neighborhoods. It also charges that Penn is responsible for the opening of a new McDonald's restaurant on 43rd Street that, allegedly, Penn has promoted in an effort to close a McDonald's on 40th Street, closer to the heart of the campus. According to this claim the university wants to move the fast-food restaurant, with its low-income clientele, away from its own planned retail improvements.

6. The Philadelphia City Council practices a form of "councilmanic courtesy," refusing to act on any bill opposed by the representative of the affected district. This gives a representative de facto veto power over any major development in his or her district.

References

Bissinger, Buzz. 1997. *A prayer for the city.* New York: Random House.

Dean, Mensah M. 1998. Not always academic. *Philadelphia Daily News,* September 29: 8.

Goodman, Howard. 1995. Apollo project languished under cloud of mistrust. *Philadelphia Inquirer,* November 5: B4.

Gorenstein, Nathan, and Cynthia Burton. 2001. New city agency will work to lure high-tech firms. *Philadelphia Inquirer,* February 8: 1C.

Initiative for a Competitive Inner City and CEOs for Cities (ICIC). 2002. Leveraging colleges and universities for urban economic redevelopment: An action agenda. April (www.icic.org).

Kantor, Paul, and H.V. Savitch. 1993. Can politicians bargain with business? A theoretical and comparative perspective on urban development. *Urban Affairs Quarterly* 28(3): 230–255.

Lussenhop, Tom. 2001. University community development, *CUED Economic Development Quarterly,* Summer.

Rodin, Judith. 2001. Common cause: Investing in the community. *The Presidency.* Spring.

Temple University. 1986. *The Academic Plan.* Philadelphia: Temple University.

Weyrich, Noel. 1998. The trouble with Temple. *Philadelphia Weekly,* August 26: 16–21.

Young, Earni. 2000. Tech center raises hope. *Philadelphia Daily News,* September 25: 13.

8

The University as an Engine for Downtown Renewal in Atlanta

Lawrence R. Kelley and Carl V. Patton

Several billion dollars in development is under way in downtown Atlanta, including numerous projects initiated by Georgia State University. Working to make itself part of the community, Georgia State, along with its private foundation and business partners, has developed a variety of building projects that are breathing life into the downtown area. Without a city master plan for the central core, the university took on a planning process and became the lead institution in redeveloping the downtown area. This chapter describes the university's learning process with its partners, how it built support, utilized two private foundations to float bond issues, leveraged private funds, and developed the expertise required to rebuild itself and downtown Atlanta.

Georgia State now serves 40,000 students annually from 145 countries, but it was founded by the Georgia Institute of Technology in 1913 as its evening school of commerce with an initial class of six students in rented downtown office space. The school quickly developed a strong reputation for its academic training in business and moved several times to accommodate increases in enrollment and academic scope. It eventually located permanently just east of Atlanta's central downtown Five Points area (see Map 8.1).

By the late 1960s the school had become Georgia State University, with six colleges, a campus of a dozen buildings, and an annual enrollment of 12,000 students. Throughout the 1970s and 1980s the university continued to grow but the downtown business community surrounding the campus lost much of its vitality. Many downtown corporations relocated to new space outside the downtown core. The state, county, and city government operations continued to expand south of the campus, but remained physically isolated from the business community.

Map 8.1   **Georgia State University Campus**

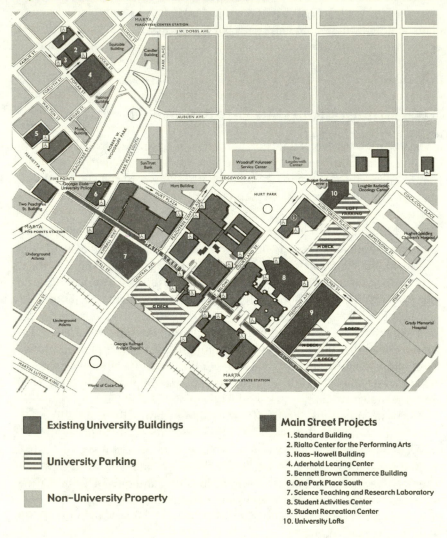

Existing University Buildings

University Parking

Non-University Property

Main Street Projects
1. Standard Building
2. Rialto Center for the Performing Arts
3. Haas–Howell Building
4. Aderhold Learing Center
5. Bennett Brown Commerce Building
6. One Park Place South
7. Science Teaching and Research Laboratory
8. Student Activities Center
9. Student Recreation Center
10. University Lofts

Source: Used by permission of the Sizemore Group, Atlanta, Georgia.

A Vision for Growth

Carl Patton became president of Georgia State in 1992. An urban planner and academic leader, he had extensive experience in urban planning, university campus planning, and economic development. He wanted the university to be a part of the community and believed that the university should focus on measurable results and be accountable. These themes guided Georgia State's initial academic strategic plan that included not only annual action plans and budgets for the university but also began to articulate a broader urban plan as well. This approach strengthened the bond between the university and the community and forged personal relationships that would prove to be decisive in future development opportunities. The focus on measurable results and accountability helped assure supporters, donors, and lenders that the university would deliver the projects it proposed.

To better position the university for development, Patton moved into active leadership roles with community organizations. This involvement also allowed him to help reshape much of the downtown environment. Under Patton's leadership, Centennial Olympic Park Area, Inc. (COPA) leveraged housing development around Centennial Olympic Park and began to create a lively twenty-four-hour environment. Patton went on to serve as chair of Central Atlanta Progress (CAP), a business coalition striving to make Atlanta a more livable, workable, and safe twenty-four-hour city. Both COPA and CAP have developed initiatives that enhance the projects Georgia State has undertaken.

The Plan for Development

Many universities, even those located in the center of cities, have tried to separate themselves from the community. Sometimes they have done so with gates and fences. Georgia State did this with platforms and catwalks. The platform system at the center of the campus raised it above the streets and sidewalks and created sitting areas and plazas intended only for faculty, staff, and students. Today the philosophy at Georgia State is quite different. The university's academic, strategic, and fiscal plans focus on being intertwined with the community.

A conceptual master plan for future campus growth was developed in 1994, leading to the university's ten-year blueprint for development, the Main Street Master Plan. The conceptual master plan was based on academic policies developed through the university strategic planning process led by the university's provost and voted into policy by the university senate. These policies were then translated into physical needs using a student-faculty team of planners and architects from neighboring Georgia Tech's city and regional planning and architecture programs. Faculty, students, and staff from the university as well as downtown stakeholders and alumni participated in the planning process. This plan gave physical form to the concept of being part of the community by opening new and existing campus buildings to the city and its streets using large windows and new, inviting community-based spaces in which to sit, walk, and congregate.

This conceptual master plan was further developed when the University System of Georgia mandated a template to guide planning at all of its thirty-four institutions. Because of the jump start with its conceptual plan, Georgia State was able to use the template to devise a more complete plan for its downtown campus. The refined master plan sought to transform one of the downtown streets that crosses through the heart of the campus into a pedestrian-friendly "Main Street" corridor by using a traffic-calming project that made it even easier for students, faculty, and staff to be a part of the urban experience.[1]

This plan was the product of widespread participation by faculty, students, staff, and neighbors, and it was presented widely in the local community and around the state and nation to alumni groups. It was placed on the university Web site where comments could be received and shared. The plan as finalized focuses on creating an inviting campus, outlines the construction of several new academic buildings, and is based on the following principles:

- Integrate institutional buildings and their use into the city environment.
- Use existing and planned structures to help define and connect campus spaces.
- Use housing opportunities to attract the population necessary to create a viable community.
- Support transportation patterns that encourage pedestrian traffic and enhance the safety and convenience of Georgia State for students, faculty, and staff.
- Create a sense of place and identity.
- Establish a central core of campus facilities and a secondary zone of support services.

The projects described below respond to these principles in various ways. They are either buildings that place activities at the center of campus or at street level, facilities that encourage pedestrian traffic along important corridors or define the Main Street area, or projects that attract people to the campus for living or recreation.

Funding the Projects

Georgia State's dramatic growth in the early 1990s increased the need for more teaching, research, and administrative space, and these needs were then specified in the Main Street plan. With a rapidly growing state university system of thirty-four institutions, however, public funding was not available to meet Georgia State's facility needs. In a good year the state might provide a total of $100 million for capital projects for all of the state's public colleges and universities combined, but a typical project at one of the research universities could be $50 million or more.[2] Since individual institutions in Georgia are prohibited from issuing bonds themselves, Georgia State had to find other funding sources to supplement state appropriations. This challenge led to a decade of new institutional practices in leasing, acquiring, and building new facilities, with each deal being more complicated than the last.

To gain financial flexibility, the university worked through its private foundation, the Georgia State University Foundation (GSUF), which played several important development roles ranging from financial intermediary to bond issuer to funding source. State of Georgia entities are not allowed to contract for services for more than one year at a time. Thus a university by itself is not able to float a bond issue or enter into an agreement to lease a facility for more than one year at a time. This situation makes it impossible for a university to enter into a real estate deal without a third party that is willing to act as an intermediary and accept the risk of one-year contracts. This is one of the roles that GSUF played.

An entity such as GSUF can also serve as a source of risk capital, helping to finance up-front costs of development, such as title searches, options on land, and legal fees. GSUF directly funded some of these costs for the university and loaned the funds for other expenditures to be paid back from project costs. GSUF also helped raise private funds to cover the gap between state funding and total costs for some projects and arranged bond financing for others. In addition the foundation purchased property outright that it later leased to the university to meet pressing space needs that could not be met by the state.

The first GSUF project was the acquisition in 1992 of a 136,500-square-foot office building that it now leases to the university. The university pays a square-foot rental cost. The facility houses office, classroom, and research functions and creates a net cash flow for the foundation. GSUF leases the facility to the university on a year-to-year basis since, as mentioned above, state law prohibits the university from entering into multiple-year leases.[3]

GSUF in 1994 acquired control of three buildings and the land under two of them to support the university's music program and the development of a center for performing arts. The project included the renovation of the three buildings. Financing was achieved through $10 million in private contributions to GSUF and $4 million in bonds issued by the Downtown Development Authority of the City of Atlanta, with the proceeds assigned to The University Financing Foundation (TUFF), an independent foundation supporting higher education development.

GSUF leases the facilities from TUFF and sublets them to the university through a series of one-year renewable leases. The lease payments are serviced with operating revenue from the performing arts center as well as the university's general operating budget. The fifty-year ground lease for the performing arts center site will result in the reversion of the building to the owner of the land at the end of the lease period. Ownership of the other two buildings, which house the School of Music, will revert to GSUF when the debt is expired.

Also in 1994 the university acquired part of the site for its new student activities center through an agreement with the City of Atlanta, negotiated between the mayor and the university president. The university paid half of the cost of the needed site in the form of a $500,000 line of credit against which city employees could draw to finance their education at Georgia State. The city's new police chief will be the most recent city employee to take advantage of this arrangement. The bond issue for the student activities center is being paid off through a dedicated student activities center fee.

Another real estate deal in which the university was involved enabled the former downtown Atlanta headquarters of First Union Bank to become a condominium development. GSUF was offered the building as a gift, but concluded that renovation for academic needs would not be feasible. A deal was struck in which First Union traded the bank building to a local newspaper in exchange for a line of advertising credit; the newspaper then gave the building to GSUF, which then sold the building to a local developer at a price that allowed the building to be converted into condominiums. The bank gained advertising and wrote the building off of its books at its basis value. The newspaper gained a charitable contribution, and the new housing near campus benefited the university and added a little more life to the downtown.[4]

The university next stepped up to answer the question about what would happen to downtown Atlanta in the wake of the 1996 Summer Olympic Games. Georgia State had served as a commuter school for decades, but that would change with the establishment of a housing department in 1993, in anticipation of the 1996 Summer Olympics. Historically being prohibited from developing housing by the Regents of the University System, the university agreed to purchase the Olympic Village after the games for use as undergraduate housing when other potential users backed out. The Regents issued $85 million in debt for the purchase. Student rent payments service the debt.

The Georgia State Village opened in fall 1996 with a 2,000-student capacity. Operated as an auxiliary service, the facility has developed an annual waiting list of 400 to 800 students. The village is located on nine acres one-and-a-half miles north of the campus on the edge of downtown and along one of the city's rapid rail transit lines; each resident receives a transit pass as part of his or her rent.

To construct a student recreation center as the next phase of adding student life to campus, GSUF leased a campus parking lot from the university in 1998 as the development site.[5] The Atlanta Development Authority (ADA) issued twenty-year bonds with the proceeds loaned to GSUF for the construction and equipping of the recreation center and the expansion of an existing parking deck to replace the lost parking. The recreation center is located across the street from the student activities center that had been built in 1995.

The recreation center bonds are special limited obligation bonds payable pursuant to a promissory note between the ADA and GSUF, which leases the facility to the university on an annual basis. A recreation fee paid by the students provides the revenue stream for payment of the lease. Ownership of this building will revert to the university when the bonds are retired. The recreation center was opened in August 2001 and serves approximately 2,500 users a day.[6]

Over the years the campus had grown westward across Peachtree Street to acquire office space to house a growing faculty. Because there was no classroom building serving the three colleges housed west of Peachtree Street, it was deemed essential that a classroom facility be constructed in this vicinity. Virtually all of the city blocks in this area were occupied by recently renovated or older substantial buildings, save one block with vacant structures scattered among retail and office uses.

The Regents agreed to provide $23 million toward a $40 million classroom building, but following a long-standing practice would not provide funds to purchase land in downtown because of its high cost and an antiurban bias of the legislature. This financial shortfall left the university with the challenge of finding private funding for the acquisition of the block, demolition of the existing structures on the site, and construction of part of the new facility.

The acquisition of the city block was controversial since some of the derelict buildings had historical connections. One was a former restaurant that had been the site of sit-ins during desegregation. Another was a building designed by the firm of a famous local architect. A small but vocal group of historic preservationists held that the university should renovate the old buildings. The university's position was that the result would be an inefficient and costly structure yielding poor results for its students and an equally poor accounting of both public and private funds.

The preservationists held a small rally opposing the university's acquisition of the block, and members of the university who would benefit from the new building held an anti-rally punctuated by music played by students and faculty of the School of Music, which would have practice rooms on the top floor of the proposed building. A flurry of pro and con letters appeared in the local paper, and one newspaper writer, whose architect father had added a false facade to one of the buildings decades earlier, took on opposition to the project as a personal cause. The irony was that all but one of the landowners was happy to sell. An old, well-loved "greasy spoon" on the block was even guaranteed a relocation space in the new building. The lone holdout would not negotiate a selling price.

The university successfully acquired the block using a court-appointed Special Master to resolve the price of the last parcel. Because of the controversy over acquiring the site, the university president appointed a citizen advisory committee to give advice to the architects. The committee was chaired by a highly regarded local businessman and included the dean of the College of Architecture at Georgia Tech, individuals who had sold their property on the block to the university, preservationists, alumni, and downtown business owners. The committee reviewed the architectural design of the building and provided continuing input to the architectural firm. This process assured that the building would fit into the context of the neighborhood and maintain the street fabric in the historic area. The result was a building that even former critics describe as breathtaking.

GSUF succeeded in raising more than $13 million so the land could be gifted to the university for the construction of the classroom facility. The building opened for classes in the fall of 2002, bringing 3,000 students per hour to the center of the city.

Tackling a Complicated Housing Deal

Building on its experiences thus far, the university wanted to tackle another important need—housing for graduate and international students. By 2000, 30 percent of total student enrollment was graduate students, and international students from 145 countries accounted for 6 percent. In addition Georgia State had experienced a tripling of research funding during the 1990s, with an accompaning increase in the number of graduate research assistants. Expecting continued growth in research and enrollment, the master plan called for doubling the number of students in university housing to a total of 4,000 by 2007.

The plan for graduate, family, and international student housing would become the most complicated deal yet. The reality of the situation was that the university lacked both money and land to commit to a housing project, as well as a substantial endowment or a long history of fund-raising. Furthermore it did not want to accept risk for itself or its foundation. The university decided to use two foundations to structure a nonrecourse project that would be built for the university on land it did not own and that the university would operate. This approach allowed the university to provide input on the location, design, and construction, even though it might not own the new housing. The university also wanted GSUF to benefit from any net proceeds from the project.

A market study and demand analysis conducted in 1999 identified the need among existing graduate students for up to 700 beds near campus. Under ordinary circumstances the university could have worked with any number of developers to procure privatized housing built on university land with arranged financing. In these situations the university's role has been to demonstrate the demand and agree to refer students. Unfortunately at that time Georgia State owned no vacant land, and none of the major players in student housing development had control of land near the university.

Nonetheless Georgia State was determined to get a high-quality, handsome building near campus at the lowest possible rental costs to students. In addition the university wanted to be able to operate the facility since it would be seen as responsible for anything that might occur there. Essentially the university was willing to accept a more complicated deal in order to get more control over the finished product, which it did. The housing that has been built is in the popular loft style with open floor plans, high ceilings, fully furnished kitchens, and individual bathrooms. In addition the university's housing office has an annual contract to operate the facility.

To create this housing the university engaged an experienced development management firm to oversee the project. The development manager took the university's specifications and selected TUFF as an independent foundation to be both the financing vehicle and the owner of the facility. The firm designed prototype housing units for the students, defined a search area for the project in close proximity to the university, prepared an initial budget for the project, created a request for proposals (RFP) and gathered proposals from developers. The development manager also conducted a second demand study that confirmed the previous study's finding that existing graduate students wanted student housing and would pay a market rate for it.

With advice from the university housing and facilities staff, the development manager called for potential contractors and developers to identify sites and development concepts acceptable to the university. The response identified only a few locations to be considered, and none was on land owned or controlled by the university or the developers. The most attractive location turned out to be a 1.5-acre surface parking lot contiguous to campus that was owned by a local hospital, which was interested in maintaining ownership of the land while increasing revenue from the location. The hospital and TUFF subsequently agreed to a forty-year lease of the land for the student housing.

The hospital was receiving revenue from the leased operation of the parking lot on which the university wanted to build the housing. The deal included a buyout of the agreement with the private parking lot operator and a promise to the hospital of increased future revenue. The hospital board was cautious about the change of use and the forty-year lease, but the development manager worked closely with the hospital staff and board to build a deal that was acceptable. Georgia State President Patton had already established a good relationship with the hospital's president, governing board, and legal team during his previous service as board chair of the hospital's HMO. When it came time for the housing deal to be developed, these relationships helped when the negotiations hit the inevitable bumps in the road.

There also were issues related to city restrictions on the size of the building, the related setbacks, and property tax exemptions that needed to be addressed. If the existing restrictions were accepted, the building could not have been large enough to generate the needed revenue to service the debt and cover operating costs. The development manager and university staff helped the government agencies understand and approve the project. One particular concession involved having the city define the structure as a long-term-stay facility similar to a hotel. In doing so the setbacks were reduced and the footprint of the lofts could cover the entire parcel of land.

With the land and the owner identified, construction proposals for the facility could proceed. Independent estimators tested construction costs, and negotiations led to a fixed-price contract for the new facility. Financing for the project was expected from bond proceeds, and work began on selecting underwriters, bond counsel, and insurers. The Fulton County Development Authority issued the bonds. Ambac Assurance Corporation of New York issued an insurance commitment to insure the timely payment of the principal and interest on the bonds, and the bonds were sold with an AAA rating from Standard and Poor's. The insurance and AAA rating reduced the interest rate at which the bonds could be marketed. The final structure of the ownership and operation of the facility includes:

- an inducement agreement between the university and the owner (TUFF)
- a ground lease from the hospital to TUFF
- a facility lease between TUFF and a limited liability corporation (LLC) formed by GSUF
- a management agreement between that LLC and the university.

The inducement agreement was critical to obtaining tax-exempt status for the bonds by providing evidence of the relationship between the university's mission and the project, since this status allowed the cost of the project to be reduced and the resulting rent to be more affordable. In the inducement agreement Georgia State encouraged TUFF to develop housing primarily for graduate and married students attending the university and promised to identify this housing to students as part of the inventory of student housing. The university also promised, as a part of this agreement, not to enter into another private development agreement for a student housing project without first conducting a market demand study to identify need. That market study would include the graduate housing facility in the inventory of existing space.

The bonds were sold on April 25, 2001, and ground was broken that same day for a fourteen-story loft-style housing facility for graduate and international students and their families. The structure includes 231 fully furnished units for 460 residents with attached parking and street-level retail space. While the project resulted in a beautiful building for Georgia State's students on land not owned by the university and without using university funds, the lease-up did not go as well as expected. Ownership issues changed as the project developed, governing authorities expressed positions focused on their organizations' sometimes-narrow viewpoints, and graduate housing was a new kind of endeavor for Georgia State.

When the Georgia State Village had opened to undergraduates a few years before, the university anticipated only partial occupancy in the first year. A number of factors were at work to promote the facility, however: the novelty of its history as Olympic athlete housing, the hyperpublicity of the Olympic Games, and a backlog of demand from students. The Village leased quickly the first year and was fully occupied for subsequent years with a waiting list of hundreds of students. The university expected a similar demand for units in the Lofts project.

Prior to development of the University Lofts, demand studies indicated a need for housing among the university's current graduate and married students. Probable prices were shown in the demand studies and the response was favorable, but several factors were not recognized. For example, when graduate and married students move into a complex, they generally do not move again during their academic careers. Consequently initial demand for the lofts was overestimated. Furthermore since graduate and married students are operating in the larger marketplace to identify and select housing, graduate student housing must be marketed in a more aggressive and competitive manner than is the case for undergraduate housing. The university housing division was not experienced with the necessary level of full-fledged marketing, and the Lofts opened in fall 2002 without a full complement of tenants.

Timing was not in the university's favor either. The downturn in the economy caused other competing private housing venues to cut their rents, offer various concessions, and generally appear, on the surface, to be better deals than the Lofts. Potential renters may not have looked past the quick price comparisons of base rents advertised by competitors to see that the loft rents included furniture, all utilities, local phone service, Internet connections, and no commuting costs.

The fast track established for completion also hurt the university's ability to show finished units early enough to attract some potential residents. With no model units to show, many potential residents made other housing decisions. The advertised guarantee of housing in nearby hotels in the unlikely event the Lofts building was not finished, which seemed like a good idea at the time, promoted a sense of uneasiness among potential renters and frightened some away. Meanwhile the local economy continued to decline, numerous companies had layoffs, and the rental housing marked in the city collapsed. Apartment complexes continued to cut their prices and offer several months of free rent and other inducements such as entering new renters into raffles for SUVs. In an attempt to be competitive and attract tenants, University Lofts offered a free month's rent as an inducement, but this was too little and too late. The Lofts were only 65 percent rented the first year. On the plus side the university needed additional faculty offices and was able to rent one floor of the new facility to meet that need.

A beneficial financial deal and a beautiful new facility are not necessarily sufficient conditions for success, and demand studies can be misleading if not completely inaccurate. Even with these difficulties, the Lofts project is an important addition to the campus and the downtown neighborhood, and fortunately the project pro forma is being met. To assure full occupancy for the 2003–4 academic year, the university president convinced the financial partners in the deal to reduce their revenues from the project and thus lower the rents an average of $100 per month per unit. In addition the university's presidential and honors scholars and scholarship athletes were housed in the Lofts instead of receiving a housing allowance to be used elsewhere. The local housing market has now recovered, and the Lofts have a waiting list.

Using what it learned from these projects, GSUF is now preparing to develop 2,000 units of undergraduate housing several blocks north of the campus on a six-acre site it recently purchased from an auto dealership that closed. The demand for this housing has been measured, accurately we hope, and ground will be broken in 2005.[7]

Lessons Learned

Success with any project begins with a clear vision of the future and an institutional commitment to make that future happen. A track record of measurable successes and financial accountability also helps to convince stakeholders that a certain level of risk is acceptable. For Georgia State, being a part of the community and working to build a relationship with the downtown business community formed a solid base for success. The university has learned a number of lessons through these increasingly complex projects.

First, build foundations inside and out of the institution. For Georgia State it was important to build a firm foundation within, involving the entire university community in creating a shared vision. Since the growth of the university depends heavily upon the ability to acquire quality facilities, it was important that the university community, especially the faculty, understand the vision and not waver when the going became difficult. Equally important was building foundations outside the institution. This lesson proved particularly helpful by the time the university reached the University Lofts project, which involved numerous governmental and independent agencies. This strategy places the university in a sensitive position, however. Having called on these friends also means that they call on the university to give back to their causes, including fund-raising, serving on boards, and delicate issues involving requests that the university purchase their services. It also requires occasional explanations that the business of the university is available on a competitive basis and that friends have open opportunities for that business but are not specifically advantaged.

Second, build on successes. Creating a shared vision, building relationships, being aware of the opportunities, and relating them to the vision of the university helped Georgia State. The time spent in master planning and preparation earned credibility and acceptability in each of the projects. Georgia State could not have entered the deal for the complicated University Lofts project without previous successful experiences in leveraging funds and issuing nonrecourse bonds. In the smaller, earlier projects, the university gained experience and built confidence among its business partners. The relationships, funding mechanisms, and legal solutions developed along the way allowed administrators to find the means to make the more complicated deals work.

Third, be flexible. During the Lofts project, the operating structure changed late in the deal. Originally TUFF was to own and operate the facility, and GSUF was not involved at all, since a specific goal had been to assure that the university and GSUF accept no risk in the project. However, bond counsel identified a concern about the tax-exempt-status eligibility of the bonds, which required closer involvement by GSUF. If the bonds were not tax-exempt, interest rates would have been significantly higher, resulting in higher project costs and higher rents. In response to this issue, documents were drawn for risk protection, and GSUF became the leaseholder through a limited liability corporation it created. Thus GSUF found the flexibility to accept a new role, and the creativity of those involved kept the project on course.

Fourth, strengthen the university foundation board. In the early 1990s the university and GSUF did not have the expertise to address the complicated issues involved with projects that came later. The early, less-complex projects strengthened the abilities and confidence of the GSUF board members and university administrators, preparing them for the twists and turns of future deals. GSUF board members developed a clear understanding of the university vision, and this strong buy-in to the university vision resulted in more creative development approaches. Over ten years GSUF moved from a foundation that essentially provided stewardship over private funds raised for the university to become a dynamic foundation that aggressively supports the university's development plan as financier, developer, and business partner.

Fifth, develop private giving and the ability to secure bond funds. Time and again Georgia State relied on the skill of its private foundation and development officers for help with private support. Financial targets established for development remained somewhat fluid and the ability to generate support rose to meet the needs. But since GSUF believed in and was committed to supporting the university's development program, funds were always located to finance the needed projects. In addition Georgia State found a way to issue bonds through GSUF and cooperating foundations when state funds were not available.

Conclusion

Georgia State University has served as an engine for downtown renewal in Atlanta. The leadership of the university worked closely with the business community and the city, thus allowing Georgia State to develop the facilities it needs to meet its mission. The university's master plan, which identified its academic goals and advanced the university as an active member of the downtown community, led to a mutual understanding that helped to promote success.

The university involved community leaders and neighbors in developing the physical plans for the campus. Community advisory groups worked with the university to be sure facility designs fit with the neighborhood, and business leaders helped Georgia State in its capital campaigns both by giving and by opening doors to gifts from others. Positive relationships with the mayor and city staff led to assistance with certain projects and flexibility in code interpretation.

To some extent Georgia State has been its own worst enemy in these development endeavors. The university's initial investments in downtown renewal did keep the lights on, but at the same time these investments pushed up the price of the real estate for the university and other stakeholders. Georgia

State's actions that resulted in new life for old buildings also whetted the community's desire to have the university take over other old buildings that would "save the downtown." Even though Georgia State made it as clear as possible that university projects would be focused on meeting the academic and service goals of the institution, some projects have been brought to the university "for the good of the community" and have been rejected.

To meet the mission of the university and serve the students, faculty, staff, and guests who enjoy the campus each day, Georgia State has been an active player in renewing downtown Atlanta. Students, faculty, and staff are now involved in and are a part of the community. The Georgia State presence is obvious on the streets. This involvement has certainly been a benefit to the university, and, we believe, to the entire downtown community.

Notes

1. The Atlanta Regional Commission has provided funding to plan for the traffic-calming project for the Decatur Street corridor, with drop-off lanes, wider sidewalks, and landscaping. Construction is being supported by federal and university funds.

2. The four research universities in the state system are the University of Georgia, Georgia Institute of Technology, the Medical College of Georgia, and Georgia State University.

3. Another project at that time involved upgrading the former C&S Bank headquarters office building. The facility was a gift to the university from NationsBank in 1992 as it moved out of downtown to its new headquarters building and became Bank of America. This historic and architecturally significant building became the home for the university's J. Mack Robinson College of Business.

4. The university has since also acquired the historic Commerce Building, housing the Commerce Club, a private club where many important civic decisions have been made. Acquiring the building allowed the Commerce Club to downscale and rent a reduced amount of space from the university, enabling it to stay in business. The university uses the balance of the building for meetings and office space. The building acquisition was financed by gifts from NationsBank, now Bank of America, and a private foundation. Substantial legal work went into clearing up the ground leases under the building, including canceling a provision that the building be torn down at the end of the ground lease and the land be returned to the original owners.

5. Also in 1998 GSUF acquired land in Alpharetta, a northern suburb of Atlanta along the high-tech corridor, and built a classroom building for graduate education, continuing education, and outreach efforts of the university to replace an existing closer-in facility. Funding for this project came from bonds issued to GSUF by the Development Authority of Alpharetta. GSUF sublets the facility to the university with annual leases. The ownership of the facility and land will remain with GSUF even after the debt is expired. In this case university staff members developed strong working relationships with the Alpharetta mayor and city council and helped campaign for the bond issue referendum to finance this development. Public speaking, lawn-sign distribution, and other public relations efforts paid off when the bond issue referendum passed by an overwhelming majority.

6. A pending project involves a city block adjacent to campus that had been ac-quired by the state through a land swap with the city. The governor at that time agreed with Georgia State that the property was ideal for university use. Approaching the end of his term and wanting to move quickly, he initiated efforts to transfer the entire block to the university by executive order. However, one staff member at the Board of Regents expressed concerns about accepting any land without full due diligence re-lated to soil conditions. Even with a benign Phase I environmental report, the staff member prevailed and the property was not transferred to the university. Since that time other state agencies have come forward to seek the land in question. The discus-sion continues on this issue, as do the frustrations. Two governors later, as this book was going to press, the land had been transferred to the university for construction of a $200 million science park.

7. The foundation is also helping to raise $25 million in nonstate funds to match $45 million from the state for a new $70 million science teaching laboratory to be located on the campus Main Street.

9

University Involvement in Downtown Revitalization

Managing Political and Financial Risks

Scott Cummings, Mark Rosentraub, Mary Domahidy, and Sarah Coffin

A Tale of Three Cities: Downtown Revitalization and the Urban Crisis

Indianapolis, Louisville, and St. Louis have much in common, in addition to their geographic proximity in America's heartland. By 1960 all three cities were beginning to experience serious changes in the demographic characteristics of their residents and were rapidly losing business and industry to the suburbs. The downtowns in all three cities were rapidly declining and the fragmented nature of local politics made it difficult to achieve consensus among business and political leaders about how to address these increasingly serious problems. The magnitude of the problems facing each city and its leaders reflected all the component parts of what planners and policy analysts throughout the 1970s and 1980s pessimistically labeled the "urban crisis" (Ames et al. 1992). Irrespective of debate over the accuracy of the term, by 1980 the downtowns of Indianapolis, Louisville, and St. Louis were deep in crises, and were being labeled by many observers as "rustbelt cities."

Early in the 1960s political and corporate leaders in Indianapolis publicly agonized over their city's declining influence in its regional economy and its lackluster national image. During an appearance on a late-night talk show, favorite son Kurt Vonnegut described the city as a cemetery with lights that came to life one day a year for the Indianapolis 500. Earlier John Gunther (1949, 387) in his book *Inside U.S.A.* described Indianapolis as "an unkempt city, unswept, raw, a terrific place for basketball and auto racing, and a former pivot of the Ku-Kluxers." In the mid-1970s a national survey by a local community group found the city had "no image" in the national media or among

147

conference planners (Walls 1999). While the "no image" label was a bit better than some representations of the city, by the late 1970s it was clear to local leaders that something dramatic would be needed to change the view of Indianapolis held by both residents and outsiders.

Approximately ninety miles to the south, Louisville was undergoing similar changes in its fortunes. In 1950 the population of Louisville was 369,129; by 1960 it had grown to 390,636; by 1980 only 298,451 people lived in the city; and by 1990 this figure dropped to 269,063. These population shifts mirrored the underlying growth of the suburbs surrounding the city, the flight of business and industry to other regions of the country, and the changing racial composition of Louisville's residents. The cumulative effect of deindustrialization, capital migration, and disinvestment radically changed the city's occupational structure (Cummings and Price 1997). Louisville lost 16 percent of its manufacturing jobs during the 1970s (Birch 1982). The city's decline in manufacturing was matched only by the experiences of other rustbelt cities devastated by deindustrialization (Akron, Youngstown, Gary, and Jersey City).

Crouch (1989) estimates that by 1988 Louisville's manufacturing workforce was approximately 88,000, a figure representing the loss of about 32,000 manufacturing jobs over a fifteen-year period. Major layoffs occurred at General Electric's Appliance Park and the Ford Motor Company, two of the city's largest industrial employers. International Harvester, Seagrams, and Brown & Williamson, all major industrial employers, simply left the city. Even the city's legendary tobacco and distillery industries, traditionally assumed to be "recession proof," experienced major downturns (Yater 1987).

In the face of this deindustrialization and radical demographic transformations, Louisville's downtown deteriorated; only one major office complex was completed between 1953 and 1968. For almost two decades in the 1960s and 1970s, development activities in the central business district (CBD) remained at a virtual standstill and numerous offices, hotels, department stores, restaurants, and commercial establishments closed their doors. The Urban Land Institute reported that between 1963 and 1982, the number of retail establishments in the CBD declined from 811 to 387 (Yater 1987). The city participated in various urban renewal projects during the 1960s and received numerous federal grants through the Community Development Block Grant (CDBG) program, the Model Cities program, and related programs during the Johnson, Nixon, and Carter years. Local corporate and political leaders, however, did not systematically address Louisville's downtown revitalization until the early 1980s.

Between 1960 and 1980 St. Louis also plunged deeply into crisis. Unlike its sister river city 250 miles to the east (Louisville) and its neighbor 220

miles to the northeast (Indianapolis), St. Louis, along with Detroit, Philadelphia, and New Orleans, emerged as a poster city symbolizing the worst aspects of the nation's urban crisis. The infamous freeze-frame photograph
capturing the implosion of the Pruitt-Igoe public housing project in 1972
branded St. Louis as the prototype of what was wrong with American cities.
St. Louis was often identified as a place where racial polarization and economic decline conspired to produce extreme forms of racial inequality, poverty, and downtown deterioration. Between 1970 and 2000 the St. Louis region
grew by less than 150,000 people, but between 1950 and 2000 more than
500,000 people abandoned the city proper.

During this same time frame, business and industry were significantly
restructured and the city's dominant position in the region's economy was
radically undermined (Cummings, Tomey, and Flack 2004). In 1951 more
than 85 percent of the region's jobs were located in the city of St. Louis, but
by 1997 less than 30 percent of jobs were located there. Between 1970 and
1990 the city lost approximately 82,061 manufacturing jobs while the surrounding counties gained more than 44,000 manufacturing jobs.

The current political fragmentation in the St. Louis Metropolitan Statistical Area (MSA) reflects long-standing disparities of wealth and power across
the region. Jones (2000) reports no less than 92 separate political jurisdictions in the St. Louis metropolitan region. In St. Louis County alone, local
government service delivery is divided among more than 150 political jurisdictions. According to Jones (2000) these separate governments insulate the
wealthy from the myriad of urban problems left behind in St. Louis city.
Jones contends that upper- and middle-income whites create political and
legal barriers between themselves and the African American poor living in
the city through maintenance of strict building codes and restrictive land use
policies within their separate suburban jurisdictions.

University Involvement in Downtown Revitalization

Throughout the 1980s and 1990s all three cities attempted to revitalize their
sluggish urban cores and reposition their respective downtowns as vital components of their regional economies. While Indianapolis has clearly been
more successful than Louisville or St. Louis, all of them enfranchised major
institutions of higher education in their redevelopment strategies. The cities
followed similar paths in response to the challenge to redevelop their downtowns, but the various institutions played quite different roles, reflecting the
particular dynamics of local politics as well as their own respective political
positions. Their chosen roles also reflect the political landscapes within which
university administrators must operate as they attempt to interface with the

development and leadership coalitions responsible for promoting and designing local redevelopment strategies.

In Indianapolis and Louisville the major institutions of higher education are part of the public sector: Indiana University-Purdue University at Indianapolis (IUPUI) and the University of Louisville (U of L). Saint Louis University (SLU), the institution of higher education most extensively involved in redevelopment efforts in St. Louis, is a private Catholic institution with a substantial endowment and is driven by a Jesuit mission linked to social justice and community outreach. Despite significant variations in mission, political constituencies, and sources of funding, all three institutions are strategically situated in parts of their cities that have been targeted for revitalization and occupy parcels of real estate that are vital to redevelopment efforts. Additionally all three institutions administer medical schools that make critically important contributions to their local and regional economies. The very different roles played by each institution take on added policy significance in light of the similar development challenges faced by their cities and the redevelopment strategies adopted and implemented.

The experiences of these three universities represent important cases in which large areas of urban real estate were cleared and redeveloped through various public-private partnerships in which the universities were critical intermediaries. In addition to the large amounts of land acquired and redeveloped by the institutions, the cases have other important policy elements in common. All three institutions were part of, and continue to be important players in, larger urban development agendas in which arts, entertainment, tourism, and sports facilities are central to their cities' redevelopment strategies (Turner and Rosentraub 2002). While all three institutions found it advisable to create innovative developmental arrangements and public-private partnerships with private investors, federal agencies, and municipal and state government, two of them (SLU and U of L) were more independent in designing and implementing their developmental agendas. Nonetheless all three cases placed university administrators in a position of being major political players in the urban regimes and coalitions promoting redevelopment. There are both political and financial risks that must be strategically managed when universities become players in larger redevelopment agendas.

In some projects university interests and objectives are not always compatible with those being pursued by other development partners and political constituencies. In the case of private institutions, these conflicts may not always entail extensive political costs. For public institutions, however, conflict with other development partners may generate loss of political capital and erosion of legislative support, and may compromise their relationships with corporate donors. All three cases entailed varying degrees of community controversy due to the number of residents or businesses displaced by university land acquisition and the associated changes in the racial and social class composition of former land users. In all three cases the management of these issues raised significant challenges for university administrators and officials.

The political costs of community controversy, however, may not be as significant as the costs associated with the political mismanagement of a development agenda. When universities enter the development arena, they are often asked to compromise an educational mission in favor of benefits incurred largely by private-sector interests. University administrators are often asked to reconcile decisions that appear incompatible with their educational constituencies and the philosophical mission of the institution, as well as the needs of community groups and the economic interests of private investors. How universities manage these competing political pressures, obligations, and constituencies are important but largely unexplored areas of inquiry.

Rebuilding Downtown Indianapolis: Higher Education as Part of a Comprehensive Redevelopment Plan

Indianapolis established a new form of government in 1969 to oversee the economic development program that led to the rebuilding of its downtown core (Rosentraub 1997). The consolidated city and county government, UniGov, administered a plan for redevelopment anchored by Indiana University-Purdue University at Indianapolis, which became the western boundary for the redevelopment effort and sought to establish itself as a first-rate public institution to complement the private institutions of higher education already located in the city.

The development of IUPUI and the associated Indiana University Medical School and hospital infrastructure involved the acquisition of many acres of land to permit expansion, demolishing a neighborhood that was the historical center of the black community of Indianapolis. The land acquisition and redevelopment completely changed the class and racial compositions of land use and was accomplished with considerable controversy. Map 9.1 shows the land occupied by IUPUI and its location relative to downtown Indianapolis and other key facilities.

The use of this land for the western anchor of the development program placed higher education, the university, and the State of Indiana as full partners in a program that included sports, entertainment, and the establishment of an arts center and a premier convention facility. In later years a new and successful mall, upscale residential units, and a full set of retail and restaurant facilities were added to the downtown resurgence (the Circle Center). By the 1990s downtown Indianapolis was hailed as a "miracle" and the perfect

152

Map 9.1 Indianapolis—Indiana University-Purdue University at Indianapolis and the Indiana University School of Medicine

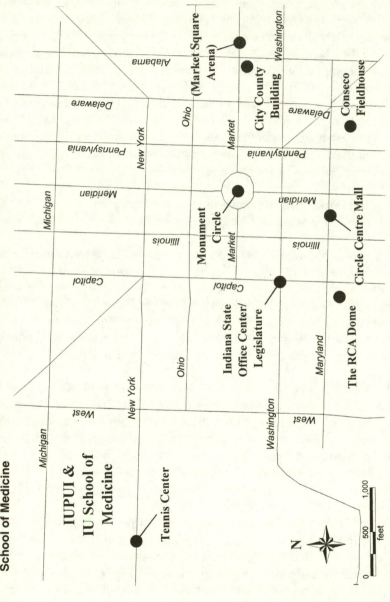

Source: Northern Ohio Data and Information Service, Cleveland State University. Used by permission.

example of a rebuilt downtown area that was the envy and model for cities throughout the Midwest and the nation (Rosentraub 1997).

The scale, scope, and success of the redevelopment programs is detailed in Table 9.1, which identifies the projects undertaken across more than twenty years to transform downtown Indianapolis. Largely reflecting a sports and entertainment strategy, the magnitude of the redevelopment plan reflected the mobilization of state government, the new UniGov structure, and the widespread participation of local corporations and private foundations. Additionally the university was a fully enfranchised partner in a powerful development coalition. In fact the university was the primary intermediary in whose name much of the land was acquired and redeveloped.

In the physical plan for a new downtown, two buildings framed the initial reconstruction efforts as the eastern component: a new city-county building to house the consolidated government and Market Square Arena as the 16,950-seat home for the Indiana Pacers basketball team. While it is quite likely that the city-county building would have been developed even without the creation of a new governing structure, the placement of Market Square Arena in downtown Indianapolis was a direct result of UniGov and the downtown development plan (Rosentraub 1997). In the absence of UniGov, the facility probably would have been built in a more suburban location, as that was the conventional pattern for arena construction in the 1970s (Rosentraub 1997).

From 1974 through 1999 more than fifty major development projects were initiated for the downtown area. The State of Indiana developed its new Government Center at a cost of $264 million, and Indiana University's investment in its Indianapolis campus totaled more than $230 million during this period. Seven of the projects were completely related to the sports identity that Indianapolis hoped to establish. In 1984 Indianapolis opened the 61,000-seat Hoosier Dome (RCA purchased the naming rights in 1994), which became the home for the Indianapolis Colts football team. The Dome has hosted the National Collegiate Athletic Association (NCAA) Men's Basketball Final Four three times; Market Square Arena was the one-time site of the tournament before the Dome opened. Other new sports facilities included a tennis stadium for the annual professional hard-court championships, the Indiana University Natatorium, the Indiana University Track and Field Stadium, the Velodrome (bicycle racing), and the National Institute for Fitness and Sports. By 1989 a total of seven national organizations (Athletics Congress of the USA, U.S. Canoe and Kayak Team, U.S. Diving, Inc., U.S. Gymnastics Federation, U.S. Rowing, U.S. Synchronized Swimming, and U.S. Water Polo) and two international organizations (International Baseball Association and International Hockey League) had moved their governing offices to Indianapolis. In 1999 the NCAA moved its headquarters to the city.

Table 9.1

Sources of Funds for Selected Downtown Indianapolis Economic Development Projects

Development projects	Year	Source of funds					Total investment (millions)
		Federal	State	City	Private	Philanthropic	
Market Square Arena	1974	0	0	16	0	0	16
Children's Museum	1976	0	0	0	0	25	25
Hyatt Hotel/Bank	1977	0	0	0	55	0	55
Sports Center	1979	0	0	4	1.5	1.5	7
Indiana Theater	1980	1.5	0	0	4.5	0	6
Capitol Tunnel	1982	1.4	0	0	0	0	1.4
IU Track and Field Stadium	1982	0	1.9	0	0	4	5.9
IU Natatorium	1982	1.5	7	0	0	13	21.5
Velodrome	1982	0.5	0	1.1	0	1.1	2.7
2 W. Washington Offices	1982	1.2	0	0	11.8	0	13
1 N. Capitol Offices	1982	3.2	0	0	10.4	0	13.6
Hoosier Dome	1984	0	0	48	0	30	78
Lower Canal Apartments	1985	7.9	0	10.3	0	2	20.2
Heliport	1985	2.5	0.1	0.6	2.4	0	5.6
Walker Building	1985	2	0	0	0	1.4	3.4
Embassy Suite Hotel	1985	6.45	0	0	25	0	31.5
Lockerbie Market	1986	1.8	0	0	14	0	15.8
Union Station	1986	16.3	0	1	36	0	53.3
City Market	1986	0	0	0	0	4.7	4.7
Pan Am Plaza	1987	0	0	5.7	25	4.5	35.2
Lockfield Apartments	1987	0	0	0.6	24.6	0	25.2
Canal Overlook Apartments	1988	0	0	0	11	0	11

	Year					
Zoo	1988	0	0	0	0	37.5	37.5
National Institute of Sports	1988	0	3	3	0	3	9
Eiteljorg Museum	1989	0	0	0	0	60	60
Westin Hotel	1989	0.5	0	0	65	0	65.5
Indiana University	1975–90	0	231	0	0	0	231
Farm Bureau	1992	0	0	0	0	36	36
State Office Center	1992	0	264	0	0	0	264
Lilly Corporate Expansion	1992	0	0	0	242	0	242
Circle Centre Mall	1995	0	0	290	0	10	300
Other Projects	1974–98	0	0	0	1,066.90	0	1,066.90
Property Tax Abatements	1974–98	0	0	98	0	0	98
Victory Field	1997		5	9	9		23
Conseco Fieldhouse	1999		38	71	69		178
USA Funds				16.6			16.6
NCAA Headquarters	1999		5			70	75
Total		46.7	555	558.3	1,689.80	303.7	3,153.50
Percentage		1.5	17.6	17.7	53.6	9.6	100

Several important points emerge from a review of Table 9.1.[1] First, more than $3 billion worth of capital development was invested in downtown Indianapolis, representing a substantial commitment of funds targeted to a specific area and in support of a comprehensively designed policy program. Second, there was an extensive commitment of private funds to the strategy. Indeed, more than half of the funds invested, 53.6 percent, were from the private sector. Third, the nonprofit sector was another active participant responsible for almost one dollar of every ten invested. Taken together, then, the private and nonprofit sectors were responsible for approximately two-thirds of the funds invested in redevelopment. Fourth, the City of Indianapolis's investment amounted to less than one-fifth of the total investment.

Finally, the investments by the State of Indiana and Indiana University[2] were virtually equal to the expenditure made by the City of Indianapolis. As a result the city was quite successful in leveraging funds for its redevelopment strategy. Basically a $3.2 billion rebuilding program for the downtown area was secured with only about $550 million from the city. For every dollar invested by the city it was able to leverage approximately $5.82. The Indianapolis downtown area that people visit today is far different and a vast improvement from the one described in unflattering terms by critics in earlier decades (Hudnut and Rosentraub 1995).

Several observations about IUPUI's role in the redevelopment of downtown Indianapolis are important here. First, the land acquisition policies and programs that permitted IUPUI to fulfill its role in this redevelopment effort were strongly supported by local corporations and business leaders, the Lilly Foundation, and state government. With these powerful actors united behind a comprehensive redevelopment plan, the university probably bypassed significant legal, racial, and political controversy as well as the associated financial costs related to its land acquisition and clearance activities. Additionally the new UniGov governmental structure was integral to the development effort. Because much of the land clearance and acquisition was undertaken in the name of higher education expansion, political controversy over competing interpretations of the public-interest component was undoubtedly reduced. While a historic section of the city's black community was destroyed and its residents displaced, the development of a new institution of higher education and an expanded medical research and hospital infrastructure was promoted as compatible with the public good. In this sense the university played a pivotal ideological role in justifying the land acquisition and clearance aspect of the city's redevelopment plan.

Second, these actions established the IUPUI campus as one of the principal economic development engines for downtown Indianapolis and the entire region. A recent report estimates that the research activities of the Indiana

University School of Medicine have an annual economic impact of $242,811,227 on the state (Przybylski 1998). The report contends that this economic impact is produced by the $94,766,483 in external research funds brought into the state or retained by the medical school. In terms of economic multipliers, Przybylski (1998, 1) contends that "for every $1 of research funding attracted to Indiana, medical school employees, suppliers, and their employees generate an additional $1.56 of sales for businesses throughout the state."

Third, and unlike the universities in Louisville and St. Louis, IUPUI was not a direct competitor with the professional sports and entertainment franchises in the city. The development of the campus complemented the city's overall development plan, and the sports facilities on the campus (track and field, natatorium, and tennis) were designed to both accommodate external tourists markets and cater to college and other amateur sports enthusiasts. These strategies ensured that the interests of the university did not conflict with those being pursued by other developers and investors, compromise the political interests of state and local government, or undermine their relationships with the corporate and business community. As a result university administrators have been able to expand their educational mission and interests by fully cooperating with downtown development interests.

Rebuilding Downtown Louisville: Higher Education as an Independent Actor in a Fragmented Development Plan

Like Indianapolis and many other cities seeking to secure a postindustrial future, Louisville's corporate and political leaders have been drawn to redevelopment strategies based upon sports, arts, tourism, and entertainment. Unlike Indianapolis's political regime, however, a fragmented business and civic leadership structure in Louisville has had difficulty creating a comprehensive downtown redevelopment plan and mobilizing the political support required to implement it (Boyd 1999). While consensus exists about the need to reverse the downtown's fortunes and reinvent the CBD as an arts and entertainment center, the identification of a strategic path of action has been a slow and contentious process.

Louisville has redeveloped its downtown in a fragmented and uncoordinated manner and without the full participation of the University of Louisville. In fact the university has often pursued its own interests in a manner that is not always compatible with those political and financial actors promoting the resurgence of the downtown. Unlike most urban universities, the U of L occupies a unique position as a major sports venue for the Louisville metropolitan region. Map 9.2 shows the major development projects sponsored by U of L in relation to the CBD.

Map 9.2   **Louisville**

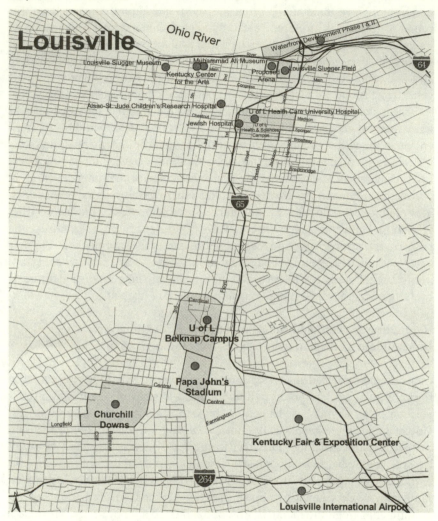

Source: Prepared by Carrie Bundy, Norman Stupp GIS Lab, Saint Louis University.

The University of Louisville has two campuses within the central city. The main campus, Belknap, is situated on the southern edge of two major historic districts: Old Louisville and Limerick. The northern edge of these historic districts gradually blends into the downtown, which is located on the banks of the Ohio River. The main campus is bounded on its eastern and western edges by a declining and largely abandoned industrial and warehouse district, and a major interstate highway (I-65) borders its eastern edge.

The Health Services Campus (HSC), with its medical and dental schools and nursing and allied health programs, is situated about three miles to the north within the city center and business district. The HSC is part of Louisville's hospital district, an area that is vital to the region's economy. Both campuses have expanded significantly in recent years and present two different and at times contradictory pictures of the university's real estate operations. Driven largely by its own calculation of self-interest, the university has played both a supportive and independent role in response to downtown development strategies.

Since the mid-1970s redevelopment of Louisville's downtown has been characterized by a series of benchmark development projects, most of which reflect pursuit of a sports, arts, entertainment, and tourism theme. In 1979 private entrepreneurs in partnership with city officials initiated the Broadway Renaissance Project, which targeted redevelopment of an historic hotel, three historic theaters, more than 1,000 new residential units, and 400,000 square feet of commercial and office space (Cummings, Koebel, and Whitt 1989). The redevelopment area covered more than three square blocks of the downtown, encompassed approximately thirty-five acres of real estate, and entailed more than $154 million of private and public funds. The university was asked to assist in the effort by expanding its downtown operations and assuming tenancy in one of the newly renovated office spaces, but declined to do so.

Inspired by the festival market concept pioneered by the Rouse Company, the city and private investors attempted to revitalize the downtown's sluggish retail sector by architecturally combining several adjoining buildings in an area close to the Broadway Renaissance Project. Opened in 1983, the Louisville Galleria has struggled unsuccessfully to retain a series of high-profile tenants, including Dillards, Laura Ashley, The Limited, Victoria's Secret, and the Fashion Shop. In 1998 Mayor David Armstrong declared the Galleria was "moments away from being empty." In 2002 an effort was launched to reinvent the retail complex as an urban entertainment center. With the addition of the Hard Rock Café and Border's Books and Music, the mayor expressed hope that the newly named "Fourth Street Live" and a $70-million-dollar renovation plan would transform the Galleria into "a 24-hour entertainment and shopping venue like none other in America." The university has never participated actively in efforts to stabilize or assist the Galleria effort or its more recent reinventions.

Largely with the support of private investors and state government, a new Kentucky Center for the Arts (KCA) was constructed in the early 1980s at a cost of approximately $28 million. Opened in November 1983, the KCA serves as the principal facility for the Louisville Orchestra and the Louisville

Ballet, as well as the host for the national Broadway Series and other concert and entertainment events. The facility is located in the heart of the historic downtown just a few blocks from other important arts and entertainment facilities including Actors' Theater, the Louisville Science Museum, and the Louisville Slugger Museum. This latter facility was an outgrowth of the successful effort by private developers and city officials to bring the Hillerich & Bradsby Company (maker of the legendary Louisville Slugger baseball bat and other sports equipment) back to its historic location in downtown Louisville. Again the university was not directly or extensively involved in efforts to renovate historic Main Street, nor did it show any interest in becoming a major player in the arts, sports, and entertainment strategies related to these initiatives.

Other significant development projects reflect Louisville's arts and entertainment strategy to revitalize the downtown. For example the Louisville Waterfront Development Corporation was created in 1986 to oversee development efforts along the Ohio River, including the design, construction, and maintenance of Waterfront Park, an area of about 100 acres of largely contaminated land located between the downtown and the river. In 1999 a major $72 million renovation of the city's convention center added approximately 449,000 square feet to existing space. In May 2000 the Louisville Slugger Field was completed at a cost of approximately $28 million. Modeled after Camden Yards in Baltimore, the Triple A baseball stadium seats 13,000 and is located on a former brownfield and warehouse facility near the river. Efforts are also under way to construct a Muhammad Ali Museum and significantly expand new residential, condominium, and office facilities close to the redeveloped waterfront.

The continued absence of university involvement in these recent sports- and entertainment-driven projects is significant for several reasons. University participation in downtown development efforts appears to take place only when its immediate economic interests are clearly affected. Since 1980 the university has invested approximately $343 million in real estate development. More than $198 million has been spent on the Belknap Campus, with $77 million of that amount invested in sports facilities. NCAA athletics are integral to the university's identity as vital components of its financial and political portfolios, and sports-centered facilities highlight much of the real estate development initiated by the university. Cardinal Park, for example, is a recently completed complex of sports fields, including major new facilities for women's sports and the Miller-Rudd Tennis Center, with indoor courts that are available for an hourly fee to both the university and the Greater Louisville community.

On the Health Services Campus the university has spent approximately

$145 million, the bulk of which has been invested in expanding medical research facilities in the downtown (see Table 9.2). Louisville's large medical complex, of which HSC comprises a considerable portion, serves as one of the city's major employers. Between 1996 and 2000 the total amount of external university research grants and contracts rose from $41 million to $60 million, mostly from medical school research activities. The HSC expansion, with new research facilities, offices, and dormitories for the health sciences students, has taken place within the context of the medical services sector, which was targeted as a major part of the city's overall downtown economic development plan. These real estate activities have removed significant blocks of blight close to the CBD and, with the recently constructed and proposed biomedical research buildings, serve to advance the city's strategy in targeting the high-technology sector. It is understandable why the university has been extensively and visibly involved in this component of downtown redevelopment, although its absence from other initiatives has generated political costs.

While both campus expansions serve private property development interests by generating new values and occupying lands that might otherwise remain underutilized, vacant, or contaminated, some university initiatives have been criticized as being too project-specific with little or no collaboration or sustained economic development planning on behalf of the city and region as a whole.

Most pertinent to the recent history of the university's lack of involvement in downtown redevelopment, and its independent pursuit of a separate agenda, is its reluctance to fully embrace the professional sports and entertainment strategy aggressively being pursued by business and political leaders in the city. Fully persuaded by rhetoric that a major-league city requires a major-league team (Rosentraub 1997), the political and corporate leadership in the city has unsuccessfully courted several professional basketball franchises (Vancouver Grizzlies, Houston Rockets, and Charlotte Hornets) over the past five years. Recent policy debate over how to attract a basketball franchise opened serious rifts among business, political, and university leadership in the city. While efforts have been made to camouflage these rifts, they have frequently erupted into heated exchange in the local press and television.

Because Louisville is a small metropolitan market, it has had great difficulty attracting a professional franchise. Buoyed by its successful effort to bring back the Louisville Slugger manufacturing operation from rural Indiana to downtown Louisville, the construction of Slugger Field, the groundbreaking for the Muhammad Ali Museum, and the transformation of the waterfront, private investors and public officials believe that a downtown

Table 9.2

University of Louisville Development Projects: Belknap Campus and Health Sciences Campus

Development projects	Year	Total investment (millions)
Belknap Campus		
New music school	1980	9.75
Playhouse renovation	1980	1.46
Chemistry building	1981	7.75
Education building	1981	5.40
Ekstrom Library	1981	12.00
Information Center-South	1984	0.13
New business school	1985	8.11
Information Center-North	1986	0.24
New engineering building	1987	3.23
Kersey Library addition	1990	1.42
Residential dormitory	1990	6.00
Student Activities Center	1990	23.81
Faculty and Alumni Club	1990	3.62
Honors Building renovation	1992	0.25
Theatre arts building	1993	1.10
Belknap parking garage	1994	8.30
Ford renovation	1994	0.87
Miller renovation	1994	3.74
Stevenson Hall renovation	1994	0.68
New classroom building	1995	15.00
University Tower renovation	1995	2.35
Life Science Lab renovation	1996	0.91
New EHS storage facility	1998	1.22
Papa John's Cardinal Football Stadium*	1998	63.20
Soccer field*	1994	0.20
Bass Rudd Tennis Complex*	1994	3.65
Cardinal Sports Park A*	2001	10.90
Cardinal Sports Park B*	2001	2.80
Total Belknap campus investments		198.06
Health Sciences Campus		
New consecrated care building	1980	36.69
New ambulatory care building	1981	11.60
Research resource center	1990	3.20
Abell Administration renovation	1991	3.17
Building demoliltion	1991	0.96
Kidney Dialysis Building renovation	1992	0.85
Health Science Center Parking Garage	1994	6.27
Kidney Dialysis Building renovation	1994	1.41
Medical/Dental Apartment renovation	1994	1.97
K Building renovation	1995	4.03
MDR Laboratory renovation	1995	0.92
High rise sprinklers	1996	0.78
K Building renovation	1996	4.83
Lion's Eye building addition	1997	4.92

Dental School simulation lab	1998	1.37
Baxter Biometical Research Building	2000	21.00
New research building	2002	41.00
Total health sciences investments		144.97
Total University Investments		343.03

Source: B. Traughber, former director of ULH, Inc., University of Louisville.
Note: *Denotes sports-related development projects.

basketball arena is required to bring a professional franchise to the city. Despite the presence of the Triple A Louisville Bats baseball team in the downtown and visions of a professional basketball team in a new downtown arena, the U of L Cardinals baseball team is for all practical purposes the primary professional sports franchise in the city. Furthermore, university officials are not enthused about losing their franchise and monopoly control over the local market to an outside professional competitor. Clearly the sports interests of the university are not necessarily compatible with those interests driving downtown redevelopment.

During the early 1990s the university, with corporate and political backing, initiated activities to move its football enterprise to a parity position with its nationally prominent basketball program. After successfully recruiting Howard Schnellenberger to head the expansion of its football program, and following a series of postseason bowl successes in the 1990s, the university initiated efforts to build a first-class football stadium on campus. The stadium, with seating for 42,000, was completed in 1998 at a cost of $63 million and entailed redevelopment of a brownfield site located south of the Belknap Campus. As a result the city now has two major sports facilities anchoring the real estate approximately three miles south of the downtown but situated on or very close to the U of L campus: Papa John's Cardinal Stadium (U of L football stadium) and Churchill Downs racetrack, the home of the Kentucky Derby. Compared to the more recent debate over efforts to secure a professional basketball franchise, the Papa John's project was carried out with a high degree of consensus among university officials, corporate leaders, and state and local politicians.

Throughout the 1980s the U of L basketball program brought significant recognition to a city that usually stood in the national spotlight for only two minutes each year during the running of the Kentucky Derby. Basketball games at Freedom Hall (a facility located at the Kentucky Fair and Exposition Center) were always at peak seating capacity, however, and the decline of Louisville's dominance in college basketball in the 1990s coincided with increased interest in courting a professional basketball franchise. Convinced that the city could never attract a professional team without a new arena, local officials, corporate leaders, and private investors placed considerable pressure on the university to get in line behind efforts to build a new downtown facility. Some local boosters privately reasoned that because the university received major support for its new football stadium, they could expect university support for the downtown arena.

Over the past two years, tough and very public negotiations ensued over the university's current contract to play basketball in Freedom Hall, a campus or downtown location for a new arena, and the financial terms of a long-term contract that would place U of L basketball in the new arena. The university's new and high-profile basketball coach, Rick Pitino, initially made it clear that he did not support pursuit of a professional franchise, but in the face of political criticism he later changed his position (Timmermann 2001a). University President John Shumaker publicly supported the new arena but preferred it be located on campus. He eventually withdrew support for the campus arena but demanded a lucrative contractual arrangement before agreeing to house the basketball program in a downtown facility.

These policy controversies came to a head in 2001 during negotiations with the Charlotte Hornets, before the franchise eventually selected New Orleans over both Louisville and St. Louis. Several local officials commented in the press and complained privately that the university's unreasonable position on the arena had cost Louisville a professional franchise and its president had squandered the region's opportunity to become a major-league city.

Some public officials interviewed during the course of this study commented that the university negotiated too hard on the downtown arena, a fact that one official thought caused the Hornets' ownership to select New Orleans over Louisville. A financial consultant for the Board of Alderman, an individual directly involved in the negotiations, commented during an interview for this study that "the arena deal did not have a chance if the university was not on board; the university had too much power during the negotiations." There appears to be a fair amount of lingering ill will over the collapse of the downtown arena deal. In fact the new downtown development plan for the Louisville region suggests that the University of Louisville should try to play ball differently the next time a professional franchise is courted:

> It is critical that the recently demonstrated support for a facility downtown—at the right time and cost—be maintained and that the city, the university, and the business community begin plans to develop an acceptable construction and financing plan for a downtown facility on the proposed site (City of Louisville, Downtown Development Corporation, Louisville Central Area, Inc. 2002, 76).

Rebuilding Downtown St. Louis: Higher Education
as a Leader in a Targeted Redevelopment Plan

In another river city four hours to the west, a private, Catholic university also has struggled to balance self-interest with a sports and entertainment downtown development agenda. In a region characterized by racial polarization and inequality, disinvestment and decline, and extreme forms of governmental fragmentation, Saint Louis University occupies a unique position of independent power and influence in local politics. The university is located in the heart of Midtown St. Louis, an area linking Forest Park (site of the 1904 World's Fair) with the downtown. This section of St. Louis is part of what is called the Central Corridor and has been the focus of long-term efforts to revitalize the downtown. Economic development strategists in the city reason that the Central Corridor, the "spine of the city," has to be secured first in order to revitalize the larger and more deteriorated urban areas to the north, which is predominately African American, and south, which is predominately white. The Central Corridor is a large geographic area running from the Arch on the banks of Mississippi River through the traditional downtown to the eastern edge of Forest Park (see Map 9.3).

The Central West End part of the corridor is one of the most fashionable historic residential districts in the city, with several historic hotels and a revitalized café and restaurant district. This area has been significantly gentrified over the past two decades and now houses numerous members of the city's business and civic elite. Another major private educational institution, Washington University (WashU), is located in the suburb of Clayton and is adjacent to University City, two upscale residential communities located just outside the city limits but close to Forest Park and the Central Corridor. Clayton is a chic edge city development several miles from the center city and is viewed as a major threat to downtown revitalization plans. Washington University's medical campus anchors the western edge of the Central Corridor and is located in the heart of Central West End's commercial district. Because of their strategic locations, WashU and especially SLU were destined to play major roles in the revitalization of this part of the city.

Both universities are significant engines of development and redevelopment for the regional economy. Although WashU is often criticized for its lack of involvement in local affairs, its research activities make significant contributions to the area. In fiscal year 1999 WashU ranked eighth among all private universities receiving federal support for research and development. In fiscal year 2000 the university received more than $364 million in research support from federal and state governments, corporations, foundations, and individuals. During fiscal year 2001 WashU received approximately

Map 9.3   **St. Louis Central Corridor**

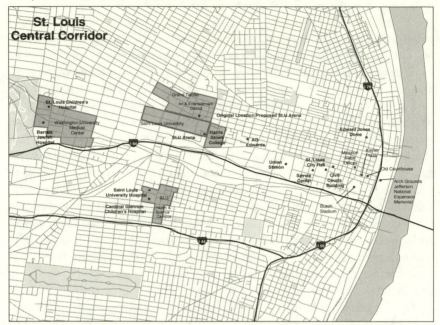

Source: Prepared by Carrie Bundy, Norman Stupp GIS Lab, Saint Louis University.

$411 million in total research support from external sources, and SLU gener-
ated approximately $37.8 million in research revenues. The medical schools
of both universities generate the bulk of the external research funds, and
both also have substantial endowments. Combined with their real estate activities, the research dollars received by the two universities produce significant multipliers in the local economy.

The presence of SLU and WashU's medical complex in the Central Corridor has stabilized demographic change in the area, strengthened the vitality
of the retail and service sector situated there, increased the volume of private
investment, and elevated the value of residential and commercial real estate.
To a large extent the real estate and development activities initiated by these
private universities are the result of independent actions made possible by
their lack of dependence on public-sector resources for financial and political support.

The direct real estate activities of SLU, however, have been the most important to the revitalization of the Central Corridor. In the late 1960s SLU
was drawn into redevelopment activities as the beneficiary of a controversial
urban renewal project. As a result the university became extensively involved

in a variety of public-private partnerships designed to address the seriously deteriorated community in which it was located. Faced with the momentous decision to relocate to suburban St. Louis or to revitalize its immediate environment, SLU administrators chose the latter option, although local political activists did not always appreciate their real estate initiatives.

One of the most monumental development projects in the history of St. Louis occurred directly across Grand Avenue on SLU's eastern border. The Mill Creek Valley renovation was one of the largest urban renewal projects ever sponsored by the federal government and possibly one of the most contentious. The area consisted of 465 acres and was frequently referred to as the city's worst eyesore. Political leadership in the city supported demolition and clearance of the area because it was the first impression of St. Louis obtained by visitors arriving at Union Station, a major St. Louis landmark. The valley was also home to approximately 19,700 residents, 95 percent of whom were African American, and it contained 839 businesses and institutions, including churches, theaters, community centers, grocery stores, and a baseball park for the St. Louis Stars, the city's historic African American baseball team (Fagerstrom 2000).

The urban renewal plan for redevelopment of this area called for a mix between residential, industry, and business uses and the expansion of the SLU campus. The original plan set aside 165 acres for industrial development; 22 acres for SLU; 20 acres for commercial development; 75 acres for residences (1,700 units); and 165 acres for expressways and roads (Fagerstrom 2000). The plan provided a convenient opportunity for the university to expand and SLU ultimately submitted a bid for the twenty-two acres of land. Three local taxpayers associated with the Protestants and Other Americans United for Separation of Church and State contested their bid. The sale was upheld by the circuit court and SLU acquired the twenty-two acres for the price of $535,742.

Participation in the Mill Creek Valley Project, despite the intensity of the controversy surrounding it, was a precursor to the university's increased involvement in real estate acquisition and development activities throughout Midtown. Indeed many thought the future of SLU itself was directly tied to the long-term success of its redevelopment activities. The intense political controversy and racial conflict accompanying the Mill Creek Valley project, however, eventually tempered university enthusiasm for direct involvement in land acquisition and expansion (Reinert and Shore 1996). Former SLU President Father Paul Reinert worked with local businesses and political leaders to form a nonprofit development corporation, New Town/St. Louis, Inc., partly as a way of deflecting political controversy away from the university while it aggressively pursued the stabilization of Midtown.

In January 1973 the Planning Commission of the City of St. Louis recommended approval of a plan for redevelopment in a 1,400-acre area identified as the New Town/St. Louis initiative. Partial support came from the federal government through the Urban Growth and New Community Development Act of 1970 (Canfield 1973). The goal of New Town/St. Louis was to revitalize Midtown by improving the quality of life for its residents, businesses, and institutions by assuring the safety and the appearance of the area. The group facilitated strategic public-private partnerships, assisted in the preservation and renovation of existing buildings, and stimulated interest and investment in the area (Reinert and Shore 1996). The formation of New Town/St. Louis led to the creation of three separate, independent redevelopment organizations: Lafayette Town Redevelopment Corporation, Midtown Medical Center Redevelopment Corporation, and City Center Redevelopment Corporation (New Town/St. Louis, n.d). SLU played vital financial and leadership roles in all three organizations.

The City Center Redevelopment Corporation (CCRC) was established in 1980 and is currently known as Grand Center, Inc. The original shareholders were SLU, the Urban League of Metropolitan St. Louis, Saint Louis Symphony Society, Third Baptist Church, Scottish Rite Masons, Mercantile Bank, and Centerre Bank (Reinert and Shore 1996). The focus of this development coalition was to utilize the existing buildings to recreate an arts and entertainment district for St. Louis. The university ultimately embraced this strategy, publicly proclaimed its presence in the heart of the city's "urban renaissance," and widely promoted its commitment to rebuild the Grand Center arts and entertainment district. The Midtown Medical Center Redevelopment Corporation focused its activities on the area immediately surrounding SLU's medical campus, and the Lafayette Town Redevelopment Corporation focused on residential revitalization immediately south of the medical campus (New Town/St. Louis, n.d).

The activities initiated by New Town/St. Louis contributed to a series of major development projects in the Midtown section of the Central Corridor and led to additional land clearance and real estate acquisitions by the university. Table 9.3 summarizes the more significant development projects located in the original area targeted by the New Town/St. Louis initiative and those in the expanded area that includes the eastern edge of Forest Park and the western edge of downtown St. Louis. The projects in the table represent a variety of investors and do not necessarily have their origins in the New Town/St. Louis initiative, although most have been influenced in some manner by SLU's leadership or financial support. Between 1980 and 2002 approximately $1.76 billion was invested in the Midtown area, and more than 47 percent was invested by SLU ($300 million) and WashU ($529 million).

Table 9.3

Investments in the Central Corridor of St. Louis by Saint Louis University, Washington University, and Other Investors

Development projects	Year	Total investment (millions)
Saint Louis University campus expansion	ongoing	300.0
WashU Medical School and Barnes Jewish Hospital:		
BJC Cancer and Outpatient	2001	320.0
BJC South Campus	ongoing	90.0
St. Louis Children's Hospital	2000	30.0
McDonnell Research Building	2002	89.0
Harris-Stowe State College campus expansion	ongoing	37.0
Other Investments: Public, nonprofit, and private		
A.G. Edwards	2002	180.0
Adams School	2001	14.0
Argyle Garage and Library	2001	12.0
Blumeyer Housing	ongoing	166.0
Cardinal Ritter High School	2002	25.5
Center for Emerging Technologies	2001	14.9
Central Institute for the Deaf	2001	11.6
Chase Park Plaza	1999	100.0
Childgarden Child Care Center	2001	1.9
Chouteau and Compton (future manufacturing site)		17.0
Continental Building	2002	25.0
Coronado Hotel	ongoing	27.0
Federal Bureau of Investigation Building	1999	7.5
Forest Park Hotel	2002	20.0
Forum for Contemporary Arts	2003	7.6
KETC/ Channel 9	1998	13.0
Lofts at Lafayette Square	ongoing	15.7
Maison Lofts	2002	5.5
McCormack House (part of Westminster Place)	2000	9.1
Mississippi Lofts	2001	10.0
Newstead Condos	2000	4.5
Otis Elevator Building	2001	2.1
Phyllis Wheatley YWCA	2003	7.2
Pulitzer Foundation	2001	30.0
Sheldon Theater Annex	1998	5.0
Sigma Aldrich Corporation	2002	55.0
SJI Building	2000	9.2
SSM Cardinal Glennon Children's Hospital	2003	56.7
St. Vincent Park	2004	20.0
Welsh, Flatness, and Lutz Building	2001	6.5
Westminster Place	2001	7.0
Wireworks Loft	2002	14.5
Fox Theater	1982	2.0
Total investments		1,769.0

Sources: Development Strategies Report, Recent Investments, City of St. Louis, USA, City of St. Louis Development Activities (http://stlcin.missouri.org/devprojects/).

SLU has dramatically expanded its campus eastward and in the process has cleared and redeveloped the earlier Mill Creek Valley project. Over the past two decades, campus real estate development at SLU has transformed a deteriorated urban landscape into spectacular green space complete with gardens, flowers, ponds, fountains, and sculptures. Over the past five years, direct SLU investments and the aggressive political leadership of its current president, Dr. Lawrence Biondi, SJ, have been credited with stimulating the redevelopment of a vacant office tower (Continental Building) and an abandoned historic hotel (the Coronado) and the construction of a new private educational facility (Cardinal Ritter High School), all on the edge of SLU's main campus.

Some vestiges of political resentment remain over SLU's earlier land clearance and demolition activities, but the university's relations with local minority leaders have been largely repaired and most local observers regard the university as one of the most important political and financial leaders in St. Louis's downtown redevelopment initiatives. When the city was immobilized by the politics of racial conflict or hampered by ongoing fiscal crises, the university was able to take independent action to organize, design, and implement plans to revitalize its immediate and surrounding environment. While revitalization, pursued largely through acquisition, demolition, and land clearance, was not without controversy, few critics currently question the path of action taken by the university or argue that the public interest was not effectively served (Thompson 1997).

Interestingly, the pursuit of the Charlotte Hornets basketball franchise by local investors pulled SLU administrators back into the turbulent waters of downtown development politics. SLU's relationship to the courtship of the Hornets, however, was very different from the events that characterized the Louisville case. Unlike at the U of L, NCAA athletics at SLU has a very small market share of the disposable income spent on sports as an entertainment venue. While its basketball team has a loyal fan following and the soccer program is always nationally competitive, SLU is inclined to boast more about having the largest share of scholar athletes of any school in Conference USA.

Moreover St. Louis (especially in comparison to Louisville) has probably overinvested in a sports and entertainment strategy (Timmermann 2001b). The city has three professional sports franchises: the Blues (hockey), the Cardinals (baseball), and the Rams (football). It has a downtown football dome (Edward Jones Dome), a downtown baseball stadium (Busch Stadium), a downtown arena that houses the St. Louis Blues (Savvis Center), and casino gambling on the riverfront. The Savvis Center and the Edward Jones Dome also serve as the major venues for concerts, trade shows, conventions, and other live entertainment extravaganzas. Notwithstanding the abundance of entertainment and sports options, efforts to lure the Charlotte Hornets basketball team by the owners of the Blues compelled SLU administrators to reevaluate their wholesale support of the city's downtown redevelopment strategies (Carey 2001). Ironically, controversy over an on-campus or downtown basketball arena opened rifts between university officials and private developers not unlike those that surfaced in Louisville.

Like their private-sector counterparts in Louisville, St. Louis Blues owners Bill and Nancy Laurie have worked aggressively to lure a professional basketball franchise. They unsuccessfully courted the Vancouver Grizzlies and competed forcefully with Louisville, Norfolk, and New Orleans for the Hornets. According to local accounts, "St. Louis University officials watched nervously . . . as Laurie . . . tried to add the Grizzlies to his sports holdings" (Carey 2001, F1). University concern was driven by the fact that the men's basketball program schedules seventeen to twenty games each year at the Savvis Center, a facility also operated by the Laurie family. Should the effort to bring a professional team to the city be successful, university officials feared significant compromises in scheduling flexibility and a drop in potential television revenue.

While President Biondi has often expressed interest in having a top-fifty basketball program, university officials have never been altogether positive about playing in the Savvis Center. This cavernous facility is much too large for an NCAA basketball program that consistently draws only between 10,000 and 12,000 fans (Gregorian 2002). As a result university officials have periodically considered building a smaller on-campus arena. Some downtown development interests have been lukewarm about the idea, arguing that it might compete with established concert venues and undermine existing revenues that might be harvested by the Savvis Center or other facilities. Even within the university community, support for a new arena has been controversial. Some faculty groups have argued that SLU's educational mission might be compromised by the need to reallocate funds away from academics and into an expensive arena.

During the negotiations for the Hornets, the debate over the wisdom of building an on-campus arena again surfaced within the university, and administrators became concerned as they watched the Laurie family make numerous concessions to the Hornets' owners. While university administrators made few public statements about the negotiations, it was clear that SLU's interests were not necessarily tied to the Lauries' vision to house four professional sports franchises in the city. Shortly after the bid to attract the Hornets failed, university officials placed the on-campus arena issue back on its active real estate development agenda.

With its current contract to play at Savvis due to expire in the 2003–4 season, SLU had to make a decision, and in January 2003 SLU administrators announced their intention to construct an on-campus arena. The Board of Trustees approved the plan in February 2003 to build a 12,000- to 14,000-seat facility at the estimated cost of $80 million. The university left no ambiguity about its intentions to compete directly with other concert and entertainment venues such as the Savvis Center and the Family Center in St. Charles (Munz 2003). The area targeted for the new arena was initially a several block site located in the heart of the Grand Center arts and entertainment district directly across from the SLU campus (see Map 9.3). The university began rapidly acquiring land and buildings in that area and initially teamed up with the arts and entertainment facilities already located there, including the Fox Theater, Powell Symphony Hall, Sheldon Concert Hall, and the Black Repertory Theater. In fact expansion into this geographic area was totally consistent with SLU's prior history of real estate development and compatible with its promotion of an arts and entertainment district close to campus. President Biondi reinforced this view when he stated, "This project will keep the momentum in this area moving forward" (Munz 2003, B1).

Expansion in this area, however, was stalled due to the cost of land acquisition and the associated price of real estate being charged by entrepreneurial developers, speculators, and landowners. As a result the SLU administration recently moved the location of the new arena to a second area identified in Map 9.3. The proposed new arena is close to the original location and requires SLU to acquire less land. In a recent press release, the university contended that "the new arena will be located two blocks from Grand Center, which will allow people, who come to the arena for an event, to also spend time in the arts-and-entertainment district" (Saint Louis University 2003). The 13,000-seat basketball arena will also accommodate numerous other activities, including 13,000 patrons for stage concerts, with 10,000 seats having 180-degree seating; 6,800 seats to accommodate smaller concerts; 14,000 seats for boxing, wrestling, and concerts in the round; 12,000 seats for circus and family shows; and 100 booths to accommodate trade shows and exhibits with more than 18,000 square feet of floor space (Saint Louis University, n.d). The new arena will also accommodate other university events such as meetings and graduation exercises, cultural extravaganzas, national conferences and conventions, masses and religious events, high school athletic contests, as well as large trade shows and exhibits.

As distinct from the U of L case, SLU has the financial and political independence to construct an on-campus arena without public-sector support. It also has the political independence to move the location of its arena in order to bypass the financial pressures being exerted by entrepreneurial developers and speculators. Nonetheless both universities were faced with strategic development choices tied to political and financial interests that were not necessarily consistent with the educational mission of the academy. In the case of Louisville, it seems apparent that a downtown arena is inevitable, irrespective of the wishes of university administrators or high-profile coaches to build an on-campus facility. In the case of St. Louis, however, failure to accommodate the university will likely produce a competitive set of entertainment choices and stimulate additional clearance and redevelopment of the Midtown arts and entertainment district. Development of the on-campus arena will also likely add to the growing reputation of SLU as an independent and progressive force transforming the Midtown section of its namesake city.

Notes

1. The projects identified in Table 9.1 do not include all development that took place in the downtown area. Some developments (the city's monuments, new fire stations, etc.) were not considered here because they would have taken place even if a new downtown strategy had not been developed and implemented. Other investments where property tax abatements were not provided also are not included in the table.

2. Indiana University is the managing partner of the joint campus with Purdue and is responsible for all fiscal matters.

References

Ames, D., N. Brown, M. Callahan, S. Cummings, S. Smock, and J. Ziegler. 1992. Rethinking American urban policy. *Journal of Urban Affairs* 14(3/4): 197–216.

Birch, D.L. 1982. Who creates jobs? In A forum for small businesses. Transcription of a presentation in Louisville, KY. November 3.

Boyd, T. 1999. The downtown puzzle: How should the pieces fit? *Business First,* March 5. Available at http://louisville.bizjournals.com/louisville/stories/1999/03/08/story2.html.

Canfield, M. 1973. $320-million neighborhood upgrade program urged. *St. Louis Globe-Democrat,* January 23: 12A.

Carey, C. 2001. Experts suggest Hornets, Blues, Savvis should be run as one: If NBA team comes here it should be part of larger operation. *St. Louis Post-Dispatch,* December 2: F1.

City of Louisville, Downtown Development Corporation, Louisville Central Area, Inc. 2002. *Downtown Redevelopment Plan.* Louisville, KY: Authors.

Crouch, R. 1989. Metropolitan Louisville's human capital: Our future workforce at risk. Unpublished manuscript, University of Louisville Urban Studies Center, Louisville, KY.

Cummings, S., T. Koebel, and A. Whitt. 1989. Redevelopment in downtown Louisville: Public investments, private profits, and shared risks. In *Unequal partnerships: The political economy of urban redevelopment in postwar America,* ed. G. Squires, pp. 202–221. New Brunswick, NJ: Rutgers University Press.

Cummings, S., and M. Price. 1997. Race relations and public policy in Louisville: Historical development of an urban underclass. *Journal of Black Studies* 27(5): 615–649.

Cummings, S., A. Tomey, and R. Flack. 2004. Workforce development policy in the St. Louis metropolitan region: A critical overview and assessment. In *Workforce development politics: Civic capacity and performance,* ed. R. Giloth, pp. 176–211. Philadelphia, PA: Temple University Press.

Fagerstrom, R. 2000. *Mill Creek Valley: A soul of St. Louis.* St. Louis: Missouri Historical Society.

Gregorian, V. 2002. Biondi eyes new arena: I hope it's going to be reality. *St. Louis Post-Dispatch,* April 13: 4.

Gunther, J. 1949. *Inside U.S.A.* New York: Harper and Row.

Hudnut, W., and M. Rosentraub. 1995. *The Hudnut years in Indianapolis, 1976–1991.* Bloomington: Indiana University Press.

Jones, E. T. 2000. *Fragmented by design.* St. Louis: Palmerston and Reed Publishing Co.

Munz, M. 2003. SLU arena will compete for events. *St. Louis Post-Dispatch,* February 24: B1.

New Town/St. Louis. (n.d.). New Town/St. Louis [Brochure]. St. Louis, MO.

Przybylski, M. 1998. *The annual economic impact of the research activities of the Indiana University School of Medicine on the Indiana economy.* Indiana University: Center for Urban Policy and the Environment.

Reinert, P.C., and P. Shore. 1996. *Seasons of change.* St. Louis: University of Saint Louis Press.

Rosentraub, M. 1997. *Major league losers: The real cost of sports and who's paying for it.* New York: Basic Books.

Saint Louis University. 2003. *SLU snnounces arena location.* Saint Louis University News Release, December 18. Available at www.slu.edu/readstory/newinfo/3611.

———. n.d. *First tip-off. Arena stats.* Available at http://arena.slu.edu/arena4.html [May 2004].

Thompson, S. 1997. Man with a mission: The Reverend Lawrence Biondi hasn't wasted any time during his 10 years at the helm of Saint Louis University. *St. Louis Post-Dispatch,* April 17: C1.

Timmermann, T. 2001a. Sauer preaches caution on NBA team: The meeting showed "complications" to moving the Hornets. *St. Louis Post-Dispatch,* October 26: D1.

———. 2001b. Can the NBA court success in crowded St. Louis market? *St. Louis Post-Dispatch,* October 28: D1.

Turner, R., and M. Rosentraub. 2002. Tourism, sports and the centrality of cities. *Journal of Urban Affairs* 24(5): 487–92.

Walls, J. W. 1999. *Onward and upward: The story of the greater Indianapolis progress committee.* Indianapolis: Greater Indianapolis Progress Committee.

Yater, G. H. 1987. *Two hundred years at the Falls of the Ohio: A history of Louisville and Jefferson County,* 2nd ed. Louisville, KY: The Filson Club.

10

Ryerson University and Toronto's Dundas Square Metropolis Project

David Amborski

Ryerson University, a public university serving approximately 16,000 students, is located in the central part of the City of Toronto.[1] This case study describes a joint university-city project adjacent to a public square in downtown Toronto: The Dundas Square Metropolis Project. The university became involved because it possesses a key land parcel on the northern edge of the square.

Circumstances fostered by the City of Toronto's desire to revitalize a stagnant retail area adjacent to the Ryerson campus presented a unique opportunity for the university to enter into a public-private partnership with the developer, Pen Equity. Specifically, Ryerson transferred development rights to the developer in exchange for access to twelve new movie theaters for classroom use. Participation in this project provided Ryerson with much-needed classroom space and a prominent location on the new public square. The City of Toronto Official Plan and the Ryerson University Campus Master Plan offered the institutional and regulatory context for the development of the project because they permit the transfer of development rights between campus land parcels.

The case study examines conditions and negotiations leading to an anticipated mutually beneficial outcome for the three key participants: the City of Toronto, Ryerson University, and Pen Equity. The study begins with the context for the project, including the development partners and their motivations, followed by the planning and structuring of the deal and the eventual components of the project, and concluding with the lessons learned from the negotiations and the resulting outcome.

The Context

Dundas Square represents Toronto's first public-square project in twenty-five years, providing an important urban design and redevelopment opportunity for the city. It is located at the intersection of Yonge and Dundas streets,

Map 10.1   **Ryerson Campus**

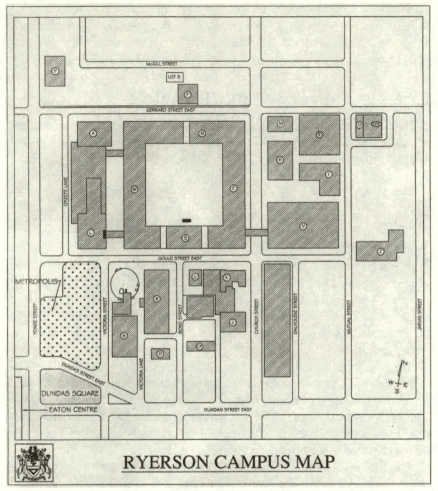

Source: Ryerson University Campus Planning Documents. Used by permission.

a vibrant corner that is estimated to have the highest pedestrian traffic levels of any intersection in Canada, with an annual flow of approximately 50 million people (see Map 10.1). The redevelopment plan is a response to the recent declining condition of the area, including concerns over increased drug transactions and other criminal activity. The area surrounding Dundas Square was comprised largely of marginal land uses and undesirable retailers, such as about thirty "dollar stores" within three blocks of the redevelopment site.

Several assets are notable exceptions to overall district decline: Eaton Centre and two Victorian theaters that will complement the Dundas Square development. The Eaton Centre is a downtown galleria-style shopping mall that attracts a large percentage of shoppers via public transit. It is located on the southwest corner of Yonge and Dundas streets, at the southwest corner of the square. The original Eaton Centre design turned its back on Yonge Street by focusing activity on the interior of the mall, with negative results on the retail environment in the vicinity of what is now Dundas Square. In recent years a city initiative has transformed the mall's blank wall into vibrant Yonge Street storefronts that are contributing to the downtown retail revival. The refurbished theaters, located on the block south of the square, are significant because Toronto ranks third behind New York and London in terms of live theater. Various policies and land use controls are employed to preserve and nurture this activity.

The Participants

The key participants in the development of Dundas Square and the Metropolis Project are the City of Toronto, Ryerson University, Pen Equity, and their lead tenant AMC Theatres of Canada, as well as the business and residential community.

With a population of 2.5 million people, Toronto is Canada's largest city and its downtown is the economic and cultural center of the country. The entire city is regulated by the City of Toronto Official Plan (master plan) as well as the zoning bylaws. All cities in Ontario are required to prepare and regularly update their official plans under the requirements of the Ontario Planning Act. Plans may be amended under the process specified in the act at the initiation of a property owner or the city. The act has a provision for appeals to the Ontario Municipal Board (OMB) by "interested parties" who disagree with city council decisions regarding a new plan or amendments to an existing plan. The OMB is a quasi-judicial body set up under provincial legislation to hear appeals regarding a range of planning decisions. As noted below the OMB held a hearing with respect to the planning and development of Dundas Square.

Ryerson University, like all universities in Ontario, is a public institution. University tuition fees are regulated, which means schools rely on the provincial government for both operating and capital funds, augmented by other fund-raising activities. Furthermore Ryerson has the lowest amount of space per student in Ontario, which is significant because of the unusual increase in enrollment in the fall of 2003. This sudden change occurred because the Ontario secondary school system reduced the number of years in the high school curriculum from five to four. Consequently students completing the new four-year curriculum in 2003 were graduating and applying for universities at the same time as those graduating from the former five-year curriculum.

To meet this demand Ryerson developed a building program that included new space for the Faculty of Community Services, Graphics, and Communication Management, as well as new buildings for the Engineering and Continuing Education departments and the Business School. In addition to a general need for more space, Ryerson also required larger classrooms. Under Ryerson's historical unionized teaching contract, class sizes have been kept relatively small. Consequently the old physical plant created and maintained classroom sizes that were consistent with that institutional structure. However, recent amendments to the faculty contract permit larger class sizes, requiring larger classrooms to capitalize on potential efficiencies.

Ryerson's 1997 Campus Master Plan is regulated by and consistent with the City of Toronto Official Plan. An important provision in the Toronto plan permits Ryerson to transfer development rights, meaning the university can consolidate unused air rights onto one parcel of land. Air rights are defined as unused permitted building space defined by city zoning bylaws. In exchange for this ability to transfer development rights, Ryerson must agree to maintain two historic properties, Oakham House and O'Keefe House (Ryerson University 1997).

The site for the proposed Metropolis development in Dundas Square integrates Ryerson's existing four-story parking structure and its associated air rights. The structure was built in 1986 and includes two ground-floor retail uses: the Ryerson Bookstore and a Tim Horton's donut shop. The site forms the eastern half of a block that borders on Yonge Street, and Ryerson officials have long recognized the potential to undertake a joint venture to incorporate the Ryerson property with valuable Yonge Street frontage (see Map 10.2).

Pen Equity is a wholly Canadian-owned asset manager that undertakes residential, commercial, office, and retail development on behalf of its pension fund clients. The city conducted a competitive process that resulted in the selection of Pen Equity as the developer to acquire and construct the Metropolis site, including use of Ryerson's transferred development rights. The firm had experience in Toronto, Ottawa, and Vancouver, but the Dundas Square site was its first major large-scale downtown development project. Pen Equity's lead tenant, AMC Entertainment International, is a large-scale business owning 226 theaters in the United States consisting of 1,719 screens located in 22 states and the District of Columbia. Through its subsidiary, AMC Theatres of Canada, the company is developing entertainment centers in Ontario, Alberta, and British Columbia.

Residential groups and business organizations also have been significant players in the development of Dundas Square. Kyle Rae, the city councilor

Map 10.2   **Dundas Square**

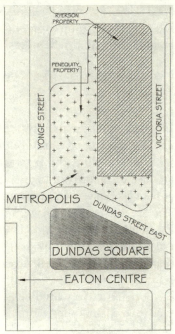

Source: Ryerson University Planning Documents. Used by permission.

representing the area, led community input into the planning process and worked collaboratively with all parties in the formation of a development strategy for the square. The Toronto East Downtown Residents Association (TEDRA), a citizens' organization speaking for the broader community, and the Yonge Street business community and property owners all articulated strong interest in the project. Together these stakeholders formed the Yonge Street Business and Residents Association (YSBRA) in the summer of 1995. Their concerns focused on the area's declining condition and an ongoing desire to create an enhanced retail environment. A January 1996 consultant's report (Soskolne 1996) was submitted to the city on behalf of the two associations in an effort to promote Yonge Street revitalization in the vicinity of the Dundas Street intersection, and the author played a significant role in representing the business association in subsequent planning and negotiations.

The Process

Ryerson became most deeply involved in the planning of Dundas Square at the final stage, when it became opportune for the university to exchange development rights for a negotiated set of benefits. In addition to its direct interests in the Metropolis development, Ryerson's concern for the ongoing functioning of the square pushed the university to become a member of the management committee that would oversee the square's ongoing programming.

Planning for the Area

The City of Toronto initiated a planning study for the revitalization of the Yonge and Dundas area in response to a redevelopment application filed for a nearby site in 1992. The resulting analysis was incorporated into the city's new official plan that was approved in July 1993 and later amended for the development of Dundas Square. In the summer of 1994, responding in part to the desire of Eaton's department store to strengthen its downtown retail presence, the city council approved a community development plan. This plan was the catalyst for the Downtown Yonge Street Regeneration Program, which was approved in March 1996 and included Dundas Square (City of Toronto 1996).

TEDRA and YSBRA became actively involved with the city council during the initial efforts to adopt the Community Improvement Plan Area Bylaw that was used to implement the proposals developed in the earlier development plan and subsequent regeneration program (City of Toronto, Planning and Development Department 1996). This regeneration strategy was a collaborative and jointly funded effort between the city and YSBRA and was directed by a steering committee chaired by Councilor Kyle Rae. Ryerson was not involved at this stage, but the plan introduced the Dundas Square concept and instituted a joint public-private approach to the development of the plan. The plan stated the desirability of combining the Ryerson parcel of land on the north side of the square with the adjacent privately owned sites to the west that border Yonge Street. This combination created a parcel of significant dimensions for a major anchor project to be built adjacent to the square.

The city apparently doubted the willingness of the Ryerson administration to participate in the Dundas Square project. Originally the city intended to assemble a large-scale development site on the eastern side of Yonge Street using its expropriation powers to acquire the privately owned properties.[2] The key Ryerson parcel was the subject of correspondence indicating that the Ryerson land could also be subject to expropriation if the university was unwilling to participate in the project. Ryerson was not approached regarding its participation in the project until 1997. Despite the expropriation threat, that outcome would have been in doubt anyway, because Ryerson is a public institution with a similar power to acquire property.

Ultimately Ryerson and the city both viewed Dundas Square as an opportunity to obtain important benefits through a negotiation process. Ryerson still needed access to the parking facilities on the parcel and the city needed the parcel to implement its large-scale redevelopment plan. Subsequent negotiations led to Ryerson retaining the existing land and parking garage while giving up the development and air rights associated with the site.[3] The preparation of the Dundas Square redevelopment plan required the city to amend its official plan and zoning bylaw amendments. Preparation for the plan began in 1997, with the city gaining expropriation permission from the Province of Ontario to begin its aggressive site assembly of ten Yonge Street properties, including those adjacent to the Ryerson parcel that were targeted for the development of the Metropolis project.

The city met significant resistance from property owners over the proposed expropriation and the approved plan and zoning bylaw amendments. The landowners claimed they were not receiving fair and full compensation for the expropriation of their properties. The objections came largely from long-term property owners who were upset over their inability to benefit from the anticipated property value increases associated with the Yonge and Dundas redevelopment. They questioned whether the city should be able to expropriate their land and then sell it to a private developer without giving them the opportunity to participate in the redevelopment scheme. Consequently nine of the ten expropriated property owners and one tenant exercised their right to appeal both the amendments and the expropriation to the OMB. Ryerson had a vested interest in the outcome of these actions, so it was considered a party to the hearing and was represented by legal counsel to protect its interests if necessary.

The hearing concluded in May 1998, and the written decision on the matter was released in June 1998. The OMB decision dismissed all of the planning appeals and approved the official plan and zoning bylaw amendments as well as the Community Improvement Plan. The OMB found that the proposed project constituted "good planning," meaning that the redevelopment objectives were deemed to be in the public interest. Furthermore the OMB agreed with the argument that the project would act as a catalyst for improving the economic and social well-being of the area. The city's application for expropriation was deemed to have merit and it was approved. However the OMB approval was conditional upon the city's endorsement of a commitment to proceed with the entire project, including funding, land expropriation, final agreements between the city and Pen Equity, a final lease between AMC Theatres of Canada and Pen Equity, and a number of other associated planning conditions (Ontario Municipal Board 1998).

Designing the Square and the Metropolis Development

The OMB approval permitted the city to move forward on initiatives related to the development of the Dundas Square area. First, during the summer of 1998, the city held a design competition for the square itself; and second, it called for expressions of interest in the development of the Metropolis land in conjunction with the Ryerson property. The design for the 3,250-square-meter open space was expected to include a 250-space underground parking garage, to be built by the Toronto Parking Authority, and a new entrance to the Dundas subway station. The plan had to account for both new development and redevelopment on adjacent sites. The first phase qualification documents were to be submitted by October, and the deadline for those selected for the second phase was the end of November. Among the forty-eight entries to the first phase of the competition, six were selected to participate in the second phase. By the end of 1998 the city selected the Toronto-based firm Brown and Storey Architects, which also won a national Award for Excellence from *Canadian Architect* magazine for the project.

After agreeing to participate in the Metropolis project, Ryerson and the City of Toronto negotiated a memorandum of understanding that ultimately evolved into an agreement for the transfer of the university's air rights. This agreement would ultimately be assigned to the developer selected to purchase and develop the site. Three companies responded to the request for qualifications issued in early 1997, and a consulting firm completed a detailed financial analysis of the proposals. A requirement placed on all Metropolis development proposals was the inclusion of movie theaters that would fulfill the city's agreement to provide Ryerson with theater seating for classroom use.

Pen Equity was selected to undertake the development of the site, including the use of Ryerson's development rights. This part of the site was integral to the success of the square, so the city wanted to ensure that the development would be built and would be a successful venture. The selection and evaluation was also important for Ryerson, to ensure that the project could support the university's classroom needs. Pen Equity entered into an agreement with AMC Theatres of Canada to be the primary tenant in the development, building on their previous working relationship in some suburban developments. The details of the proposed development are in Table 10.1.

Following the selection process, the city assigned the Ryerson development rights agreement to Pen Equity, but retained a central role in this public-private partnership. The general requirements resulting from these negotiations are:

Table 10.1

Metropolis Theatre Project, Toronto

Project: A 340,000-square-foot entertainment-based retail center anchored
                by an AMC 30-screen megaplex theater.

AMC 30   115,000 sq ft
Ancillary   225,000 sq ft
Total   340,000 sq ft

Parking for 6,100 spaces within a three-block radius.

Tenant Mix: AMC 30-screen/6000-seat megaplex theater, entertainment-based
                retail, interactive retail, leisure retail (books, music), leading fashion,
                themed restaurants and bars.

- The city and Pen Equity will enter into a development agreement and in conjunction AMC and Pen Equity will enter into a lease. Ryerson also will enter into an agreement with Pen Equity concerning the Ryerson land/development rights.
- The city will assemble the six lots of retail property on Yonge Street and secure air rights above the Ryerson lands.
- The city will transfer the retail property on Yonge Street and the air rights above the Ryerson lands to Pen Equity.
- Pen Equity will develop and finance the theater and the retail space, and be responsible for permanent financing of the development. Pen Equity will cover the costs of an incentive payment to Ryerson up to an agreed limit.
- AMC will operate the theater and pay rent to Pen Equity.
- Retail tenants will pay rent to Pen Equity.
- Pen Equity will provide participation payments to the city in accordance with the agreed formula.

The benefits that Ryerson will receive in exchange for relinquishing its development potential on the parking garage site to Pen Equity are specified in Table 10.2. It is important to note that the parking garage itself will remain in Ryerson hands, as will the retail space for the bookstore.

Ryerson would be granted weekday access to the twelve theaters from 8:00 a.m. to 1:00 p.m. daily, which had an estimated annual value of $3.6 million. A minimum estimate could be valued as low as $1.3 million, which would have a downward impact on the total benefits. The cash amounts for the Victoria Mall and Lake Devo infrastructure improvements were fixed. The parking and Tim Horton's revenues were estimated from the project at current rates.

Table 10.2

Ryerson University Benefits, July 1997

Theater access (12 @ 5hrs/day)	$3,600,000
Cash (area improvements)	$1,000,000
Refurbishing Victoria Mall	$900,000
Parking revenue (20 Years)	$10,000,000 (+ increases)
Tim Horton's Donut Shop (10 years)	$650,000 (+ increases)
Lake Devo refurbishing	$700,000
Tax indemnity	Unknown
Total	$15,850,000

Source: These figures were prepared by Ryerson staff and presented to the Ryerson Board of Governors.

Note: The theater benefits were based on the building cost of Ryerson classroom space prorated to the percentage of the day that they may be used. The parking and Tim Horton's Donut Shop revenues relate to guarantees above the actual rents over the specified time periods.

In addition to the development rights transfer, negotiations between Ryerson and Pen Equity led to agreement on several other issues. In conjunction with AMC, Ryerson formed a committee of classroom users to participate in finalizing a theater design that would be appropriate for classroom activities. Additionally Pen Equity wanted to alter the existing parking structure, and Ryerson agreed to the changes in exchange for a large electronic billboard on the east side of the building near the north end that is central to the Ryerson campus. Ryerson also gained less quantifiable benefits associated with the development of the new square and the Metropolis project: a long-sought subway linkage to the university; and a new Dundas Square address that was a reasonable alternative to its long-time desire for exposure on Yonge Street.

Establishing a Management Committee

Ryerson felt it deserved a role in the management of Dundas Square based on its participation in the Metropolis project, as well as the university's influence over the success of the areawide revitalization effort. Subsequently Ryerson and the City of Toronto organized a Yonge-Dundas Square Symposium in May 2000 to seek community input regarding the operation and management of the square. The symposium addressed a broad range of issues including security and safety, maintenance, programming, and crowd and noise control. A report by the city's Policy and Finance Committee (2001) considered several management models but recommended a board of management model made up of thirteen members including a city councilor, business and community group members, city staff, police, and Ryerson University.[4] In December 2001 the city council adopted the report's recommendations as the governance model for the square.

The Board of Management has a program planning and operational oversight role in managing the square. In accordance with its prescribed bylaws, the committee must periodically review the operating guidelines, develop a sponsorship program, identify issues and seek solutions related to the square's management, and formulate a business plan and annual budget (City of Toronto Policy and Finance Committee 2001). The expectation is that the Board of Management be financially self-sufficient within three years of becoming responsible for Dundas Square.

Status of the Metropolis Project

The original expectation was that Pen Equity would begin the project immediately after receiving approvals in 1998, but it was delayed continuously and some observers questioned whether the project would ever be constructed. By mid-2003 the public-square component of the development had been completed, programming was taking place on a regular basis, and some additional improvements and development had been initiated. In June 2003 Pen Equity obtained permits for excavation and shoring work for the construction of the Metropolis Theatre project on the north edge of the square. These permits reflected the initial plan that had been approved for development, and the expectation was that the construction would proceed on a continuous basis until completion, although no specific time frame was announced. The lead tenants remained in place for the major retail component and AMC was committed to the theater component.

Because of the delays Ryerson was seriously impacted by lack of access to the theaters for classroom space. To address this deficit the university found a solution by using the Pen Equity/AMC project as its model. It negotiated with the owners of the Carlton theater complex to make alternations to their nine theaters, which are located a short distance from the campus. Ryerson has use of those theaters from 8:00 a.m. to 1:00 p.m., Monday through Friday. Presumably, after the Metropolis project is completed, Ryerson will assess their need for the continued use of the Carlton theaters.

Analysis of the Outcomes

An assessment of Ryerson's benefits from this development partnership should consider the following:

- Should Ryerson have participated in this venture?
- Did Ryerson receive a fair exchange for its development rights?
- How did the delays affect the current status of the project?

Any evaluation must acknowledge that strong redevelopment pressures in the area based on a city policy initiative drove the development of the Ryerson site, with support from local business and residents groups. Hints at a possible expropriation of Ryerson's land if the university was uncooperative strongly motivated the university to participate and negotiate the best deal possible. A prime benefit for Ryerson is the ability to use the Metropolis Theatre complex for classes. This innovative approach provides Ryerson with classroom space that is appropriate in size and in terms of quality and equipment for lectures.

Even if the Ryerson parcel were not part of the designated redevelopment, the university should have been involved in the planning and design of the square, for two reasons. First, as an applied learning and research institution, Ryerson is already actively involved with its surrounding downtown community through studio courses and workshops conducted in programs such as urban planning, social work, early childhood education, architecture, and environmental health. Second, Ryerson needs to have a voice in the development and management of all areas adjacent to its campus. For example construction of the new square and the associated development around it could potentially have negative traffic and crime impacts on the Ryerson campus. Traffic impacts may affect adjacent streets and parking facilities, especially during the peak periods of the university's large continuing education program. Crime and drug problems in and around the square also may lead to additional university policing costs if criminal activity gravitates into the green spaces on the Ryerson campus.

Ryerson requires ongoing input into the Dundas Square decision-making process to address issues related to the development of the square, and more specifically the programming that should be consistent with the educational use of the theaters. This input has been achieved by granting a Ryerson representative a position on the Management Committee. If Ryerson had not cooperated in the development of the property around the square, it could have been excluded from participation in the committee.

Assessing whether Ryerson's benefits as a result of the transfer of development rights were a fair exchange requires viewing the partnership from several different perspectives. First, the partnership must be considered in the context of Ryerson's financial position and the availability of capital funding. Despite fund-raising efforts and some capital grants from the Province of Ontario, the university would have had great difficulty funding a new building on the Metropolis site at the time the deal was negotiated. Consequently having a partner shoulder the capital financing cost for the new facilities was very attractive, especially based on the university's immediate needs and the student enrollment pressures anticipated for 2003 and beyond.

A valid assessment must also compare the value of air rights sold to Pen Equity relative to the benefits received by Ryerson. This may be difficult to assess since the sale of air rights is relatively unique in Toronto, particularly for universities. Early versions of Toronto's planning regulations permitted density transfers in designated parts of the city for small sites and the theater district. However, based on the expected Ryerson benefits of close to $16 million, and comparing that figure to the development potential for the 340,000 square feet on the Ryerson site, one can make a rough analysis of the benefits and opportunity costs. If the development value at the time of the agreement (1997) is estimated in the range of the low $30s per square foot, the value of the development potential would be in the $10 to $11 million range, which is less than the almost $16 million in benefits to the university. A more conservative estimate of $13.5 million, based on a lower economic benefit for the use of the theaters, would still be greater than the opportunity forgone. Despite this apparent positive trade-off for the development rights, some may still wonder if a greater financial benefit could have been achieved if Ryerson had been able to deal directly on a competitive basis with the site developers.

Finally, have the delays in the development of the Metropolis project had important impacts on the project? This question is relevant because the Metropolis development took out permits and began construction only in the summer of 2003. Given an original projected start date of 1998, the project is already five years behind schedule, directly affecting Ryerson's need for use of the theaters for classrooms. Some parties have been concerned that the project would be aborted and began questioning the likelihood that the development would ever be completed. However, throughout the period of delays, there were positive signs that Pen Equity would not walk away from its commitment to build the entire project. The deal structure specifies certain payments to be made by the developer to the City of Toronto over time. In September 2002 the developer made a scheduled $10 million payment, bringing the grand total of payments received by the city to $30 million.

Uncertainty about the future of the Metropolis project has persisted since it was first announced and throughout the delays. Reports began to surface that the theater industry was curtailing some of its plans to build new megaplexes across North America, and it appeared that some markets, including Toronto, could be overbuilt. Astute negotiations on behalf of the city and Ryerson should have included a compliance time frame in the

final agreement or a penalty clause for noncompliance. This would have
been especially beneficial for Ryerson because of its need for access to the
AMC theaters in the fall of 2003.

Conclusion

Ryerson University's role in the development of Dundas Square is not
surprising given the typical consultative process undertaken by communities affected by major developments, nor in terms of the university's
mandate for local community involvement. However, when considering
the specifics of Ryerson's participation through the transfer of its development rights to the Metropolis Theatre project, the university's role and
approach are not standard but rather innovative and probably unique in
Ontario, if not Canada. Transfers of development rights have been a part
of previous city plans, but they have typically been "as of right" rather
than through a negotiated deal brokered by the city and involving more
than two parties. The city appeared to use a carrot and stick strategy,
suggesting the possibility of expropriation while at the same time entic-
ing Ryerson with some needed benefits; that is, large well-equipped classroom space and infrastructure improvements. It appears that the sharing
of commercial movie theater space with university classroom use is unprecedented. This approach is especially attractive since many institutions such as Ryerson not only need additional space, but also have a
shortage of funds for capital expenditures.

Concerns over the desirability of this arrangement are nonetheless justified, based on the protracted time to initiate and complete the project. When
universities negotiate for this type of joint venture in the future, they need
to consider when the benefits will begin to accrue. The delayed time frame
in this case introduced a serious element of uncertainty, as the availability
of classroom space remained unknown and ultimately the university had to
lease alternative space in the Carlton theaters. Additional costs also must
be considered, such as those incurred by Ryerson to lease the Carlton space,
provide additional multimedia facilities, and locate technical and security
staff on an off-campus site. This case study also may raise questions about
the desirability of universities entering into agreements with developers in
any situation.

The Ryerson case appears to demonstrate a positive net benefit from this
joint venture. However, universities should carefully consider the timing of
the disposition of their limited landholdings, particularly when undertaking
a collaborative project contingent upon the use of their most valuable devel-
opable property.

Notes

1. The "new" City of Toronto was created in 1998 when the provincial government required the six municipalities that formerly constituted Metropolitan Toronto to be united into a single-tier governmental unit.

2. Expropriation powers given to municipalities in the Province of Ontario are similar to the power of eminent domain.

3. The Metropolis project was designed and constructed over the top of the Ryerson parking garage. It uses the physical space of the air rights above the structure plus the transferable development rights from the campus lands.

4. The committee consists of the ward councilor, four members from the business community, one from the neighborhood association, one from Ryerson University, one from the Toronto Parking Authority, one from the Yonge Street Mission, one from the Toronto Theatre Alliance, two city staff (economic development, and facilities and real estate), and one from the Toronto Police Services. For the operation of this committee see City of Toronto, Policy and Finance Committee (2001).

References

City of Toronto, 1996. Downtown Yonge Street regeneration program, Yonge-Dundas redevelopment project, project plan. Toronto.

City of Toronto, Planning and Development Department. 1996. New planning amendments for Downtown Yonge Street. Toronto.

City of Toronto, Policy and Finance Committee. 2001. Yonge/Dundas Square–Operations resulting from urban development services and governance model. Report No. 16. Toronto.

Ontario Municipal Board. 1998. Yonge Street regeneration project decision and reasons for decision. The Joint Consolidated Hearings Act. Toronto.

Ryerson University. 1997. Campus Master Plan. Toronto

Soskolne, Ronald L. 1996. Downtown Yonge: A program to promote the regeneration of Toronto's main street. Prepared on behalf of the Yonge Street Business and Residents Association (YSBRA). Toronto.

Part III

University Development Practices: Acquisition, Finance, Development, and the Deal

11

An Overview of University Real Estate Investment Practices

Ziona Austrian and Jill S. Norton

To understand the role of the university as developer, it is important to investigate the issues that affect a university's acquisition and development practices and how these issues manifest themselves in day-to-day activities. This chapter explains the various approaches used by universities to acquire and develop real estate around their campuses and proposes a framework within which universities' real estate investment practices can be understood. The framework is based on case studies and in-depth investigation of real estate investment activities at five universities across the United States. While their experiences cannot be expected to represent those of all universities, the case studies provide valuable insight into the broad issues that affect university real estate investment activities.

The five universities selected for study are The University of Arizona, Portland State University, Marquette University, Wayne State University, and the University of Pittsburgh. The criteria used to select them included public versus private status, size of student enrollment, location, and characteristics of the surrounding neighborhoods. The five cases include both public and private institutions with wide-ranging student enrollments. They are located in different regions of the country, and their surrounding communities vary in terms of their economic stability and their designation as residential, commercial, or mixed-use environments. In addition to the formal criteria, the authors selected universities whose real estate activities were not well studied previously; except for Marquette University and the University of Pittsburgh (see chapter 2 of this volume) this criterion was satisfied. Information was collected from a number of sources including Internet sites, newspaper reports, planning documents, policy documents, and in-person interviews with key individuals associated with the universities and surrounding neighborhoods (see Appendix 11.1).

Table 11.1 presents background information about each university. The University of Arizona is a public university with nearly 37,000 students. It is located northwest of downtown Tucson and is surrounded by residential neighborhoods. Portland State University is a relatively young public university located in downtown Portland in a commercial area adjacent to the central business district. Student enrollment has grown steadily since the university was founded in 1955 and now exceeds 20,000. It is currently the largest university in the Oregon University System.

Marquette University, founded in 1881, is a private Jesuit university of about 11,000 students located west of downtown Milwaukee, Wisconsin. It is surrounded by expressways to the south and east and by primarily low-income, renter-occupied residential neighborhoods to the north and west. Wayne State University is a large public university with an enrollment of more than 31,000. It is located in Detroit's Midtown district, which lies north of downtown and is also home to many of the city's cultural institutions. The area is bounded by expressways and the neighborhoods that lie within it are primarily low-income and have high renter occupancy rates.

The University of Pittsburgh is located in the city's Oakland neighborhood, the educational and cultural center of Pittsburgh and location of other universities, large health care facilities, museums, and other cultural institutions. The University of Pittsburgh is a state-related university, that is, a hybrid of public and private institution. Its Oakland campus enrolls more than 27,000 students, and the university also has a smaller branch campus outside Pittsburgh. Oakland includes four distinct residential neighborhoods (north, west, central, and south) with varying demographic and economic characteristics that include both low-income and upper-income households; some areas are primarily renter occupied, while others have high home ownership rates.

Following a brief description of the analytical framework guiding the study, the chapter describes four factors that shape four distinct aspects of the real estate investment practices of universities, using examples from the fives case studies to demonstrate how this occurs. The chapter concludes by highlighting these connections and discussing the importance of understanding university real estate investment activities in this context.

Analytical Framework

The analytic framework that emerged from the five case studies suggests that four primary factors influence the real estate acquisition and development practices of universities. These factors are referred to as the independent variables: motivation for investment, characteristics of the physical environment surrounding the campus, degree of policy oversight facing the

Table 11.1

Case Studies in University Real Estate Investment Practices

Institution	Location	Census division (region)	Type of university	Student enrollment	Surrounding neighborhoods
The University of Arizona	Tucson, AZ	West (Mountain)	Public	36,847	Residential
Portland State University	Portland, OR	West (Pacific)	Public	20,110	Commercial
Marquette University	Milwaukee, WI	Midwest (East North Central)	Private	10,988	Residential
Wayne State University	Detroit, MI	Midwest (East North Central)	Public	31,168	Mixed-use
University of Pittsburgh	Pittsburgh, PA	Northeast (Middle Atlantic)	State-related	27,190	Mixed-use

university, and leadership styles and vision of university and civic officials. The real estate acquisition and development practices of universities are driven by these factors and are referred to as the dependent variables: the nature of the decision-making process, type of projects undertaken, financing mechanisms employed, and dynamics of university-community relations (see Figure 11.1). It is the complex interaction of motivation, physical environment, policy oversight, and leadership that shapes how universities make decisions about real estate acquisition and development, the types of projects in which they choose to invest, the financing mechanisms they utilize, and how they manage university-community relations.

University Real Estate Investments: The Independent Factors

Although there were many differences among the five universities selected for study, it became apparent that many common issues affected their real estate acquisition and development practices. In all cases the motivation for development, physical environment of the university, the types of policies that govern university actions, and leadership styles of university administrators and local officials were important to understanding the development process.

Motivation

Recognizing what motivates universities' real estate development activities is important in studying the development process. Motivation obviously affects the types of projects that universities undertake, but it can also affect the structure of the decision-making process, availability of various financing mechanisms, and the nature of university-community relations.

The prime motivation for physical expansion by many universities is steady growth in student enrollment. A greater national emphasis on postsecondary education, accompanied by broader access, has resulted in dramatic increases in the number of people attending institutions of higher education. Over the last three decades, total fall enrollment in degree-granting institutions in the United States increased nearly 70 percent (Snyder, Hoffman, and Geddes 1998). Increased enrollment leads to higher demand for classrooms and laboratories, office space, student housing, and recreation facilities. For example The University of Arizona experienced a steady rise in student enrollment, growing from 6,200 students in 1950 to almost 37,000 by 2002. Portland State University had about 16,000 students in the mid-1990s, but by 2002 had more than 20,000, and the number is projected to grow to 35,000 by 2012.

Figure 11.1 **Analytical Framework**

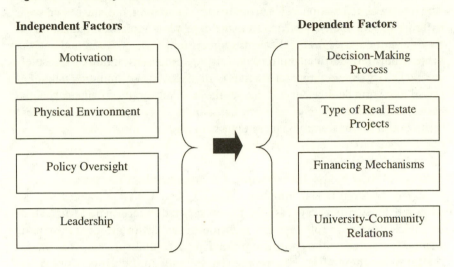

Another motivation for much of the construction on campuses is the need for top-notch facilities to attract and retain faculty and students. This is true for universities that have traditionally had a strong research component, such as The University of Arizona, and for those that want to build their research capacity or transform themselves from commuter schools to more traditional universities, such as Wayne State and Portland State. Both universities traditionally served a large number of commuter students, but are making an effort to attract more students to live on campus and create a twenty-four-hour community around the university. They share a common vision, although Portland State is located in a vital downtown district and Wayne State is located in an area undergoing significant redevelopment.

While many universities engage in real estate development to accommodate or facilitate growth, others are motivated by a concern about student recruitment and retention that stems from problems in surrounding neighborhoods. Some colleges and universities, once part of vibrant urban centers, have seen their neighborhoods decline (primarily from the 1960s to the 1980s) and are now surrounded by urban blight. University leaders often responded to neighborhood decline by constructing physical and symbolic barriers around the campus in an attempt to isolate themselves from the conditions plaguing those outside the academic community. This response generally failed to satisfy students and their parents, who wanted a safer and more stimulating environment for learning, and led to a greater willingness among institutions to engage in large-scale efforts to improve the surrounding physical landscape. The prime example among our case studies is Marquette University, which established two development organizations to revitalize the residential and commercial base of the neighborhood and devoted considerable financial resources to the effort. Its actions were solely motivated by the need to improve the condition of the surrounding neighborhood following declines in student enrollment that stemmed from fears about neighborhood safety. By most accounts, both students and residents benefited from the university's investment.

Physical Environment

A university's physical setting has a direct influence on its property acquisition and development process. If a university needs additional space, is there sufficient room to grow or will expansion put pressure on the surrounding land area? What are the specific types of land uses that surround the campus and how do they affect the process? The answer to these questions determines what types of projects are possible, what funding mechanisms are available, who will be involved in decision making, and how community members will react. Rural and suburban campuses often have open land available for development, but urban campuses are often landlocked by property that has been developed for other purposes or presents impediments such as expressways, waterways, or railroads.

Surrounding land uses can represent a variety of problems. As might be expected, universities adjacent to residential neighborhoods often encounter the greatest obstacles in acquiring and developing real estate. Residents may appreciate universities for the many amenities they bring (e.g., cultural and sporting events and community outreach services), but the dominant presence of a university in a residential neighborhood often leaves neighbors feeling wary. When a university is in a growth mode, this wariness intensifies, because residents may believe their homes and quality of life are threatened by campus expansion. Community opposition can affect the development process in various ways, depending on how the university chooses to respond and whether residents have political power to fight the university. The universities in Pittsburgh and Tucson are bounded by both upper-income and lower-income neighborhoods, but in both cases the lower-income neighborhoods have borne the brunt of university expansion. As expected, the stable, upper-income neighborhoods are less vulnerable to university expansion. They generally have the resources and political influence to fight encroachment, and the higher market values make it more difficult for the universities to acquire properties.

Assembling tracts of land is also particularly challenging. Since residential lots in urban areas tend to be small, it can take years to assemble enough land to build a needed facility. The university must aggressively pursue properties when they become available and wait patiently for others. This not only makes it difficult for the university to meet its objectives, it also adds fuel to an already contentious situation. Residents generally oppose properties being land banked for future development. A major complaint among neighborhood residents in Tucson is that the university uses houses it acquires for purposes not appropriate for residential neighborhoods (such as maintenance or storage facilities) or demolishes houses only to leave the lots vacant or use them for surface parking. Even if residential structures are maintained to house office activities, a scattered pattern of university versus resident ownership changes the character of the neighborhood.

Universities located in commercial districts encounter different issues in the acquisition and development process. Portland State University faces less opposition to campus expansion, but confronts another set of obstacles, including intense competition for property in the city's vibrant commercial zones. The university must be able to compete on the open market for available properties, which means garnering the financial resources needed to match offers of private developers. Furthermore universities are large bureaucracies and not always structured to make decisions quickly, which is a serious disadvantage in a competitive market. To address this challenge, all universities in this study have developed efficient decision-making processes for actions involving real estate acquisition and development.

While surrounding land uses can present obstacles, they can also provide opportunities. Wayne State University, which is located in a deteriorated urban area, is able to benefit from underutilized land by converting vacant buildings or industrial sites to meet its real estate needs. The university's plans generally cause little opposition, because the City of Detroit and some of the neighbors favor any form of investment over no investment. Moreover, acquisition costs are generally low. Wayne State faces other challenges in the development phase, however, because the time and expense associated with demolition, conversion, and environmental cleanup can derail projects. At the same time some members of the community would like to see less demolition and more historic preservation and high-quality projects. They think the attitude that any development is better than no development has resulted in poorly designed buildings that are out of character with the neighborhood.

The physical environment introduces another set of difficulties for universities with a rigid campus boundary, such as a major thoroughfare, expressway, waterway, or railroad. Both Marquette University and The University of Arizona have attempted to reroute streets, although they failed because of strong community opposition. These types of boundaries have also led to creative development strategies. For example Portland State University is exploring the possibility of capping a low-level highway to allow construction overhead and is considering an aerial tram as a river crossing.

State and Local Policy Oversight

State and local policies relating to real estate acquisition and development have a less visible but significant impact on university development activities. The extent to which policies facilitate or restrict a university's ability to operate in the real estate market varies considerably. Furthermore, oversight of university activities can originate from multiple sources.

There are often significant differences in the extent to which formal policies govern a university's actions with respect to real estate development. Private universities, for example, are generally subject to the restrictions placed upon them by their boards of trustees. While the possibility exists for disagreement between board members and administrators, both groups are ultimately responsible only to the university, lessening the likelihood that other considerations would interfere in the decision-making process. This independence reduces delays, facilitates funding approval, and makes it much easier for the university to compete in the real estate market. In the case of Marquette University the president's decision to invest large sums of university funds to revitalize the neighborhood required only board approval. It should be noted that some private universities arrange bond finance through a public entity, and under such circumstances must consider public comment; however, their decision-making process involving real estate development remains primarily internal.

The level of autonomy granted to public institutions differs widely from state to state. Some public universities enjoy a level of independence that is more characteristic of private universities; they do not have to go beyond their own board for project or funding approval. For example Wayne State University (like all public universities in Michigan) is constitutionally autonomous and the governing responsibility lies with the university's board. Wayne State does not face state-imposed restrictions on the amount it can offer for real property and is not required to wait for approval from a statewide body. The university issues its own bonds, is responsible for the debt service, and has its own bond rating.

In other states the board that governs all public institutions of higher education (e.g., a board of regents, a board of higher education) must approve capital budgets, agree to property acquisitions over a specified amount, and authorize the sale of bonds. In some cases universities must also obtain approval from the state legislature before they can move forward with real estate acquisition and development plans, and some public universities face restrictions with respect to the price they can pay for real estate. Portland State, for example, operates under the policies of the Oregon University System and the state legislature. These policies include a restriction on how much the university can bid for a property relative to the appraisal price (the bid cannot exceed the average of two appraisals); a requirement for approval from the board of the Oregon University System when the purchase price of a property exceeds $100,000; and approval from the state legislature when the price exceeds $1 million (Oregon Secretary of State n.d.). Similarly, The University of Arizona must receive approval from the Arizona Board of Regents (ABOR) for real estate transactions valued at more than $250,000 (Arizona Board of Regents 1983). The restrictions on acquisition price and the time delays involved in obtaining these approvals can be substantial obstacles in the development process, limiting the university's ability to compete in the market.

Some universities may also face restrictions on the amount of bond debt they can issue (or can be issued on their behalf), which clearly influences the feasibility and timing of development plans. For example the Oregon University System issues bonds on behalf of Portland State, but bond sales also must be approved by the state legislature. In Arizona the Board of Regents issues bonds on behalf of the state's public universities. The state legislature must not only approve bond sales, but also authorizes the amount of debt that the Board of Regents can issue over several years. Even if some debt has been retired, additional bonds cannot be issued during that time period.

State policy can be particularly restrictive if it limits where a university can acquire property. Portland State University's real estate acquisitions are guided by boundaries negotiated by the university and the city (Portland State University District Partnership for Community Development 1993). Although the university can purchase property outside the limits for student housing or investment purposes, most acquisitions occur within the agreed-upon boundaries. All public universities in the State of Arizona are required to restrict property acquisition to a clearly defined area (University of Arizona 1988, 2000). As a result greater importance is placed on acquiring land when it becomes available within the planning area, and universities are forced to carefully consider optimal land uses. The University of Arizona can purchase properties only within negotiated boundaries and is subject to even stronger limitations. In some areas within the defined boundaries the university cannot buy property unless the owner initiates contact and expresses interest in selling.

Local governments tend to have little direct control over university real estate acquisition and development plans, but may be able to influence how projects are developed through the design review process. Some universities in this study were required to submit their plans to the local planning board for review. This mandate gives public officials and citizens an opportunity to voice concerns about how proposed projects might affect their community and may help ensure that proposals are sensitive to surrounding architecture and land uses. Design review can also be used as a tool to ensure community involvement and acceptance of university development activities. The City of Pittsburgh has used this approach effectively to encourage the University of Pittsburgh and other large institutional developers to involve residents and community groups in their decision-making processes.

University Leadership

The direction that a university takes with respect to real estate acquisition and development ultimately depends on its leadership. The university president and top-level administrators set the agenda for physical development. Their vision for the future of the university and their perception of the role of the university as a civic partner determine what they do and how they do it.

Real estate development is sometimes driven by a new vision for the university, as when a change in leadership results in a dramatic shift in the focus and priorities of the institution. For example, at The University of Arizona, an increased emphasis on the biosciences has created the need for new high-tech laboratory facilities. At Portland State and Wayne State, the desire to transform from commuter campuses to more traditional residential campuses is precipitating the construction of additional university-owned housing.

Leadership also plays the key role in determining how the university moves through the development process. Leaders who see the university as an important part of the neighborhood and city are more responsive to the needs and concerns of the larger community. The neighborhood revitalization effort initiated by Marquette University occurred because the institution welcomed a new president who recognized that the university's fate was intertwined with that of the neighborhood. He knew that fast and drastic action had to be taken to address the poor condition of the neighborhood in order to preserve the university's future. The president was able to convince the university board to devote the necessary resources to make a difference in the neighborhood, and redevelopment activities were carried out in a way that addressed the needs of local residents while stopping the downward trend in enrollment.

Some university leaders assess their plans in light of broader community goals, show willingness to partner with public agencies for mutually beneficial outcomes, and ensure avenues for community participation in decision making. When the University of Pittsburgh named a new chancellor in 1996, it ushered in a new era in university-community relations. The chancellor placed greater importance on establishing positive relationships with residents, neighborhood organizations, and city officials, and he communicated this vision to his top administrators. In contrast, other universities act quietly on issues involving real estate, hoping to avoid complications and controversy. The approach that a university selects appears to be a direct reflection of how the core leadership views the role of the institution in civic affairs.

University Real Estate Investments: The Dependent Factors

This section explores the decision-making process in some detail, including what guides decisions, who is involved in decision making, and how barriers to development are addressed. It also identifies the types of real estate development projects that are undertaken, how they are financed, and how the development process affects university-community relations. It is in these discussions that the impact of the independent factors becomes apparent.

Decision-Making Process

University real estate investment decisions are guided by long-term academic needs as well as short-term opportunities. As explained earlier, many universities are experiencing growth in student enrollment and are increasing academic offerings. They also recognize that cutting-edge research facilities and a safe, vibrant campus environment are needed to attract top students and faculty. All universities in this study are located in central cities and some are in or near the downtown area. As such they are landlocked by residential neighborhoods, other large institutions, freeways, or other physical barriers. Some of the universities are located in growing cities where real estate is in high demand, while others are in redeveloping areas where some competition exists for the most favorable sites or for new or rehabilitated buildings. These issues affect how universities act in the real estate market.

Many universities have a master plan that guides long-term decisions and takes into account the factors that affect the real estate acquisition and development process, whether directly or indirectly. The motivation for new development, opportunities and obstacles that exist in the physical environment of the campus, policy restrictions, and the vision of university leaders are generally reflected in the master plan. Wayne State University's master plan, completed in 2001, supports the objectives to enhance the research capacity of the institution and to develop a more traditional, residential campus. It identifies where expansion opportunities exist and where further development would be more problematic. The master plan includes elements that support the vision of the current leadership to better connect the campus with the surrounding community by creating a twenty-four-hour university district (Wayne State University 2001).

Portland State University's master plan not only addresses the institution's long-term academic needs, but also reflects how leaders envision the role of the university in the larger community. The university's plan is integrated with the city's Central City Plan, which includes a university district (Bureau of Planning 1988). Portland State led the planning effort for the district, working alongside residents and other stakeholders. The result of this process was a plan that addressed the needs of the university while respecting the interests of those outside the academic community.

Although universities are guided by master plans that address long-term needs, they must be able to respond to opportunities as they arise in the local real estate market. How do universities structure decision-making processes that guide real estate acquisition and development? Because most institutions compete with private-sector developers or other large institutions, they find ways to streamline their decision-making processes to respond quickly to opportunities. Universities are known as slow-moving bureaucracies when it comes to curriculum changes, educational innovations, and hiring practices, but the institutions in this study developed strategies that have allowed them to act quickly on decisions involving real estate acquisition. In both public and private institutions, the decisions are usually made by a handful of top administrators who have easy access to the university president.

For example, at the University of Pittsburgh, a state-affiliated (quasi-public) university, the assistant vice chancellor for business continuously receives information on real estate opportunities and can approach the vice chancellor and chancellor when needed. Administrators have the authority to approve deals of less than $1 million. More expensive deals require approval from the Board of Trustees' property and facilities committee, but this group also works quickly to authorize deals. Because the university is located in a densely populated area where real estate is relatively scarce and other large institutions compete for the same properties, the university's current administration and Board of Trustees have structured themselves to act quickly when making decisions on real estate.

As described previously, universities are guided by different policies concerning real estate acquisition. Universities frequently need to circumvent the restrictions imposed on them and develop mechanisms that enable them to be active players in the real estate market. A university foundation can be an important partner in this effort. As state government agencies, the public universities in this study were generally restricted to making an offer at or below the average of two appraisals. In localities with a competitive real estate market, increased demand may push the price beyond appraised values, making it impossible for a university to compete with the private sector. As an independent organization, a university foundation does not face the same type of restrictions and, with the appropriate resources, can make a more competitive bid.

The University of Arizona and The University of Arizona Foundation have used this approach to their mutual advantage. The foundation purchases properties of interest to the university and then enters into an agreement whereby the university leases the property for a period of time. At the end of the lease the foundation deeds the property to the university. The foundation benefits because rent payments are structured to provide a good rate of return on the investment, and the university benefits because it gains immediate access to the property and eventual ownership. This arrangement has also been used when the university has been interested in property outside its planning boundary, and when quick action is required and the university cannot wait for approval from the board of regents or state legislature. This type of partnership is possible only when the foundation has adequate financial resources. Portland State University, for example, has not yet been able to rely on its foundation because the university is relatively young, it does not have a large, well-established alumni base, and the foundation's assets are fairly limited.

Type of Real Estate Projects

Most universities invest in different types of real estate projects, including student housing, office and academic buildings, research labs, research parks, parking garages, recreation and athletic facilities, and mixed-use structures. The specific types of projects in which a university chooses to invest reflect its motivation for development, the opportunities and constraints in the physical environment, and the agenda of university leaders.

All five universities in this study have recently developed, or have plans to develop, new residential units for students. Motivated by either rapid growth in enrollment or the desire to bring more students to campus, all are focused on developing more university-owned housing. Wayne State University opened a new dormitory-style undergraduate housing complex in 2002, its first newly constructed residential building in almost a decade, and additional units are planned as part of the effort to create a twenty-four-hour campus community. The University of Arizona has multiple housing projects under way to meet the needs of its growing student body.

More students means increased demand for parking, and both The University of Arizona and Wayne State have had to make substantial investments in parking facilities. Portland State, despite its rapid growth, has been able to focus its investments on classrooms, office space, and research facilities because it benefits from a highly utilized public transportation system. The University of Arizona and Wayne State also boast new student centers. The University of Arizona opened a student union and bookstore in November 2002 to replace a smaller, outdated facility, and Wayne State University recently completed a 700,000-square-foot welcome center that includes a bookstore and serves as a one-stop-shop for new or prospective students.

The University of Pittsburgh has undertaken a number of projects to meet the demands brought on by continuous growth over the last several decades. Student housing was a top priority because the large influx of students in surrounding neighborhoods was having a negative impact on the local housing stock. A 500-unit, garden-style apartment complex was recently completed to address that need. The university also built a large convocation center to host basketball games and special events; and it provides a student recreation center and space for retail establishments and restaurants. Another recent project is a multipurpose academic complex that provides space for classrooms and offices as well as ground-floor retail (Gallinger 2001; Schacknew 1999).

The University of Arizona took advantage of an unusual opportunity in the real estate market to develop a research park that supports its research mission. IBM was having difficulty finding a buyer for the property in 1994, and the university was able to negotiate a very favorable financing arrangement for its acquisition. Located several miles from the university, the Science and Technology Park is considered its most valuable real estate holding outside the main campus.

Portland State's real estate investment strategies must capitalize on the limited development opportunities that exist in the campus's densely populated downtown location. The university carefully monitors the local real estate market and strategically acquires property as it becomes available. This policy has allowed the university to build some new facilities and to adapt many existing buildings for academic use. Portland State recently constructed a new building to house the College of Urban and Public Affairs; other projects under way include a new student housing facility and a Native American student and community center.

To accomplish its goal of improving and stabilizing its surrounding neighborhood, Marquette University (through the development organizations it created) invested in hundreds of properties over a period of several years. Most of their acquisitions involved multiunit apartment buildings, which were renovated and then leased to responsible tenants. Marquette also invested in a large mixed-use complex in an effort to revitalize the commercial base of the neighborhood. The $30 million Campus Town project included 88,000 square feet of retail space and 153 units of student housing (Carlson 1994; Farbstein and Wener 1996; Tijerina 1994).

Financing Mechanisms

Universities rely on a variety of methods and tools to finance real estate acquisition and development, such as general obligation and revenue bonds, state capital budget allocations, partnership agreements, tax increment financing, commercial loans, and university endowment and operating funds. Specific funding choices are affected by various factors, including in large part the policies regulating the university.

Bonds

The most popular means of financing large real estate development projects is the sale of bonds. They are generally issued by the university or a state-wide administrative body (such as a board of regents), but may be issued by other entities, such as a dormitory authority. General obligation bonds pledge the full faith and credit of the institution to secure the debt. The bonds may be tax-exempt (that is, the interest payments to bondholders are tax-exempt) if proceeds of the sale are used to construct academic facilities; bonds are taxable if used for for-profit enterprises, such as retail space. Revenue bonds are secured by a specific revenue source and are therefore used for revenue-producing projects, such as student housing complexes or parking garages.

For some public universities the state legislature must approve the sale of bonds, which may influence the financing mechanism selected. For example the Arizona legislature restricts the amount of debt that the Arizona Board of Regents (ABOR) can issue in the form of general obligation bonds (referred to as system bonds in Arizona) for a given period of time. When the debt limit is reached, ABOR must go back to the legislature to request more bonding authority. Because of these limitations The University of Arizona also uses instruments similar to revenue bonds called Certificates of Participation (COPs), for which a specific project serves as the collateral. COPs have a slightly higher interest rate, but they do not put the institution at risk, because they pledge only the building being financed. Furthermore, COPs must be approved by the Board of Regents and reviewed (but not approved) by the legislature. Debt issued through COPs does not reduce the amount of debt that ABOR can issue on behalf of the university in the form of general obligation bonds.

Portland State also must contend with state policy when considering the use of bonds to finance real estate development. Since the Oregon University System must issue the bonds, its board must approve the sale; in addition, state legislative approval is required. The system has two types of bonding authority: Article XI G Bonds, for which the state pays the debt service; and Article XI F Bonds, which place responsibility for debt service with the university for which the bonds were issued. The choice of debt instrument is clearly influenced by policies and decisions made at the state level.

By contrast Wayne State University is solely responsible for its debt service and is able to issue its own bonds and maintain its own credit rating without state involvement in financing decisions. Similarly the University of Pittsburgh, a state-related but not a public university, issues its own bonds according to how much debt it needs and its credit rating allows. About 70 to 75 percent of the university's buildings have been funded through tax-exempt bonds.

State Capital Budget

All public universities in this study also use some state capital funds to finance their real estate acquisition and development. The availability of state funds determines the extent of need for alternative funding mechanisms. In Michigan, public universities submit a five-year capital outlay request to the state each year. Over the last ten years the state funded five or six major projects at Wayne State University, although it did not budget any money for capital expenditures in the past two years. Michigan has a 75/25 rule, which means that for approved capital outlay projects the state provides 75 percent of the cost and the university must finance the remaining 25 percent. The University of Pittsburgh's status as a state-affiliated university allows it to fund real estate acquisition and development through the capital budget of the commonwealth. Each year the university identifies its top ten capital budget priorities and submits them to the state. The governor guarantees a specific amount over a period of time, which allows the university to proceed with its highest priorities; most recently, the university was guaranteed $100 million over five years.

Partnerships Agreements

Partnerships are an increasingly popular way for universities to finance real estate development, and all of the universities in this study worked with private-sector developers or other entities to meet their development objectives. The reasons for doing so varied, but generally were related to funding limitations or policy restrictions that made it difficult for the university to act alone.

The University of Arizona frequently relies on private-sector developers and local foundations as development partners because of its own debt limitations, time delays associated with seeking state approval, and restrictions on where the university can acquire property and how much it can offer. For example the university partnered with the private sector to finance its research park at a site built by IBM as a research and production center. The property was purchased for $98 million, financed by bonds floated by the Arizona Research Park Authority, a nonprofit organization created to help acquire, develop, and finance research parks in the state. IBM agreed to lease back 60 percent of the space in the park for twenty years; the annual lease payments received from IBM are sufficient to repay the annual debt on the bond. At the end of the twenty-year period, the park will belong to the Arizona Board of Regents. The university is now planning a large development around the medical campus and is again looking to partner with a private developer in a lease-back arrangement.

Portland State University provides another interesting example of the benefits of partnering with the private sector. A private company financed and installed the electrical, heating, and telecommunication distribution systems in the building that houses the College of Urban and Public Affairs. The company retained ownership of the equipment and distribution systems, and the university entered into a thirty-year lease for their use. At the end of the lease the university takes ownership.

A new type of partnership arrangement used by universities and private developers to build student housing involves a special-purpose financial entity established solely for this purpose (Brick 2002). The University of Arizona serves as an example. The university obtained permission from ABOR to form the Southern Arizona Capital Facilities Finance Corporation, which operates as a distinct nonprofit entity with the authority to issue tax-exempt bonds. The corporation sold the bonds needed to finance a housing complex, the university leased the land to the corporation, and the corporation hired a private developer to build the complex for a one-time fee. Revenue received from rents is used to repay the debt issued by the corporation and to make payments to the university for the ground lease. The university will take ownership of the building in twenty years. The advantage of this type of arrangement is that the university does not have to cover the cost of development. It is considered "off-balance-sheet financing." The controversy relates to the question of who is ultimately responsible for the debt should revenue fall and default occur. The finance corporation is essentially a creation of the university; however, as a separate legal entity it carries its own debt. Despite concerns by outside financial analysts, this remains a popular financial tool for The University of Arizona and other public universities in the state.

Tax Increment Financing

Tax increment financing (TIF) allows property tax receipts that governments receive from new development in a defined area to be diverted to pay for the area's development costs. Any future growth in property tax revenue is used to pay for the development. Once an area is formally designated as a TIF district, the initial assessed property valuation serves as a baseline. As the area is developed and property values increase, the tax increments (the difference between the initial assessed value and the increased value) pay for the bonds that were issued to finance improvements. Universities may enlist the support of the city in which they are located to establish a TIF district to finance development costs, but the project must involve a public purpose and therefore opportunities are limited.

Marquette was the only university in this study to use TIF. One of the largest efforts of Marquette's redevelopment initiative was Campus Town, the $33 million project that included residential and commercial space. The development organizations charged with managing the effort worked with the City of Milwaukee to arrange for TIF to support the commercial development portion of the project. The TIF was only one source of funding for this project, accounting for about 13 percent of its cost.

Commercial Loans

Most universities do not use commercial loans to finance their real estate acquisition or development, although the organizations working on behalf of Marquette University used standard commercial loans and mortgages to acquire and renovate properties. In several cases they agreed to fifteen- or twenty-year mortgages at market rates, but only where they believed the property would earn a rate of return sufficient to cover mortgage payments.

Endowment Funds and Other University Funds

Some universities, especially those with large endowments, use endowment funds to finance portions of their real estate investments. During the 1960s the University of Pittsburgh's Board of Trustees decided to designate one-half of all unrestricted endowment funds for property acquisition. Recently its endowment funds were used to finance the for-profit portion of a multipurpose academic building otherwise funded by tax-exempt bonds. Marquette University also made a large investment in its redevelopment initiative, committing $9 million of unrestricted funds to get the effort under way.

University-Community Relations

Universities are large and powerful institutions with their own visions and agendas. The real estate acquisition and development activities that support these agendas have an important impact on university-community relations. There is often an expectation that universities should work for the betterment of the surrounding community and that they should be active "civic partners." In many cases universities do make important contributions to the larger community; however, a university's real estate acquisition and development activities often create conflicts that offset those contributions. For each of the universities we studied, effectively managing university-community relations was an important part of the real estate development process.

A university's motivation for development is critical in this context. Marquette University managed to maintain positive relations with the surrounding neighborhood because its efforts involved rehabilitation of neighborhood structures, and most stakeholders believed the university's redevelopment activities would benefit the community. The university was generally able to dispel concerns about gentrification by promising that rents would be held at a rate affordable to neighborhood residents. In contrast The University of Arizona has struggled to establish positive relations with its neighbors who fear encroachment caused by the university's rapid growth.

The character of the physical environment can create challenges and have an important impact on university-community relations. By all accounts Portland State has maintained a very positive relationship with stakeholders in the downtown area surrounding the campus and the city as a whole. Whenever possible the university has used existing buildings to meet its growing needs, and has done so with little displacement of businesses. Neighborhood residents commonly expressed the view that the university has actually contributed to the vitality of downtown.

The importance of leadership in shaping university-community relations was apparent in each of the five case studies, and in all cases the current leadership is believed to be more sensitive to the university's neighbors than previous administrations. Some of this sentiment stems from the realization that a healthy neighborhood is important to the future of the institution and the recognition that information sharing can go a long way toward improving the university-community relations. The University of Pittsburgh's neighbors took a more favorable view as a result of some key changes in administrative processes. The university established a single point of contact to whom neighbors could direct their concerns and thus eliminated internal communication gaps. That individual also was given adequate authority to represent the university and make decisions on its behalf.

While the leaders at the five universities in this study showed varying degrees of sensitivity toward their neighbors, they all recognized the importance of at least informing neighbors about their development plans to avoid speculation. There were no instances where community opposition caused universities to significantly change their overall development agendas; however some specific projects were blocked or concessions were made to satisfy community stakeholders. For example community opposition to The University of Arizona's proposed purchase of an apartment building created such negative public relations that ABOR refused to approve the purchase. The University of Pittsburgh altered design plans on a student housing complex to meet residents' request to have doors face the street rather than an inner courtyard, resulting in the complex being better integrated with the neighborhood.

The extent to which community groups can affect the development process is partly a function of their sophistication. Well-organized groups with highly skilled leaders are better able to exert pressure and more equipped to negotiate with the university. In Tucson, leaders from the neighborhood south of the main campus were able to negotiate a memorandum of understanding with the university that established guidelines for acquisition of properties (with greater specificity than the state-imposed policy relating to acquisition within the planning boundaries). The agreement also defined acceptable and unacceptable land uses for university-owned property within the residential area (Memorandum of Understanding 1996). In contrast the neighborhood north of the campus lacked strong community leadership and the university expanded more rapidly in that direction.

Good communication between the university and community groups can provide benefits for both parties. For example the university can benefit from neighborhood knowledge of the real estate market. A community group in Pittsburgh's Oakland area notified the university of a run-down bar that might be going on the market because they preferred to have the university acquire it rather than another bar owner. The mayor of Pittsburgh believes in empowering the neighborhoods, and his policies encourage collaboration between large institutions and residents affected by their development patterns. Institutions also can create some goodwill with the neighborhood by providing grants for youth programs, workforce training, and facade improvements. The University of Pittsburgh Medical Center, for example, allocates $100,000 annually to fund a residential facade improvement program for the areas surrounding its main medical campus.

University-community relations and the development of trusting and consistent relationships with residents and neighborhood organizations take time. Resentment generated from past wrongs can linger for a long time, and one controversial act by a university can erase years of progress.

Conclusions

This chapter is based on the premise that four key factors influence the real estate acquisition and development practices of universities. Case studies illustrate the importance of the motivation for investment, characteristics of the physical environment surrounding the campus, degree of policy oversight facing the university, and leadership styles and vision of university and civic officials in shaping the development process. Specifically they affect the nature of the decision-making process, type of projects undertaken, financing mechanisms employed, and the dynamics of university-community relations.

Motivation for development—that is, whether to address needs brought by growth or decline—clearly determines the type of projects that universities undertake. The universities experiencing growth in student enrollment tended to focus on classroom, office, research, athletic, and student housing facilities, whereas the one institution motivated by declining enrollment and the need to stabilize its neighborhood concentrated on residential and commercial development. The case studies also demonstrate the impact of motivation on university-community relations. Universities undergoing expansion must contend with neighbors' fears of encroachment, which adds tension to university-community relations. Marquette University had to address concerns about gentrification, but generally had the support of neighborhood residents. Similarly some residents and stakeholders around Wayne State are wary of the university's activities, but support the overall goal of bringing more people to the neighborhood to create a more vital district.

The implications of motivation on decision making and financing may not be as immediately obvious, but are nonetheless important. The parties involved in decision making tended to vary in accordance with the motivation for specific projects. For instance, universities were more likely to involve outsiders in the decision-making process when planning for the development of residential or commercial units than when planning for academic facilities. Marquette University serves as an example of how motivation can have implications for financing. Because the project benefited the public, the city allowed for tax-increment financing, and Marquette was able to leverage funding from local companies and private donors.

The degree of policy oversight varied considerably among the five universities studied. Marquette, Wayne State, and the University of Pittsburgh were guided primarily by internal policies, whereas The University of Arizona and Portland State were subject to policies adopted by statewide governing bodies. The most significant impacts of policy oversight were on the decision-making process and choice of financing. Universities with strict oversight faced lengthy approval processes and were often required to seek approval at various phases of the project and obtain authorization from multiple parties, including both administrative and legislative bodies. The ability to draw upon various funding sources also depended upon the policies that governed the institutions. For example the bonding capacity of The University of Arizona and Portland State was determined not by the bond market but by statewide bodies governing the institutions. Finally, policy oversight can play a role in university-community relations. For example the planning boundaries for The University of Arizona, adopted by the ABOR on behalf of the university, were intended to alleviate tensions with residents and business owners in the surrounding neighborhood by providing greater certainty about the university's acquisition plans.

The physical environment of universities can provide both opportunities and constraints for the development process. The types of projects that universities are able to develop depend in large part on the availability of land in and around the campus. Wayne State has been able to take advantage of underutilized properties in the surrounding neighborhoods to support its development agenda. In contrast The University of Arizona struggles to assemble land in its predominately residential area. The University of Pittsburgh was forced to demolish its football stadium in order to build an events center because large plots of land are scarce in its neighborhood. The physical environment also has a critical impact on university-community relations. Universities located in residential areas, such as The University of Arizona, will likely experience greater difficulty in establishing positive university-community relations. In this respect, the physical environment may also affect the decision-making process. The length of time required to obtain project approval and the parties involved in decision making will often vary depending on how the project is perceived to impact the neighborhood.

The importance of leadership in shaping development agendas was evident for each of the universities studied. The specific projects that were developed depended on motivation, but they also reflected the broader vision of the institutions' leaders. For most of the universities studied, development priorities changed substantially with the introduction of a new administration. The role of leadership in shaping university-community relations was also apparent, depending on how leaders perceived the role of the university in the community. Leadership can also affect the decision-making process by determining the inclusivity or exclusivity of the process, and it can have an influence on project financing by encouraging creative strategies rather than relying on more traditional financing mechanisms. Furthermore, charismatic leaders may be more effective in attracting funding from outside sources.

Examining university real estate investment activities through this framework reveals important connections that affect the acquisition and development process. For example consideration of a university's motivation for development leads to thoughts about university-community relations. Some would argue that universities have an obligation to serve those in surrounding communities, particularly when located in low-income neighborhoods. But the question can be raised as to whether a university can meet both its own needs and the needs of the larger community. This study also drew attention to how characteristics of the physical environment of universities facilitate or limit development and, in part, determine the amount of controversy that accompanies the development process. A review of policies governing real estate acquisition and development revealed that universities often adapt their approaches to circumvent restrictions. Some would credit universities with developing creative financing strategies, while others might be concerned that they are engaging in riskier ventures. The importance of effective leadership was apparent in all aspects of the development process, but especially with respect to university-community relations. Leaders who perceived the university and members of the larger community as civic partners were better able to establish positive relationships with those outside the university and more adequately address concerns involving the institution's development activities.

Universities are key players in the physical development of their communities, and their actions have important implications for the economic well-being of neighborhoods, cities, and regions. It is important to be aware of the factors that affect the development process and understand how they shape what universities are willing and able to do.

Appendix 11.1

The University of Arizona

Jaime Gutierrez
Assistant Vice President, Office of
 Community Relations
The University of Arizona
88 N. Euclid Avenue
Tucson, AZ 85721-0158
Interview: March 11, 2002

David Harris
Assistant Executive Director for
 Financial Affairs and Capital
 Resources
Arizona Board of Regents
2020 North Central Avenue,
 Suite 230
Phoenix, AZ 85004
Interview: March 14, 2002

Mark Homan and Joseph Esposito
Rincon Heights Neighborhood
 Association
1619 E. 8th Street
Tucson, AZ 85719-5518
Interview: March 12, 2002

Melodie Peters
Rincon Heights Neighborhood
 Association
1416 E. 10th Street
Tucson, AZ 85719-5809
Interview: March 12, 2002

Chuck Pettis
Real Estate Consultant
The University of Arizona Foundation
1111 N. Cherry Avenue
Tucson, AZ 85721-0109
Interview: March 11, 2002

Charles Poster
Associate Professor
College of Architecture, Planning
 & Landscape Architecture
Director, Community Planning
 & Design Workshop
Roy P. Drachman Institute
The University of Arizona
819 East First Street
Tucson, AZ 85721-0483
Interview: March 11, 2002

Joel Valdez
Senior Vice President for
 Business Affairs
The University of Arizona
1401 E. University Boulevard
Tucson, AZ 85721-0066
Interview: March 11, 2002

Mercy Valencia
Director, Space Management
The University of Arizona
800 E. University Boulevard,
 Suite 326
Tucson, AZ 85721
Interview: March 12, 2002

Bruce Wright
Associate Vice President, Economic
 Development
Chief Operating Officer, University
 of Arizona Science and
 Technology Park
P.O. Box 210458
Tucson, AZ 85721-9007
Interview: March 13, 2002

Portland State University

Gary Aas
Chief Operating Officer
College Housing Northwest
2121 SW Broadway, Suite 111
Portland, OR 97201
Interview: August 14, 2002

Steve Dotterer
Principal Planner
City of Portland Bureau of Planning
1900 SW Fourth Street, Suite 4100
Portland, OR 97201
Interview: August 13, 2002

Abraham Farkas
Director of Development
Portland Development Commission
1900 SW Fourth Avenue, Suite 7000
Portland, OR 97201
Interview: August 13, 2002

Susan Hartnett
Project Manager
City of Portland Bureau of Planning
1900 SW Fourth Street, Suite 4100
Portland, OR 97201
Interview: August 13, 2002

Jay Kenton
Vice President for Finance and
    Administration
Portland State University
207 Extended Studies Building
Portland, OR 97207-0751
Interview: August 15, 2002

Daniel Potter
Vice President
College Housing Northwest
2121 SW Broadway, Suite 111
Portland, OR 97201
Interview: August 14, 2002

Erika Silver
Vice Chair
Downtown Community Association
P.O. Box 1534
Portland, OR 97207
Interview: August 14, 2002

Nohad Toulan
Dean, College of Urban and Public
    Affairs
Portland State University
POB 751
Portland, OR 97207-0751
Interview: August 15, 2002

Marquette University

Steve Cottingham
Assistant Vice President and
   Counsel
Office of the General Counsel
Marquette University
615 North 11th Street
O'Hara Hall, Rm. 015
Interview: April 2, 2002

Juli Kaufmann
Campus Circle Project (1991–1994)
Executive Director
Village Adult Services, Inc.
Aurora Health Care
336 W. Walnut Street
Milwaukee, WI 53212
Interview: April 1, 2002

Theo Lipscomb
Director of Community Development
West End Development Corporation
3034 W. Wisconsin Avenue
Milwaukee, WI 53208
Interview: April 2, 2002

Patrick LeSage
Director, Campus Circle Project
   (1992–1995)
Principal, Pettibone Group LLC
126 N. Jefferson Street
Milwaukee, WI 53202-6120
Interview: April 2, 2002

June Moberly
Executive Director
Avenues West Association
2040 W. Wisconsin Avenue, Suite 778
Milwaukee, WI 53233
Interview: April 1, 2002

James Sankovitz
Vice President Government Relations
   (1987–1996)
Marquette University
4057 N. Prospect Street
Milwaukee, WI 53211-2121
Interview: April 1, 2002

Allison Semandel
Associate Planner
Department of City Development
City of Milwaukee
809 North Broadway
Milwaukee, WI 53202
Interview: April 1, 2002

Carol Winkel
Director of Community Relations
Marquette University
Holthusen Hall, 419
P.O. Box 1881
Milwaukee, WI 53201-5936
Interview: April 1, 2002

Wayne State University

Marsha Bruhn
Director
City Planning Commission
Coleman A. Young Municipal
  Center
2 Woodward Avenue, Suite 202
Detroit, MI 48226
Interview: August 20, 2002

Andrea Zack Burg
Assistant Director
Design & Construction Services
Wayne State University
5454 Cass Avenue
Detroit, MI 48202
Interview: August 20, 2002

Sue Mosey
President
University Cultural Center
  Association
4735 Cass Avenue
Detroit, MI 48201
Interview: August 19, 2002

Jim Sears
Assistant Vice President
Facilities Planning and Management
Wayne State University
5454 Cass Avenue
Detroit, MI 48202
Interview: August 20, 2002

Michael Solaka
President
New Center Area Council, Inc.
3011 West Grand Boulevard
Detroit, MI 48202
Interview: August 20, 2002

Carol Wells
Director
Community Affairs
Wayne State University
3006 Faculty Administration
  Building
Detroit, MI 48202
Interview: August 20, 2002

University of Pittsburgh

David Blenk
Executive Director
Oakland Planning and Development
  Corporation
235 Atwood Street
Pittsburgh, PA 15213
Interview: November 29, 2001

Sabina Deitrick
Associate Professor
Graduate School of Public and
  International Affairs
University of Pittsburgh
3E25 Posvar Hall
Pittsburgh, PA 15260
Interview: November 16, 2001

Richard Florida
Professor of Regional Economic
  Development
Heinz School of Public Policy
Carnegie Mellon University
4800 Forbes Avenue, Room 2508
Pittsburgh, PA 15213
Interview: November 15, 2001

Martha Garvey
President of the Board
Oakland Planning and Development
Corporation
235 Atwood Street
Pittsburgh, PA 15213
Interview: November 29, 2001

Susan Golomb
Planning Director
City of Pittsburgh
200 Ross Street
Pittsburgh, PA 15219
Interview: November 30, 2001

Scarlet Morgan
Executive Director
Breachmenders Ministries
200 Robinson Street
Pittsburgh, PA 15213
Interview: November 29, 2001

Arthur G. Ramicone
Vice Chancellor Budget and
  Controller
University of Pittsburgh
1817 Cathedral of Learning
Pittsburgh, PA 15260
Interview: November 30, 2001

Eli Shorak
Associate Vice Chancellor for
  Business
University of Pittsburgh
124 Cathedral of Learning
Pittsburgh, PA 15260
Interview: November 16, 2001

Tracy Soska
Co-Director, Community Outreach
  Partnership Center
Director of Continuing Professional
  Specialties, School of Social Work
University of Pittsburgh
2025 Cathedral of Learning
Pittsburgh, PA 15260
Interview: December 4, 2001

John Wilds
Director
Community and Governmental
  Relations
University of Pittsburgh
4227 Fifth Avenue
Pittsburgh, PA 15260
Interview: November 30, 2001

References

Arizona Board of Regents. 1983. *Arizona Board of Regents policy manual.* Available at www.abor.asu.edu/1_the_regents/policymanual/index.html.

Brick, M. 2002. Big deals on campus: Special-purpose entities. *New York Times,* July: Section 3, 6.

Bureau of Planning, City of Portland, Oregon. 1988. *Central City Plan,* August.

Carlson, J. A. 1994. Neighborhood resurrection: Marquette University tackles inner-city redevelopment in Milwaukee. *Chicago Tribune,* April 24.

Farbstein, J., and R. Wener. 1996. *Building coalitions for urban excellence.* Cambridge, MA: Bruner Foundation.

Gallinger, J. 2001. There's something about Oakland: And Pitt projects drive development. *Pittsburgh Business Times*, March 9. Available at http://pittsburgh.bizjournals.com/pittsburgh/stories/2001/03/12/focus5.html.

Memorandum of Understanding Between The University of Arizona, Rincon Heights Neighborhood Association, and City of Tucson. 1996. Available at htttp://w3.arizona.edu/~ cfp/adopted_campus_plans/lrdvp_plans/scap/mou.htm.

Oregon Secretary of State. n.d. *Oregon administrative rules, Oregon University System, Division 50, real property, facility, and campus planning.* Available at http://arcweb.sos.state. or.us/rules/OARS_500/OAR_580/580_050.html.

Portland State University District Partnership for Community Development. 1993. *Vision for a university district: a working concept.*

Schacknew, B. 1999. Couple gives $10 million to Pitt. *Pittsburgh Post-Gazette*, June 23. Available at www.post-gazette.com/regionstate/19990623pitt1.asp/.

Snyder, T., C. Hoffman, and C. Geddes. 1998. U.S. Department of Education, National Center for Education Statistics. *State comparisons of education statistics: 1969–70 to 1996–97* (November). Available at http://nces.ed.gov/pubsearch/pubsinfo.asp?pubid=98018/.

Tijerina, E. S. 1994. Housing work, tot lot planned for West Side. *Milwaukee Journal*, August 17: B1.

The University of Arizona. 1988. *The University of Arizona comprehensive campus plan, April.*

———. 2000. *FY2002-2005 capital improvement plan biennium update.*

Wayne State University. 2001. *2020 Campus master plan.*

12

Leasing for Profit and Control

The Case of Victoria University at the University of Toronto

Larry R. Kurtz

How does a small arts and theological university come to be a major land-owner and commercial landlord in the middle of Toronto, Canada's largest city and Ontario's provincial capital? What does it take to turn university property into endowment real estate? And what impact does the university as developer have on its surrounding community? Some answers to these questions can be found by analyzing three different real estate initiatives of Victoria University. The projects have two common elements: each represents a decision to use property to generate revenue to support the academy rather than for facilities of the university; and each represents a decision to generate revenue by leasing university property rather than by selling it and converting the proceeds to other assets commonly found in endowment portfolios.

By way of general background, Victoria was established by pioneering English Methodists in 1837 in the small town of Cobourg east of Toronto. In 1892 Victoria sought to improve its prospects by moving west and federating with the larger University of Toronto (U of T) on a block of land leased from it on the edge of the Queen's Park, then at the outskirts of Toronto (see Map 12.1). Federation meant an initial pooling and later almost total integration of academic resources, while maintaining independent corporate financial and business structures. The first academic building on Victoria's leasehold block, dating from 1892, is now surrounded by other academic and residential facilities added since 1908. The last readily buildable site on this block was used to construct a 500-seat theater and small office complex that opened in 2001. Victoria today has about 110 faculty fellows and about 3,800 full-time students (of whom some 775 live on campus).

Map 12.1 **Victoria University**

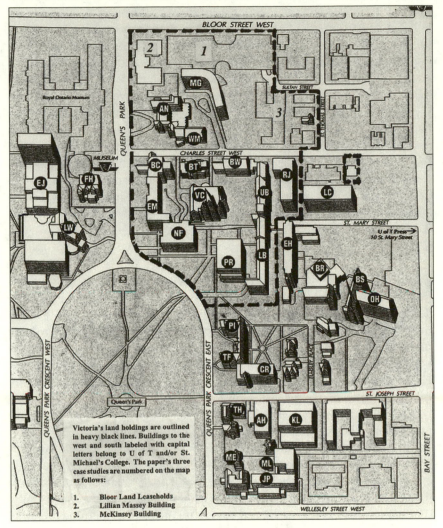

Source: Used by permission of Victoria University in the University of Toronto.

Less than a decade after the move to Toronto, and several years before doing any more building, Victoria's Board of Regents began acquiring additional properties to the north and east, some on a freehold basis and others on a leasehold basis. These properties, acquired from U of T and small private landholders as opportunity offered and in a few cases by gifts or trade, cover an area slightly larger than the original leasehold block. The university itself used all of them at one time for office space, student and family housing, service buildings, and so forth. About half of the actual land on this north block still is devoted to Victoria facilities. The balance, for now, is viewed as endowment real estate serving the university's purposes by generating income.

The change in thinking about how Victoria's property holdings could or should be used evolved gradually. Because Victoria is a church-affiliated institution, it has no direct access to the provincial government grant funding, which is the financial mainstay of most Ontario universities. Thus it has had to look to private sources of support to cover a large proportion of its ongoing operating and capital expenses. In this context it is not surprising that Victoria's board frequently turned its thoughts to the possible exploitation of property assets to bolster the institution's financial position, especially as Toronto's economy boomed, commercial development crowded the edges of the campus, and property values escalated dramatically.

Case Study 1

On July 1, 1960, Victoria executed a 100-year land lease with private interests to allow the building of a mixed-use commercial/residential project on Toronto's Bloor Street West, then developing a reputation as the city's premier shopping district. The site with a street frontage of 480 feet and a depth of 150 feet had been cleared of buildings. The new project was leased to yield a rent at 6 percent of its market value for an initial term of thirty years, with rent thereafter to be revisited every twenty years as a 6 percent function of market value on the renewal dates.[1]

This land, originally owned by U of T, was leased in the 1890s to private individuals who built themselves substantial single-family houses. Starting in the 1920s Victoria began acquiring the leasehold rights to individual properties in this block, and by the late 1940s had gained control of them all. In 1949 Victoria bought freehold title from U of T for $240,000, with a proviso in the title deeds that the lands would be used for educational purposes only; if Victoria later no longer wished to use them for such purposes, U of T would repurchase the lands at the 1949 sale price. No long-term plan for this major parcel of land appears to have informed the decisions to acquire it on a piecemeal leasehold basis, or to negotiate for its conversion to freehold in 1949. If there had been any plan to exploit its commercial potential, it is unlikely that Victoria would have agreed to the restrictive covenant in the 1949 deed. Yet just a decade later the wheels were in motion to do a major commercial lease of this property.

As early as 1950 there are references in board proceedings to the possibility of exploiting this parcel commercially.[2] Unsolicited expressions of interest from private parties to buy or lease provided stimulus to internal discussions about how the property might best serve the university's goals. Board members closest to these discussions were well aware of the restrictive covenants in the 1949 title deeds, and in early 1953 set about getting the U of T to agree to their removal. After an initial rebuff the U of T agreed in 1956, after what appears to have been some informal arm-twisting by Ontario's provincial premier of the day, to issue a quitclaim deed in this regard, opening the door to eventual commercial use.[3]

In the interim the board's Finance and Property Committee in 1955 commissioned a consulting study from a prominent local realtor who, after considering various alternatives for use of the lands, concluded that the immediate annual income was likely to be greater from leasing than selling the land and investing the funds in other assets, noting that leasing would take advantage of increasing capital values over time and act as an inflation hedge.[4] Just a month after receiving this consulting report the board resolved to explore private development of the property. Their explorations, despite success in removing the restrictive covenants in 1956, proceeded slowly, but in 1959 action on this project finally went into high gear.

Since commercial use of the Bloor lands would require a zoning change from the prevailing residential and institutional permissions then in effect, the chairman of the board in June 1959 directed staff to work on a rezoning to allow the same commercial uses as the lands across the street and down the block to the east. Within a month Victoria's solicitors had made the requisite rezoning application to the City of Toronto's Committee on Buildings and Development.

An outside valuation report dated September 30, 1959, recommended that the property be listed for lease at "a rental based on $35 sq.ft. on the 72,000 sq.ft., which produces a value of $2,520,000 and at 6% represents a net rental of $151,200." The report went on to say "an aggressive campaign of canvassing and advertising in Toronto and other cities should be made to produce a lease or leases."[5] The board soon thereafter approved a recommendation of its Finance and Property Committee to take immediate steps to lease the property on the terms recommended.

Plans to use these lands as endowment real estate were proceeding even as Victoria was laying ambitious plans for new facilities of its own. A women's residence was started before the Bloor leases were assured. A new library and a new administrative and faculty office building would follow within a few years. All of these projects would shrink the remaining supply of land for future buildings. Nonetheless, in those more deferential times there appears to have been no significant opposition from students, faculty, or alumni to the board's planning for these lands to generate commercial revenue.[6] The availability of other sites to accommodate planned university facilities and the prospect of new revenue from a land lease to help pay for them no doubt helped in this regard. Nearby property owners were evidently happy to see Victoria's stretch of Bloor Street develop commercially. The only recorded opposition to the rezoning application came from the city's planning commissioner who was overruled at the political level. On December 2, 1959, Toronto's *Globe and Mail* reported as follows:

> Under a zoning change approved yesterday by the Toronto Planning Board, a 25-story office building with more than twice the floor space at the new city hall could be built on the south side of Bloor St. east of Queen's Park. The board approved a request from Victoria (University) to rezone a strip of its property to C1V4, the highest commercial density allowed, despite a warning from Planning Commissioner M.V. Lawson that there was no justification for rezoning to C1V4. (He) said that the high density requested by the university appeared to be out of proportion to possible demand.

By the time of the board's meeting of April 21, 1960, an outside consulting report was in hand recommending a lease to a consortium of three local businessmen, one of whom was the owner of a small hotel nearby.[7] While there were three other bidders, none apparently was prepared to pay the land rent requested. Even before the meeting's formal approval to proceed, however, the lessees were working with Victoria to secure another zoning variance, this time to permit a mixed-use commercial/residential project on the land that was now officially rezoned for commercial uses only. The lessees had concluded that the highest and best use would be a mixed-use project with a substantial residential rental component. The prevailing orthodoxy of local planners at the time did not welcome such mixed uses (i.e., people living above stores or in commercial areas). Approval for a second zoning change was nonetheless given by the Ontario Municipal Board[8] on June 10, 1960, even though this variance also was opposed by the city's planning commissioner, who gave evidence at the hearings to the effect that he did not believe a mixed residential/commercial development was practical in Toronto, and that existing bylaws in any case had no provisions to cover this situation.

Two buildings were later constructed: a twelve-story office tower with ground-floor retail space; and a mixed-use building with three floors of office and high-end retail space (Chanel, Prada, and Max Mara are among the current tenants) and eleven floors of luxury rental apartments. The latter is now listed as a local heritage building precisely because it blazed a trail for other mixed-use commercial/residential developments in modern Toronto, bringing people to live in high-density commercial areas.

Notions about what constitutes good urban planning and zoning bylaws to safeguard the public interest obviously evolve over time. While the decision to seek this additional variance was driven by the lessees' market sense about what would maximize return rather than any university sensibilities about progressive urban planning, Victoria's willingness to cooperate with the lessees to challenge the conventional planning wisdom of the day had an entirely salutary influence on the direction of future urban development in Toronto.

Since this was the first of Victoria's commercial real estate ventures and now has a track record of more than four decades, it is worth taking stock of the decision to lease rather then sell. Nothing in the statutes by which Victoria is governed prevents it from selling land, but there is nothing in the formal records of the board or its committees indicating there was ever a direct or extended debate on this lease versus sale question, which at several points in the 1950s appeared to be entirely open. Professional advice given to the board in 1955 did suggest that leasing was likely to yield more revenue than selling. The consultants assumed that the probable alternative investments would be heavily tilted to fixed-income securities then typical of university endowments (long-term bond and mortgage rates at the time were in the 5 to 6 percent range).

We know that continued ownership of the land asset was seen to have the additional advantage of being a hedge against inflation; that pursuit of any scheme to sell the land would likely have met some active opposition in the board[9]; that Victoria decision makers were well aware that other commercial and high-density residential rental projects were then being undertaken on leased land sites in Toronto[10]; and that the potential uses of the site and consequently its market value would not have been materially affected by offering it only on a leasehold basis.

Was leasing the better choice? Long before the first thirty-year term was up, and with inflation soaring in the late 1970s and early 1980s, many wondered. Cumulative ground rent paid up to 1990 was just $4.5 million. But when the market value of the lands was reassessed in 1990, rents as a 6 percent function of market value for the next twenty-year term jumped from $151,000 to $3.653 million per year. Securing this increase required a lengthy arbitration followed by court proceedings when the tenants launched (ultimately unsuccessful) legal appeals against the arbitrators' findings. After the rent increase in 1990, the rent over forty-one years (through 2001) totaled $44.7 million.

If the land had been sold at 1960 market value and the proceeds invested in the Toronto Stock Exchange (TSE) 300 Index, used here as a proxy for the most aggressive alternative investment that might then have been considered by a Canadian endowment fund, the cumulative payout would have been some $9.2 million over thirty years and $17.5 million over the forty-one years to 2001 (i.e., assuming the capital in the initial index purchase had been held whole against inflation as measured by the consumer price index and total index returns over this time were achieved at a constant or annualized rate). We cannot know the future TSE 300 Index return, but the lease provides that the rent going forward in the next renewal period cannot be less than what is now being paid, so there is downside protection against the possibility of declining realty values. Because land rent under the lease terms cannot be subordinated to any other claims on the property and nonpayment triggers default, the current rent is virtually guaranteed into the future.

Except for the time and cost of the proceedings to reset rents from 1990, this investment to date has required little effort by Victoria as lessor, apart from scrutiny of the lessees' periodic renovation plans, mortgage refinancings, and changes in ownership structure over time. Where this scrutiny has required outside legal or other professional help, the lessees have paid the costs. The buildings on site and their tenants form part of a varied, urbane backdrop to the campus with almost no friction between town and gown.

From hindsight, we would write land leases differently today with much more frequent rent review dates, perhaps at five- or ten-year intervals; in 1960 commercial and residential mortgages with thirty-year fixed terms were still commonplace. Nonetheless the leases struck in 1960 are widely seen as far-sighted investments (especially after the stock market meltdown of 2002), producing excellent returns and giving a future generation a chance to rethink how this property abutting the campus can best serve the university. The relative illiquidity of the land asset has removed that temptation to dip into capital in difficult times, which can occur when highly liquid paper securities are the asset at hand.

Case Study 2

With one successful foray into commercial property development behind them, Victoria's board spent the next two decades acquiring additional small property holdings nearby and, at intervals, considering more unsolicited offers to develop university land and possible realty initiatives of their own to increase revenue. The second actual development initiative came in 1979 when Victoria "inherited" a three-story, neoclassic academic building of some 50,000 square feet, containing a faded gymnasium, classrooms, kitchen/laboratories, faculty offices, and a disused swimming pool under its rear courtyard. The building was located at a prominent intersection just west of the Bloor Street lands leased in 1960 and bordered by other Victoria properties to its south. Built in 1908 as a School of Household Science for U of T, which owned the land under it, the building was a gift of an heiress of the former Massey agricultural machinery empire. The donor, whose family also had been major benefactors to Victoria, specified that if the school should ever be closed, U of T would have the option of "purchasing" the building by making a cash payment to Victoria approximating its then market value, or selling the land under it to Victoria (also at market value).

Neither Victoria nor U of T had any practical academic use for the structure at that time. From the outset of negotiations about the eventual fate of the property there were differences about the respective market values of the land and the building. Victoria was initially reluctant to contemplate buying the land because of the cash outlay required and considered simply accepting cash for its claim to the building. U of T wanted to pursue the sale of both land and building to a third party, giving Victoria that portion of the proceeds attributable to the building's value. The terms of the donor's bequest had spelled out arbitration provisions in the event U of T and Victoria could not themselves agree on values. Perhaps fearing that a final cash payout for the building would yield less than hoped, Victoria proposed that the two institutions jointly find a tenant, lease the building for a period of fifteen to twenty-five years and split the net revenue in order to keep long-term control of the property in university hands. When U of T's hope for a quick third-party offer to buy the property did not materialize and they turned down Victoria's proposal for a joint leasehold venture, Victoria decided to buy the land and try to finance the acquisition by leasing the building itself. Although the building had style and an eminently commercial location, it was zoned for institutional uses only.

While negotiations over land price dragged on, a government agency decided to rent most of the space in the building. Victoria then undertook major renovations to adapt the space for institutional office uses and the tenant moved in on February 1, 1981. Another leasehold followed for the balance of the space, and a second government tenant took occupancy on April 1, 1982. The cost of leasehold improvements was $2.6 million; coupled with a land purchase price of $1.7 million (finally agreed in a 1982 settlement), Victoria's out-of-pocket investment to gain control of the property and make improvements totaled some $4.3 million. Part of the agreement on price was that U of T, in the event the property were ever to be sold by Victoria, would receive 50 percent of any increase in land value attributable to any subsequent rezoning permitting additional density on the site.

By the early 1990s the smaller of the two government agencies had outgrown its premises and gave notice to vacate, at a time when local office vacancy rates were approaching 15 percent and rents had plummeted.

Fortunately the space vacated comprised only part of the overall leaseable space in the building and it had direct access from Bloor Street, by now Toronto's most fashionable shopping precinct. Nonetheless the institutional zoning on the property and the lack of demand for office space at the time meant that the premises vacated would sit idle for almost two years before being leased again as commercial retail space. The institutional zoning in the university area did allow for a limited range of commercial uses, such as banks, retail stores, or bookshops seen as serving the campus community, provided such premises did not occupy more than 5,000 square feet of space in the building. To lease 6,500 square feet of vacant main-floor space for one of the permitted commercial uses required a zoning variance from Toronto's Committee of Adjustment. City planners, recognizing that long-term preservation of heritage buildings may require some flexibility in their uses, were helpful in securing the variance needed.[11]

Negotiations to relet the vacant space as commercial premises proceeded in tandem with the zoning variance processes. The new tenant would be Club Monaco, a trendsetting and growing fashion retailer with more than 100 stores in Canada, the United States, and the Far East. The company wanted space in the neoclassic building with its high-profile location to create a Toronto flagship store. They accepted the space on an as-is basis and agreed to make all leasehold improvements and pay Victoria market rates for retail space, which were significantly higher than local office rents. Their renovations opened up a cluttered floor plan, reclaimed the disused swimming pool as store space, and won them a local heritage award for "sensitive insertion of a retail store into a heritage structure"[12]

In a second round of zoning negotiations with city officials a few years later, Victoria was successful in getting commercial zoning permissions for the entire building by signing a formal heritage preservation agreement[13] for the building's exterior for a twenty-year period, and agreeing that any further retail expansion in the building take its access from Bloor, the commercial street where the building's secondary entrance was then located. The main entrance around the corner is directly opposite one of Canada's most important museums and close to other institutions such as the provincial parliament at Queen's Park. This newly won commercial designation for the entire building then allowed Victoria's remaining government tenant to surrender some office space in a time of public-sector cost cutting. That space was simultaneously taken up by Club Monaco (now a wholly owned subsidiary of Ralph Lauren, Inc.); the firm currently rents all three floors and basement of the building's north wing (about 40 percent of the building).

In this second venture into using university property as endowment real estate, Victoria had two options: buy the land on opportunity and lease the building to pay the cost of acquisition and improvements in order to gain control of a key corner of a major city block owned almost entirely by Victoria, or see the property sold into other hands by U of T, albeit with Victoria sharing in the proceeds. While the move to close the School of Household Science had generated some controversy within U of T, particularly among alumnae of its programs, there was no opposition within the Victoria community to treating it as endowment real estate because the property had not previously belonged to or been used by Victoria.

In this case Victoria is the landlord and property manager to office and retail tenants, with direct exposure to their financial health and market success. Such exposure is mitigated by the quality of the government tenant's covenant and by Club Monaco's agreement to rent on an as-is basis and convert outdated institutional space to first-class retail space at its own expense. In a worst-case scenario, if the retail tenant defaults the leasehold improvements remain for the landlord's benefit; the risk of default is itself minimized because the retail tenant has a major immovable investment in the building.

In private hands this property would long since have been under pressure for higher-density commercial redevelopment. Indeed there have been unsolicited approaches in this regard. Both Victoria and the community benefit from preservation of a low-rise historic building in this particular urban context, and the municipality gains property tax revenues from its commercial use, which would not obtain if the property were being used directly by the university or other tax-exempt institutions.

Net annual income over the first ten years represented a return of between 6 and 7 percent on Victoria's original out-of-pocket investment. With significantly higher rents today, and with the cost of the original improvements fully amortized over twenty years, the net annual dollar income is now more than 2.5 times that obtained in the 1980s. Apart from this income Victoria has the benefit of knowing that as early as 2006 it could reclaim some 60 percent of the building for its own institutional uses if its nearer-term priorities suggest such a course, and it could reclaim the balance of the building from Club Monaco in 2015.[14] None of the leases written for these premises over the years has ever exceeded twenty years, even with renewal options.

Case Study 3

Over several decades Victoria consolidated its hold on a sizable rectangular block at the northeast fringe of its campus bounded by three city streets and a Victoria playing field. On part of that block sat an unsightly (but profitable) surface parking lot. The larger part of the block was occupied by a series of

aging turn-of-the-century townhouses and a pair of low-grade service buildings. Victoria's board decided in 1987 that these properties were surplus to
any current institutional needs. They executed an agreement to lease the site
to a developer (selected in an invitational competition) and set about securing zoning amendments to permit mixed-use commercial/residential development. The rezoning process became a messy political exercise when student
opposition to commercial development of the lands surfaced after the agreement to lease had been signed. It took more than three years to be resolved,
from 1987, when local realty markets were thriving, to early 1991, when
they were nearly comatose.[15] The developer, who proposed to build a 270-
room luxury hotel, was given extra time by Victoria to wait out the market
downturn in exchange for removing all conditions on his leasehold deposit.
Ultimately he defaulted with nothing built, forfeiting a $2 million deposit in
its entirety.

With a partial recovery in commercial real estate in the mid-1990s, Victoria
began anew the search for a development partner to take advantage of the
market potential of this block. In late January 1997 a chance encounter brought
to the door the Toronto partners of McKinsey and Co. Inc., a prominent international management consulting firm, looking for a site to build an "office
of the future." In a series of blue-sky discussions with their staff and a local
architect who had previous experience working on major university research,
college, and library facilities, the McKinsey partners determined that they
would like something that looked and felt like a college building, located on
or adjacent to a university campus if possible. Within little more than six
months Victoria and McKinsey reached agreement on major business terms,
approved design and development drawings, hired construction managers,
and began demolition of three small structures on site. Excavation and construction work began in earnest at the end of 1997, and McKinsey moved
into its new Toronto offices in June 1999.

This time around there was no serious opposition to commercial development, either inside or outside Victoria, in part perhaps because the scale of
the building proposed was much reduced from the earlier hotel plans. The
new facility is a 60,000-square-foot, modernist, three-story structure in stone
and glass with teak windows, a sky-lighted atrium, one level of underground
parking, and a walled garden, sited at the eastern edge of a Victoria playing
field. The university's board and internal community see this project as a
possible college building-in-waiting, and are especially pleased with that
prospect given several glowing architectural reviews and awards the building has received since its opening.

Designed to McKinsey's specifications, the project was built by an established construction management firm under contract to Victoria, which secured

construction and takeout financing from the university's banker. McKinsey is leasing the building for an initial fifteen-year term and is paying annual net rents sufficient to amortize the entire capital and interest cost of the project over that period. Thereafter, they have three five-year renewal options at pre-set annual net rents. At the end of thirty years (at the latest), use of the building reverts to Victoria.

This third venture in endowment real estate raised several issues for Victoria, but the sale/lease debate for this site took place long before McKinsey's representatives came calling. As early as 1986 Victoria's board had hired professional planning consultants to do a site-plan study for the commercial possibilities of this northeast corner of its landholdings. The consultants suggested that mixed-used commercial/residential uses would probably be the easiest to achieve in political and zoning terms, and would likely also maximize the site's land value. But to capitalize on the residential potential of the site, the possibility of selling a portion of the property was to be left open for discussion. This aspect of the report was the only one the board saw fit to change. After reservations about the sale option were voiced, the board voted to delete any mention of a possible sale, even a portion of the site. The consultants had explained that if any sale of land was entirely ruled out, Victoria might well compromise the residual land value for up to two-thirds of the site's density potential. The reason for this had to do with the market's keen interest in condominium sites and almost complete lack of interest in sites for residential rental buildings; condominiums could not at that time be built in Ontario on leased land.

McKinsey's approach did not require revisiting the possibility of sale, because the company had no interest in buying the land. The original hope was to craft a land lease in which some developer would be the actual lessee and would construct facilities that McKinsey would rent. Victoria was entirely prepared to lease land for the sort of building proposed, but the McKinsey project would not require all of the available site—an L-shaped plot about two-thirds of which bordered a midblock playing field and the remaining third having a valuable corner exposure. McKinsey wanted the midblock part of the site, desirable because it abutted the playing field, but in some respects the least interesting part of the site from the standpoint of having a conventional commercial address. After considerable discussion about splitting the parcel into two pieces, Victoria's board agreed in principle to lease the midblock portion and take its chances on a later redevelopment of the remaining smaller corner site.[16] Negotiations then began with respect to a suitable land rent formula.

Meanwhile McKinsey's hope of finding a commercial developer to realize its office building stalled, in part at least because the firm wanted options for a lease of up to thirty years, but the ability to leave after twelve years, on suitable notice, if their business needs changed. Given the highly particular single-tenant building they had in mind, the somewhat unusual location for a commercial office building, and the relatively short time frame (twelve years) to which they were prepared to commit absolutely, no commercial developer appeared ready to take on the project.

In these circumstances the question for Victoria was whether it would itself assume an active developer's role. From the outset McKinsey's covenant to pay rent for at least twelve years looked very solid to all concerned, including Victoria's and McKinsey's separate bankers, both of whom were prepared to lend Victoria money to finance the project, and indeed competed to do so. The only significant risk to Victoria appeared to be the possibility that McKinsey might exercise an option to vacate after twelve years, leaving Victoria with many years of mortgage payments still to go to pay for the project, and no guarantee of a replacement tenant.

The way out of this dilemma was a lease in which rent payments were in a sense front-end loaded. McKinsey agreed to pay level annual net rents adequate to amortize the building fully in just fifteen years, rents that on a square-foot basis were as high as almost any in the city, and well above the going rate for first-class office space in Victoria's midtown neighborhood when the project was started. If the tenant were to leave after twelve years, Victoria would have just three years of amortization payments remaining to be free and clear of any debt on the project. Because net annual rent payable in the first five-year renewal term (i.e., after the initial fifteen years) is substantially lower than rent now being paid, there is a considerable incentive built into the lease for McKinsey to stay on and profit from the front-end loading of rents in the first fifteen years. Should the tenant nonetheless leave after twelve years, Victoria will have the option of renting to another commercial tenant on entirely new terms, or using the building itself. In any event three years of uncovered amortization payments are a known and manageable burden because interest rates on the borrowed funds are guaranteed for a fifteen-year term.

In this case the tenant has chosen to do its own property management, including custodial, maintenance, and grounds services, and pays municipal property and business taxes directly. Now that the project is up and running, Victoria's ongoing role as developer and landlord is minimal. The university and local community benefit from an attractive new midblock public walkway separating the building from the adjacent playing field.

This development project required Victoria to take a long-term view on financial return because the tenant's rent for fifteen years is devoted entirely to amortizing the cost of the building; only when this ambitious amortization schedule is ended will the university enjoy the benefit of rent that it can treat as disposable income. This aspect of the lease arrangement was, however, seen as a way of mitigating significant risk for a future generation in the event the tenant exercises its option to leave after twelve years; it would have been possible to extend the amortization term to twenty or twenty-five years, for example, and in doing so take some portion of the current rental income stream as a land rent from the outset for immediate operational priorities.

Conclusion

The three cases detailed above suggest that Victoria has created, in opportunistic fashion, a sizable endowment real estate portfolio from properties it acquired more by acquisitive, expansionist instinct than any conscious decision to invest in real estate per se. Properties acquired to secure possible future needs, or simply to ensure control of development on Victoria's periphery, have themselves acquired the status of a quasi-sacred trust in the university's internal mythology. This makes any discussions of sale fraught with emotion in a way that seldom obtains in discussions about the relative merits of holding or selling assets in a securities endowment portfolio.

Fortunately for Victoria its center-city location has allowed it to turn property assets to financial advantage by leasing; sale was not required to realize respectable investment returns. Ownership allows the university to control what gets built at the edges of its campus, and if future academic priorities suggest physical expansion it will have some options at hand.

Finally, the income stream from Victoria's endowment real estate, given the nature of the leaseholds in it, has come to be recognized as having many of the characteristics of yields from a fixed-income portfolio. This recognition in turn has recently led to changes in the asset mix of Victoria's securities endowment, boosting equity allocations to some 75 percent (at the expense of fixed-income allocations) because the stability of its realty income stream can serve as a counterbalance to the variability of returns inherent in seeking higher yields with equities.

Notes

1. All information on property transactions, leasehold terms, and revenue streams is derived from property and financial records maintained by the Bursar's Office, Victoria University.

2. All references to proceedings and decisions of the Victoria University Board of Regents and its various committees, consulting reports they commissioned, and correspondence are taken from formal minutes and papers filed with them lodged in the United Church and Victoria University Archives in Toronto.

3. A letter of February 2, 1953, from O.D. Vaughan for U of T to Leopold MacCaulay, then chairman of Victoria's board, indicates that U of T's board was not at all happy with the request to waive the restrictive covenant and reminded Victoria it had agreed to a repurchase clause in the event it no longer wished to use the lands for academic purposes. Accompanying MacCaulay to make the request for waiver was E.W. Bickle, a well-connected member of Victoria's board who regularly hosted Ontario's provincial premier, The Hon. Leslie Frost, at Sunday dinner in his home (interview with Mrs. W. Wilder, Bickle's daughter). Bickle's next-door neighbor, Henry E. Langford, was active in the board's affairs in the early 1950s and chairman when the 1960 lease was agreed. His son Alex Langford, later also very active as a Victoria board member, avers that it took behind-the-scenes intervention by Frost to convince authorities at U of T to give way and allow Victoria to serve the federated university cause by using the lands to generate revenue rather than for academic facilities in a narrow sense.

4. For full details see the report of W.H. Bosley, October 5, 1955 (filed with Board of Regents papers in the United Church and Victoria Archives in Toronto). Bosley was in the 1950s and remains today a prominent local realty firm.

5. Report from the Real Estate Department, The Chartered Trust Company, which had been commissioned to give advice to Victoria and were subsequently appointed as the university's agents to market the property on a leasehold basis.

6. Board and committee minutes of discussions record no serious opposition, and Victoria's president of the day, Dr. A.B.B. Moore, remembers none of consequence apart from a few students who suggested the land might better be used to create a green park (interview with Dr. A.B.B. Moore).

7. For details see the report of February 15, 1960, from the Real Estate Department, The Chartered Trust Company.

8. The Ontario Municipal Board is a quasi-judicial agency with power to rule on appeals against planning decisions by municipal councils in Ontario. Victoria and its lessees were the appellants in this case.

9. At the board meeting of April 11, 1957, when commercial development of the lands was under discussion, one prominent member of the board, Mrs. Clara F. McEachren, wanted it officially noted that she was "utterly and completely opposed to selling any part of the Bloor St. frontage." She had grown up in her family's mansion just a block away at the edge of Queen's Park. The board chairman of the day, Henry E. Langford, was a firm advocate of leasing. He had met the Duke of Westminister on a visit to London and been much impressed with the duke's fortunes in property and his advice never to sell land (interview with Alex Langford, son of H.E. Langford).

10. Donald Mills, part of the legal team that drafted the leases for Victoria, had worked on a major commercial leasehold development just across the street from these lands only a short time earlier (interview with Donald Mills). That legal team also included his father, Ralph Mills, who later served as chairman of Victoria's board (1962–1970).

11. Victoria had over the previous decade built a store of good will with Toronto heritage and planning officials in the course of considerable work to restore and preserve three significant heritage structures in the inventory of its own campus buildings.

12. Citation from Heritage Toronto Award of Merit, June 9, 1997.

13. Historic designation of a building by city authorities in Ontario does not guarantee preservation; it provides for a period of delay if the owner of a designated

property seeks to demolish or make unsympathetic changes, during which time local officials can insist that all avenues to advance preservation be explored. Heritage preservation agreements are frequently the price a property owner pays in exchange for zoning concessions being sought in respect of commercial use and/or additional density permissions.

14. While the leasehold rental payments applicable to Victoria's Bloor Street lands detailed in Case Study 1 above are a matter of public record because of the parties' resort to arbitration and court proceedings in the early 1990s, lease rents and other business terms in this instance, as with the McKinsey case that follows, are described only in very general terms to respect commercial confidences.

15. Victoria from the outset worked with city planning officials and gained their cooperation in issuing a positive planning report recommending the zoning and official plan changes permitting higher density and commercial use permissions being sought by the university. The Toronto City Council initially approved the planners' recommendations in principle, but later, after student opposition surfaced and a municipal election intervened, refused the changes sought. Victoria appealed the decision to the Ontario Municipal Board and, with the help of city planners who were subpoenaed to testify on Victoria's behalf, won the case.

16. Victoria has since obtained formal zoning approvals to permit a luxury hotel or residential building of 125 rooms or suites on this corner site, and in the spring of 2003 issued a request for proposals with the hope of finding a development partner to build out this corner property on a land-lease basis. Victoria is now working with a prominent local developer to obtain rezoning permissions for a new luxury rental building on the site.

13

The Little Fish Swallows the Big Fish

Financing the DePaul Center in Chicago

Kenneth McHugh

In the late autumn of 1988, DePaul University in Chicago was well along its path toward transformation from the "little school under the El tracks" to its position as the largest Catholic and ninth largest private university in the nation. DePaul had experienced continuous enrollment growth since the 1970s, mostly at its two major campuses in Chicago—the Loop Campus downtown and the Lincoln Park Campus in a neighborhood experiencing gentrification on the city's North Side. Driven by a state-of-the-art enroll-ment management function, on-campus housing on the Lincoln Park Cam-pus had tripled, with the building crane replacing the Blue Demon as that campus's mascot. However, the university's response to growth on the down-town Loop Campus had been less effective.

The Loop Campus was home to the university's central administration, and more than 8,900 students were enrolled in the four colleges at that loca-tion: College of Law, College of Commerce, School for New Learning (for adults returning to earn degrees), and the Computer Science Department of DePaul's College of Liberal Arts and Sciences. The total administrative and academic space contained in the three buildings of the Loop Campus—the Administration Center, O'Malley, and Lewis buildings—was 568,000 square feet (see Map 13.1). The university had adopted a facilities master plan for the Loop Campus, which provided for renovation of the existing buildings into new and modern facilities. However, the master plan was deficient; it could not be implemented because there was no flexibility in the existing campus space, nor was there readily available rental space in the area to allow the university to begin a staging operation for the implementation of the master plan (*The DePaulia* 1989). This chapter discusses the unique op-portunity and financing plan that allowed DePaul to overcome these chal-lenges and expand its Loop Campus.

Map 13.1 **DePaul University**

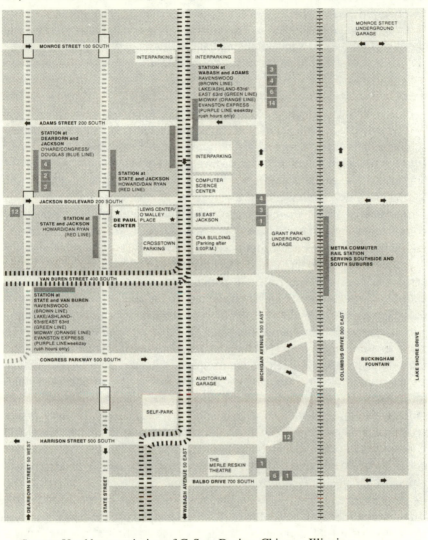

Source: Used by permission of G-Spot Design, Chicago, Illinois.

The Building

Out of a window in the office of DePaul's then president, the Reverend John T. Richardson, one had a clear view into the abandoned and deteriorating Goldblatt Department Store. The building, abandoned for more than a decade, had once been a proud member of the "battleship" department stores that flanked State Street, Chicago's "Great Street" for downtown retail. Constructed in 1911 as the Rothschild Department Store and designed by Holabird and Roche, the building contained more than 700,000 square feet, including basement space. The structure stretched a full city block from Jackson Boulevard to Van Buren Street along State Street in Chicago's South Loop. Each of the first ten floors contained 50,000 square feet and the eleventh floor added 37,500 square feet. It was placed on the list of buildings on the National Register of Historic Places in 1989.

A downturn in Chicago's economy in the 1970s led to the closure of some of its grand State Street department stores so that by the early 1980s the Goldblatt Building had been empty and deteriorating for a decade, while the City of Chicago pondered its future. In 1982 Mayor Jane Byrne, with the city council's approval, purchased the building for $10 million and designated it as the site for the city's new central library.

By 1986 the city had a new mayor, and politics and public opinion were complicating the project. The city had spent almost $15 million preparing the building for conversion and faced a projected $80 million in additional expenses to complete the project. Mayor Harold Washington, saddled by the project he had inherited from the previous administration, said "Let's go ahead and make the best we can on a bad deal, but don't forget who did it to us" (Strong 1986). By the summer of 1986 the *Chicago Sun-Times* and the Union League Club had mounted a negative public opinion campaign against using the site for the central library. Joseph Cardinal Bernadin and A Better Government Association joined that campaign (Camper, Kass, and Crimmins 1986). The negative sentiment grew from fears that the building was structurally unsound for use as a library, that the renovation would cost $121 million, $17 million more than originally projected, and that the city deserved a better site and building for its central library (Camper, Kass, and Crimmins 1986). Finally, at the end of that year, the Chicago Public Library Board voted unanimously to build the library on city-owned land one block away from the Goldblatt site.

The change in plans finally led the city to seek a buyer for the Goldblatt Building in 1988, opening the door for DePaul to purchase the building (Houston 1988). To assist the university in studying the feasibility of acquiring and using the building, the university established a "blue ribbon committee" made up of trustees, civic leaders, and real estate experts to help it formulate a plan (DePaul University 1988b).

The resulting plan proposed a vertical subdivision of the building into three distinct uses. Approximately 300,000 square feet of the building on floors 6, 7, 8, 9, and 10, and three quarters of the building's penthouse would house DePaul's Graduate School of Business, a student union, the central library for the College of Commerce, additional classroom space, and a conference center. To provide the expansion space that the university required to address its growth, the plan would link the Goldblatt Building to DePaul's current academic facilities via a series of sky bridges linked to the Lewis-O'Malley complex (DePaul University 1988a). Floors 2, 3, 4, and 5 and a portion of the basement would serve as commercial office space for the rental market. The third mixed-use element dedicated 75,000 square feet on the first floor to incorporate light retailing into the cultural and educational district of South State Street, which was promoted by the State Street Plan, a blueprint for area development created by civic leaders. The remaining space accommodated the mechanical systems of the building as well as certain maintenance functions and general storage.

University administrators worked with the city to create a new subdivision called the McHugh Re-subdivision to facilitate the DePaul Center Development. Using architectural drawings as a guide, a survey was prepared, dividing the facility into separate pin numbers that would accommodate the horizontal and vertical adjacencies necessary to construct and operate a mixed-use facility. It was important that the ownership mechanism accommodate both for-profit and not-for-profit uses. The result was the creation of three separate functions within the building: an academic building, a commercial office building, and a retail center.

A total project budget, covering hard construction costs, soft costs, and land acquisition costs, was set at $70 million dollars (Long and Spielman 1991). The real estate experts who served on the blue-ribbon committee assisted in the establishment of the budget and made sure that it contained a generous developer fee, which was later eliminated in the value engineering process. A number of individuals interpreted the size of the budget as an indication that the project was not feasible for DePaul (*The DePaulia* 1989). One notable DePaul trustee memorably described the project as "the little fish trying to swallow the big fish." Therefore, while the mixed-use facility envisioned in the early planning phase appeared to be the ideal solution for DePaul's space needs, it could only move forward with an equally creative financing plan.

The Financing Plan

Purchase Price

The first focus of the financial plan was to make a decision as to the purchase price. This became a matter of substantial debate, since the City of Chicago had paid an estimated $10 million for the building and had spent considerable amounts of additional money studying the facility for use as the central library. In the course of the debate, three different strategies for determining the purchase price emerged. The first was to make the city whole by offering what it had invested into the building, with a possible reduction justified by the loss in value during the city's ownership, including loss associated with not heating the building over the harsh Chicago winters. This strategy was quickly abandoned when it was determined that keeping the city whole plus the projected cost of renovation exceeded the cost of new construction on the land, if acquired at market value after the building was demolished.

The second approach was to offer what the development community had been proposing—the fair market value of the land after demolition of the building. The value of raw land in the South Loop ranged from $200 to $300 a square foot at that time; additionally it was argued that the building had a negative value to be deducted from the value of the land to arrive at a fair market purchase price. This approach also failed to provide the necessary purchase price to make the plan work.

The third method argued that because of the historical nature of the building and the public opposition to demolishing it, the purchase price should be reduced not by demolition costs, but by renovation costs. Due to the poor maintenance and high renovation costs, and the need to save the building, a case was made that the site had little value.

After carefully analyzing all three strategies for determining a purchase price and considering the likelihood that someone could acquire the site and demolish the building in the face of mounting public opposition, the university decided that the financing plan should contain a purchase price offer indicating that the university would be undertaking a significant risk to place this historic building back into service (Davis 1988; *Chicago Sun-Times* 1989; DePaul University 1989). Additionally, DePaul administrators felt that the purchase price should reflect the university's past, present, and future commitment to the citizens of Chicago. Underscoring the university's credibility was the fact that DePaul's campuses had remained a stabilizing force in the South Loop and in Lincoln Park in past eras when these neighborhoods were blighted. This legacy allowed DePaul to make a strong statement regarding the university's willingness to partner with city officials and with city residents in the restoration of this historic building (DePaul University 1989).

To reflect those critical points, the purchase price had three elements. The first was a cash payment that would make a statement with regard to the university's good-faith commitment without creating a burden on the overall project budget. It was determined that a payment of $1 million in cash upon the closing of the transaction would make such a statement.

To demonstrate the university's confidence that the building could be restored not only within the predetermined budget, but also after value engineering could produce a savings to the budget, the university agreed to share expected cost savings with the City of Chicago as part of the overall price of the building. Therefore it agreed to make available 25 percent of the savings off the project budget to a maximum of $1 million as additional payment to the city for the building (Scott 1989).

Finally the university wanted to demonstrate a commitment to the city and its residents who had been the lifeblood of DePaul since its inception. To honor that relationship the purchase price included a ten-year guarantee to issue partial scholarships to Chicago residents who choose to attend DePaul University. This scholarship program, appropriately named The Mayor's Scholarship Program—Leadership 2000, would provide $250,000 a year in DePaul scholarships for a ten-year period.

The university wanted to increase its commitment to institutional financial aid as part of its enrollment management program, so the annual $250,000 payment was easily absorbed as part of the university's strategic enrollment plan. As a result this scholarship program was not dealt with as a separate line item of expense to the project. Through value engineering the university was able to reduce the project budget by $5 million; in effect this generated an additional $1 million payment to the city. Later the city reinvested this $1 million for improvements in the floors they eventually occupied. In the final analysis of determining the purchase price, it could be said that the university's true cost of acquiring the building and land was a cash payment of $1 million.

Yet, as a strategy was developed to garner public support for the city's decision to sell the building, the city was able to say that the purchase price for the benefit of the citizens of Chicago had been in reality $4.5 million. Thus the city was able to satisfy those who felt the price of $1 million was too low and, in effect, the project benefited from the fact that the $1 million paid for the building and the land was a symbolic purchase price, not a true burden to the project.

The "Estate for Years" Concept

The next section of the financing plan was probably the most critical element to the success of the project. Not unlike the university, the City of Chicago's office needs had grown significantly. The city had a sizable number of offices scattered across downtown Chicago in various rental properties (Spielman 1989). At one point the city had considered turning the Goldblatt Building into City Hall South and would have used the entire building for its purposes. For some undetermined reason the idea was abandoned and the city continued to rely on rental space elsewhere. The city had commissioned a study to justify the notion that another city-owned building would eventually be required to support the growth of city government. The study reported the commercial rental locations of certain city offices. It then analyzed the lease terms and projected future costs resulting from increased rent due to built-in increases in the lease rate plus the estimated increase in the pass-through operating cost. Also of note was the fact that when the city rents property from a commercial landlord, the city is required to pay its prorated portion of real estate taxes the same as any commercial tenant would pay. This study was a public document available during the formation of the financing plan for the DePaul Center. It quickly became apparent that the city would gain a substantial benefit by occupying space in the DePaul Center. The aggregate amount of space available was a rentable square footage of 225,000 square feet.

The concept of simply leasing space to the city as a tenant had significant drawbacks for DePaul. Because of the commercial nature of the space, the university could not rely on tax-exempt financing for the city's space. Another difficult aspect in leasing to a municipality was that the underlying credit of the municipality, while certainly rated high, was problematic from the standpoint that most leases are subject to annual appropriation. In effect a lease can be canceled in a tight budget year. Therefore a lease with the City of Chicago for the long term did not appear to be the ideal solution unless the university was willing to take on the risk for financing the entire 225,000 square feet of commercial office space.

The university's appetite for assuming such a risk was significantly low. It had just begun to design and construct a new library on the Lincoln Park Campus, which had a budget of $25 million. It was clear that the financing plan had to be more creative in dealing with the commercial office space. A suggestion of simply selling the space to the city after the vertical subdivision was completed was discounted for two reasons. The university had a long-term goal to own the building and was reluctant to consider a structure where it would share ownership. The city was equally hesitant to accept a structure in which it would be only a partial owner of a building housing its offices. The city wanted the benefits of leasing, but was unable to provide a long-term commitment. From these concerns an idea sprang forth that has become the hallmark of the DePaul Center financing plan.

The city was offered the right to purchase the 225,000 square feet under a legal concept called an "estate for years" or a "fee simple determinable" (DePaul University 1989). This provided all the elements of ownership but with a definite date of expiration of those ownership rights. Coupled with the estate for years was a service agreement by which the university contracted with the city to provide services to the city space, which would be at actual cost plus a management fee and would be allowed to escalate as those expenses increased in cost. Furthermore the university agreed to provide an allowance to be used for interior improvements and offered to serve in the role of construction manager. As noted earlier, the university had generated an additional $1 million from the project budget to be applied to the purchase price when the city agreed to accept the concept of occupying DePaul Center under the estate for years. The city also agreed to invest the $1 million in its own tenant improvements.

The concept of purchasing an estate for years allowed the city to finance the purchase using tax-exempt bonds. The estate for years was not subject to annual appropriation, allowing the city to offer its own tax-exempt bonds and yet on its books treat the debt service as lease payments over a thirty-year period.

One of the most significant elements of the estate for years was that the rental payments would not escalate. That enabled the city to make payments into the project fund for approximately $30 million and negated the university's need to borrow that portion of the project fund. When presenting the estate for years concept to the city, the university relied heavily on the tremendous potential savings for the city in comparison to its then current rental position, whereby it was paying real estate taxes plus rent that escalated on an annual basis. Because of the ownership structure for this building, the city would not be required to pay real estate taxes on its space in the building. Over a thirty-year period the comparison yielded a gross savings to the city, and therefore to taxpayers, estimated to be as high as $177 million (DePaul University 1989; *Chicago Sun-Times* 1989). Clearly the city had yet another factor to point to in justifying the low purchase price to DePaul for the sale of the Goldblatt Building and site.

At the closing DePaul University presented a $1 million check to the City of Chicago, a promise to provide an additional $1 million depending on project savings, and a commitment to issue $2.5 million of DePaul scholarships dollars to the citizens of Chicago over a ten-year period. The city turned over to the university the deed to the building plus an obligation to pay approximately $30 million for the estate for years in the building, which would be the future home to 225,000 square feet of city government offices.

Early on it became apparent the city would finance its estate using a general obligation bond issue. This could have put DePaul in a precarious financial position during the construction period. However the city agreed to pay for its estate in advance. Working with the city's controller, DePaul prepared a sophisticated financial model to predict and allocate acquisition, construction, and financing costs between the tenancies so the parties could negotiate a draw schedule against the purchase price. Payment of the purchase price in installments would ensure the university always had sufficient resources to fund development costs as they arose.

Value Engineering

The financing plan set the purchase price, and a strategy to deal with the rent-up risk for the commercial office space was in place. Therefore the construction risk became the next element to receive substantial discussion and debate. Because of the history of the building, its age, the previous study of its renovation as a potential library, its abandonment, and its deteriorating condition, there probably was not another Chicago building that had been subject to more evaluation. Embedded in all of the data and the studies was an underlying concern about the unknown versus the known. The designers of the financing plan therefore made two fundamental decisions regarding the construction risk.

The first decision was to exercise extreme caution in preparing the budget. All the normal construction contingencies had been developed, but when the budget was being incorporated into the proposal, an additional $5 million was added to provide for yet another contingency. While it was contemplated that the normal contingencies could be used to improve the project, if available, the additional $5 million was available to reduce the potential overbudget exposure, but was never intended to be spent. Hence this $5 million was a project risk reserve fund.

The second decision involved the construction process. The university was to serve as general contractor for architectural exterior design and the demolition work, including environmental issues. The goal was to reduce the building interior to its historical framework. The intent was that contractors and subcontractors bidding the project would not view it as a problematic renovation with all kinds of unknowns. By eliminating the old interior build-out, contractors would see open spaces with building conditions exposed. As a result of this strategy, the university was successful in its goal to maintain the $5 million reserve, and was able to turn other contingencies into project improvements.

Tax-Exempt Bonds

The financial plan next dealt with that portion of the building that would be the expansion space for the university. The plan called for the university to exclusively use approximately 300,000 square feet on floors six through ten and three-quarters of the space on floor eleven. The price tag for the university's space was approximately $25 million (McRoberts 1989). As previously mentioned, the university had committed to the construction of a new library on its Lincoln Park Campus for a similar cost. The first choice for a plan to pay for both the DePaul Center renovation and the new library was to make both projects elements of the university's recently announced $100 million capital campaign. While this idea generated enthusiasm, it was generally conceded that the university had to backstop the capital campaign with a different financing vehicle that needed to incorporate some characteristics of a bridge financing. The financing was viewed, particularly in the case of DePaul Center, as being needed for a period of approximately ten years. A decade would be the time that the campaign would require for soliciting and receiving pledge payments. To avoid a bond issue of thirty years in duration, the university conceived a program to issue general obligation tax-exempt bonds with the maximum flexibility.

The university issued $57 million of adjustable demand bonds through the Illinois Educational Facilities Authority on February 7, 1992 (First Chicago 1992). The unique feature was that each bond was capable of operating at any time in one of five modes: a daily mode, a weekly mode, a commercial paper mode, an adjustable long mode, or a fixed mode. Bonds in any mode could be converted to one or more of the other modes. The bonds were then subject to optional redemption from the date of the original issuance. The bonds in the daily, weekly, commercial paper, and adjustable long modes were secured by a transferable, irrevocable, direct-paid letter of credit from a Triple-A-rated bank. When a bond was placed in a fixed mode it was not secured by the credit facility. A remarketing agent was selected to reissue bonds, which came to maturity in any of the shorter modes. The rationale behind the structure was to first take advantage of the lower variable short-term interest rate and then provide for ease of redemption in the event that payments for the project were received via the capital campaign (First Chicago et al. 1992).

Not all things contemplated by the financial plan worked as designed. The $100 million capital campaign for the university, although successful in the aggregate, failed to generate specific capital gifts for the projects designated to benefit from the campaign. For example the College of Commerce graduate program, which would become a primary occupant of the DePaul Center, received an almost $10 million naming gift for what became the Kellstadt Graduate School of Business, but donor restrictions prevented use of any portion of the gift for bricks and mortar. The gift could not help the project by serving as budget relief, thus freeing up university funds, because of resistance by the academic unit. As a consequence, at a future point the university refunded this bond issue with another one and converted it to a fixed-rate general obligation of the university, and continues to make principal and interest payments to pay for the projects.

The Music Mart

Developing a strategy to deal with financing the retail space was another element of the financing plan. The university had committed in the redevelopment agreement with the city for the building to maintain approximately 75,000 square feet of retail space on the first floor and lower level of the building. A plan was developed for financing this space through a partnership with a private developer who had experience in marketing retail space. This space did not qualify for tax-exempt financing. In addition the 4- to 5-percent portion of the tax-exempt bond issue that might have qualified for taxable use had been previously committed to the eleventh floor cafeteria in order to facilitate a contract with the food-service vendor. The retail space also was subject to real estate taxes.

After reaching agreement with the city, the university began to implement its financing strategy for this space. A carefully prepared request for proposals was submitted to a number of notable real estate developers who had expertise in the rental of retail properties. After an extensive selection process, a letter of intent was signed with a retail developer who had proposed a single payment to the university equal to the cost of the shell and core improvements to the building for the retail space. The developer also agreed to enter into a long-term lease by which the university would receive additional rental payments from the developer after a successful retail marketing effort. The developer would then bear the financing cost of any tenant improvement costs necessary to secure retail tenants.

The due-diligence period gave the developer time and opportunity to test the marketplace to ensure the validity of the underlying assumptions regarding the ability to attract financing based on lease agreements. It became clear that the location of the real estate and the developer's own experience and expertise would not result in a successful project. At the same time the university became more sensitive to assuring that the retail component was compatible with the academic function of the building. There was a growing concern that substandard retailing would be the only business attracted to the location. In response to this concern and the ineffectiveness of the developer, the university embarked on an alternative approach.

Armed with a willingness to finance the retail portion of the project with university funds and accept rental income as a return on its investment, the university formed a concept for marketing the retail space called the Chicago Music Mart. The theme of Chicago Music Mart was borne from the history of the university's buildings in the South Loop. At one time the South Loop was called Music Row because it was home to a substantial number of music manufacturers and stores. For example one of the university's buildings, the Lewis Center, was the former Kimball Piano Factory. The building that housed the university's administration and growing computer science department had once been the Lyon and Healy Harp factory. Such prominent names as Steinway and Steger also had outlets in the area (Frantz 1996).

The university implemented the Music Mart plan by establishing an internal department to deal with retail tenants, including retailers already using space in other university buildings. DePaul also engaged the services of a retail broker and a public relations firm. An enhancement to the plan was the addition of a stage in the lower area of the Music Mart and the plan to offer community groups the opportunity to present noon concerts or other performances (Shutt 1993). To this day, this popular attraction is referred to as "Tunes at Noon." While the concept required a great deal of patience and created some trepidation about concern for using university funds, the result was and is a very successful investment.

Public Opinion

The financing plan at this point clearly had developed six strategies that were expected to be sufficient to accomplish the objective. It had a strategy with regard to the proper purchase price. The estate for years plan for the office space offered a win-win situation for both the city and the university. The budget was well protected from unforeseen and unanticipated events, and a construction strategy was in place to implement the plan. The university's own financing was acceptable to its Board of Trustees and the board willingly took on responsibility for the portion to be funded from the capital campaign gift receipts. The retail portion provided a creative solution for proceeding with the project. The final element of the plan did not necessarily deal with financing but with success in selling the idea.

The complexity of the project and the uniqueness of what it offered required a very positive campaign to promote the plan. The purchase price was anticipated to generate negative public opinion. The removal of 225,000 square feet of city space from the commercial property inventory could have created resistance. On the positive side, providing space for the university to continue to grow and the return of music retailing to the South Loop were considered positive elements (*Independent Quarterly* 1991). The overriding positive outcome of the project was the renovation of the blighted Goldblatt Building into a viable anchor of the South Loop, using renovation rather than demolition to bring a landmark building back to life (DePaul University 1989).

For this message to be clearly communicated, the university's media relations department scheduled a series of editorial meetings with three major and influential city publications, the *Chicago Sun-Times*, the *Chicago Tribune*, and

Crain's Chicago Business. The plan was shared with each of the editorial boards in great detail, and in all three cases there was a high level of interest and general support in what was beginning to be characterized as a mutually advantageous endeavor (*Chicago Sun-Times* 1989; *Crain's Chicago Business* 1989a). The project certainly was going to be a win for the university because it would enable needed expansion and additional state-of-the-art facilities at an affordable cost. The project was a win for the city of Chicago because it presented an opportunity to creatively deal with an eyesore on State Street. The plan also turned out to be a win for taxpayers because of the tremendous savings generated in accommodating city offices in the building. All three newspapers published editorials in support of the project and set the stage for positive public opinion and success for the project. Perhaps the best accounting of the support could be found in the following editorial that appeared in *Crain's Chicago Business* (1989b).

Take the money and run

Richie Daley is one lucky politician.
      Consider: The fate of the Goldblatt's building has bedeviled every mayor since Jane Byrne, who was conned into buying it nearly a decade ago. Since then, the building has had starring roles as a future library and a newspaper scandal; today, it's an unheated hulk that is deteriorating badly. Now comes a plan that would take the building off the city's hands without bulldozing a landmark; help revitalize the south end of the State Street Mall; and meet the space needs of a growing educational institution. . . . The proposal would leave retail space and an urban park at street level, six floors for the university and 214,000 square feet of office space. . . .
      . . . The time has come to end the long-running Goldblatt's disaster. We hope Daley administration officials accept the DePaul plan.

There was never a word of objection made with regard to the university's plan to renew the white elephant on State Street, and early praise for the project was reinforced after the building was completed (see Table 13.1). In November 2000, the Urban Land Institute presented the DePaul Center with its prestigious Award for Excellence for Rehabilitation.

Conclusion

Are there lessons to be learned from the plan to acquire and renovate the DePaul Center building? Or were the circumstances so unique that it was a one-of-a-kind project? While the specific details would indicate that the elements in place came together in a fashion that cannot be replicated, there are

Table 13.1

Summary Status of the DePaul Center, 1989

The property	700,000-square-foot building, 11 stories; former department store
Historic significance	Built in 1911 and listed on the National Register of Historical Places in 1989
Previous owner	City of Chicago, 1982–89. Abandoned, empty, and unheated during that time
Location	Adjacent to DePaul University Loop Campus
The financing plan	• Offer purchase price: $4,500,000 • Paid price: $1,000,000 in cash; $2,500,000 in DePaul scholarships to Chicago residents ($250,000/year for ten years); and $1,000,000 from project savings
Source of funds	• $25,000,000 tax-exempt bond issue by DePaul University • $30,000,000 one-time payment for thirty-year real estate interest in 225,000 square feet of office space in the building • $10,000,000 internal investment by DePaul University to finance the retail space
Use of funds	$65,000,000 project fund to acquire and renovate the Goldblatt Department Store building

Source: Used by permission of G-Spot Design, Chicago, Illinois.

certain aspects of the financing plan that can be applied to other projects. Risk is always present; a good plan does not eliminate it but mitigates against it. In the case of the DePaul Center, DePaul University undertook the development risk, the construction risk, and the retail risk. At the time the university was well-positioned with internal experience and skills to manage these risks. More important, there was a clear inside knowledge of both the city and the university that did not exist even with the developers on the blue-ribbon committee.

Without the benefit of the creative financing plan, the economics would not have worked, and the opportunity to sell the idea and the potential benefits to the many skeptics would not have existed. The city needed to be convinced that the project would have public acceptance and that DePaul had the in-house expertise to manage a project that at the time was almost as large as the annual university budget. In the final analysis the financial feasibility and the mutually beneficial economics of the space for both the university and the city proved to be the deciding factors. It was the kind of plan that renowned Chicago architect and city planner Daniel Burnham would have endorsed because it had "magic to stir men's blood."

References

Camper, John, John Kass, and Jerry Crimmins. 1986. Library may close book on Goldblatt's. *Chicago Tribune*, August 14: 1.

Chicago Sun-Times. 1989. Editorial. Act on good plan for vacant eyesore, October 1: 54.

Crain's Chicago Business. 1989a. Editorial. DePaul scores big with win-win plan, March 13: 10.

———. 1989b. Editorial. Take the money and run, September 25: 10.

Davis, Robert. 1988. Goldblatt's demolition rumors raise concern on State Street. *Chicago Tribune*, September 16: 11.

DePaul University. 1988a. Blue ribbon committee notes, November 16.

———. 1988b. DePaul University planning meeting minutes, October 27.

———. 1989. Proposal to the City of Chicago for redevelopment of the Goldblatt building. September 15.

First Chicago, William Blair & Company, and The Northern Trust Company. 1992. Illinois Educational Facilities Authority: Adjustable Demand Revenue Bonds–DePaul University. Series 1992. February 7.

Frantz, John. 1996. Chicago Music Mart, Chicago IL . . . It's coming. *Music & Sound Retailer,* September/October: 23–24.

Houston, Jack. 1988. City to seek buyer for old store. *Chicago Tribune*, December 2: 4.

Independent Quarterly-Federation of Illinois Independent Colleges and Universities, 1991. DePaul initiates cornerstone program, Fall.

Long, Ray, and Fran Spielman. 1991. Goldblatt building's sale to DePaul OK'd. *Chicago Sun-Times*, October 3: 40.

McRoberts, Flynn. 1989. DePaul is lone bidder for Goldblatt building. *Chicago Tribune*, September 17: 2C3.

Scott, Chris. 1989. DePaul seals deal for Goldblatt's building. *Crain's Chicago Business*, November 27: 8.

Shutt, Craig. 1993. Anatomy of a rehab: DePaul Center, the adaptive re-use of an historic department store. Compiled by Daniel P. Coffey & Associates, Ltd. from articles that appeared in *Commerical Renovation* from August 1992 to October 1993.

Spielman, Fran. 1989. City looks for ways to trim lease costs. *Chicago Sun-Times*, July 11: 10.

Strong, James. 1986. Library site bad, but set, mayor says. *Chicago Tribune*, March 14: 8.

The DePaulia. 1989. Master plan looks good on paper, but questions remain, February 24: 7.

14

No Such Thing as Vacant Land

Northeastern University and Davenport Commons

Allegra Calder, Gabriel Grant, and Holly Hart Muson

Davenport Commons is an innovative model of community housing for both students and local residents that was developed on behalf of Northeastern University by a partnership of three local developers in Boston, Massachusetts. The project was developed in the neighboring community of Roxbury because the university has little available land inside its traditional campus boundaries. The completed project consists of 125 units of housing for 595 students and 15 staff; 75 owner-occupied townhouses; and 2,100 square feet of retail space. From start to finish the project was controversial, and it highlights a number of challenges faced by urban universities with a need to expand.

University-led real estate development in Boston, and this project in particular, is controversial for at least two reasons. First, the shortage of available vacant land in the city politicizes virtually all large-scale development. Second, local universities are thought by some to hold inordinate influence on the city's economy and land use patterns. This power has contributed to feelings of resentment among neighboring populations.

This chapter describes how the Davenport Commons project evolved to surmount several obstacles and seeks to provide insight for real estate developers, city and university officials, community members, and activists. Particular attention is paid to the structure and the workings of the developer, Madison Davenport Partners, and the other major stakeholders, in an effort to explain who was involved and how they contributed. The project has been heralded as a success by virtually all stakeholders and offers a number of valuable lessons.

Background

Home to world-famous institutions such as Harvard University and the Massachusetts Institute of Technology, Greater Boston has more than sixty institutions of higher education. These institutions play a vital role in the city's economic and cultural life and significantly impact the housing market. For example in 1998 there were approximately 135,000 higher education students living in Boston.[1] Of that number, only about 28,000, or 20 percent, lived in university-provided housing (Tong 2000). Local politicians and urban policy experts have called upon local universities and colleges to provide more student housing to help stabilize the housing market. A recent report on housing in Boston suggests that adding 7,500 student housing units over five years could ease the pressure on the housing market and benefit the institutions as well (Bluestone et al. 2001).

Northeastern University is a private, nonprofit, coeducational institution of higher education founded in 1898 at the Boston branch of the Young Men's Christian Association. Today Northeastern has about 22,500 students and is a national research university that is student-centered, practice-oriented, and urban. According to Richard Freeland, president of Northeastern, "We are totally the opposite of Harvard. We celebrate our open edges so nobody can miss the point that we are open to the city" (Klenotic 2000). Over the past decade Northeastern has undergone tremendous change, transforming itself from a little-known school catering primarily to local students to one with a national reputation that draws students from across the country and around the world. As a result of this change, a primary focus of the school's mission has been the creation of high-quality student housing to respond to intensifying demand for university-operated housing.

It is not only the presence of university students that accounts for the Boston region's tight housing market. Demand far exceeds supply, and rent control ended in 1994, resulting in rental prices that are among the highest in the nation and on par with New York and San Francisco.[2] It is within this environment of rapidly increasing rents, gentrification, and the constant pressure of university expansion that the Davenport Commons project was proposed in Roxbury, one of the last bastions of affordable housing in the city (see Map 14.1).

The Planning Process

The planning process that resulted in the construction of Davenport Commons was extraordinarily complex, characterized by periods of vocal community opposition, numerous revisions responding to political and financial requirements, and intense public scrutiny.[3]

In 1996 the City of Boston had two major housing-related goals: the creation of more student housing and the development of more affordable housing. In addition it was eager to sell a surface parking lot bordering the

Map 14.1 **Northeastern's Campus**

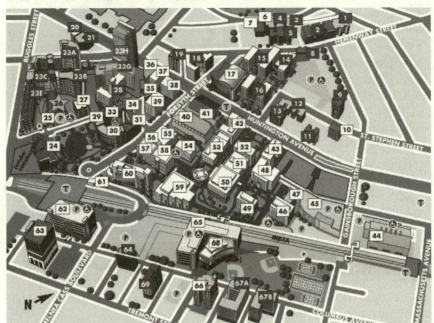

Source: www.campusmap.neu.edu/. Davenport Commons=67A, 67B. Used by permission.

Northeastern campus that it had been unable to divest in previous attempts. Opinions differ on whether the city approached Northeastern about buying the land or if the university initiated the deal. Either way, the land was eventually sold to the university in a process that project opponents contend was an inside political operation intended to serve the interests of both the city and the university, but devoid of any legitimate public participation.

In fact Mayor Thomas Menino did discuss development possibilities for the site with Northeastern, including student dormitories, although he understood that student housing would be contentious in that neighborhood. This left the university scrambling to find a creative solution to accommodate more students without building only dorms. According to Tom Keady, then Northeastern's vice president of government relations and community affairs, two viable solutions emerged: (1) build dormitories, despite the understanding that the mayor would not publicly support such development, and make a considerable linkage payment to placate the city; or (2) develop both affordable rental housing and student housing, which would provide an internal subsidy for the affordable units. The university knew that it lacked the capacity to handle the complexities of financing an affordable housing deal, so it began discussions with a select group of nonprofit and private developers to gauge interest in the idea. While in hindsight this was the right approach, it generated opposition from other interested parties who wanted to participate in this potentially lucrative project.

At a community meeting in 1996, a Northeastern official inadvertently disclosed plans for Davenport Commons, unleashing the first wave of opposition. Negotiations had been ongoing for about six months when the community was finally notified of the plans, and much of the initial protest focused on the lack of transparency. Some sensed that the university thought it was doing the community a favor. They objected to the condescension and were skeptical that the university would be a true partner.

Some in the community maintain that the city, through the Boston Redevelopment Authority (BRA), drafted the request for proposals (RFPs) for purchase and development of parcels 14, 14A, 15, and 16A specifically tailored to Northeastern's plan, thereby preventing any real competition. They also believe that the BRA deliberately established a short time frame and did not adequately publicize the RFP because it planned on awarding Northeastern its approval. Tom O'Malley of the BRA contends that while the city and Northeastern held extensive discussions about development options for the parcels, the RFP was legitimate and yielded one other proposal for a mixed-use development that included market-rate housing and a Walgreen's drug store. Furthermore this was not the first time an RFP had been issued for the land; previous attempts had produced no results. Nonetheless few in the community were aware that the project was in the planning stages and many were angered over the lack of information offered to the public.

On the day of the RFP deadline in the spring of 1997, a *Boston Globe* article (Anand 1997) confirmed the plans for Davenport Commons, and the community protested. The perception that project approval had been negotiated behind closed doors was a serious setback. In response to the uproar the BRA extended the RFP deadline.

It was clear from the start that Davenport Commons would be a complicated undertaking, politically and financially. It was also clear that the university needed to cede a degree of control over the development to local partners in whom the community had greater trust. In recognition of these challenges, Northeastern chose to work with a local community development corporation and two developers with links to the local community and public-sector experience. A development team called Madison Davenport Partners (MDP) was formed to carry out the project on Northeastern's behalf, consisting of Madison Park Development Corporation and Housing Investments, Inc., and Trinity Financial, both Boston-based real estate developers and consultants that specialize in affordable housing. After reviewing this team's proposal and one other submission, the Boston Redevelopment Authority in 1998 designated MDP as developer of the four parcels.

Although Northeastern was no longer the "developer" of the project, it remained a vital force in providing its long-term vision as well as substantial predevelopment capital. President Freeland was deeply committed to the project and commissioned an internal team to help ensure the project's successful completion.[4] This team's ability to navigate shifting political environments helped keep the project moving forward, and its determination to see the project through and its ability to handle the numerous internal and external obstacles were critical to the outcome.

Madison Park Development Corporation (MPDC) is an African American-led community development corporation (CDC) with a history of successful housing and commercial projects in Roxbury. Danette Jones, executive director at the outset of the project, was an early advocate for the project, which proved pivotal to its eventual success. Jones viewed involvement with the Davenport project as an opportunity to exercise control over where and how the university located its student housing and as a way to increase housing opportunities for low-income households in their target service area of Roxbury. MPDC leaders contributed a great deal to the development team, working to build trust between the local community and the university.

Trinity Financial's expertise lies in assembling complex real estate deals and managing development projects. Trinity's solid reputation as an affordable housing developer and the leadership of firm principals Jim Keefe and Patrick Lee, the latter a widely respected African American business leader, also were critical to the success of the project and its ultimate acceptance by the community.

Housing Investments, Inc. provided valuable guidance in the project's early stages and helped to bring all of the necessary parties to the table to negotiate a workable deal. Firm President Amy Anthony, a former secretary of the Massachusetts Executive Office of Communities and Development, added deep political experience and affordable housing finance expertise. For this project the two development firms filled different roles, with Housing Investments, Inc. focused on the strategic planning and "deal structure" stages of the project, and Trinity Financial involved throughout as day-to-day project manager for the development. The proposal envisioned Madison Davenport Partners developing the site using predevelopment funds and debt secured by Northeastern, and then leasing the site to the university for a thirty-year term, after which the university would acquire the property.

In the beginning the idea of using a team of highly regarded local organizations to develop student and affordable housing on vacant land appeared to all involved to be a financially viable approach that was unlikely to encounter significant opposition. Furthermore Mayor Menino and the staff at the BRA actively supported Northeastern's efforts to work cooperatively with the city's growth objectives. Nonetheless, as the project evolved, varying degrees of opposition came from local government officials, community organizations and grassroots activists, and segments within the university itself.

Community Opposition

What MDP and the city did not fully comprehend early on was that many community leaders and residents believed that decisions related to the future of the parcels should, as a matter of law and as a matter of principle, require their approval. Community members wanted a greater say in the process and a greater role in shaping change in their neighborhood.

Roxbury is a predominately African American community, many of whose residents had long felt ignored by Northeastern and marginalized by the city. The four vacant parcels in question were the result of a city-led urban renewal project in the late 1960s to construct an interstate highway. After homes were razed and former residents were forced to find housing elsewhere, the highway was never constructed. Although various redevelopment proposals were put forward over the next thirty years, none came to fruition and the property languished. Discounting this history at the outset of the process proved to be a mistake. Jeanne Pinado, current executive director of Madison Park Development Corporation, put it aptly: "There is no such thing as vacant land." Land means different things to different people, but it is never a blank slate.

Opposition to Davenport Commons, while never uniform, was rooted primarily in two concerns: the community's right to be heard and Northeastern's encroachment into Roxbury. Many perceived the development to be an institutional land grab. This was a particularly sensitive issue due to the history of the land, but also because it had recently been revealed that Harvard had secretly purchased fifty-two acres in the neighboring community of Allston. "The struggle for affordable home ownership in Roxbury and the struggle to get Northeastern University to stop land banking its land is an economic human rights issue" stated Pat Cusick, director of the South End Neighborhood Action Program (SNAP) (Massachusetts Welfare Rights Union 1998). Cusick went on to file a suit, which was later dismissed, with HUD's civil rights department over the lack of community process. As a participant in the working group that was formed to come up with a more amenable plan, Cusick would eventually become part of the solution.

Community concerns ranged from issues directly related to the design of the project to the threat of gentrification and displacement. Those who opposed the project wanted different things and few had the same message. Support for the project came from local churches, union members, and many of those on waiting lists for rental housing. In the face of seasoned community activists, however, these groups' messages rarely came through.

The proposed project increased hostility toward the university but also within the community itself. Boston has few peers with respect to the number and strength of its CDCs, and expectations are exceedingly high. One developer joked, "Whatever you propose in Boston, it will never be enough. If you proposed the Sistine Chapel, they'd want two Sistine Chapels." The struggle over Davenport brought to the fore territorial disputes between CDCs with overlapping target areas, as long-time collaborators found themselves on opposite sides of the debate. This question of territory became important because groups from the adjacent South End neighborhood claimed the parcels fell under their jurisdiction and were some of the most vociferous opponents.

For its part Northeastern recognized the need to negotiate issues at a community level, as opposed to simply dealing with the mayor's office, and began to formulate new ways of communicating with the public. External opposition was not the only obstacle facing the university, however, and Keady maintains that at times the internal opposition proved more difficult to address than the community politics.

Internal Politics

Northeastern had a long-standing set of procedures for managing construction projects, and Davenport Commons marked the first time that the university gave up control by employing outside developers with ultimate decision-making authority. This arrangement inevitably challenged some of Northeastern's institutional norms, was threatening to some inside the university, and resulted in internal opposition. Others inside the university questioned whether the use of university resources to build affordable housing was consistent with the school's mission. Vince Droser of Trinity Financial felt that the involvement of private-sector developers forced the university to question some of its institutional standards and assumptions, which resulted in greater efficiency, overall savings, and institutional learning.

The academic culture is vastly different from the real estate development culture. Consequently expectations related to procedures and time lines often differed, and relations had to be managed carefully. When the architect's plans were presented, representatives from the Student Housing and Physical Plant departments expressed concern that the plans did not meet certain institutional standards related to door widths, toilets, and accessibility for disabled, among other things. Meetings held over the previous six months had been open to all university departments, yet some waited until the plans were complete to participate in discussions. Others within the university collaborated with the various community opposition groups.

Internal dissent eventually reached a point at which President Freeland decided to call a meeting to rally support. Freeland had been the victim of several very public "smear campaigns" waged by disgruntled community residents. Yet his perseverance and resolute support for the project, both within the university and publicly, helped to keep it on track.

Design Revisions

The initial plans for Davenport Commons called for 879 student beds, 40 rental units, 20 home ownership units with 20 surface parking places, and 1,000 square feet of commercial space. Many in the community felt the neighborhood didn't need more rental units since it already had a large share of Boston's subsidized housing. They believed new home-ownership opportunities were a way to help stabilize the area. Other community opposition to affordable rental housing was driven simply by a "not in my back yard" response. Once the rationale for home ownership had been articulated, the wider community embraced it. The planned rental units were converted to home-ownership units and the sale prices for these units were lowered to increase affordability. Although rental units would have generated greater subsidy, the development team recognized the importance of home ownership to the community and the university made up the difference in cost.

Throughout the process of public hearings and community meetings, MDP continually revised plans for Davenport Commons by making reductions in the number of student beds, increases in home-ownership units and commercial space, and changes to the architectural design. Despite attempts to include the community in the design decision-making process, it eventually became clear that some opponents sought to paralyze the process indefinitely. Mayor Menino issued a challenge to all the interested parties involved to reach an agreement by a target deadline. His attention and support sent a strong signal to the community and its leaders and they did refocus their efforts. Were it not for Menino's unwavering support and intervention, the project may have languished. Patrick Lee of Trinity Financial praised the mayor's efforts: "In any other city, the mayor would have walked away."

Toward Resolution

At the mayor's behest a working group made up predominately of African American civic leaders was assembled to reach a solution.[5] The group met every few weeks over several months to craft a proposal that would meet the community's needs while still allowing the project to go forward.

Vincent Haynes, president of the MPDC Board of Directors, proved to be a key influence in this group. A longtime civic leader and resident of Roxbury, Haynes is highly respected within the community. During a critical impasse in the working group's deliberations, he persuaded Mel King, an influential Roxbury community activist opposed to the project, to attend a meeting and participate in seeking a resolution. King's involvement indicated to other community leaders that the project had worthwhile benefits and that a resolution could be found. An article in the *Boston Globe* quoted Tom O'Brien, former director of the BRA, praising Haynes, "There was a split in the community; he was able to be a bigger individual than just a partisan of one side. He pulled all the leaders together and caused them all to say, 'How do we find a way?' It was his stature, his long-term activism, that caused people to come together" (Radin 1999, B1).

The group proposed dividing the parcels in half, allocating equal land for 125 units of student housing (accommodating 595 students, a significant reduction from the total of 879 that was first proposed) and 75 owner-occupied townhouse units. The planned home ownership units were for moderate-income families, a difficult group to serve in constrained housing markets such as Boston's, since there is little federal or state money available to serve this group. An internal subsidy from student rents was used to bridge the funding gap for the home-ownership units, a strategy that increased support for the project.

The 50/50 split of the land was generally accepted and became highly symbolic for the community as a way to reclaim the land for public benefit. While the division of land was comforting to many, some remained highly skeptical of Northeastern's motives and feared that students would occupy the home-ownership units. When it became clear that the site could accommodate only sixty units of community housing, the partners looked for more land on which to build additional units; a reduction in units certainly would have met resistance. Fortunately MPDC owned a small parcel nearby and it became the site for fifteen units, known as Shawmut Estates, thus avoiding a reduction in the agreed-upon number of seventy-five units.

The long development process generated a number of additional changes to the scope of the project. For example, in the original design student and community housing was intermingled in one unified development. As a result of community involvement, a new plan separated student housing from the community home-ownership units, creating two distinct living environments. In addition to changes in the mix of unit types, the building height was increased but the overall density of the student housing was reduced.

Through its attempts to gain community approval for Davenport Commons, the university ultimately made several concessions beyond the scope of work at Davenport. Northeastern agreed to release to the community a list of all the properties it owned and to produce a community-approved area master plan prior to acquiring more property (Walsh 1998).

The Davenport Commons design process was extensive and involved more stakeholders and more complex negotiations than the university originally anticipated or had dealt with on previous development projects. Despite the numerous delays that resulted from this level of community participation, Keady believes that as a result both the project and the university were strengthened.

Project Financing

At the same time as the negotiations related to design, scale, and programming mix were taking place with the various stakeholders, the project's financing package was being crafted. Because Davenport's mix of affordable and student housing was a first in Massachusetts and the country, none of the traditional affordable housing or student housing development financing sources immediately fit the project. The development team, which had worked with Massachusetts Housing Finance Agency (MHFA) when Davenport was being planned as affordable rental housing, had to convince MHFA to consider financing a student housing and home-ownership deal, something it had never done before. Once the development team convinced MHFA of the innovative nature and economic viability of the project, however, MHFA saw the Davenport model as a potential source of new business and moved to broadly interpret its charter in order to include student housing, thus enabling the agency to participate in the project.

To finance Davenport MHFA issued 501(c) (3) bonds on behalf of Northeastern, a nonprofit organization. The proceeds of these bonds ($33,171,000 in tax-exempt debt) was loaned to the project, along with $4,757,000 in shorter term taxable debt. The project also signed a thirty-year lease with Northeastern for the student housing portion, which effectively guaranteed the 501(c) (3) bonds. This feature of the deal exposed Northeastern to some risk but allowed the project to benefit from lower interest rates. In addition Northeastern provided a significant contribution of $1,850,000 to cover up-front predevelopment costs. Northeastern's financial strength proved critical to the deal.

Without the university's ability and willingness to guarantee the 501(c) (3) bonds and to make a substantial equity contribution, it is unlikely that the project would ever have been completed. Finally, a variety of federal and local government grants, gap financing, and proceeds from the sale of home-ownership units combined to make up the remaining funds for the project (see Appendix14.1).

The involvement of Trinity Financial and Housing Investments proved invaluable during the financing and deal-making stages. Northeastern had traditionally financed its developments in far more conventional ways and therefore lacked experience dealing with the numerous federal, state, and city funding agencies that contributed to the project. The two firms were seasoned veterans of complex layered funding and community coordination.

The general structure of the transaction was complex. The deal was structured to have MDP serve as developer of both the student housing and home-ownership units, but grant Northeastern a large degree of control over the student housing development with the university acting as neither owner nor developer. In order to accomplish this, the parcels of vacant land to be used for student housing were acquired from the BRA by MPDC, which then transferred the land to Northeastern and developed the student housing under the direction of MDP and in close consultation with Northeastern. Once completed, Northeastern owned the land, which it leased to MPDC for a term of thirty years and MPDC owned the student housing, which it leased to the university for thirty years for an annual amount equal to the tax-exempt debt payments. At the end of thirty years, once the tax-exempt debt has been paid off, MPDC will sell the student housing portion to Northeastern for $1, giving the university control of both the land and the student housing. On the home-ownership side, MDP acquired the vacant land directly from the BRA, developed the units, and sold them to buyers selected in accordance with an agreement with the community.

Construction and Occupancy

Construction began in October 1999 and by spring 2001 the home-ownership units were ready for occupancy. Demand for the units was so great that a lottery was implemented to determine who among the almost 700 applicants would be chosen. Eligible applicants had to meet strict income requirements and owners agreed to restrictions governing rental and occupancy of the units.[6]

Resale conditions, an increasingly common provision in tight housing markets, were also instituted. Homes may be sold only to buyers in the same income bracket under which the seller qualified. In addition the value of the home cannot increase annually by more than 5 percent. Prices for the homes ranged from $85,000 to $225,000.[7] MPDC helped the home owners set up a condominium association and provided technical assistance and first-time home-buyer education.

Students moved into Davenport Commons in fall 2001. The units accommodate three to six students and include bedrooms, bathroom, kitchen, and common living area. The response from both the community and students has been uniformly positive. Outreach and cross-programming between students and home owners has resulted in open communication and generated heightened respect among students for the surrounding community. The addition of high-quality housing close to campus has enhanced the housing options available to Northeastern students.

Lessons Learned

There are certain factors, including the strength of community development organizations and the tight housing market, that are particular to Boston and therefore unique to how the development of Davenport Commons unfolded. The combination of these factors will not necessarily be present in university-sponsored development projects taking place in other parts of the country. However, many of the factors that influenced the Davenport development do exist in other locations and as a result there are many broad lessons that can be learned.

Strong Leadership Is Critical

During the development of Davenport, the leadership at Northeastern University was deeply committed to developing a stronger image and standing for itself in Boston's competitive and politically charged institutional community. As a means of achieving this, the president and key staff members mapped out long-range goals and identified key advocates to marshal the school's resources toward achieving its goals. In addition to President Freeland's unwavering support, this project benefited from the stewardship of Tom Keady rather than simply the oversight of an in-house construction manager. Equally important was the strong support of Mayor Menino and the Boston Redevelopment Authority.

Find Partners with Important Skills and Relationships

Outside consultants were chosen specifically for the value of their pre-existing relationships in local government and embedded community organizations, and they played key roles in bridging the gaps between the university and community. These partnerships benefited the school in several ways: by providing access to respected community members who were key to gaining broad support; by diffusing opposition by spreading responsibility for development among multiple parties; and by providing funding and regulatory agencies a basis for confidence in an untried development model. The development team also identified and allied itself with influential neighborhood leaders who were able to bring opponents on board. The involvement of these community leaders brought credibility to a project that originally was viewed with suspicion.

Financial Strength and Long-Term Vision Are Key

Northeastern's financial strength and stability provided the developers with what was for them an unusual opportunity—the possibility of financing the construction of moderate-income homes through bonds issued against the school's strong credit rating. Like many urban universities, Northeastern's long-range success is strengthened by the health of the residential communities that surround the school and their mutually supportive relationship. This reality helped shape the strategic decision to create home-ownership opportunities for local residents rather than using the vacant land entirely for student housing. The seventy-five new home-ownership units benefit the university by helping to weave the surrounding neighborhood and university together and by demonstrating the university's sincere effort to be a good neighbor.

Create "Win-Win" Outcomes

Virtually all of the Davenport stakeholders were able to claim success. The university added nearly 600 beds to its strained inventory; the city successfully disposed of long-underused parcels of land in a manner that helped the city's affordable housing problem; and the local residents won a number of concessions, including home-ownership rather than rental units, a lower overall density, and greater transparency with respect to the university's master plan. While it was not an easy process, the fact that all involved were able to claim some level of victory allowed the project to be built and will make it easier for Northeastern to pursue future development in the area.

Appendix 14.1. General Structure of the Transaction

The Davenport Commons project was structured in the following manner:

- Madison Park Development Corporation (MPDC) acquired the title to the student housing portion of the property (vacant land) from the Boston Redevelopment Authority (BRA) and transferred it to Northeastern University. Northeastern, as owner of the student housing portion of land, then leased it to MPDC through a thirty-year ground lease.

- MPDC, Trinity Financial, and Housing Investments, Inc., jointly called Madison Davenport Partners (MDP), developed the project according to agreed-upon terms and specifications, limiting the development risk to Northeastern.
- The completed student housing building is owned by MPDC, which rents it to Northeastern according to a thirty-year student housing lease. Debt payments made by MPDC to Massachusetts Housing Finance Agency are equal in rent to the amount Northeastern pays to MPDC. The student housing is committed to remain student housing as long as the 501 (c)(3) bonds are outstanding.
- As a tenant leasing the student housing from MPDC, Northeastern participated as a client in the development process. A university representative went to weekly job meetings, approved change orders, and provided a ten-day punch list at completion, which MPDC, as owner, was responsible for satisfying.
- When the thirty-year lease expires, Northeastern will acquire student housing for $1 from MPDC, which will give it ownership of both the land and the building.
- MPDC also acquired from the BRA parcels for home-ownership units, which MPDC developed, with the assistance of MDP, and sold to buyers selected by lottery in accordance with a community agreement.

Notes

1. This number refers to Boston proper and does not include Cambridge. In the 2000 Census, Boston's total population was 589,141. Available at www.census.gov.

2. According to a report by the National Low-Income Housing Coalition (2003), Boston is the fifth least affordable metropolitan statistical area.

3. Community is used throughout to describe opposition or support from outside the university, its partners, or the city. However, it should not be interpreted as a unified voice of dissent or support as there were various factions within the community.

4. The Northeastern team included Tom Keady, then vice president of government relations and community affairs, and members of the Administration and Finance Office including Laurence Mucciolo, senior vice president; Joseph Murphy, treasurer; Vin Lembo, vice president for university counsel; Jeff Doggett, assistant director of government relations and community affairs; and various members of Facilities Management.

5. Working group members included Patrick Lee, principal of Trinity Financial; Jeanne Pinado, Madison Park executive director; State Senator Dianne Wilkerson; State Representative Byron Rushing; Pat Cusick of SNAP; Syvalia Hyman, president of United South End/Lower Roxbury Development Corporation; and Vincent Haynes, then president of Madison Park's Board of Directors.

6. Shawmut Estate's fifteen units were for households at or below 80 percent of the area median income (AMI). Thirty-seven of the Davenport home-ownership units

were also set aside for families at or below 80 percent of the AMI; eleven units were reserved for those earning 81 to 120 percent of AMI and the remaining twelve were for those earning 121 to 175 percent of AMI. According to HUD, AMI for a family of four for the Boston Metropolitan Statistical Area was $82,600 in 2004, but at the time the units were sold it was approximately $66,000.

    7. In 2001 the median price for a condominium in Roxbury was $287,000 (Pikounis 2001).

References

Anand, Geeta. 1997. Northeastern plan combines dorms, community housing. *Boston Globe,* May 2: A1, A19.

Bluestone, Barry, Charles C. Euchner, Gretchen Weismann, and Center for Urban and Regional Policy. 2001. *A new paradigm for housing in Greater Boston.* Boston: Northeastern University. Revised Edition, February.

Klenotic, Deborah. 2000. Grand design: The new master plan. *Northeastern University Magazine,* January. Available at www.numag.NU.edu/0001/campus.html.

Massachusetts Welfare Rights Union. 1998. Press Release, May 29.

National Low-Income Housing Coalition. 2003. Out of Reach 2003: America's Housing Wage Climbs. September. Available at www.nlihc.org/oor2003/.

Pikounis, Aglaia. 2001. Development mixes affordable, student housing. *Banker & Tradesman,* October 1. Available at www.bankerandtradesman.com/pub/3_42/residential/108393-1.html.

Radin, Charles A. 1999. Roxbury's quiet hero; Behind scenes, Haynes a proud peacekeeper. *Boston Globe,* January 14: B1.

Tong, Kathryn. 2000. Campus crisis: Thousands of student returning to area colleges scramble to find housing. *Boston Globe,* August 20: H1.

Walsh, Christine. 1998. Davenport Commons a done deal. Project to provide student beds, home ownership. *Northeastern News Online,* December 2. Available at www.nunews.NU.edu/nu-news/Issues/120298/n1.html.

Interviews

Amy Anthony, President, Housing Investments, Inc. October 25, 2001.

Jeffrey Doggett, Assistant Director, Office of Government Relations and Community Affairs, Northeastern University. March 1, 2002.

Vince Drosser, Vice President, Development, Trinity Financial. November 28, 2001.

Vincent Haynes, long-time community resident and former Board of Directors chairman, Madison Park Development Corporation. February 8, 2002.

Tom Keady, Associate Vice President for Government and Community Relations, Boston College. June 7, 2002.

Patrick Lee, Executive Vice President, Trinity Financial. February 21, 2002.

Tom O'Malley, Boston Redevelopment Authority. February 26, 2002.

Jeanne Pinado, Executive Director and David Price, Director of Real Estate and General Counsel, Madison Park Development Corporation. November 9, 2001.

Robert Pyne, Director of Rental Development, Massachusetts Housing Finance Agency. February 22, 2002.

Dianne Wilkerson, Massachusetts State Senator. April 11, 2002.

15

Campus Partners and The Ohio State University

A Case Study in Enlightened Self-Interest

David Dixon and Peter J. Roche

The Ohio State University (OSU) is a public university with growing national stature as a center of learning and research. Located about two miles north of downtown Columbus, OSU became increasingly convinced during the 1990s that it needed to address previous disinvestment in the neighborhoods around its campus, both to protect its ability to attract students, faculty, and staff and to fulfill its historic mission of public service as a land-grant institution. The university has a long tradition of civic engagement: it is the largest employer in Columbus; the campus accommodates a combined student, faculty, and staff population of almost 50,000 (greater than the city's downtown workforce); as a land-grant university it is interested in shifting its traditional public service focus from agricultural issues to urban problems; and large numbers of its alumni occupy leadership positions in local government, business, and civic affairs.

This chapter describes a commitment to community revitalization that emerged in the first half of the 1990s, took shape and matured in the latter half, and continues in full force in the early twenty-first century. This account also provides analysis of two significant university-sponsored community redevelopment projects now under way: the South Campus Gateway, a mixed-use development on High Street, the university district's principal "Main Street"; and the Broad Street Revitalization Initiative, a neighborhood housing plan. These activities have moved the university into a position of far greater engagement with the economic, social, and physical qualities of the surrounding district and to the forefront nationally of educational institutions that have involved themselves in community revitalization.

Map 15.1 **Ohio State University District**

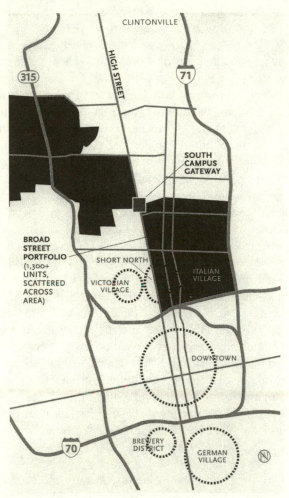

Planning Context

OSU sits in the center of a university district bordering High Street, which defines the eastern edge of the campus and is a primary artery for the city of Columbus. Across High Street is a highly diverse mix of shops, bars, entertainment venues, and food businesses. The university district itself extends along High Street for roughly one mile to the north and south of the campus (see Map 15.1).

High Street flourished as a university- and community-oriented Main Street for more than four decades before World War II, a period when university enrollment grew from fewer than 10,000 to more than 25,000. By the late 1920s High Street was known as one of the liveliest commercial districts in Columbus, and its growing array of shops, entertainment, and services transformed the street into a highly popular center for OSU's community life. Since World War II, however, OSU, like many urban universities, has seen the neighborhoods around its campus change dramatically. Middle-class families moved to the suburbs and the businesses and services supported by those families largely followed. Initially students and lower-income residents moved in, but by the 1980s students began to abandon the district as well.

In the 1960s the pace and extent of change along the street began to be visible, and the university's reaction further accelerated the neighborhood's decline. Unnerved by rioting along High Street in protest of the Vietnam War, the university consciously began to close itself off from the street and adjacent neighborhoods, severing direct vehicular connections from the neighborhoods into the campus. The most symbolic and devastating closing was of 15th Street, the traditional front door of the campus for the larger Columbus community. The university closed the street and then sited a new performing arts center in such a way as to cut off much of the visual connection between the campus and High Street and the rest of the university district. With bunker-like planters and service docks, the arts center—and OSU—abruptly turned its back on High Street. Extensive investment in landscaping, streetscape improvements, new buildings, and other facilities intentionally shifted the campus's focus west toward Route 315.

At the end of the twentieth century, OSU turned its attention to raising its national stature as a major public university, but a series of highly troubling trends began to undermine its ambitions:

- The university community—students, faculty, and staff—left the university district in large numbers. By the mid-1990s more than 70 percent of students owned cars, compared with roughly 10 percent in the 1970s, and more than 60 percent of undergraduate and graduate students lived outside the district. Many other students increasingly sought on-campus housing.
- A mix of students and low-income residents—predominantly people of color—replaced departing middle-class families, who had been largely white. In the wake of the student exodus in the 1980s, the southeastern quadrant of the university district came to house Columbus's highest concentration of Section 8 housing. Home ownership in the district dropped from 50 percent in 1950 to roughly 12 percent by the late 1990s.

- Concerned that its downtown was losing jobs and tax revenue to increasingly ambitious suburban office parks, the city converted High Street into an arterial to enhance accessibility from northern suburbs, removing curbside parking essential to retailers and closing streets that connected residential neighborhoods to High Street.
- As disposable income along High Street declined and suburban competition exploded, the street lost most of its anchor retailers. Smaller retailers moved out, and strip retail began to replace traditional pedestrian-friendly retail to the north and south of the campus.
- Crime became an increasing concern, particularly east and southeast of the campus, accelerating the departure of students and long-time residents.

Why the University Changed Course

In 1992 OSU inaugurated a new president, Gordon Gee, formerly a senior administrator at Brown University. Brown had benefited greatly from the "renaissance" of Providence's College Hill neighborhood, a resurgence that had spread across the downtown and had made the city an exciting place to live, work, shop . . . and study. President Gee often remarked that when he was being introduced to OSU his guides were very selective in the routes they took on the way to the campus, avoiding the university district. Within a year President Gee took a strong leadership position, urging the university and the city to launch a comprehensive revitalization strategy to "stem the tide of neglect" across the university district. He cited five key reasons:

- *Responding to rising crime.* The 1994 kidnapping and murder of a first-year student one-half block from High Street received national publicity. Gee stressed that the university could not guarantee the safety of its community without addressing crime in the larger community.
- *Enhancing student quality of life.* As students sought suburban apartment housing miles from campus, the university was less able to present itself as a vital living and learning center.
- *Attracting top students and faculty.* OSU's academic plan envisioned a place among America's top ten public universities. Increasingly, however, alumni and the admissions office reported that high-performing potential students were declining admission offers because of the environment around the university.
- *Living up to OSU's mission as a land-grant institution.* Gee advocated shifting the university's public involvement focus from the traditional agricultural concerns of a land-grant university to social, economic, racial, and other issues.

- *Breaking the cycle of neglect.* Gee argued that if the university did not intervene, the university district's problems would only grow steadily worse.

Forming Campus Partners

President Gee launched a series of discussions and was instrumental in bringing about early decisions that set the stage for the formation of Campus Partners. While leaders in the community, city, and university all saw the need for revitalization, no leadership for this effort had emerged. To address this lack, the president advocated that the university form a partnership with the city, with the university taking the lead in planning and funding. Gee worked with community leaders, many of whom were deeply suspicious of the university's motives and who were quick to point to a record of community removal rather than revitalization. He convinced them that OSU was committed to an inclusive planning process, to improving quality of life for all residents, and to supporting the needs of businesses along High Street and elsewhere. As evidence of that commitment, he set up a task force to shape a strategy and included members from across the university community, as well as neighborhood and city representatives.

The task force considered a wide range of options, from direct university participation in revitalization efforts to creation of a for-profit entity independent of the university. The task force recommended the formation of Campus Partners for Community Urban Redevelopment under an Ohio statute that confers on "community redevelopment corporations" a wide range of public powers—most notably the ability to carry out eminent-domain takings. The task force determined that the university would provide essentially all funding and that it would appoint a majority of the board; the other members would be city and community representatives.

The task force found many arguments for establishing a new entity:

- The revitalization should be led by an entity with a clearly defined mission and full-time staff dedicated to this task. Flexibility and effectiveness in conducting planning and real estate development activities would also be key, and the university itself could not provide that expertise.
- Clear authority for making decisions, independent of the very collegial decision-making process of the university, would be critical.
- Distance from the university structure would be important, both to shield OSU from potential controversy and to inspire community acceptance. While President Gee had allayed much of the concern among community organizations about the university's intentions, OSU remained associated in the public mind with the wrecking ball.

- Despite the need for distance, it would be equally important to take advantage of the university's relationships with alumni who constituted so much of the political, business, and civic leadership of Columbus and central Ohio, and to convey instant credibility and leverage with the city and with major agencies such as the U.S. Department of Housing and Urban Development (HUD).
- Finally, Campus Partners would need to live up to private-sector expectations by playing the dual role of the redevelopment authority (assembling land and handling relocation, demolition, and environmental cleanup) and the source of "patient capital" (taking early risks related to planning and market studies, land purchases, etc.).

Incorporated in January 1995, Campus Partners for Community Urban Redevelopment was charged with developing a comprehensive neighborhood revitalization plan and implementation program for the university district. Campus Partners' mission extended to engaging in series of quality-of-life initiatives that included enhancing delivery of public services; implementing a university-sponsored home-ownership initiative; and promoting another initiative (Campus Collaborative) for improving education, employment, and health service. The staff of five was led by a president with a notable record in public- and private-sector redevelopment, and it included professionals with development, public relations, and community outreach experience. OSU committed $3 million in initial operating funds, followed by a $25 million investment from the university endowment for direct real estate investment purposes such as land assemblage. The university expected long-term financial rewards as well as other benefits from this larger investment, but with minimal returns for at least a decade.

Launching Campus Partners . . . and Meeting the Other Players

Campus Partners almost immediately selected a consultant to prepare an encyclopedic, district-wide compendium of neighborhood revitalization programs and strategies. The University Neighborhoods Revitalization Plan: Concept Document, completed in late 1996, was officially adopted by both the university and the city as the basis for further planning and revitalization activities. Controversy marked the Concept Document planning process, however, making it clear that even though the Campus Partners model might be inherently sound, the organization needed to develop far more effective approaches to community outreach and planning to achieve its goals.

First, Campus Partners needed to learn more about other key players and to develop working partnerships with local residents, business owners, the City of Columbus, and local property owners and developers. The highly diverse group of local residents—including Section 8 tenants, long-term residents, newer home owners, students, and others—had a wide range of sometimes conflicting goals. They did not necessarily set a high priority on the kinds of university-oriented businesses that Campus Partners' initial leadership envisioned. Instead they focused on enhanced services and neighborhood retail establishments, historic preservation, avoiding university expansion into the neighborhood, neighborhood political issues, and other concerns.

The city's planning professionals, meanwhile, recognized that they needed to inject public-sector concerns into the planning process, including economic development goals such as fiscal benefits and job creation; district design guidelines comparable to those developed in other neighborhoods; and troubleshooting to prevent political problems related to issues raised by other stakeholders. Finally, housing developers, while initially very supportive, grew concerned about competition from new development, possible eminent-domain takings, and access to potential development activities. The perceived lack of a community-based planning process and the wide range of issues raised by the initial planning effort combined to bring early momentum to a halt by the end of 1996.

In early 1997 Campus Partners' first president resigned and was replaced by Terry Foegler, who has planning and development experience in both the public and private sectors. He made two critical decisions: (1) to lead with more community-based planning and to let decisions reflect that broader involvement; and (2) to step back from a district-wide approach to implementation and proceed with a series of sequential projects that could be reasonably supported by community-based planning and more readily backed by the stakeholders identified above in addition to the university itself. Foegler decided to start by focusing on decline along High Street. After looking at both local and national examples, including the Short North and German Village districts in Columbus and "LoDo" in Denver, Campus Partners outlined a strategy in which the amenities, jobs, and services of a revived Main Street would attract students, faculty, staff, and other residents back to the district while creating a high-profile symbol for the university and the district.

Following a national search, Campus Partners hired Goody, Clancy & Associates (GC&A), a Boston-based planning and design firm, to create a vision and strategy for revitalizing High Street. Leading a team of real estate, retail development, transportation, and historic preservation consultants,

GC&A worked closely with Campus Partners over a two-year period. Two aspects of this process were critical to its success: effective community outreach and a development strategy that blended university, city, and private-sector capabilities and resources.

Outreach began when Campus Partners convened an Advisory Steering Committee chaired by the executive director of the University Community Business Association. The inclusion of many voices both lengthened and strengthened the public process, building into the resulting vision and strategy a strong sense of community, city, and university ownership, as well as strengthening financial feasibility. The final plan was forged during five days of continuous meetings with the steering committee. The larger community was kept informed through regular coverage in a monthly newspaper for the university district, the business association newsletter, and the *Columbus Dispatch*. The consultants and Campus Partners staff made frequent public presentations to university staff and neighborhood groups, and Campus Partners maintained an open office where it regularly briefed students, residents, and other visitors.

The development strategy combined complementary roles for the university, the city, and the private sector. The team's real estate and retail consultants affirmed projections that the right combination of university, city, and private investment could unlock considerable demand for retail, entertainment, housing, and services. The consultants identified demand for roughly 1 million square feet of new space in existing and new buildings along a two-mile stretch of High Street. The strategy focused on:

- *forming a parking authority* through a partnership joining the city, the university, and local property owners and businesses to respond to the area's severe parking shortage;
- *establishing a special improvement district* with seed funds and staff provided by Campus Partners, but ultimately supported by property owners and businesses, to insure that High Street remained "clean and safe" and to lead private-sector initiatives;
- *preparing development and design guidelines* funded by Campus Partners and officially adopted by the city to preserve the street's lively, often historic character;
- *offering facade- and building-improvement incentives* shaped by the guidelines; funded by the city, the university, and private sources; and supported by city-funded design services;
- *initiating strategic redevelopment projects*, including a major mixed-use "destination," to be known as South Campus Gateway, to anchor revitalization together with additional strategic redevelopment efforts; and

- *enhancing the public realm* through more than $5 million in streetscape and similar improvements, funded by the city in response to the plan and in accordance with the vision and guidelines.

Structuring a Redevelopment Strategy: Community Development as Enlightened Self-Interest

Two Campus Partners projects illustrate the risks and opportunities associated with the assumption of direct responsibility for community-based real estate development by universities.

The first, South Campus Gateway, is a 500,000-square-foot mixed-use center between the university's law school and the neighborhood Empowerment Zone. It represents an attempt to transform the image and substance of a marginal commercial district that has served as a primary gateway to campus for generations of students and faculty. The second, the Broad Street Revitalization Initiative, represents an equally bold foray into community-based real estate development by acquiring, renovating, and repositioning 1,385 units of severely distressed low-income housing. Despite striking differences between these two projects, certain clear lessons emerge from the attempts to transform a distressed urban neighborhood in the name of enhancing the university setting and sparking regional economic development.

South Campus Gateway

The centerpiece of the High Street revitalization strategy, South Campus Gateway, represents the culmination of more than five years of planning, public participation, and site assemblage. Designed as a bridge from campus to community and firmly rooted in the principles of comprehensive urban development, the 500,000-square-foot center mixes retail, office, and residential uses. Anchored by a Barnes & Noble College Bookstore and 70,000 square feet of OSU office space, it serves as a unique, high-quality destination for more than 70,000 people who live, study, work in, or visit OSU neighborhoods each day. By mid-2003, with retail tenants committed and other project elements in place, the site had been cleared and the project was moving through final design; construction was scheduled to begin in spring 2004. To reach this point, Campus Partners needed to learn a series of lessons about the role it could and should play in the development process.

Based on a presumption of market interest, the scale and complexity of the development task, and the university's preference for avoiding exposure to market risk, Campus Partners issued a nationwide RFP for firms interested in developing the proposed center. The RFP process invited leading design and development firms to propose a variety of uses, capital structures, and design characteristics within the guidelines established for the project by the planning process. An experienced firm with a national reputation for creating urban mixed-use centers was selected.

From the start, however, tensions began to appear between the university's own design, public benefit, and financial goals and the developer's investment objectives. Upon being designated, the developer launched a detailed assessment of Columbus's overbuilt retail market and at its conclusion advised Campus Partners that OSU would need to take additional steps to ensure the economic success of the development. These extra steps—from subordination of the university's ground lease interest in the land to acquisition of a college bookstore in order to attract a national bookstore chain as a retail anchor—raised fundamental questions about the financial viability of the proposal under the private development model. Perhaps more significant, the recommendations forced the university to reexamine its financial expectations for the development.

The difficulty of assuring adequate financial return on land and improvements is hardly news to firms engaged in urban real estate development, particularly for projects that must achieve significant public purposes in inner-city locations. Assembling multiple, privately owned parcels, relocating businesses and remediating existing conditions all can drive land costs above the residual land value associated with proposed improvements. In this case it became clear that a $20 million investment in site assembly was not the only cost the university would have to assume. OSU would need to defer and deeply subordinate its investment returns and security in order to achieve the developer's yield expectations and to attract private capital.

Faced with this challenge, Campus Partners began to explore alternative models: turnkey development (hiring a firm to develop the property with a guaranteed profit, although OSU would own the finished project); various joint-venture structures uniting the university and a private developer, which would open the door to a substitution of university investment for private debt/equity capital; and OSU serving as owner/developer, with an outside firm overseeing development for a fee. Campus Partners saw three advantages in these alternatives:

- maximized use of university resources, particularly resources that were not considered "scarce" (i.e., debt/bond capacity);
- protection of the university's public-purpose goals for the project, including the mix of uses, the quality of design, and the achievement of economic development goals for the community; and

- more accurate reflection of the respective contribution of each party in allocating investment benefits and generating fee revenue for Campus Partners.

With these alternatives under consideration, the university found itself taking on tasks that normally fall to a developer. In its attempts to attract a major bookstore as a retail anchor for the development, for example, OSU took the unusual step of acquiring an off-campus bookstore with a dominant share in the local textbook and booksellers market and with extensive real estate holdings in the commercial district. Further, the university entered into an agreement that made Barnes & Noble College Bookstores the sole operator of all campus bookstores. Finally, Campus Partners successfully procured approximately $15 million in public subsidies (including tax-increment financing) to underwrite significant public improvements, including a parking garage. These steps persuaded Barnes & Noble to sign a long-term lease as a tenant at South Campus Gateway.

If the university was acting in many ways as a developer, what was the advantage of continuing to work with—and subordinating the university's financial interests to—a master developer? In resolving this question, Campus Partners decided to assume the role of owner/developer, subject to a contract with a third-party fee developer. This decision reflected the increasing commitment and capacity of Campus Partners and struck a more appealing balance between the university's long-term expectations and the realities of the marketplace.

Broad Street Portfolio Revitalization

In its acquisition, redevelopment, and repositioning of 1,385 scattered units of distressed low-income housing, Campus Partners took on an even more unusual project. The properties in the Broad Street portfolio comprised more than 240 buildings scattered across the city's East Side that were home to nearly 1,000 young single women with children and a median income of less than $6,000. The revitalization of those homes had a pronounced effect on the climate for reinvestment within university neighborhoods.

The impact on the university district of the distressed portfolio, together with the destabilizing effects of high concentrations of off-campus student housing, cannot be overstated. Since the assembly of the Broad Street portfolio by a private developer in the mid-1970s, university neighborhoods had watched as home ownership dropped and crime rose dramatically. Unchallenged, these trends threatened to undermine the economic viability of the revitalization strategies proposed by Campus Partners, including South Campus Gateway.

Like most institutions engaged in direct development within urban communities, Campus Partners' first inclination was to avoid active redevelopment of the portfolio in favor of a more passive advocacy role. A HUD proposal to change the contract rents paid for units in the portfolio, however, was a clarion call to action. The change would have set rents at levels far below what was needed to support quality asset management, jeopardized the financial stability of the portfolio, and precluded rehabilitation. Acting just weeks before the mandatory imposition of this "mark to market" restructuring plan and a thirty-year contract extension, Campus Partners engaged Peter J. Roche to explore alternative directions for the portfolio and to negotiate an option agreement to acquire the thirteen partnerships that constituted the Broad Street portfolio.

The intervention by Campus Partners radically changed the political dynamic in the university neighborhoods by galvanizing dozens of civic and community organizations to become involved in the proposed restructuring. A nine-month deferral of the restructuring plan enabled Campus Partners to conduct due diligence, consult with residents and other stakeholders, raise capital, and propose an alternative vision for the restructuring. In June 2001, in collaboration with the Columbus Empowerment Zone, the City of Columbus, and dozens of community groups, Campus Partners unveiled an alternative proposal for revitalizing the Broad Street portfolio, including:

- preservation of 1,385 subsidized housing units, together with an unprecedented relocation of up to 500 of them to less distressed neighborhoods;
- a dramatic increase in the proposed scope of rehabilitation work (from $1 million to $37 million—sufficient to provide essential renovations in the low-construction-cost Columbus market), setting a new standard for reinvestment in this fragile urban neighborhood;
- reconfiguration of thirteen ownership entities into portfolios designed to reflect and reinforce the social geography of existing neighborhoods; and
- an agreement by HUD to negotiate a more sustainable rent level consistent with market conditions for comparable properties in more desirable settings.

Although not without controversy, this aggressive revitalization plan struck a balance between the goals of affordable housing advocates and neighborhood revitalization proponents (including OSU and the Empowerment Zone) who sought to reduce the concentration of low-income housing. Throughout this process Campus Partners was consistently viewed with varying degrees of mistrust rooted in a perception that the university secretly sought to displace poor residents, then convert vacated affordable units to student housing. To counter that perception, Campus Partners undertook a concerted community relations effort that culminated in the issuance of a Statement of Values calling for preservation and enhancement of a vulnerable community asset. This investment in community relations yielded significant public and political support.

Campus Partners initially assumed all of the development responsibilities for acquiring and restructuring the portfolio. In particular the organization secured site control, conducted due diligence, and secured significant financing commitments for the revitalization work. Additionally Campus Partners played an essential role in developing congressional support for the plan, including passage of earmarked budget legislation for the project.

Due to the project's complexity and dimensions, Campus Partners later entered into a joint venture with an experienced affordable housing owner/operator, Ohio Capital Corporation for Housing. This statewide nonprofit developer assumed the role of managing general partner and directs the day-to-day operations of the project. Campus Partners retains authority to oversee the portfolio operation and the option to exercise a right of first refusal for units located in university neighborhoods in the event of a default in project ownership or operation.

Lessons Learned

The Campus Partners model may serve other universities seeking to move beyond their campuses into community planning. At least five lessons can be drawn from the organization's experience.

First, certain characteristics of the organization proved key to its success in shepherding these two projects to development:

- an entrepreneurial culture that allowed the organization to exercise independent judgment and take decisive action, and a dedicated staff with specialized skills in the fields of planning, real estate, and community development;
- a clear, comprehensive, market-based vision and business strategy;
- a commitment to investing in time-consuming community-based planning and assuring the substantive involvement of the community in all aspects of development; and
- an ability to strike a balance between the political stature necessary to attract resources and the tyranny of mandatory consensus.

Second, no university should take on a community development project lightly. Although it is reasonable to expect a healthy return on investment, a university is not a conventional investor/developer. It should think of its investment as patient capital, with returns calculated over many years. It should anticipate investing in both thoughtful planning and serious community outreach. It should stand ready to assume unfamiliar roles and responsibilities. Institutions like OSU may have access to vast reservoirs of goodwill and technical, financial, and political resources, but these should not be squandered on poorly conceived projects that ignore local market conditions. Above all, while proceeding with care, a university should also understand that its greatest risk might lie in doing nothing.

Third, as both OSU projects demonstrate, the potential rewards of community-based development can be substantial—and may not always be defined in dollars. In the short term, meaningful investment in internal development capacity and a sincere engagement with local communities can yield extraordinary financial and political leverage. South Campus Gateway, for example, will generate $10 million to $15 million of public and social investment through such mechanisms as tax-increment financing districts, business improvement districts, new markets tax credits, and direct appropriations of public funds for infrastructure that supports community development. The Broad Street project represents even more substantial leverage: Campus Partners' modest early-stage investment in site control and predevelopment activity will unlock tens of millions of dollars in public and private capital, much of it directly supporting the overarching goals set out by OSU and Campus Partners for the campus community.

Fourth, a university undertaking a community development project may have to embrace many of the functions of a planning agency. Even with early efforts to establish a strong partnership with the city government in Columbus, for example, Campus Partners found that it could not rely on the city alone for community outreach. It needed to establish its own relationships with the myriad of neighborhood, advocacy, and business groups, churches, local planning boards, and other stakeholders that would play a role in planning and implementing revitalization. The university's first steps were not uniformly successful, despite a long history of community outreach. The scope and ambition of the developments that OSU proposed required an increased investment in community relations and planning, and a commitment to sharing decision making.

Finally, the indispensable element is leadership at the highest level. For Campus Partners it came directly from the OSU trustees and the president's office, which institutionalized community development as a core element of the effort to increase the school's standing among public universities in the United States. On another level universities themselves can take a leadership role in their communities. Particularly where public-sector planning capacity is limited, universities often prove to be the institutions best positioned to catalyze larger planning efforts. Backed by strong internal support, a university development initiative can renew the campus, energize faculty and students, and strengthen the community that the university calls home.

Part IV

Lessons Learned

16

Private Choices and Public Obligations

The Ethics of University Real Estate Development

Rachel Weber, Nik Theodore, and Charles Hoch

Current assessments of university real estate development typically describe projects that are jointly planned and sponsored by university administrators and private developers. Such case studies tend to celebrate mutual gains and exhort participants to build on modest beginnings. Although analysts may recognize that conflicts can arise because of construction delays or the exact allocation of returns, the fundamental interests of the university and the development community are assumed to converge around these joint community-building efforts.

The contemporary research university is not a typical development partner, however. The expectations placed on it by a large and diverse group of stakeholders, the loose hierarchy to which it aspires, and its mission to serve broad public interests give universities, and in particular public universities, a unique organizational form and decision-making structure. The contracts signed by developers and universities to govern their deals are but one expression of the trust necessary to sustain relationships with the multiple stakeholders that comprise the university community. Moreover, such agreements have the potential to substantively ignore the broader purposes of the university and to subvert other ends to which members of the different communities may be committed. University officials must ask whether real estate development is an objective worthy of realization in light of the means it may require. In other words they must address the ethical ambiguities and challenges encountered when their universities act as developers.

In this chapter we make the argument that ethics matter in university real estate deals and then suggest examples of what we call "practical ethics" that can assist us in evaluating such transactions. To illustrate how practical ethics are either ignored, undermined, or operationalized in specific instances, we examine the case of the University of Illinois at Chicago, describing its development goals and the changing means through which those goals were pursued. We do not seek to provide an exhaustive list of "commandments" that must be followed for any deal to be considered ethical. Nor do we attempt to set out principles whose application can and should be constant or universal across cases. Our hopes are more modest: we wish to demonstrate how ethical principles can be part of the tool kit that university dealmakers use to craft good development agreements.

The Ethics of University Real Estate Development

The Urban University

The contemporary research university is itself a community of communities—multiple colleges and departments bound together by a campus bureaucracy. The university administration primarily attempts to meet the demands of competing colleges. When the leadership of the research university looks beyond the immediate campus, it also attends to the responsibilities and rewards of national and international research communities. University leadership and administration must manage uncertainty about their own success and the survival of the institution. Put simply, each administrative regime seeks security and predictability both on and off campus to pursue improved national and international stature among peer institutions.

These goals translate into two sorts of demands for physical facilities: those that enhance the effectiveness and prestige of the research disciplines, and those that satisfy local demands for student and employee housing, security, and other campus amenities. The university uses its economic power and social influence to acquire property for these facilities and to negotiate favorable development contracts for the expansion and redevelopment of the campus.

Urban settings pose a special challenge for campus expansion because universities must plan and build in areas that already are densely developed (Berube 1978). Implementation of the pastoral campus ideal, with low-rise buildings and ample open space, is constrained by high land costs, proximity to neighboring property owners and residents, and city officials for whom universities represent but one of many corporate-institutional constituents. Moreover, because of changes in the demographic composition of many North American cities, universities often find themselves in or surrounded by low-income neighborhoods of color. These communities often resent what they view as the institution's privileged position and disregard for their well-being, both of which conspire to limit their access to university resources.

While the university leaves a large footprint on the urban landscape, it also generates economic impacts that spread across the region and the globe. Its influence increases the number and demands of potential stakeholders, which include a large assortment of neighborhood associations, donors, employees, students, governmental units, and vendors (Gills 2002). For instance, local nonprofit community development organizations advocate for the interests of residential neighbors; business and trade associations lobby for university contracts; and unions seek to improve the working conditions of staff. University administrators are in the difficult position of balancing and prioritizing the multiple and sometimes competing interests of these stakeholders.

We believe that those university employees and officials responsible for planning, negotiating, and implementing development projects shoulder significant responsibilities not only for their own conduct, but also for the broad impact of their policies and practices. The university may possess similar legal status as other large corporations, but the university often enjoys greater public authority. This authority flows from a mission that involves much more than selling educational services; universities are responsible for nurturing creative arts, harboring intellectual freedom, inspiring public service, subsidizing innovative research, and the like. This authority also imposes obligations on the university administration when it acts to improve the physical infrastructure of the campus. In sum, university dealmakers need to do more than meet the conventional standards of good real estate practice; they also need to draw upon the norms that give the university its civic authority and status.

Moreover, many believe that public universities should be held to even higher standards of conduct. Their missions to serve broad public interests are legislated by charter, particularly in the case of land-grant universities. They receive tax revenues and special legal considerations that, for example, allow them to issue debt at rates lower than other corporations. Such benefits and privileges support the notion that the public university should make special efforts to accommodate the greater diversity of demands articulated by those affected by its conduct.

Three Ethical Norms and Two Guiding Principles

Ethics refers to the values different university officials and employees use to guide their conduct in making deals. Ethical conduct is situational; it is negotiated by deliberation among a shifting set of stakeholders inside and outside the university. People act ethically within the framework of institutional roles that combine moral and political considerations.

When the university and its employees or contractors engage in development deals, they should pay close attention to three particular norms: legitimacy, efficiency, and fairness. These norms correspond to three overarching questions: Does the deal fit the basic purposes of the university and those it serves? Does the deal offer good market value for the university as a competitor in the real estate market? Does the deal treat the relevant parties fairly?

Translating these values into the complex web of relationships among different stakeholders requires principles to foster organizational and social trust and agreement. We think two principles are especially important for building trust: reciprocity and transparency. No matter how ethical an individual university negotiator may be, if important members of the relevant stakeholder groups do not trust him or her, resistance is likely to ensue. Universities, especially public universities, enjoy special powers and authority because people believe that the university administration will act in ways that take the interests of others and of a greater good into account. Yet the very size and authority of universities makes it difficult for different stakeholders to fully submit themselves to such authority—especially in a society with strong democratic traditions.

Applying the principles of reciprocity and transparency anticipates the problems of organizational indifference and complexity. Reciprocity requires that all partners achieve some form of mutually advantageous exchange through sustained cooperation. It does not imply that development partners start out from similar positions of power (i.e., equal footing), but that they agree upon the distribution of benefits as well as the conditions that must be satisfied before those benefits are realized. Transparency requires that information channels allow partners to comprehend the interests, intentions, and capabilities of each partner. It does not mean that all information is disclosed indiscriminately (which, in fact, may constitute a dereliction of fiduciary duty), but rather that information be relevant, actionable, and delivered on a timely basis.

Additionally our approach emphasizes practical deliberations that improve the legitimacy, efficiency, and fairness of the deal among the relevant stakeholders. Good university deals may flow from the enlightened self-interest of intermediate negotiators, but few people touched by such deals want to rely on this ideal alone. We think that negotiators and stakeholders create more ethical deals when their collaborations put the principles of reciprocity and transparency to practical use, clarifying how the intentions of the university translate into more legitimate, efficient, and fair improvements for relevant stakeholders.

The ethical distinctions we make in this chapter build on those elaborated by the Center for Ethics and the Professions at Harvard University. The center identifies three significant dimensions of practical ethics. First, practical ethics involves the use of moral principles rather than relying upon either the deductive application of norms or intuitive judgment of normative fit. Second, practical ethics focus on institutions and the ethical relevance of the complex roles that link individual conduct, policy, and administration. Third, practical ethics relies on deliberations that may change both how we conduct our roles and the norms that guide the roles we play (CEP 2003). Additionally our treatment of efficiency and fairness draws upon the ideas of justice from the work of Michael Walzer (1983), authority from Charles Anderson (1985), reciprocity from Peter Marris (1996), and transparency from Amartya Sen (1999).

Efficiency

That a good development deal relies upon the norm of efficiency hardly requires elaboration. The parties to any financially successful agreement respond to competitive pricing based, ideally, in unfettered exchange. If parties to the deal obscure important information to blind the judgment of competitors and partners (e.g., knowledge about environmental contamination), they will foster inefficient outcomes. If partnerships are based only on kinship or favoritism, instead of a notion of reciprocity and exchange mediated through market prices, outcomes may be similarly inefficient.

The university administration enters deal making in much the same way as do realtors, developers, and contractors: that is, instrumentally. Contracts provide a framework for negotiations that seek to ensure that the distribution of risk does not undermine the prospects for profitability. But exclusive concern for competitive economic gains among the players discourages attention to either longer-term consequences of the deal or the needs of the marginal and weaker parties unable to enter the negotiations with standing. Challenging the privileged position of profit making becomes an important ethical practice.

Large university projects are both complex and relatively unique, often making them expensive and risky. The profit-seeking players involved in the deal will seek to shift the risk to others, especially to future risk bearers. The clever deal maker seeks to find ways to shift risk to others and, in doing so, avoid costs and responsibility for undesirable consequences. In contrast the ethical deal maker seeks to identify and allocate risks in ways that calibrate the burdens and the benefits over time. Such reciprocity often extends beyond the bounds of the written contract.

Legitimacy

We expect developers to make deals that will generate profits. When universities enter the marketplace, however, we expect that their deal making will do more than earn a return on investment. Universities typically pursue land development not as an end, but as a means of achieving other goals that satisfy the interests of their many communities. Those who participate and benefit from their relationships with the university do so as employees, contractors, clients (e.g., students, patients), or neighbors. These are relationships based mainly not only on contract, but also on service and proximity.

The university acting as developer must possess the authority to pool, prioritize, and represent the interests of these different stakeholders. University leadership, usually the administration and governing board, authorizes a proposed real estate deal. For all universities, the legitimacy of such authority flows from legal statute and charter as well as the consent of the different parts of the universities (e.g., boards of trustees, college faculties, staff, and students). Public universities also must attend to communities outside the university itself, including governmental bodies such as state legislatures and the wide assortment of civic communities affected by university policies and practices.

University deal makers must offer justifications to the communities within the university regarding the value and importance of the development project as a worthy means of furthering university goals. Additionally they must offer justifications to those communities outside the university whom the proposed project will impact. These justifications may appear in plans, redevelopment agreements, or other public documents. When universities make these justifications of the development deals transparent to the relevant parties inside and outside the university, they legitimize their authority to carry out a deal "in the public interest."

Fairness

The fair development deal addresses the interests of those who face a disproportionate burden given their limited access to potential rewards. This makes practical moral sense because the deal makers take steps that reduce the potential suffering of the most vulnerable. In doing so they learn how current arrangements reinforce such vulnerability and what might be done to remedy these arrangements. For instance, if a small group of powerful deal makers keeps secrets from other relevant parties, this increases the exposure of such parties to undue hardships. Sharing this knowledge reduces the discretion of the powerful and enables the weaker parties with a stake in the outcome to influence the outcome by shaping the deal.

Including the weaker parties in the negotiations may improve the legitimacy of the deal, but does not ensure more reciprocal outcomes. University
deal makers might establish a more inclusive process, but then avoid establishing meaningful reciprocity by taking only symbolic actions to ensure
that benefits accrue to weaker parties. These actions might include making
committee appointments, forming advisory groups, or promising future benefits to marginal or weaker parties whose members bear the brunt of the
negative consequences (e.g., displacement). The clever deal maker co-opts
the weaker parties. The ethical deal maker builds into the agreement incentives to take these parties' interests into account.

The Case of the University of Illinois at Chicago

In this case study we evaluate the degree to which the creation and development of the University of Illinois at Chicago (UIC) met the ethical standards
outlined above. As an urban renewal project in a densely populated urban
core, the development of the Circle Campus of the University of Illinois
system seemed destined for controversy and community opposition over the
course of its lifetime. However, UIC's willingness and ability to work with
its immediate neighbors and the City of Chicago has evolved and improved
over three distinct phases. As we will argue in the conclusion, the university
did not undergo an ethical conversion during this period, but rather gradually
adopted greater transparency and reciprocity to both enhance its effectiveness as a developer and to respond to demands presented by its stakeholders.

Expansion, 1960–1980

During the university's expansion phase, the ethical principles of reciprocity
and transparency were consistently subordinated to the priorities of big-city
machine politics. Patronage and closed-door deal making between state authorities (such as the Illinois Housing Board), leading civic organizations,
the mayor's office, federal agencies (such as the Federal Housing and Home
Finance Agency), and the university's Board of Trustees precluded meaningful input into the decision-making process by residents, community organizations, and local business owners (Rosen 1980).

The City of Chicago and Mayor Richard J. Daley, in particular, took a
leadership position in bringing a campus of the University of Illinois to Chicago. The interests of the state university system and the City of Chicago
coalesced around a site on the city's Near West Side. The university wanted
an urban campus to accommodate the surging demand for higher education,
and Mayor Daley sought to use such a development to shore up the western

flank of the city's ailing downtown and protect the Loop and the area north of the campus, viewed as the city's Skid Row, from further deterioration. Unable to secure rights to the vast rail yards abutting downtown, the mayor settled for the Harrison-Halsted site with its concentration of urban renewal property and low-income inhabitants.

In seeking to expedite the construction process, several channels for community participation were closed down, violating the principle of transparency. For example, the city initiated the land disposition process without notifying key representatives of the local community. As Ferman (1996, 69; emphasis added) reveals, "Daley's top planners were researching the Harrison-Halsted site and were under strict orders not to reveal anything to the public *or even to university officials*. By the time Daley announced that the Harrison-Halsted corridor was an alternative site, it was, in fact, the only site." Moreover, such actions preempted the possibility of an organized neighborhood response and shifted all venues for decision making from the community level to the city council, the state legislature, the Illinois Housing Board, and the courts. Bennett (1989, 169) notes, "In none of these places could proponents offer alternative proposals or debate the substantive merits of the UIC-city proposal." Although an injunction suit was filed by an organization of residents in 1963, the Illinois Supreme Court ruled against the resident group and the campus was built.

Involving the federal government in the redevelopment scheme and using land that the city controlled as part of a federal urban renewal project satisfied two objectives: (1) it avoided the need for approval of the necessary action by a local group other than the city; and (2) it enabled the city to get the federal government to take over most of its financing obligation to the university (Rosen 1980, 161). It also redrew the lines of accountability, favoring one set of reciprocal relations (i.e., city-federal) over others. For example, Daley's strong support for the new Democratic president, John F. Kennedy, was rewarded with the federal government's willingness to provide the urban renewal funds to subsidize land acquisition and clearance. This exchange of political favors was made at the expense of the city's prior commitment to neighborhood leaders to support grassroots development (see Bennett 1989; Rosen 1980).

During the expansion phase, as was the norm in this era, the principle of transparency was largely disregarded by powerful public actors working in concert. Community organizations as well as project partners were denied critical information and access that would have allowed them to have any meaningful input into the planning process. In particular the residents' inability to influence the process was not proportionate to the burden they were forced to bear. By the completion of the project, the area had lost approximately 14,000 residents and 630 businesses (Cohen and Taylor 2000).

Consolidation, 1980–95

The decline in federal funding for urban renewal combined with the death of Mayor Daley reconfigured the stakeholder relationships through which the university sought to achieve its development objectives. In 1983, after the Chicago Circle campus officially merged with the Medical Center, the president of the University of Illinois system asked the then 182.5-acre Chicago campus to begin its own planning process. University administration projected a need for an additional 2.3 million gross square feet within the next twenty years (UIC 1984). New proposals for campus buildings began to appear in departmental budgets.

Surrounded on all sides by the low-income neighborhoods of color that urban renewal had spared in the previous period, the university's expansion plans confronted problems associated with land acquisition and community relations. At first it chose to deal with the challenges surreptitiously (Gerut 1990). In 1988 the university set up a private trust fund to acquire property in a depopulated commercial area south of the campus. The site of the historically important Maxwell Street Market, this area was home to an outdoor flea market and more than a dozen retailers. Here the ethical principle of transparency conflicted with accepted market practices. Understandably the university did not want to signal its expansion intentions to private real estate developers or property owners, which would have set off a frenzy of speculative buying and selling. In addition to securing cheaper land, the secrecy accorded by the trust would allow the university more time to come up with a stronger master plan for the area. Secrecy, officials believed, would help them avoid rekindling the tensions of the past, since many community members had not forgotten the earlier betrayal.

The university's expansion plans were heavily dependent on the city's landholdings, planning authority, and aldermanic influence on community relations. However the city was unsure of how the university's vague objectives meshed with its own goals and the well-being of the neighborhood. UIC requested that the city put an end to the sale of all city-owned land in the targeted area until its planning process could be completed. The city balked at the suggestion, unwilling to cede its authority without receiving assurances as to how and when the land would be used. The city demanded that the university put together a master plan before additional concessions would be made.

The election of Richard M. Daley (son of Richard J. Daley) as mayor dramatically improved city-university relations and again saw the city as an active player in (as opposed to regulator of) the university's expansion plans. Expressing its interest to engage in "joint planning for the area," the city obtained title to tax-delinquent properties in the area and demolished those that were deteriorated. The city then sold its land in the expansion area to the university via quitclaim deeds. It also agreed to vacate certain streets and alleys at no cost to the university, relocate the Maxwell Street Market, and undertake street improvements. In return the university agreed to finance the market and land use analysis for the area when the city's budget for such activities was cut.

The university's consolidation phase saw a change in stakeholder relations. Although in many ways UIC still enjoyed the support of city hall, officials were increasingly prepared to use the city's regulatory authority to safeguard the public interest. The city held the university to a higher standard of transparency than had been required during the expansion phase, demanding that UIC reveal its plans before further development would be approved. The city was especially concerned that UIC live up to its responsibility as one of the largest landowners on the West Side, understanding that the institution's development decisions would have far-reaching impacts on current and future land uses in the surrounding area.

Revitalization, 1995–present

During this phase UIC's priorities shifted dramatically from expanding the institutional boundaries of the university to meet the space needs of academic departments and students to, in the words of Stan Delaney, executive director of the project, "building a new community almost from ground zero" (cited in Corfman 1999). In 1996 the interim chancellor intimated that the campus expansion would require more than an arm's length relationship with a developer. The state legislature did not appear willing to allocate sufficient funds to pay for the project's additional land acquisition and infrastructure as envisioned and asking for these funds might have come at the expense of other traditional academic budget items (UIC 1996a). Therefore a joint venture with a private developer was proposed that would add private, market-rate housing and commercial development to the original proposal for residence halls and academic and recreational facilities. Controversial legislation was passed to give the university authority, as a public institution, to enter into a private development deal, permitting activities such as selling university-owned property to private parties.

The request for proposals for the joint venture reflected this shift in focus. It stated that the university was willing to

> entertain proposals for privately developed housing that will meet needs of faculty and staff, *as well as address community housing goals*. This

program element would help to attract more faculty to the area adjacent to the university and foster development of a more traditional campus atmosphere . . . an explicit strategy for community building activity should be identified if the developer includes this element as part of the proposed development (UIC 1996b, emphasis added).

Encouraged by the buoyant housing market, the possibility of building one of the largest new construction projects in Chicago's densely developed core, and the apparent compliance of city and state administrations, the winning development team (eventually) proposed to build 900 units of market-rate housing. As negotiations progressed, it became apparent that this housing was intended not only to contribute to UIC's community building effort but also to help foot the bill for an increasingly expensive undertaking, which came to be known as University Village. All of the responses to the RFP assumed that the university would finance the bulk of project costs. Few, if any, were willing to contribute their own equity. In addition the university would have to install new infrastructure and purchase an additional 15.2 acres (at inflated prices) to accommodate the project. This was land it would eventually sell back to the developers.

Instead of hiring fee developers and paying them with funds from standard-issue capital improvement bonds, the university turned to the city for support. The City of Chicago designated the proposed development site as a tax increment financing (TIF) district. This designation allowed the University of Illinois system to receive 95 percent of the new property tax revenues that would be generated in the project area over a twenty-three-year period to pay back new bond issues. These tax revenues (i.e., the "increment") would help the university repay almost $100 million of the $525 million development (Shields 1999). Because state-owned buildings do not generate any property taxes, market-rate housing became a financial necessity.

Bringing the activities of the private real estate market to bear on the repayment of publicly issued debt subjected the university system to the scrutiny of the financial markets. Moody's gave the new TIF bond issues a slightly lower bond rating because the expansion pushed the university's debt capacity to the limit. Standard and Poor's noted that "universities are not usually in the business of improving neighborhoods, and having a role in private development is rare. But if UIC's goal is to dramatically improve the campus environment, they can't do it alone" (Shields 1999; see also Brick 2002). The expansion-related bonds constituted the largest borrowings in years for the university system and increased the amount of the operating budget that debt service will consume to 3 percent (from 2 percent).

As the interests of private developers, city planners, and financial actors came together around the new community-building objective, some began to wonder if the public status of the university was being used for inappropriate private gain. Moreover the universe of potential stakeholders expanded, and the demands they made of each other became increasingly complex. Committing a substantial amount of public funds to this quasi-private deal also brought new obligations and demands for transparency and a more equitable distribution of benefits.

Facing questions about the legitimacy and fairness of the deal, the university and city reached out to incorporate the interests of previously excluded neighbors in the development process. The university established a committee for structuring community involvement to review the proposals submitted through the RFP process, although the university retained the right of selection. The centerpiece of efforts to involve the local residents was the "community benefits clause" of the redevelopment agreement signed by the University of Illinois Board of Trustees and the City of Chicago. This committed the university to contracting goals to ensure participation by minority and women business enterprises. UIC also agreed to double the number of Latino employees (from 8 percent to 16 percent) at the university as a whole (Washburn 1997).[1]

The city, too, took its representative role more seriously. Even though the expansion project was a high priority for Mayor Daley, the city held the university to very specific and stringent community benefits standards. For its part the city attempted to create more widespread community benefits by stipulating that a portion of the 900 units of private housing be "affordable" to households earning 80 to 120 percent of the regional median income. The sale prices for these units, as well as the relocation costs for existing merchants and residents, would be subsidized with the TIF funds.

UIC's South Campus Development Project was extraordinary in many respects. Completing such a massive project in an era of greater interdependence between public and private actors and demands for greater openness required the university to cultivate relationships of trust that extended beyond mere contractual obligations. In the process, however, new conflicts arose. For example, in extending itself to further private as well as public goals, the university found itself in an awkward position, beholden to profit-seeking private interests, to its public mandate to deliver high-quality education at a reasonable cost, and to its responsibility to minimize harm to neighboring residents and institutions. The university team had to simultaneously internalize both the market values of the financiers and the political demands of minority stakeholders.

Conclusion

The UIC development examples illustrate the ethical ambiguities university deal makers face when undertaking real estate projects. A reciprocal relationship requires that parties abide by their agreements without any hidden constraints or deceptive promises. In such cases parties should receive benefits that are proportionate to the investments they make, risks they take, or burdens they shoulder. These additional criteria for the distribution of benefits require political judgments about who has standing in the deal and their relevant needs. The university may enjoy legal corporate status, but as a social and public institution it must attend to the needs of its multiple communities.

During UIC's expansion phase, city officials engaged in machine politics that shunned transparency to close the deal, while embracing patronage-based reciprocity to build the campus. The city and university did little to offset the burdens of displacement imposed on the residents and business owners forced to move when the campus was constructed. When the deal makers used state powers to exclude relevant parties from the deal, they violated the tenets of reciprocity.

The transparency of UIC's development deals improved over the ensuing forty years, although, particularly during the land acquisition phase, it could be argued that some degree of secrecy was necessary to move the deal forward. In this case improved transparency proved crucial by helping replace routine suspicion with modest trust. This improved the legitimacy and authority of the university even as it reduced discretion. The legacy of patronage required clear signals of public disclosure to offset earlier practices of deception.

The city's role shifted from political patron to regulator to accomplice over this period. Reforms eroded the patronage machine's indifference to minorities, civic groups, and other sources of opposition. City officials shared knowledge and expanded the range of public procurement to include a wider and less docile array of contractors. The resulting improvements in the ethical dimensions of its development decisions did not reflect a self-conscious conversion, but a gradual awakening to the efficacy of democratic participation in a context of increasing political demands.

The political power of UIC grew enormously over four decades, as did its economic role in the development of the city. However the scale and complexity of the university made it both practically difficult and strategically risky to seek unilateral development authority. The university development team increasingly realized that the political disapproval of state legislators, neighbors, employees, and the city (articulated through market, political, or legal means) would trump any attempts at unilateral expansion. The increasing demands of privatization (e.g., the TIF) forced the university development team to internalize market values at the same time as increasing political demands pressured them to expand the circle of stakeholders. The UIC development staff crafted a compromise that sought to balance benefits to both the developer and previously excluded stakeholders.

The legitimacy of university development deals hinges on an authority that seeks to identify, anticipate, and include the interests of all relevant relationships both within and outside the university (Gills 2002). Public benefits that flow from deals do not arise spontaneously from private exchange, but through negotiations that combine the principles of transparency and proportional reciprocity. As transparency increases, even marginalized stakeholders can grasp the meaning of project consequences, for themselves and for others. Such inclusion enhances the legitimacy of the deal and places moral and political pressure on the university staff to ensure fairness. The UIC development team took important steps in this direction, but has traveled only a short distance so far.

This chapter shows how ethical principles can be used to inform university development deals. The case surely can be made to include additional values (e.g., sustainability) and principles (e.g., integrity) that we did not consider. Additionally, some readers might expect that arguments be made supporting the priority of one value over others in specific instances (e.g., efficiency over fairness). However, our objective was not to make such a case, but rather to emphasize the relevance of practical ethics and challenges associated with ethical conduct in the context of university development deals. Our approach opens the door for future work that builds on this foundation to connect to broader questions of university policy and administration and to the deeper ethical assumptions on which such deals depend.

Notes

The authors wish to thank the editors and contributors to this volume for their helpful comments and suggestions. We also thank Ranada Harrison and Bill Neuendorf, who provided research assistance.

1. This provision was, in fact, quite strategic. Building political support for the TIF district in city council and community support for the expanded development involved brokering deals with local Latino leaders. Redistricting had recently altered the racial and ethnic composition of the ward within which the university is located.

References

Anderson, Charles. 1985. The place of principles in policy analysis. In *Ethics in planning*, ed. Martin Wachs, 193–215. New Brunswick, NJ: Center for Urban Policy Research.

Bennett, Larry. 1989. Postwar redevelopment in Chicago: The declining politics of party and the rise of neighborhood politics. In *Unequal partnerships: The political economy of urban redevelopment in postwar America*, ed. Gregory D. Squires, 161–177. New Brunswick, NJ: Rutgers University Press.

Berube, Maurice. 1978. *The urban university in America*. Westport, CT: Greenwood Press.

Brick, Michael. 2002. Big deals on campus: Special-purpose entities. *New York Times*, July 24: C6.

Center for Ethics and the Professions (CEP). Harvard University. 2003. http://ethicstest.harvard. edu/mission/practical_ethics.html.

Cohen, Adam, and Elizabeth Taylor. 2000. *American pharaoh*. Boston: Little, Brown and Company.

Corfman, Thomas. 1999. A new course: With Maxwell Street revamp plan, UIC gets into the development biz. *Crain's Chicago Business,* October 4: 17.

Ferman, Barbara. 1996. *Challenging the growth machine: Neighborhood politics in Chicago and Pittsburgh*. Lawrence: The University Press of Kansas.

Gerut, John. 1990. The University of Illiniois at Chicago expansion plans: A history and theory of large institutional expansion. Unpublished master's project. Chicago: UIC.

Gills, Douglas. 2002. Unequal and uneven: Critical aspects of university-community partnerships. In *Collaborative Research: University and Community Partnership*, ed. Myrtis Sullivan and Marilyn Willis, 27–48. New York: American Public Health Association.

Marris, Peter. 1996. *The politics of uncertainty.* London: Routledge.

Rosen, George. 1980. *Decision-making Chicago-style: The genesis of a University of Illinois campus*. Urbana: University of Illinois Press.

Sen, Amartya. 1999. *Development as freedom.* New York: Anchor.

Shields, Yvette. 1999. Deal in focus: University of Illinois ready to ramp up debt with twin offerings. *The Bond Buyer,* December 1: 42.

University of Illinois at Chicago. 1984. A look to the future: Strategic plans for UIC.

———. 1996a. Report from the Chancellor, Chicago: Development plans for South Campus. June 13.

———. 1996b. Request for proposals. Unpublished document.

Walzer, Michael. 1983. *Spheres of justice: A defense of pluralism and equality.* New York: Basic Books.

Washburn, Gary. 1997. UIC agrees to double Latino staff; accord also calls for more contracts. *Chicago Tribune,* November 21: D9.

17

Ivory Towers No More

Academic Bricks and Sticks

Wim Wiewel and David C. Perry

University real estate development is a new area of academic and applied inquiry. As discussed in the introductory chapter, these development activities are part of the larger issue of the relations between the university and its city and community, and they raise perennial questions. But these questions have become more pronounced with the increased role of large research universities, in particular, as major employers, generators of economic development, and key components of the local, national, and global knowledge economy. This chapter sums up what we have learned about the nature of university development projects—their impact on the university's neighborhood and the city, and on the institution itself. How do universities go about implementing these projects, and what appear to be the best practices? What are the policy, practice, and research questions raised by the increasing role of universities as developers in their cities?

Shaping the City, the Neighborhood, and the Campus

The main reason universities engage in real estate development projects is that they need additional space for their core activities. This is the central motivation in fifteen of the twenty-two cases represented in the preceding chapters, while improvement of the surrounding neighborhood was the main motivation in most of the remaining cases. The biggest projects involve the construction of whole new campuses, such as the Auraria Higher Education Center in Denver, the Tacoma campus of the University of Washington, the University of Illinois at Chicago, and Indiana University-Purdue University at Indianapolis. These massive undertakings almost inevitably involve displacement of current residents and businesses, but in the end have a positive effect on their immediate area, and often the entire city. They represent a major commitment by the higher education institutions and are undertaken only with large amounts of public funding and political support.

The development of these new campuses in a sense created, in all four cases, whole new neighborhoods close to their cities' downtowns. In most cases this was not incidental, but a conscious intention on the part of key decision makers. Thus these projects were also part of each city's transformation, enabling the city to play a central role in the knowledge economy at a global or regional level. For Indianapolis the new campus became a major part of restructuring downtown, including an emphasis on athletics. In Tacoma the new branch of the University of Washington is revitalizing an obsolete warehousing district. In both Chicago and Denver, where the new campuses were started respectively in the 1960s and 1970s, low-income downtown neighborhoods slated for urban renewal were transformed, but at significant human cost. Even now this process is not yet completed. UIC's Near West Side neighborhood continues to lose low- and moderate-income housing units and gain upper-middle income housing and commercial space, as the university and many private developers convert old public housing, an old major food wholesale market, an old hospital, and other smaller buildings and sites. Demand for this housing is high because Chicago's downtown continues to offer the region's major business and financial services jobs and the city in general has once again become attractive for new or returning residents.

Construction of a whole new campus, of course, is relatively rare. More frequently, existing campuses expand by adding classrooms, office space, laboratories, dormitories, athletic facilities, or other buildings to enhance academic life. This physical expansion is the inevitable by-product of the growth of higher education generally. The research activities of universities continue to expand; student numbers are at or near all-time highs; and the expectation on universities to provide housing, social activities, and support services continues to grow. Over time these projects can have a significant effect on the neighborhoods surrounding the campus.

The primary concern for about half a dozen of the cases in this volume was improving the appearance, safety, and socioeconomic status of adjacent neighborhoods. The most well-known of these cases is probably the University of Chicago. As long ago as 1952 the university established a neighborhood organization, the Southeast Chicago Commission, to ward off the economic decline of its Hyde Park neighborhood, and the university's efforts continue to this date. The chapters on Ohio State University, University of Pennsylvania, and Columbia, and the briefer descriptions of Saint Louis University and Marquette University, give other examples.

Most striking about these cases is the levels of commitment such efforts requires. Ohio State invested $28 million from its endowment; Penn has been involved in its West Philadelphia neighborhood for several decades, involving hundreds of faculty members and thousands of students; and, while not represented in this book, Yale invested $20 million from its endowment in physical redevelopment of its adjacent commercial area. These projects also require a lot of time and concerted attention, and always run the risk of causing their own raised expectations. While these chapters were not designed as full-fledged evaluations of these efforts, it is clear that the universities' involvements with their neighborhoods have achieved many of their goals. Also the process itself has usually had intermediate beneficial effects: housing has been rehabilitated; new community facilities were built; students have gained learning opportunities; and local residents have received services. It is clear, though, that serious attempts to change conditions in adjacent neighborhoods are not for the faint of heart, and they require long time commitments .

Another effect of undertaking real estate development outside of the traditional campus boundaries is that it may help raise the institution's profile locally and even nationally. While some of this visibility in UIC's case was the result of community opposition to the project, it nevertheless helped position the university more clearly as one of the city's major institutions. DePaul gained in stature by redeveloping a major downtown department store that has now become a hub of academic and civic life. Georgia State University's role in downtown revitalization distinguished it from its older and bigger neighbor, Georgia Tech. Both Northeastern and Temple engaged in real estate development as part of their transformation from local to national institutions. Especially for younger or lower-ranked institutions such as the ones mentioned here, a major development project, apart from being necessary for their growth, may also give them a boost in their quest for higher rankings and greater visibility.

The Process of Real Estate Development: What Institutions Do and What Works

The cases represented in this book allow us to formulate some general conclusions and draw broad lessons that appear to hold true for several of them. Many of the institutions required very strong and committed *leadership* to be successful. They often had to spend some time developing the right *internal structure* in order to conduct effective real estate development. They also had to decide to act alone or with *partners and intermediaries*. Any time development takes place outside the traditional campus neighborhood, *relations with the neighborhood* become a major issue, as do *relations with city government*. Given that, it is perhaps not surprising that the development process often is a *long and winding road*, with ever-lengthening timelines and many obstacles. Finally, *financing* posed challenges throughout, although perhaps less so than might have been expected.

Leadership

Given the complexity of real estate development, it is not surprising that strong leadership seems to be a critical success factor in many of the projects described here. The preferences and style of the person in charge (usually the chancellor or president) will affect the type of projects undertaken and how relations with the community, the city, or the private sector are handled. Regardless of preferences or style, commitment to the project is often essential to get it completed at all.

For instance, presidents like Gordon Gee at Ohio State, Sheldon Hackney and Judith Rodin at Penn, and the president of Marquette University led the community involvement of their institutions. At Northeastern, President Richard Freeland had to intervene personally to overcome internal dissension. Carl Patton at Georgia State developed a close working relationship with Atlanta's power structure and was directly involved in many of the real estate projects. UIC Chancellor James Stukel cared deeply about a close relationship with the mayor and hence was willing to have the university take heat from the community for acquiring land and displacing the fabled Maxwell Street Market. However, his plan for land banking was scuttled by his successor, who was much more comfortable with the private sector and sold most of the land to a private developer. At the University of Pittsburgh, Chancellor Mark Nordenberg, appointed in 1995, focused attention on regional economic and community development, especially for adjacent communities, and he subsequently named a point person for contacts with the community related to construction projects, a move that apparently made all the difference.

The cases where strong leadership was lacking seem to have been more difficult to complete. Ryerson University's project in Toronto is very interesting in that it would give the university daytime use of movie theaters for classes. However, while the university seems to have given up some of its rights, development hit a five-year delay and the movie theaters were not built in time for their intended use in 2003, when an anticipated enrollment surge occurred. On the other hand strong leadership may also cause conflicts. An enduring conflict between the president of Temple University and a local council member stymied several projects over a period of years. In Louisville the university's president was generally seen as having been too intransigent in negotiations over its use of a new downtown basketball facility that would also be used to attract a professional franchise.

At a small number of institutions leadership seems to have been suffi-ciently institutionalized that, even without much evidence of direct interven-tion from the top, projects proceed. The development projects at Victoria University, albeit relatively small, are one example. Over a period of several decades, the university has remained committed to a practice of leasing out its real estate, to create an endowment portfolio. On a larger scale the Uni-versity of Chicago seems to have maintained a fairly consistent involvement with its neighborhoods, first Hyde Park and increasingly also Kenwood and Woodlawn. Changes in approach there appear to be related more to the chang-ing economy and political climate than presidential decisions. In Denver the work of the Auraria Higher Education Center proceeded under the authority of the Colorado legislature, based on a clear plan and mission that deliber-ately kept the chief executives of the participating educational institutions off the board.

Thus leadership clearly can have a major effect on the direction and style of real estate development. High-level attention and commitment may also be necessary to break through the inevitable obstacles. The highest achieve-ment, however, may be to inculcate the vision, objectives, and approach in an organizational structure so it can be implemented consistently and steadily.

Internal Structure

How do universities organize themselves to implement their real estate ac-tivities? While the chapters in this book do not provide detailed organiza-tional and decision-making charts, we can identify some of the key issues and characteristics. There is a clear difference between projects that are done in partnership with a private developer or other outside entity (such as an intermediary) and those implemented primarily by the university itself. In the former case, a relatively small team of top university administrators is usually in charge of the project from the university's side. For instance when Northeastern partnered with two private developers and a community devel-opment corporation, its team members included the senior vice president, the vice president of government relations and community affairs, the trea-surer, the vice president for university counsel, and others from the facilities management department. The UIC partnership team working with two pri-vate developers included representatives from capital programs, facilities, the chancellor's and provost's offices, and the budget office. In these projects faculty and student involvement tends to be limited, although at both institu-tions these groups demanded input at various times.

Elsewhere, institutions have developed strong internal capabilities. At DePaul the office of the vice president for administration played a lead role in developing the very creative concept and financing for its rehabilitation of the Goldblatt Department Store. Key issues regarding internal structure are whether there is enough in-house expertise and whether decisions can be made quickly enough. Especially for institutions operating in robust real estate markets, rapid decision making and considerable delegated authority are essential. Public institutions may be at a particular disadvantage in this regard, as public boards are more likely to restrict authority and impose limitations. Indeed, some institutions, such as The University of Arizona, are restricted in where they can acquire real estate. Georgia State University is not allowed to enter into multiyear contracts; thus most real estate deals have to be run through its foundation. (In contrast, Yale's Office of Real Estate has considerable latitude, subject to the vice president for New Haven affairs, and is able to operate without the scrutiny of public institutions. A chapter on Yale originally written for this volume was withdrawn because of confidentiality concerns.)

Clearly the ability to develop and sustain internal expertise depends in part on the size of the institution and its real estate operations. Having considerable expertise in-house seems to be advantageous. For example it is doubtful whether outside consultants alone would have had the depth of institutional understanding and the access to institutional and political decision makers that allowed DePaul to develop its unusual project. Conversely it is not clear that UIC's deal with private developers, which was necessary because the university lacked the internal expertise, has best served the university's long-term interests, since it has involved selling at modest financial gain most of the land acquired at great political cost. Another advantage of in-house expertise is that learning takes place over time, and that it is easier to develop a decision-making system that is responsive to market conditions while still remaining accountable. At the same time, having some separation between the daily operations of the university and its real estate arm may make sense. The most extreme form of this is the Auraria Higher Education Center, which has the authority to plan, construct, own, lease, operate, maintain, and manage the entire complex housing the three different institutions of higher education.

Alone or Together: Partners and Intermediaries

In undertaking their projects, universities may have the option to do so acting alone, to partner with one or more private developers, or to devolve the authority to undertake a set of projects entirely to an intermediary. In well over half the cases discussed in these chapters, universities acted primarily alone or retained the lead role. The two clearest cases of intermediaries are

Campus Partners at The Ohio State University, which is empowered and capitalized to undertake major development projects, and the Auraria Higher Education Center, which is a legislatively mandated intermediary. Other universities, such as the University of Pittsburgh and St. Louis University, have established intermediaries, but these are not generally empowered to conduct major real estate projects. Finally there are four cases where private developers played an important role. Northeastern and UIC were mentioned before; Ryerson University is only a minor partner in a much larger development involving city government and private developers; and the University of Pittsburgh case gives several examples of joint projects with a private developer to construct a dormitory, a hotel, a technology center, and parking.

There are also cases where universities tried to work with private developers and discovered it was not worthwhile. The Ohio State University issued an RFP for a 500,000-square-foot, mixed-use development, but found out that developers wanted the university to assure their profit and take on so much of the risk that it was not worth the price, and the university let its intermediary, Campus Partners, take on the developer role instead. Similarly DePaul worked with a private developer to implement the retail portion of its project, but in the end took on most of the functions in-house, including developing a retail leasing office.

The main justifications usually offered for working with private developers are that universities lack the expertise, the private sector can move more quickly and cheaply, or the private sector can provide capital. In the latter case, however, universities generally can borrow at better rates than private developers. In the first case, expertise can probably be acquired more cheaply and reliably by hiring consultants or owner representatives than by obtaining it from a development partner who has his or her own interests at heart. Thus cases where a private developer can act more quickly or at lower cost are the most reasonable opportunities for partnerships. Given the long time line of many of the projects described in these chapters, there may well have been some gains if private developers had been more involved.

Relations with the Neighborhood

Conflicts between universities and their neighborhoods are generally the first thing people think about when the topic of university real estate development arises. Town-gown tensions are as old as universities themselves. Except for drunken students, nothing riles up the "townies" as much as campus expansion. In the United States the postwar history of university expansion is also closely associated with urban renewal and its racial connotations. The chapters on Columbia, University of Chicago, Temple and Penn, UIC, and the University of Pittsburgh all refer to major conflicts going back four or five decades. Those chapters can, in fact, be read as a history of impressive social progress, as the autocratic and secretive approaches of the past have been largely supplanted by much more consultative and open processes.

As Weber, Theodore, and Hoch note in chapter 16, ethical considerations have become more important and better heeded. Clearly the way universities implement their expansion projects is significantly influenced by both their experiences during the 1960s and the secular change in society, as low-income neighborhoods have become better organized and able to demand a seat at the table. Conflict still exists, but in most cases it is better managed and does not lead to major demonstrations or occupations of university buildings. (An exception appears to be university plans for construction of biohazard laboratories, which have led to recent demonstrations in Davis, California and Ithaca, New York.)

Intermediary organizations are one way to manage university-community relations. Perhaps the most ambitious effort along these lines is Campus Partners, established in 1995 by The Ohio State University. The university appoints the majority of the board of Campus Partners, with city and community representatives making up the remainder. The university also has provided most of the funding, including an initial $3 million in operating funds and $25 million in endowment investment funds. Armed with eminent-domain powers, Campus Partners is engaging in major residential and commercial redevelopment efforts in areas adjacent to the campus. Not surprisingly this entity itself has, at times, also become the focus of conflict and community opposition. Working on a much more limited mandate, the entity established by Northeastern University to develop the Davenport Commons, including two private developers and a community-based organization, had the same experience of becoming a target for community opposition itself.

More modest forms of intermediaries are described in the University of Pittsburgh case, where a plethora of intermediary organizations brought together university, community, and city representatives at various times for discussion and planning purposes: Oakland Directions, Inc., which produced the Oakland neighborhood plan in the 1980s; Community Input in the Master Plan, which organized community input into the 1995 university master plan; the Oakland Agreement Committee, which focused on nonuniversity development in 1995 and became the Oakland Community Council; the Oakland Improvement Strategy, which produced the 1998 strategy document for housing; the Oakland Task Force, which became active in the late 1990s; and a current informal group convened regularly by staff from the university's office of the vice chancellor for business affairs.

This listing shows how often these structures need to be modified to accommodate changes in community or university circumstances. Indeed, the authors of the Pittsburgh chapter argue, and we see evidence of this elsewhere, that the process of community involvement needs to be learned and relearned repeatedly. A stylized model looks as follows: the university develops a plan to expand or wishes to acquire some major property; the community registers concern or opposition; the university forms an organizational structure or establishes some process to deal with the community and negotiate; the project is modified and implemented (or cancelled); the process or structure for community-university interaction atrophies, until a new project comes along. If too much time has elapsed, or significant leadership changes have occurred, the process starts all over; if the time lapse is short and there is good institutional memory, the next round may be smoother.

Given that development intermediaries themselves may not be shielded from community conflicts, and given the relative instability of other formal intermediary structures, universities may be just as well off to establish advisory committees for particular purposes and projects. They may require less start-up time or staff support, and may be more flexible and adaptable in the long run. At UIC such a body was formed to review the RFP for the major, fifty-acre South Campus expansion plan, to advise on the selection of the private developer, and to design the community hiring and purchasing plan that became part of the project. Constituted as an advisory committee without any further legal status, it served to neutralize what had been vehement opposition by a small number of organizations and legitimated the project because it brought together many other community organizations, many of which benefited from various existing and new university projects and programs.

There does not appear to be any clear pattern regarding the types of neighborhoods where conflict is most likely to erupt. One might hypothesize that in areas where the real estate market is strong there would be lots of conflict over land use, whereas in poor and declining areas university interest would be welcomed, and there are cases where this is true. Austrian and Norton note that Marquette University's investment in housing in its deteriorated neighborhood was generally welcomed, while the University of Arizona experienced far more difficulty in its affluent area. Similarly both the Auraria Higher Education Center in Denver and the University of Washington in Tacoma experienced relatively little opposition as they were built in areas with significant abandonment and vacancies. But Temple University, Northeastern, and UIC ran into considerable opposition when they wanted to expand into deteriorated and, in the case of Chicago, virtually vacant areas. As was noted in the Northeastern case, "there is no such thing as vacant land"—everything has a history and often an imagined or wished-for future. Conversely DePaul University, whose main campus is in an affluent and very dense neighborhood, has managed to expand in relative harmony, albeit with much community discussion. These examples suggest that the history of university-community relations, the image of the institution, neighborhood politics, and the strength of the structures and processes that shape these relations may be far more important than the actual conditions of land availability.

Relations with City Government

In small cities and towns there may be little distinction between university-community and university-local government relations. In larger places, however, these are two distinct sets of issues. One of the main areas of contention between universities and their local governments is taxes, services, and the degree to which universities are subject to local ordinances and regulation. This book does not deal much with these topics, since they are not specifically related to real estate expansion. Nevertheless they are always present. In some places the conflict over the university's exemption from property taxes and its refusal to make payments in lieu of taxes (PILOTs) has caused serious problems. For instance, Northwestern University in Evanston, Illinois, has been exempt from property taxes; due to a unique law specific to Northwestern, it is even exempt from paying property taxes on most of its commercial real estate; and it has refused to make general payments in lieu of taxes. In retaliation, Evanston at one point threatened to designate part of the campus a historic district, requiring the university to request city council approval for any change it wants to make (Walker 2003, 80-112). On the other hand, during the past decade the city and the university have collaborated on a downtown revitalization project that has been very successful and has increased taxable property in the city significantly.

This case demonstrates something that is present in many other places as well: elements of both conflict and cooperation in the relation between the university and the city. Which force prevails depends in part on the issue, as well as on the politics and attitudes of the leadership and other local political factors. For instance, Temple University appears to have suffered from adversarial relations between its president and the local city council representative. Not until a new president came in did things change. In the same city, the University of Pennsylvania seems to have benefited from more consistently harmonious relations. In Chicago, DePaul University received extraordinary cooperation and financial assistance from city government in redeveloping the former Goldblatt's store. The University of Chicago seems to have received consistent city support as well, even though it battled community organizations at times. On the other hand UIC, sited in an urban renewal area only because of the iron will of Mayor Richard J. Daley, experienced a series of conflicts with the city's planning department when it was pursuing the South Campus plan, in part because initially there was strong community opposition. However, with strong mayoral support and a new approach to community relations, some compromises regarding preserving some buildings and facades were negotiated and the conflict largely disappeared.

Other universities have experienced similar shifts in city support. The Pittsburgh case described changes that took place as a more neighborhood-oriented mayor was elected and forced the university to be much more accommodating to neighborhood concerns. Ryerson University was asked to participate in a city-led redevelopment project, but it was also made clear that there would be consequences if it didn't. Northeastern University also had to contend with mayoral threats, even though it ultimately received city support.

The importance of creating good relations with the local political, business, and civic elite is described clearly in the chapters on Georgia State University, the Auraria Higher Education Center, and the two Philadelphia universities. Georgia State's president personally played a lead role in developing multiple contacts with the Atlanta city government, ranging from hosting conferences and transition-team workshops to providing educational benefits for city employees. The leadership of the Auraria Higher Education Center was actively involved with Denver's city planning staff in revitalization plans that went well beyond the campus boundaries, as well as with the local architectural community. The Philadelphia chapter details the careful nurturing and stewardship of relations with elected representatives at the state and local levels, as well as the active participation of university officials on local and statewide boards and committees. While good relations never guarantee support, they provide multiple avenues for communication about university needs and priorities. This also suggests that while at any time the relationship may be a given, based on political vagaries and its previous history, it is subject to modification through concerted and consistent attention.

A larger question is whether the relationship between a university and its city, and particularly local government, is in some way different from any large institution's. Universities are the largest employers in many places and very significant providers of external funds, cultural opportunities, and athletic entertainment. Universities may also be a key but less visible source of entrepreneurship and other forms of economic development. On the whole, however, the chapters in this book do not dwell on this role. In the knowledge economy, universities are more important than ever, but in most of these cases neither the city nor the university appears to have wrestled with what this means for the role of the university and the physical and real estate consequences thereof. Rather, projects proceed in a piecemeal fashion, and cities treat the university like any other organization that needs building permits and other municipal services. In most cases contacts are project- and task-oriented and episodic, rather than continuous, comprehensive, and strategic. Of course much city planning occurs that way in general. Nevertheless, given the permanence of universities, it appears that a more consistent and comprehensive approach to joint planning might better serve both the universities and their cities.

The Long and Winding Road: Time Lines and Obstacles

Most large real estate development projects are complicated and tend to undergo changes between initial conceptualization and final result. University projects are not easier, and often are quite a bit harder because of the multiple constituencies involved. There is no evidence that private universities find the process notably easier than public ones; each has its own obstacles to overcome.

Austrian and Norton concluded that the development process was harder in cases where the university is land constrained, but in reality that is virtually always the case. When land has been used and is now vacant, there are often expectations related to its reuse that may conflict with the university's plans. Even for universities in rural areas, pressures for land preservation may make expansion difficult. Only if the campus itself has ample buildable space is the university spared most of the challenge of dealing with outside constituencies and concerns.

In some cases described here, the projects' difficulties relate to their very conceptualization. When the real goal of a project is to improve the quality of the neighborhoods surrounding the campus, any number of specific projects might help achieve it. Thus the first phase of such an effort inevitably involves lengthy planning processes to determine whether commercial revitalization, residential rehabilitation or new construction, or development of campus-related or other institutional facilities might be the best approach. The Pittsburgh case study describes planning for the "two-block area," a particular part of the neighborhood near campus, which started in 1968 and did not yield a new building until 2002—thirty-four years and four chancellors later! Somewhat more quickly, Ohio State's president started the planning process for neighborhood improvement in 1994, and construction for the first project (South Campus Gateway) is scheduled to begin in the spring of 2004. UIC's $550 million South Campus project may have started as early as the 1970s with secret land acquisition, but serious planning for further acquisition and development efforts did not begin until 1993 and the first leasable space became available in 2001.

In addition to the challenge of determining the development concept, virtually every component of the ultimate project in these cases was unclear at first. These elements included the nature of the development entity (the university itself, a partnership with the private sector, or some another intermediary) and the boundaries of the project area. Furthermore each case experienced various forms of community opposition at some point, as well as pressure from city government to modify plans. Some of the problems were caused by the constraints imposed by financing needs and availability; others resulted from the nature of the proposed development, from leadership changes, or from political struggles for control.

Even more limited efforts are often characterized by significant changes in concept or implementation, some of them due to the particular nature of universities. DePaul began to look at the vacant downtown Goldblatt Department Store in 1988, but the $65 million project was not completed until 1996. It required rethinking the financing and the retail component several times. On the one hand the city was willing (and politically able) to sell the building for a nominal sum because the buyer was a university; on the other hand the expectation to create a significant public and civic use for the building was much greater for DePaul than would have been the case for a private developer.

Of the three Victoria University projects described, one took three years while the other two took approximately ten years to realize, and each had changes in the nature of the buildings' uses. Many of these were driven by concerns of students, the university board, and the city government, most of which a private developer would not have had to contend with. Northeastern's project took five years from an official's inadvertent disclosure of plans for student housing to first occupancy by community residents, followed a year later by students. While the community would probably have exerted similar pressure on private developers (and might well have driven them away), Northeastern did not have the option of going elsewhere, and simultaneously was more subject to political pressure from the mayor's office to be responsive to community demands.

According to Alice Boyer (2003), a university planner at Georgetown University, the average university real estate development project will take twice as long as a similar-size project implemented by a commercial entity. This is not because of lack of competence or willingness, but primarily because of the multiple formal and informal review and approval processes, as well as the dependence on either public or philanthropic funding. This suggests on the one hand the importance of leadership and commitment to see projects through, along with the need to understand, accept, and plan for this kind of time line. On the other hand it suggests the need to choose projects wisely and to have multiple plans moving forward at once, since any one project may run into difficulties.

Financing

The chapter by Austrian and Norton gives a good overview of the standard financing mechanisms that universities use for most real estate projects. These include bonds (both revenue bonds and bonds secured by general revenue of the university or the state); certificates of participation, which function like bonds; direct public capital grants; private capital with leasing provisions; debt finance through a separate entity; tax increment financing; standard commercial loans; endowment funds and other private gifts; and internal university funds from indirect cost recovery, tuition, or other revenue. On the whole this variety suggests that financing does not present specific or peculiar difficulties for universities. There are exceptions, however, as in Georgia where universities are not allowed to contract for periods exceeding one year at a time. Long-term financing or leasing arrangements are impossible with such a restriction. Therefore Georgia State had to work through a separate foundation to be able to move forward. Similarly The University of Arizona is prohibited from paying more than the average of two appraisals to acquire property. Again, working through a foundation was the answer.

Each of these financing mechanisms has variations, which can make the deals quite complex and creative. A particularly rich example is DePaul University. Its purchase price for the city-owned downtown building it planned to rehabilitate included $250,000 per year for ten years in scholarships for city residents. In reality this was a no-cost item, since the university had already decided to increase financial aid. Georgia State used a similar mechanism to provide a $500,000 line of credit for tuition for city employees, even though the actual marginal cost to the university would be negligible. DePaul also sold part of the building back to city government as an "estate for years," which lasts only thirty years; after that period ownership reverts to DePaul. This arrangement allowed the city to finance the purchase using its own bonds, as opposed to having the city rental payments be subject to annual lease payments, requiring annual city council approval. DePaul used the purchase price as part of the financing for the major rehabilitation that was needed. Basically the city paid for the rehabilitation of its own space and agreed to turn the space over to DePaul after thirty years.

At Georgia State one interesting project involved a series of transactions: a bank sold its building to a newspaper in exchange for advertising space; the newspaper then donated the building to the Georgia State University Foundation (for which the newspaper received a charitable tax donation); the foundation then sold the building to a private developer whose condominium project improved the university neighborhood.

It is clear that some of these projects included some element of public subsidy or private philanthropy, and thus are not necessarily comparable to market transactions. However, a university's attractiveness for such donations or subsidies is one of its assets, and universities do well to seek ways to leverage it.

Conclusion: Implications for Policy and Practice and Future Research

This book was not set up to test formal hypotheses, or even to gather systematically the same information on each case. Nevertheless the review above yields several conclusions that appear to hold across a range of circumstances. We summarize them here, and then conclude by suggesting areas for further research.

1. The primary motivation for university real estate projects is the need for additional space. Improvement of surrounding neighborhoods is the second most frequent motivation, followed in very few cases by the use of real estate development for income and endowment purposes.
2. The universities that set out to improve their surrounding neighborhoods have had success, but this has generally taken a long time and required very significant and long-term commitments.
3. Most major real estate development projects require persistence and strong leadership at the highest level. Where it is lacking, success is less likely or takes longer.
4. Undertaking major projects requires considerable in-house expertise and the ability to make decisions quickly.
5. Most universities take the lead and implement projects themselves, rather than working with private developers or other organizations in a primary role.
6. Working in partnership with private developers may not always be worthwhile, since universities can obtain the required expertise and financing from other sources and at lower cost. However private developers may be able to work more quickly and reduce project costs.
7. The creation of formal intermediary organizations for planning or development purposes also may not be worthwhile in most cases. For the planning phase, advisory bodies provide more flexibility,

while it is not clear that for development activities an intermediary organization brings enough advantages to offset the costs and risk.

8. The level of university-community conflict or cooperation appears to be less a function of objective factors such as land availability or the condition of the neighborhood than of the degree of present and past collaboration, which is subject to improvement through concerted efforts.

9. The nature of university-community relations appears to have improved over the past fifty years in terms of ethical criteria and principles of fairness and transparency. But the lessons on how to conduct such relations need to be learned and relearned regularly, suggesting an upward spiral.

10. Relations between universities and city governments tend to be project- or task-oriented, episodic, and subject to political and personal vagaries. Given the importance of universities to their cities, and the importance of local government to university projects, it would make sense for both to engage in more systematic, continuous, and comprehensive joint planning.

11. Extensive involvement in civic and public affairs by the university's leadership helps identify project opportunities and improves the ability to get projects done.

12. There does not appear to be a systematic difference between private and public universities in the nature of the development process.

13. University projects appear to take considerably longer than similar-size private commercial projects, primarily because of the multiple stakeholders involved, their high expectations of the university, and the longer time line for arranging financing.

14. A range of useful financing mechanisms is readily available for university projects. Financing often takes a long time because of the dependence on public or philanthropic sources. There is also considerable scope for creative financing, in part because of the attractiveness of universities as recipients of public or private largesse.

In terms of future research, each of the fourteen conclusions above can be restated as a hypothesis that could be tested more formally. No doubt it will turn out that some items hold only for larger universities, and there are likely to be exceptions. It would also be interesting to investigate the role of universities outside of the United States and Canada. In Europe more so than in the United States, universities have been an integral part of both their cities and their national political and economic systems. Also there are very different traditions of planning, urban development, and citizen participation in other parts of the world.

Another area where more work would be useful is related to best practices and models for success from which practitioners might benefit. Clear case descriptions of planning processes, the use of intermediaries, community involvement, development of relations with local government, and financing models are likely to be helpful to universities as they continue to expand in the future.

References

Boyer, Alice. 2003. Personal Interview, Director of Facilities Planning and Associate University Architect, Georgetown Univeristy. January 2.

Walker, Cassie. 2003.The hundred years' war. *Chicago Magazine*, April: 80–112.

About the Editors and Contributors

Editors

David C. Perry is Director and Professor of the Great Cities Institute at the University of Illinois at Chicago. He is the author/editor of nine books and more than one hundred articles. He studies urban policy and the political economy of urban institutions, including universities, most recently in comparative and global contexts.

Wim Wiewel is Professor of Public Affairs and Provost and Senior Vice President for Academic Affairs at the University of Baltimore. He was previously Dean of the College of Business Administration and Dean of Urban Planning and Public Affairs at the University of Illinois at Chicago. He is the author/editor of six books and over fifty articles and chapters on economic, urban, and neighborhood development. He is a former president of the Association of Collegiate Schools of Planning, and a fellow of the Urban Land Institute.

Contributors

David Amborski is a Professor at the School of Urban and Regional Planning, Ryerson University in Toronto.

Ziona Austrian is Director of the Center for Economic Development, Maxine Goodman Levin College of Urban Affairs at Cleveland State University.

Allegra Calder works in the Fair Lending Department of Washington Mutual in Seattle, Washington. She formerly worked at Housing Investments, Inc., in Boston.

Brian Coffey is Professor and Director of the Urban Studies Program at University of Washington, Tacoma.

Sarah Coffin is an Assistant Professor in the Department of Public Policy Studies, Saint Louis University.

Scott Cummings is a Professor in the Department of Public Policy Studies, Saint Louis University.

Sabina Deitrick is an Associate Professor at the Graduate School of Public and International Affairs, University of Pittsburgh.

Yonn Dierwechter is an Assistant Professor in the Urban Studies Program, University of Washington, Tacoma.

David Dixon is an Architect and Urban Planner at Goody Clancy and Associates in Boston, Massachusetts.

Mary Domahidy is Associate Professor and Chair of the Department of Public Policy Studies, Saint Louis University.

Gabriel Grant is a Housing Developer with Beacon Development Group in Seattle, Washington. He formerly worked at Housing Investments, Inc., in Boston.

Charles Hoch is Professor at the Urban Planning and Policy Program, University of Illinois at Chicago.

Lawrence R. Kelley is Vice President for Administration and Finance at California Polytechnic State University in San Luis Obispo. He formerly served as Associate Vice President at Georgia State University.

Robert Kronewitter is a certified planner and registered architect in Colorado, Texas, and California.

Larry R. Kurtz is a retired Bursar of Victoria University in the University of Toronto.

Peter Marcuse is Professor of Urban Planning in the Graduate School of Architecture and Planning, Columbia University.

Kenneth McHugh is President and CEO of Institutional Project Management LLC in Chicago and is Executive Vice President Emeritus for The Real Estate Center at DePaul University.

Holly Hart Muson is Project Manager at Housing Investments, Inc., in Boston, Massachusetts. She is also associated with the Preservation of Affordable Housing, Inc.

Jill S. Norton is a Research Associate in the Center for Economic Development, Maxine Goodman Levin College of Urban Affairs, Cleveland State University.

Carl V. Patton is President of Georgia State University.

Cuz Potter is a doctoral student in urban planning at the Graduate School of Architecture and Planning, Columbia University.

Peter J. Roche is the Principal of a private consulting practice specializing in real estate finance and community development and consults on residential, commercial, and mixed-use real estate initiatives throughout the United States.

Mark S. Rosentraub is the Dean and Professor of Urban Affairs of the Maxine Goodman Levin College of Urban Affairs at Cleveland State University.

Tracy Soska is Director of Continuing Professional Specialties and a Lecturer at the School of Social Work, University of Pittsburgh.

Elizabeth Strom is Professor of Political Science in the Department of Political Science, Rutgers University, Newark, New Jersey.

Nik Theodore is an Assistant Professor in the Urban Planning and Policy Program, University of Illinois at Chicago.

Henry S. Webber is Senior Lecturer in the School of Social Service Administration and Vice-President for Community and Government Affairs at the University of Chicago.

Rachel Weber is an Assistant Professor in the Urban Planning and Policy Program, University of Illinois at Chicago.

About the Lincoln Institute of Land Policy

The Lincoln Institute of Land Policy is a nonprofit and tax-exempt educational institution established in 1974 to study and teach land policy, including land economics and land taxation. The Institute is supported primarily by the Lincoln Foundation, which was established in 1947 by Cleveland industrialist John C. Lincoln. He drew inspiration from the ideas of Henry George, the nineteenth-century American political economist, social philosopher, and author of the book *Progress and Poverty*.

The Institute's goals are to integrate theory and practice to better shape land policy decisions and to share understanding about the multidisciplinary forces that influence public policy in the United States and internationally. The Institute organizes its work in three departments: valuation and taxation, planning and development, and international studies, with special programs in Latin America and China.

The Lincoln Institute seeks to improve the quality of debate and disseminate knowledge of critical issues in land policy by bringing together scholars, policy makers, practitioners, and citizens with diverse backgrounds and experience. The Institute studies, exchanges insights, and works toward a broader understanding of complex land and tax policies. The Institute does not take a particular point of view, but rather serves as a catalyst to facilitate analysis and discussion of these issues—to make a difference today and to help policy makers plan for tomorrow.

L LINCOLN INSTITUTE
OF LAND POLICY
113 Brattle Street
Cambridge, MA 02138-3400 USA
Phone: 617-661-3016 x127 or 800-LAND-USE (800-526-3873)
Fax: 617-661-7235 or 800-LAND-944 (800-526-3944)
Email: help@lincolninst.edu
Web: www.lincolninst.edu

Index